edited by A.G.Wilson · London papers in regional science 3 · a pion publication

patterns and processes
in urban and regional systems

p Pion Limited, 207 Brondesbury Park, London NW2 5JN

ISBN 0 85086 035 0

Set on IBM 72 Composers by Pion Limited, London.
Printed in Great Britain by J.W.Arrowsmith Limited, Bristol.

Contents

Contributors

L. L. H. Baker — *Department of Planning and Transportation, Greater London Council, County Hall, London SE1*

M. Batty — *Department of Geography, University of Reading, Reading*

R. Bussière — *Centre de Recherche d'Urbanisme, Paris*

Erlet A. Cater — *Department of Geography, University of Reading, Reading*

J. M. Clark — *Transport Assessment Group, Cranfield Institute of Technology, Cranfield, Bedford*

E. L. Cripps — *Department of Geography, University of Leeds, Leeds*

I. Cullen — *Joint Unit for Planning Research, 171–174 Tottenham Court Road, London WC1*

J. B. Goddard — *Department of Geography, London School of Economics, London WC2*

Vida Godson — *Joint Unit for Planning Research, 171–174 Tottenham Court Road, London WC1*

W. Isard — *Department of Regional Science, University of Pennsylvania, Philadelphia*

Sandra Kendall — *Department of Planning and Transportation, Greater London Council, County Hall, London SE1*

P. Liossatos — *Graduate Group in Peace Research, University of Pennsylvania, Philadelphia*

Sandra Major — *Joint Unit for Planning Research, 171–174 Tottenham Court Road, London WC1*

V. K. Mathur — *Economics Department, Cleveland State University, Cleveland*

A. Metcalf — *Local Government Operational Research Unit, Reading*

B. Pilgrim — *Local Government Operational Research Unit, Reading*

B. G. Redding — *Department of Planning and Transportation, Greater London Council, County Hall, London SE1*

P. H. Rees — *Department of Geography, University of Leeds, Leeds*

H. S. Rosen — *The Institute of Urban Studies, Cleveland State University, Cleveland*

R. B. Smyth — *Department of Planning and Transportation, Greater London Council, County Hall, London SE1*

P. Stringer — *Bartlett School of Architecture, University College London, London WC1*

A. G. Wilson — *Department of Geography, University of Leeds, Leeds*

Preface

This volume contains the papers which were presented at the fourth Annual Conference, held in London in August 1971, of the British section of the Regional Science Association. The papers are concerned with various aspects of patterns and processes in urban and regional systems. They are organised in four sections. The first section is concerned with new concepts and techniques in regional science and contains two papers, one about social energy, the other about some modifications to the economic base model. Part 2 contains six papers on patterns and models concerned with residences, transport and demography, and model dynamics. Part 3 contains two papers which represent a different research style, concerned with survey evidence on contact flows and activity structure. The final part contains three papers concerned with evaluation methodology. The volume will provide useful material for academic regional scientists, economists, geographers, sociologists and planners as well as practitioners in the field.

AGW

Social Energy: A Relevant New Concept for Regional Science?

W.ISARD, P.LIOSSATOS
University of Pennsylvania

1 Introduction

In the papers I (W. I.) delivered at London and Philadelphia last year, I set forth a number of hypotheses and speculations concerning the way in which a social system is structured and operates over time. In doing so, I did not hesitate to draw upon general relativity theory of physics, and to suggest types of interactions among social behavioral units which parallel the interactions of bodies in the physical system. Consequently, at times I had to make passing references to such concepts as social mass, social momentum, and social energy. I promised then that I would explore the content and significance of such concepts in future manuscripts, and attempt to make precise definitions.

This paper focuses entirely upon the basic concept of social energy. Once this concept has been properly treated, it will be rather easy to pass on to related concepts such as social mass, social momentum, social acceleration, and social work.

In the argument which follows there are three main parts. In the first, I use formal mathematics to define rigorously my notion of social energy. In the second I try to develop a useful and reasonable way of interpreting social energy, beginning with highly oversimplified notions, and again drawing upon parallels in physics. The interpretation of social energy reached at the conclusion of this part must, of course, be strictly consistent with the formal definition in the first part. Finally, in the third part, I present succinctly several theories and models of how the economy works—a part of the social system which has been intensively and rigorously explored—and identify precisely specific magnitudes in these theories as social energy.

2 A formal definition of social energy

The social system may be viewed as consisting of z relevant properties and w relevant behaving units. There are many constraints which functionally relate these properties and which contain the action spaces of these units. I assume then that the number of independent variables in the system is thereby reduced to s. Among others, relevant variables might be income, housing stock, store of knowledge, real industrial capital, mineral resources, human resources, and cohesiveness. Measuring each of these variables along an axis, and thereby considering each a generalized coordinate, we can describe the *position*, or *configuration*, of the system as a point q_i $(i = 1, ..., s)$ in an s-dimensional space.

In addition to position, or configuration, I am also interested in the *path (world-line)* of the system over time, that is how the system changes its position over time. Consequently time rates of change, dq_i/dt or $\dot{q}_i$, become relevant. These time rates of change may be designated *generalized velocities* or *paces*. Further, since the position and path of the system may depend on the particular point of time at which the system is being studied, it is necessary to consider explicitly the time variable t.

Now at any point of time, t, the q_i (position), and the $\dot{q}_i$ (pace) may be viewed as describing the *state* of the system—at least to the extent that our theoretical capabilities currently permit. This means that if we are given the q_i and $\dot{q}_i$ at a given instant *and* the laws of motion implied by a theory involving the variables q_i, $\dot{q}_i$, and $\ddot{q}_i$, we can predict the q_i and $\dot{q}_i$ for any subsequent instant [1]. Of course what we predict is no better than the theory we propound or consider most relevant.

Now the most general way (consistent with a variety of theories) of expressing the laws of motion of a social system is to assume that (1) the system is characterized by some definite function of its state,

$$\mathcal{L} = \mathcal{L}(q_i, \dot{q}_i, t) , \qquad (2.1)$$

the familiar Lagrangian expression [2] and (2) the motion of the system is such that certain conditions are satisfied by this function relating the variables of basic interest to us. More specifically we assume that the motion of the system from a fixed position q_i^0 at $t = t_0$ to another fixed position q_i^1 at $t = t_1$ is such that optimization conditions (an optimization objective) are satisfied, namely,

$$\delta \int_{t_0}^{t_1} \mathcal{L}(q_i, \dot{q}_i, t) dt = 0 . \qquad (2.2)$$

Since q_i^0 and q_i^1 are fixed, it necessarily follows that $\delta q_i^0 = \delta q_i^1 = 0$. In order for the Lagrangian $\mathcal{L}$ to satisfy the extremum equation (2.2) the following Euler conditions must be met [3]:

$$\frac{\partial \mathcal{L}}{\partial q_i} - \frac{d}{dt}\left(\frac{\partial \mathcal{L}}{\partial \dot{q}_i}\right) = 0 , \qquad i = 1, ..., s . \qquad (2.3)$$

The meaning of equation (2.2) is that, if we are given all conceivable paths of the system from q_i^0 to q_i^1, the real path optimizes the integral in expression (2.2).

[1] Where a theory involves variables $\ddot{q}_i$ and still higher derivatives, then the q_i and $\dot{q}_i$ are not enough to describe a state of the system.

[2] By our notation, we mean here and subsequently:

$$\mathcal{L} = \mathcal{L}(q_1, ..., q_s; \dot{q}_1, ..., \dot{q}_s; t) .$$

For general references on the Lagrangian and Hamiltonian formulations in mechanics, which we employ extensively in this paper, see Lanczos, 1960; Landau and Lifshitz, 1960; and Goldstein, 1959.

[3] For proof, see appendix A.

We call the term $\partial\mathcal{L}/\partial q_i$ the *generalized force*, F_i, in the ith direction because if q_i represent the Cartesian coordinates of a single material particle in three-dimensional Euclidean space, the partial derivatives $\partial\mathcal{L}/\partial q_i$ represent the familiar Newtonian force acting on the particle, having dimensions of work done per unit distance. Similarly, the partial derivatives, $\partial\mathcal{L}/\partial\dot{q}_i = p_i$, are called *generalized momentum* because if q_i represent the Cartesian coordinates of a single material particle in three-dimensional Euclidean space, the three quantities p_1, p_2, p_3, become identical with the Cartesian coordinates of the momentum $mv\,(\equiv m\dot{q}_1, m\dot{q}_2, m\dot{q}_3)$. (In the general case, however, the generalized momentum does not correspond to this elementary definition and must be considered a vector in configuration space.) Thus, in the case of a single particle, equations (2.3) take the familiar Newtonian-type form:

$$F_i = \frac{d}{dt}(m\dot{q}_i) - m\ddot{q}_i , \tag{2.4}$$

where $\ddot{q}_i$ is the acceleration of the particle. Accordingly in the general case we call $\ddot{q}_i$ *generalized acceleration*.

Condition (2.2) corresponds to the *principle of least action*, or Hamilton's principle in physics, where action is defined by

$$S = \int_{t_0}^{t_1} \mathcal{L}dt . \tag{2.5}$$

Now from equation (2.1) we have

$$d\mathcal{L} = \frac{\partial\mathcal{L}}{\partial q_i}dq_i + \frac{\partial\mathcal{L}}{\partial\dot{q}_i}d\dot{q}_i + \frac{\partial\mathcal{L}}{\partial t}dt . \tag{2.6}$$

Letting

$$p_i = \frac{\partial\mathcal{L}}{\partial\dot{q}_i} , \tag{2.7}$$

so that $\dot{p}_i = \dfrac{d}{dt}\left(\dfrac{\partial\mathcal{L}}{\partial\dot{q}_i}\right)$, we have from equation (2.3)

$$\dot{p}_i = \frac{\partial\mathcal{L}}{\partial q_i} . \tag{2.8}$$

Substituting equations (2.7) and (2.8) into equation (2.6) we have

$$d\mathcal{L} = \dot{p}_i\,dq_i + p_i\,d\dot{q}_i + \frac{\partial\mathcal{L}}{\partial t}dt . \tag{2.9}$$

Noting that

$$d(p_i\dot{q}_i) = dp_i\dot{q}_i + p_i\,d\dot{q}_i$$

so that

$$p_i\,d\dot{q}_i = d(p_i\dot{q}_i) - \dot{q}_i\,dp_i , \tag{2.10}$$

and substituting equation (2.10) in (2.9) and transposing terms, we have

$$-\dot{p}_i\,dq_i + \dot{q}_i\,dp_i - \frac{\partial\mathcal{L}}{\partial t}dt = -d\mathcal{L} + d(p_i\dot{q}_i) = d(p_i\dot{q}_i - \mathcal{L}) . \tag{2.11}$$

We define the Hamiltonian H as

$$H = p_i \dot{q}_i - \mathcal{L} .$$ (2.12)

When we divide both sides of equation (2.11) by dt, we obtain

$$-\dot{p}_i \dot{q}_i + \dot{p}_i \dot{q}_i - \frac{\partial \mathcal{L}}{\partial t} = \frac{dH}{dt} .$$ (2.13)

If we assume a closed system, that is that the Lagrangian expression (2.1) does not depend on time explicitly, so that $\partial \mathcal{L}/\partial t = 0$, then it is seen that $dH/dt = 0$ and H is a constant. For the situation of a closed system we define the

$$\text{social energy} = -H = \mathcal{L} - p_i \dot{q}_i .$$ (2.14)

Note that the functional combination of the q_i and $\dot{q}_i$ making up H retains a constant value along the path of the system, although the q_i and $\dot{q}_i$ vary individually.

Later, in Appendix D, we shall extend the definition of social energy so as to be applicable to non-closed systems. In such systems, the Hamiltonian as defined by equation (2.14) is not a constant along the path of the system.

We can show that the variables, q_i and p_i, can characterize the state of the system just as well as the variables q_i and $\dot{q}_i$ [4]. The Hamiltonian H then takes the form

$$H = H(q_i, p_i, t) .$$ (2.15)

[4] We note that from equation (2.11) we have

$$-\dot{p}_i dq_i + \dot{q}_i dp_i - \frac{\partial \mathcal{L}}{\partial t} dt = d(p_i \dot{q}_i - \mathcal{L}) = dH .$$ (a)

This suggests that $H = H(q_i, p_i, t)$ from which, generally viewed, we have:

$$dH = \frac{\partial H}{\partial q_i} dq_i + \frac{\partial H}{\partial p_i} dp_i + \frac{\partial H}{\partial t} dt .$$ (b)

So, by comparison of (a) with (b) we have:

$$\frac{\partial H}{\partial q_i} = -\dot{p}_i ;$$ (c)

$$\frac{\partial H}{\partial p_i} = \dot{q}_i ; \text{ and}$$ (d)

$$\frac{\partial H}{\partial t} = -\frac{\partial \mathcal{L}}{\partial t} .$$ (e)

Hence the Euler equations

$$\frac{d}{dt}\left(\frac{\partial \mathcal{L}}{\partial \dot{q}_i}\right) = \frac{\partial \mathcal{L}}{\partial q_i} , \quad \text{or} \quad \dot{p}_i = \frac{\partial \mathcal{L}}{\partial q_i} ,$$

which is equation (2.8), together with the definition of the p_i and the Hamiltonian expression imply equations (c) and (d), generally known as the Hamiltonian equations of motion. These equations, which are $2s$ in number and of first-degree, are equivalent to the Euler–Lagrangian equations of motion, which are s in number but of second-degree.

We also show in Appendix B that the action S evaluated along a real path of the system can be viewed as a function of q_i and t, which satisfies the following:

$$\frac{\partial S}{\partial q_i} = p_i \tag{2.16}$$

and

$$\frac{\partial S}{\partial t} = -(p_i \dot{q}_i - \mathcal{L}) = -H ; \tag{2.17}$$

or in other words

$$\frac{dS}{dt} = \frac{\partial S}{\partial q_i}\dot{q}_i + \frac{\partial S}{\partial t} = p_i \dot{q}_i - H = \mathcal{L} , \tag{2.18}$$

an expression we shall find meaningful in section 4 of this paper.

3 Some reasonable ways of interpreting social energy

Given our precise definition of social energy, we may seek some meaningful interpretations. We must start from the beginning and develop interpretations from oversimplified answers to relevant questions.

First, we ask: "what are some reasonable social system properties to consider for analysis and measurement?" One obvious property is mass; and if m_j represents the mass of a particle or behaving unit j in that system, $j = 1, ..., w$, then $\sum m_j$ may be taken as a first relevant measure for the system. We view $\sum m_j$ as an *unweighted mass*.

Beyond mass we are interested in the position of each particle or behaving unit j in the z-dimensional Euclidean space of relevant properties. We may specify this position by Q_j ($\equiv Q_{1j}, ..., Q_{zj}$). If we now weight the position of each particle by its mass and divide the sum of the products by total mass, we obtain the position of the center of mass of the system: this is

$$\frac{\sum_j m_j Q_j}{\sum_j m_j} . \tag{3.1}$$

Further, we are interested in the time rate of change in the position of each particle (behavioral unit), that is in

$$\frac{dQ_j}{dt} = \dot{Q}_j \ (\equiv \dot{Q}_{1j}, \dot{Q}_{2j}, ..., \dot{Q}_{zj}) .$$

These are the generalized velocities or paces of the particle (behaving unit) j. When we multiply the generalized velocity or pace of a particle (behaving unit) j by its mass, m_j, we obtain $m_j \dot{Q}_j$, the generalized momentum of j and a measure of its potential impact when it collides with any other particle (behaving unit) or group of particles (behaving units). For the system as a whole, the sum of the momenta of its particles divided by their total mass, that is

$$\frac{\sum m_j \dot{Q}_j}{\sum m_j} ,$$

(3.2)

may be viewed as the generalized pace, or velocity of the system, or its momentum per unit mass.

The concept of total mass of a social system, $\sum_j m_j$, is frequently not the most useful concept of mass to employ. In past studies we have often weighted mass by income, say Q_d, or by years of education, say Q_e, etc., to obtain for the social system a weighted total mass, $\sum m_j Q_{hj}$ (say total income), $h = 1, ..., z$ (where m_j may refer to the mass of a political unit and Q_{hj} to the *per capita* income of its inhabitants). We may also weight mass by a velocity, $\dot{Q}_{hj}$, to obtain $\sum m_j \dot{Q}_{hj}$ (say *net change* in total income). But observe that, while *unweighted total* mass has a magnitude which is independent of position and direction of change and thus of any reference point (origin) and direction of axes which an observer may designate as appropriate, the *weighted total* mass as defined above has a magnitude which does depend on reference point (origin) and direction of axes. Since different observers may vary greatly in what they choose as relevant origins and directions, it is desirable to find another way to weight mass so that all observers obtain the same magnitude for weighted total mass.

One such way is to weight mass by the square of the time rate of change, that is by $\dot{Q}_{hj}^2$ or in general by $\dot{Q}_j^2$ to obtain

$$\sum_h \sum_j m_j \dot{Q}_{h,j}^2 \quad \text{or} \quad \sum_j m_j \dot{Q}_j^2 .$$

(3.3)

Both squares yield a scalar, independent of origin and direction, and thus a magnitude which observers and analysts in all systems can agree upon, provided they are in Euclidean space. Therefore, because of its invariance property, we are inclined to explore the use of the weighted mass, $\sum_j m_j \dot{Q}_j^2$ as one of several key components of our 'social energy' concept.

At this point, it may be helpful to draw a parallel from Newtonian physics. We may consider in the abstract a free particle j of mass m_j moving through physical space. In the Newtonian framework there exists a set of simple coordinate systems (the inertial systems) in which the path of motion of a free particle is independent of the point in space which serves as origin and the direction of the axes laid down to describe position. (That is, space is homogeneous and isotropic.) The path of motion is also independent of the point from which time is measured. (That is, time is homogeneous.) Hence the general Lagrangian expression,

$$\mathcal{L} = \mathcal{L}(Q_j, \dot{Q}_j, t) ,$$

(3.4)

which is a function of the state of the system at any moment of time reduces, in this specific context, to

$$\mathcal{L} = \mathcal{L}(\dot{Q}_j) , \tag{3.5}$$

since $\mathcal{L}$ must be independent of Q_j (position in space) and t (position in time). But the specific expression (3.5) is inappropriate since the vector $\dot{Q}_j$ has a specific direction, implying that $\mathcal{L}$ is not independent of direction. However, if we consider $\mathcal{L}$ as a specific function of $\dot{Q}_j^2$, which is a scalar, we do have a path of motion which all observers in all inertial systems would agree upon. In fact, the Lagrangian for a free particle in the Newtonian system is:

$$\mathcal{L}_j = k\dot{Q}_j^2 . \tag{3.6}$$

Since the Lagrangian is invariant up to a scalar transformation, we can conveniently use for the constant k the expression $\frac{1}{2}m_j$ so that for any particle j, $\mathcal{L}_j = \frac{1}{2}m_j\dot{Q}_j^2$ and for w non-interacting particles

$$\sum \mathcal{L}_j = \mathcal{L} = \sum \tfrac{1}{2}m_j\dot{Q}_j^2 . \tag{3.7}$$

Such an expression is recognizable as the *kinetic energy* concept of Newtonian physics.

It would, however, be completely wrong to suggest any parallel between the kinetic energy concept embodied in expression (3.7) and our concept of weighted social mass of expression (3.3). This point is immediately apparent because we cannot, even in the abstract, conceive of w behaving units in a social system without interaction. The very notion of a social system involves particles (behaving units) interacting. So, if we are to draw any parallels from Newtonian physics, we must incorporate interaction among particles.

At this point we seek to introduce interaction among particles in the simplest way possible. Interaction could be dependent on absolute positions, relative positions, absolute or relative velocities, absolute or relative accelerations, etc., or some combination of these. It would seem that dependence on relative positions alone would be one of the simplest ways to begin to study interaction, and in fact, in Newtonian physics, interaction among masses which is associated with gravitational forces depends on relative positions. So we may introduce into the Lagrangian expression the term

$$\tilde{V}(Q_1, Q_2, ..., Q_w) ; \tag{3.8}$$

but how introduce this term? Everything being the same, we look for the simplest way—namely a way which involves addition or multiplication. If the right hand side of equation (3.7) were multiplied by the expression (3.8), then if we were to want to consider the extreme case of a system of non-interacting particles for which it is reasonable to set $\tilde{V}(Q_1, ..., Q_w) = 0$, we could not recover the Lagrangian of equation (3.7); we would have $\mathcal{L} = 0$. Further, for a system of interacting particles whose direction and velocity of movement was such that at some instant of time $\sum \frac{1}{2} m_j \dot{Q}_j^2 = 0$, $\mathcal{L}$ would equal zero if the right hand side of equation (3.7) were multiplied by expression (3.8)—an inappropriate outcome since, for a non-negligible force of interaction among the particles, the Lagrangian describing the path of motion of the system should not record a zero net force at that point of time. Hence, we are led to introduce expression (3.8) into the Lagrangian of equation (3.7) by way of addition to obtain:

$$\mathcal{L} = \sum_j \tfrac{1}{2} m_j \dot{Q}_j^2 - \widetilde{V}(Q_1, ..., Q_w) , \tag{3.9}$$

the minus sign being strictly a convention. Observe that equation (3.9) represents the difference between kinetic energy and potential energy, and this new formulation of the Lagrangian has worked out well for studying mechanical systems with classical physics. Observe also that the potential energy term $\widetilde{V}$ cannot be described for one particle alone. It involves interaction among particles, and thus relates to a property which must be mutual. Further, if the position of one particle changes, the paths of motion of all other particles are instantaneously affected. In contrast, the energy of the first term of the right hand side of equation (3.9) sums the strictly independent energies (kinetic) of particles.

So far in this section we have been treating particles in a z-dimensional Euclidean space, and thus wz variables. It may well be that not all these variables are simultaneously independent and that the system must meet a number of constraints. We may then let the number of independent variables (degrees of freedom) in the system be s, representable by the s generalized coordinates q_i, $i = 1, ..., s$. Hence it follows that

$$Q_j = Q_j(q_1, ..., q_s, t) \qquad j = 1, ..., w , \tag{3.10}$$

or

$$Q_{hj} = Q_{hj}(q_1, ..., q_s, t) \qquad h = 1, ..., z ; j = 1, ..., w .$$

Also,

$$\dot{Q}_j = \frac{dQ_j}{dt} = \frac{\partial Q_j}{\partial q_k} \dot{q}_k + \frac{\partial Q_j}{\partial t} , \tag{3.11}$$

k being an index of a generalized coordinate. Since both i and k are dummy indices, and thus interchangeable,

$$\dot{Q}_j^2 = \left(\frac{\partial Q_j}{\partial q_k} \dot{q}_k + \frac{\partial Q_j}{\partial t} \right) \cdot \left(\frac{\partial Q_j}{\partial q_i} \dot{q}_i + \frac{\partial Q_j}{\partial t} \right). \tag{3.12}$$

Now if the constraints in the system do not depend on time, then $\partial Q_j / \partial t = 0$. So equation (3.12) becomes

$$\dot{Q}_j^2 = \frac{\partial Q_j}{\partial q_i} \cdot \frac{\partial Q_j}{\partial q_k} \dot{q}_i \dot{q}_k , \tag{3.13}$$

and therefore

$$\sum_j \tfrac{1}{2} m_j \dot{Q}_j^2 = \tfrac{1}{2} \sum_j m_j \frac{\partial Q_j}{\partial q_i} \cdot \frac{\partial Q_j}{\partial q_k} \dot{q}_i \dot{q}_k \tag{3.14}$$

$$= \tfrac{1}{2} \sum_i \sum_k \sum_j m_j \frac{\partial Q_j}{\partial q_i} \cdot \frac{\partial Q_j}{\partial q_k} \dot{q}_i \dot{q}_k , \tag{3.15}$$

where the summations over i and k are made explicit. Let

$$A_{ik}(q_1, ..., q_s) \equiv \sum_j m_j \frac{\partial Q_j}{\partial q_i} \cdot \frac{\partial Q_j}{\partial q_k} . \tag{3.16}$$

Then, equation (3.3) becomes

$$\tfrac{1}{2} \sum_j m_j \dot{Q}_j^2 = \tfrac{1}{2} \sum_{i,k} A_{ik}(q_1, ..., q_s) \dot{q}_i \dot{q}_k , \tag{3.17}$$

where the right hand side is a quadratic form. The Lagrangian of equation (3.9) becomes:

$$\mathcal{L} = \tfrac{1}{2} \sum_{i,k} A_{ik}(q_1, ..., q_s) \dot{q}_i \dot{q}_k - V(q_1, ..., q_s) . \tag{3.18}$$

The first term on the right hand side of equation (3.18) can be viewed as kinetic energy (energy associated with mobility) in generalized coordinates, while the second term is potential energy in generalized coordinates, the Lagrangian being the difference of the two. By making V independent of time, we assume that our system is closed.

We demonstrate in the appendix that

$$p_i \dot{q}_i = \sum_i \sum_k A_{ik}(q_1, ..., q_s) \dot{q}_i \dot{q}_k . \tag{3.19}$$

Hence from equations (2.14) and (3.19)

$$H = p_i \dot{q}_i - \mathcal{L} = \sum_i \sum_k A_{ik}(q_1, ..., q_s) \dot{q}_i \dot{q}_k - \tfrac{1}{2} \sum_i \sum_k A_{ik}(q_1, ..., q_s) \dot{q}_i \dot{q}_k$$
$$+ V(q_1, ..., q_s) ,$$

or

$$H = \tfrac{1}{2} \sum_i \sum_k A_{ik}(q_1, ..., q_s) \dot{q}_i \dot{q}_k + V(q_1, ..., q_s) . \tag{3.20}$$

Here H is precisely the sum of kinetic energy and potential energy, namely the total energy of a mechanical system of classical physics when expressed in generalized coordinates. But the Hamiltonian H for closed social systems has also been designated social energy. Thus we have a significant parallel between social energy, as we have defined it, and the energy of a mechanical system. This parallel suggests that the concepts of both kinetic energy and potential energy of classical physics may also provide some insight for the study of social systems. It also suggests that both (1) the mobility (pace) of behaving units and (2) their interaction are relevant for social energy.

However, our use of the Hamiltonian H is not restricted to systems in which social energy is a sum of kinetic and potential parts, as will appear later.

4 Social energy: specific formulation in the Ramsey model

In this section we wish to identify the concept of social energy in terms of specific magnitudes in well-defined problems. To begin with we choose the classic Ramsey model, and then consider (one or more) growth models which have been subsequently developed. It is important to stress at this point that we set forth social energy as a *general* concept. In any model the magnitude to which social energy refers is specific to the model and to the basic theory underlying the model. Like the concepts of region, industry, and payoff, the concept of social energy does not relate to any specific theory *per se*.

We follow Allen (1939, pp.536-540) in presenting the Ramsey model. In a closed economy there are two factor inputs which vary in quantity over time: labor $L(t)$, and capital $K(t)$. These two factors are each homogeneous in nature and are used to produce a single general good whose output, $Y(t)$, is governed by the production function:

$$Y = Y(K, L) . \tag{4.1}$$

The actual consumption of this good in any year, $C(t)$, is given by

$$C = Y - \dot{K} , \tag{4.2}$$

where $\dot{K}(t)$ ($\equiv dK/dt$) is the amount of the good that is saved and simultaneously invested in productive capacity (plant and equipment). Associated with consumption of the good is a utility function, $f(C)$, and with the supply of labor input a disutility function, $v(L)$. Thus for the community as a whole, the utility realized during any unit of time is $f(C) - v(L)$, and the utility function over a period of time from a beginning point t_0 to an end point t_1 at which no net saving occurs is:

$$W = \int_{t_0}^{t_1} \{f(C) - v(L)\} dt . \tag{4.3}$$

Formally we may take L and K to represent generalized coordinates and to define the configuration space of the system. The Lagrangian $\mathcal{L}$ may then be viewed as:

$$\mathcal{L} = \mathcal{L}(K, L, \dot{K}, \dot{L}) = f(C) - v(L)$$
$$= f[F(K, L) - \dot{K}] - v(L) , \tag{4.4}$$

that is, as net utility realized during a unit of time, and the action S as:

$$S = W = \int_{t_0}^{t_1} \{f(C) - v(L)\} dt , \tag{4.5}$$

that is, as total utility realized during the time period. We have:

$$\frac{\partial \mathcal{L}}{\partial L} = \frac{\partial f}{\partial C} \frac{\partial C}{\partial Y} \frac{\partial Y}{\partial L} - \frac{\partial v}{\partial L} \ ,$$

$$\frac{\partial \mathcal{L}}{\partial K} = \frac{\partial f}{\partial C} \frac{\partial C}{\partial K} \ ,$$

$$\frac{\partial \mathcal{L}}{\partial \dot{L}} = 0 \text{ since } \dot{L} \text{ does not enter as a variable in the Lagrangian,}$$

$$\frac{\partial \mathcal{L}}{\partial \dot{K}} = \frac{\partial f}{\partial C} \frac{\partial C}{\partial \dot{K}} = -\frac{\partial f}{\partial C} \text{ since } \frac{\partial C}{\partial \dot{K}} = -1 \ .$$

Thus the first Lagrange equation

$$\frac{d}{dt}\left(\frac{\partial \mathcal{L}}{\partial \dot{L}}\right) = \frac{\partial \mathcal{L}}{\partial L}$$

implies:

$$\frac{d}{dt}(0) = \frac{\partial f}{\partial C} \frac{\partial C}{\partial Y} \frac{\partial Y}{\partial L} - \frac{\partial v}{\partial L} \ ,$$

or

$$\frac{\partial v}{\partial L} = \frac{\partial f}{\partial C} \frac{\partial Y}{\partial L} \text{ since } \frac{\partial C}{\partial Y} = 1 \ ; \tag{4.6}$$

and the second Lagrange equation

$$\frac{d}{dt}\left(\frac{\partial \mathcal{L}}{\partial \dot{K}}\right) = \frac{\partial \mathcal{L}}{\partial K}$$

implies

$$\frac{d}{dt}\left(\frac{\partial f}{\partial C} \frac{\partial C}{\partial \dot{K}}\right) = \frac{\partial f}{\partial C} \frac{\partial C}{\partial Y} \frac{\partial Y}{\partial K} \ ; \tag{4.7}$$

or since

$$\frac{\partial C}{\partial \dot{K}} = -1 \text{ and } \frac{\partial C}{\partial Y} = 1 \ ,$$

$$\frac{d}{dt}\left(-\frac{\partial f}{\partial C}\right) = \frac{\partial f}{\partial C} \frac{\partial Y}{\partial K} \ . \tag{4.8}$$

Equation (4.6) states the condition that the marginal disutility of labor should be equal to the utility (through consumption) of the marginal product of labor. Equation (4.8) states the condition that the negative of the time rate of change of marginal utility should be equal to the utility of the marginal product of capital. The meaning of this condition becomes clearer if we multiply both sides of equation (4.8) by dt to obtain (after cancellation):

$$d\left(\frac{\partial f}{\partial C} \frac{\partial C}{\partial \dot{K}}\right) = \frac{\partial f}{\partial C} \frac{\partial Y}{\partial K} dt \ . \tag{4.9}$$

On taking the integral of both sides over the period from t to t_1 we obtain,

$$+\frac{\partial f}{\partial C}\frac{\partial C}{\partial \vec{K}}\bigg|_{\text{at } t_1} - \frac{\partial f}{\partial C}\frac{\partial C}{\partial \vec{K}}\bigg|_{\text{at } t} = \int_t^{t_1} \frac{\partial f}{\partial C}\frac{\partial Y}{\partial K}\mathrm{d}t \,,$$

or

$$-\frac{\partial f}{\partial C}\frac{\partial C}{\partial \vec{K}}\bigg|_{\text{at } t} = \int_t^{t_1} \frac{\partial f}{\partial C}\frac{\partial Y}{\partial K}\mathrm{d}t - \frac{\partial f}{\partial C}\frac{\partial C}{\partial \vec{K}}\bigg|_{\text{at } t_1} \,. \tag{4.10}$$

The left-hand side refers to the utility foregone because of the reduction of the consumption of the good at time t in order to use that good to produce an additional unit of capital during that time. The first term of the right side is the sum, over the points of time from t to t_1, of the utility of the additional goods produced by that additional unit of capital. The second term refers to the utility which can be realized if at time t_1 that additional unit of capital is converted back, via a reversible production process, into the consumption good, and if the resulting amount of that good is consumed. That is, the second term is the salvage value of the unit of capital. In sum, equation (4.7) implies the condition that the utility foregone by a marginal increase in capital (savings) at time t must equal the additional utility realized over the years from the consumption of goods stemming from that investment plus the utility of the goods salvageable from that investment at the end of the time period.

The negative of the Hamiltonian, $-H$, or social energy is:

$$-H = \mathcal{L} - p_i \dot{q}_i$$

$$= f(C) - v(L) - \frac{\partial \mathcal{L}}{\partial K}\dot{K} - \frac{\partial \mathcal{L}}{\partial L}\dot{L} \tag{4.11}$$

$$= f(C) - v(L) + \frac{\partial f}{\partial C}\dot{K} \,.$$

Graphically, $-H$ or social energy, which is constant for the Ramsey closed system, may be depicted as in figure 1. Since $(\partial f/\partial C)\dot{K}$ is the utility from the consumption of goods that is foregone at any time t, because those goods have been used to produce the capital goods $\dot{K}$ at that time, social energy at time t is the sum of (1) net utility realized (utility from actual consumption of goods less the disutility of actual labor) and (2) utility foregone because of investment—which may be viewed as an opportunity cost, or as virtual utility, or as utility embodied in investment goods.
In terms of a year, a unit of time that Society often employs, social energy may be viewed as the *ability to do work* during that year; that is, to yield community satisfaction realized directly from actual consumption during that year *plus* community satisfaction unrealized because goods are

embodied in real wealth (capital) during the year to achieve greater future satisfaction. In a very broad and loose sense, social energy may thus be considered, on an annual basis, as an *ability to effect social welfare.*

In order to facilitate understanding of the more complicated models to be presented later, it is useful to interpret here, in a systematic fashion, each of the terms which we have encountered. First, recall that:

$\mathcal{L}$ is the annual net value of consumption of goods and exertion of labor in terms of utility. It is represented graphically at any point in time by the height of the vertical line under the curve of figure 1.

$S = W$ is the total utility over the time period from t_0 to t_1. In the box of figure 1 it is given by the area under the curve.

$-H$ is the social energy as already defined, and is the vertical height of the box of figure 1.

q_i are the *generalized coordinates*, the relevant configuration variables, which in our case are L and K.

$\dot{q}_i$ are the *generalized velocities or paces*—the time rates of change of our configuration variables. In our particular problem, $\dot{L}$ is not a relevant velocity because according to our theory it does not have a direct effect on $\mathcal{L}$, or on the annual utility [5]. $\dot{K}$ is a relevant velocity, and in our particular problem is the annual increase in capital stock or investment.

$\dfrac{\partial \mathcal{L}}{\partial q_i}$ is a generalized force, and in our problem represents the marginal net utility resulting from a change of q_i. This marginal net utility is positive and equal to the utility of the marginal product when $q_i = K$, and zero when $q_i = L$, since the utility of the marginal product from a small increase in L is balanced by the disutility of that effort.

$\dfrac{\partial \mathcal{L}}{\partial \dot{q}_i}$ is a generalized momentum. We can understand the significance of

[5] The labor supply L is associated with a given population P, all individuals of which may be taken to have like tastes and skills, and to share equally in the product of the community. Ignoring differences in age and sex, we may arbitrarily conceive each individual to be able to work physically a maximum of 18 hours per day, 365 days per year or 6570 hours per year. Thus the maximum possible annual input of labor, $L_{max} = 6570P$. But our model does not require that each individual labor 18 hours per day, but only that amount (the same for all individuals, say 8 hours) where the marginal disutility of additional time at labor just equals the utility of the marginal product of that labor. Hence, not all potential labor is exploited, and L is a variable associated with a fixed population P which does not reach its maximum value, $6570P$, except possibly under extreme conditions.

If we were to consider a community with a changing population, we would have: $\dot{P} = \dot{L}_{max} \neq 0$. However, it should be kept clearly in mind that while the population and the maximum value which L can take may change by a certain percentage, say 10 percent, it does not follow that the actual value which the variable L takes will change by the same percent. For example, because of diminishing returns to scale, and still assuming equal shares in the total product, the members of a growing community may decide to work fewer hours per day.

this term if we recall the Lagrangian equation (2.3),

$$\frac{d}{dt}\left(\frac{\partial \mathcal{L}}{\partial \dot{q}_i}\right) = \frac{\partial \mathcal{L}}{\partial q_i} \, ,$$

which implies, as we have shown [equation (4.10)], that

$$-\frac{\partial \mathcal{L}}{\partial \dot{q}_i}\bigg|_{\text{at } t} = \int_t^{t_1} \frac{\partial \mathcal{L}}{\partial q_i} dt + \text{a constant.}$$

This last relation states that $-\partial \mathcal{L}/\partial \dot{q}_i$ at time t is equal to the marginal net utilities cumulatively summed over the point of time t and subsequent points of time up to t_1 (inclusive of change in the scrap value at t_1) due to the marginal (last unit of) increase in the stock of q_i resulting from change in $\dot{q}_i$ at time t. This relation suggests that $-\partial \mathcal{L}/\partial \dot{q}_i$ is a utility value (price or cost) to be associated with a unit of $\dot{q}_i$, in our case a unit of the capital that is invested at time t. Since we have defined $p_i = \dfrac{\partial \mathcal{L}}{\partial \dot{q}_i}$, $-p_i$ may be taken as this value (price or cost). It also follows from our basic principle that $\dot{p}_i = \dfrac{d}{dt}\left(\dfrac{\partial \mathcal{L}}{\partial \dot{q}_i}\right) = \dfrac{\partial \mathcal{L}}{\partial q_i} = a$ marginal net utility at time point t, which is positive in the case of capital, and $\dot{p}_i$ may be viewed as a value (price or cost) of the services (per unit of time) yielded by that unit of new capital at time t[6]. In the case of labor, $\dot{p}_i = 0$, since the marginal disutility of labor just balances the utility value of its marginal product.

$\dfrac{\partial \mathcal{L}}{\partial t}$ is a marginal utility related to time. Since we take our model to be time independent, in the sense that it does not matter which point of

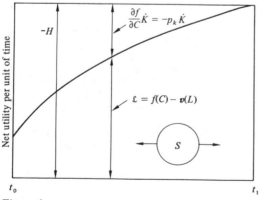

Figure 1.

[6] In order to avoid confusion, we retain the symbol p to relate to momentum and suggest the symbol π to refer to market or welfare prices. Thus $\pi_i = -p_i$ when i is a capital good and $\pi_{s(i)} = \dot{p}_i$ when $s(i)$ is the service yielded by capital good i.

real time we designate as the starting point, we are in effect assuming that $\partial \mathcal{L}/\partial t = 0$.

Previously, in defining S we considered two fixed points in configuration space at two corresponding points of time, t_0 and t_1. Also S was computed on any conceivable path joining these two points. If we fix only one of the end points, say q_i^1, at time t_1, and S is computed along an optimal path ending at t_1 in q_i^1, then S becomes a function of q_i and t. With this in mind,

$\dfrac{\partial S}{\partial q_i}$ is the change in the cumulative sum of utilities at time point t and all subsequent time points from a small change in q_i at time t. The meaning of this term is best understood when we specify the q_i^1 at the end point t_1, and then consider the partial derivative $\partial S/\partial q_i$ at the initial point of time, t_0. Then $\partial S/\partial q_i$ is depicted graphically by the bold curved strip of figure 2, which represents the difference in the two paths as a result of a small variation in q_i^0. For example, suppose $q_i = K$, so that we are identifying the change in S that would have occurred had there been one more unit of capital available at t_0. Since capital does not depreciate in the current model, the difference in S would be the cumulative sum of the utilities, over all points of time from t_0 to t_1, of the *additional* annual marginal product derived from that unit of capital (inclusive of change in scrap value at t_1). This difference in S is defined by the bold curved strip. Note that this difference is equal to

$$-\left.\frac{\partial \mathcal{L}}{\partial \dot{q}_i}\right|_{\text{at } t_0} = \int_{t_0}^{t_1} \frac{\partial \mathcal{L}}{\partial q_i}\mathrm{d}t - \left.\frac{\partial \mathcal{L}}{\partial \dot{q}_i}\right|_{\text{at } t_1} ,$$

or more specifically, from equation (4.10), to:

$$-\left.\frac{\partial \mathcal{L}}{\partial K}\right|_{\text{at } t_0} = \int_{t_0}^{t_1} \frac{\partial f}{\partial C}\frac{\partial Y}{\partial K}\mathrm{d}t - \left.\frac{\partial f}{\partial C}\frac{\partial C}{\partial K}\right|_{\text{at } t_1} .$$

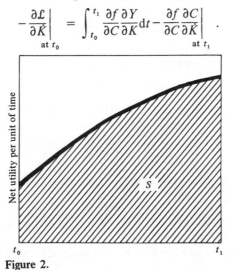

Figure 2.

This observation is, of course, consistent with the relations (2.7) and (2.16),

$$\frac{\partial S}{\partial q_i} = -p_i = -\frac{\partial \mathcal{L}}{\partial \dot{q}_i} . \quad (7)$$

Generally speaking we may view $\partial S/\partial q_i$ as equal to the price or value of a unit of investment, or a new unit of capital at time t. Also we may observe that for fixed $q_j, j = 1, ..., i-1, i+1, ..., s$, and fixed time,

$$\delta S = -p_i \delta q_i ;$$

that is, for any given increase in the stock of q_i, the rate of increase in total welfare is given by $-p_i$, which is the price of q_i.

$\frac{\partial S}{\partial \dot{q}_i} = 0$, since our definition of the action (sequence of subactions) $S = S(q_i, t)$ is independent of $\dot{q}_i$. The $\dot{q}_i$ are thus derived variables, that is, they are a function of (q_i, t) in accord with the definition of S, S being associated with an actual optimization path.

$\frac{\partial S}{\partial t}$ is a partial whose meaning can be best understood if we consider a path of motion where q_i^0, q_i^1 are specified for t_0 and t_1 respectively, and where we consider a small change in t_0. Suppose we replace t_0 by $t_0 + \delta t_0$ in such a way that q_i at $t_0 + \delta t_0$ is equal to q_i^0. Then $\partial S/\partial t$ represents the loss in total welfare from the shortening of the time period over which the economy is observed. Since by definition (2.17)

$$\frac{\partial S}{\partial t} = H , \quad (8) \qquad \text{we have} \qquad \delta S = H \delta t_0$$

for fixed q_i. That is, for any given change in the time period observed, the rate of change in total welfare is given by $-H$, the social energy per unit of time. In brief, if we consider shortening the time path by a year, the loss in welfare is equal to the social energy (actual plus virtual utility) that would have been realized in that year.

$-\frac{\partial H}{\partial q_i}$ is the marginal change in social energy consequent to a change in capital or labor at time t. By equations (a), (b), and (c) of footnote (4), $-\partial H/\partial q_i = +\dot{p}_i$ and by equation (2.8), $\dot{p}_i = \partial \mathcal{L}/\partial q_i$. Hence $-\partial H/\partial q_i$ is the marginal net utility of q_i as interpreted in our discussion of $\partial \mathcal{L}/\partial q_i$.

$-\frac{\partial H}{\partial \dot{q}_i} = 0$ since our particular definition of H as a function is independent of $\dot{q}_i$.

(7) In equation (2.16), the partial $\partial S/\partial q_i$ is evaluated for a path for which the initial point is fixed. This difference accounts for the change in sign.

(8) Observe that a change in sign is required because the end point rather than initial point is fixed in our example.

$-\dfrac{\partial H}{\partial t} = +\dfrac{\partial \mathcal{L}}{\partial t} = 0$ from definition (2.17) and from the discussion of $\dfrac{\partial \mathcal{L}}{\partial t}$.

Like $\mathcal{L}$, H is time independent in the sense that it is immaterial at which point in real time we begin our model.

Finally, we must interpret the full time-rate of change of $\mathcal{L}$, H, and S. By our definition (2.1)

$$\dfrac{d\mathcal{L}}{dt} = \dfrac{\partial \mathcal{L}}{\partial q_i}\dfrac{dq_i}{dt} + \dfrac{\partial \mathcal{L}}{\partial \dot{q}_i}\dfrac{d\dot{q}_i}{dt} + \dfrac{\partial \mathcal{L}}{\partial t}$$

$$= \dot{p}_i \dot{q}_i + p_i \ddot{q}_i = \dfrac{d}{dt}(p_i \dot{q}_i) .$$

But $d(p_i \dot{q}_i)/dt$ = the negative of the time rate of change of 'utility foregone through capital investment', or virtual utility—which is the slope of the curve of figure 1 at any point, and which is thereby the same as the time rate of change of $\mathcal{L}$, as is implied by the conservation of social energy in our particular situation.

$dH/dt = 0$, since by our definition of social energy, H is a constant.

$$\dfrac{dS}{dt} = -\mathcal{L} , \quad \text{or} \quad dS = -\mathcal{L}dt .$$

This signifies that if we change the time period over which we observe welfare for our economy, the rate of change of total welfare is given by $-\mathcal{L}$. Roughly speaking, if we shorten the period by one year, by replacing t_0 by $t_0 + 1$, the loss in total welfare is given by the utility realizable at year t_0.

5 The Ramsey model with capital replacement and increasing labor productivity

In order to obtain a model somewhat more realistic than the Ramsey model, we introduce the process of replacement of capital as it is used up in production, and the process whereby labor becomes increasingly efficient over time as it becomes more skilled, as technological advance permits the more effective use of existing stocks of capital, and as the replacement of older used-up capital plant and equipment makes available more productive plant and equipment. We thus introduce two new variables into the model, namely L_e the number of standard efficiency units which the labor force L constitutes at any time t, and D, the amount of capital which is to be replaced at time t. We also have two new relations (constraints), which in one form are

$$L_e = e^{\tau t}L , \tag{5.1}$$

where τ is a positive rate per unit of time, and where we set $t_0 = 0$; and

$$D = \rho K , \tag{5.2}$$

where ρ is a positive rate per unit of time.

The production function, consumption function, and the Lagrangian are now, respectively,

$$Y = Y(K, L_e),$$ (5.3)

$$C = Y - \dot{K} - D,$$ (5.4)

$$\mathcal{L} = f(C) - v(L) - \lambda_L(L_e - e^{\tau t}L) - \lambda_D(D - \rho K)$$ (5.5)

where λ_L and λ_D are the familiar undetermined Lagrangian multipliers. From the above relations we have:

$$\frac{\partial \mathcal{L}}{\partial D} = 0 \qquad\qquad \frac{\partial \mathcal{L}}{\partial D} = \frac{\partial f}{\partial C}\frac{\partial C}{\partial D} - \lambda_D = -\frac{\partial f}{\partial C} - \lambda_D$$

$$\frac{\partial \mathcal{L}}{\partial \dot{K}} = \frac{\partial f}{\partial C}\frac{\partial C}{\partial \dot{K}} = -\frac{\partial f}{\partial C} \qquad \frac{\partial \mathcal{L}}{\partial K} = \frac{\partial f}{\partial C}\frac{\partial C}{\partial Y}\frac{\partial Y}{\partial K} + \lambda_D \rho = \frac{\partial f}{\partial C}\frac{\partial Y}{\partial K} + \lambda_D \rho$$

$$\frac{\partial \mathcal{L}}{\partial \dot{L}_e} = 0 \qquad\qquad \frac{\partial \mathcal{L}}{\partial L_e} = \frac{\partial f}{\partial C}\frac{\partial C}{\partial Y}\frac{\partial Y}{\partial L_e} - \lambda_L = \frac{\partial f}{\partial C}\frac{\partial Y}{\partial L_e} - \lambda_L$$

$$\frac{\partial \mathcal{L}}{\partial \dot{L}} = 0 \qquad\qquad \frac{\partial \mathcal{L}}{\partial L} = -\frac{\partial v}{\partial L} + \lambda_L e^{\tau t}.$$

To insure an optimal path of growth, four Euler conditions must be met. The first Euler condition,

$$\frac{\mathrm{d}}{\mathrm{d}t}\left(\frac{\partial \mathcal{L}}{\partial \dot{D}}\right) = \frac{\partial \mathcal{L}}{\partial D},$$

implies:

$$\frac{\mathrm{d}}{\mathrm{d}t}(0) = -\frac{\partial f}{\partial C} - \lambda_D, \qquad \text{or} \qquad \lambda_D = -\frac{\partial f}{\partial C}.$$ (5.6)

That is, the Lagrangian multiplier λ_D must be equal to the negative value of the marginal utility of the good that is consumed.

The second Euler condition,

$$\frac{\mathrm{d}}{\mathrm{d}t}\left(\frac{\partial \mathcal{L}}{\partial \dot{K}}\right) = \frac{\partial \mathcal{L}}{\partial K},$$

implies:

$$\frac{\mathrm{d}}{\mathrm{d}t}\left(-\frac{\partial f}{\partial C}\right) = \frac{\partial f}{\partial C}\frac{\partial Y}{\partial K} + \lambda_D \rho,$$ (5.7)

or substituting in the value of λ_D from equation (5.6), we have

$$\frac{\mathrm{d}}{\mathrm{d}t}\left(-\frac{\partial f}{\partial C}\right) = \frac{\partial f}{\partial C}\left(\frac{\partial Y}{\partial K} - \rho\right).$$ (5.8)

This relationship is to be given the same interpretation as that of (4.8) except that net marginal product of capital, after allowance for replacement (depreciation), $(\partial Y/\partial K - \rho)$, substitutes for the marginal product of capital.

The third Euler condition,

$$\frac{d}{dt}\left(\frac{\partial \mathcal{L}}{\partial \dot{L}_e}\right) = \frac{\partial \mathcal{L}}{\partial \dot{L}} \; ,$$

implies:

$$0 = \frac{\partial f}{\partial C}\frac{\partial Y}{\partial L_e} - \lambda_L, \qquad \text{or} \qquad \lambda_L = \frac{\partial f}{\partial C}\frac{\partial Y}{\partial L_e} \; . \tag{5.9}$$

That is the Lagrangian multiplier, λ_L, must equal the utility value of the marginal product of an efficiency unit of labor.

The fourth Euler condition,

$$\frac{d}{dt}\left(\frac{\partial \mathcal{L}}{\partial \dot{L}}\right) = \frac{\partial \mathcal{L}}{\partial L} \; ,$$

implies:

$$0 = -\frac{\partial v}{\partial L} + \lambda_L\, e^{\tau t} \qquad \text{or} \qquad \frac{\partial v}{\partial L} = \lambda_L\, e^{\tau t} \; . \tag{5.10}$$

That is the marginal disutility of labor must equal the marginal product of an efficiency unit of labor multiplied by $e^{\tau t}$, a factor which indicates the increase in the efficiency of that unit of labor since year $t_0 = 0$. Observe that from equation (5.1)

$$\frac{\partial Y}{\partial L_e} = \frac{\partial Y}{\partial L}\frac{\partial L}{\partial L_e} = \frac{\partial Y}{\partial L}e^{-\tau t} \; .$$

Therefore condition (5.10) can be written, with the use of (5.9), as:

$$\frac{\partial v}{\partial L} = \frac{\partial f}{\partial C}\frac{\partial Y}{\partial L_e}e^{\tau t} = \frac{\partial f}{\partial C}\frac{\partial Y}{\partial L} \; . \tag{5.11}$$

That is, the marginal disutility of labor must equal the utility of its marginal product.

The negative of the Hamiltonian, $-H$, is:

$$-H = \mathcal{L} - p_i \dot{q}_i$$

$$= f(C) - v(L) - \frac{\partial \mathcal{L}}{\partial \dot{K}}\dot{K} - \frac{\partial \mathcal{L}}{\partial \dot{D}}\dot{D} - \frac{\partial \mathcal{L}}{\partial \dot{L}_e}\dot{L}_e - \frac{\partial \mathcal{L}}{\partial \dot{L}}\dot{L}$$

$$= f(C) - v(L) + \frac{\partial f}{\partial C}\dot{K} \; .$$

Note that this quantity is not conserved. This follows because, by equation (2.13),

$$\frac{dH}{dt} = -\frac{\partial \mathcal{L}}{\partial t} \; , \tag{5.12}$$

and from equation (5.5)

$$\frac{\partial \mathcal{L}}{\partial t} = +\lambda_L \tau e^{\tau t} L = \lambda_L \tau L_e ,$$
(5.13)

which does not equal zero. Now from equation (5.12)

$$dH + \frac{\partial \mathcal{L}}{\partial t} dt = 0 .$$
(5.14)

On integrating both sides, and substituting for $\partial \mathcal{L}/\partial t$ from equation (5.13), we have:

$$-H + \int_t^{t_1} \lambda_L \tau L_e \, dt = \text{constant} = -\widetilde{H} .$$

Here $-\widetilde{H}$ is a new integral of motion which is a constant, and may be designated the extended Hamiltonian, which we now identify as social energy for the system of our model. The interpretation of $-\widetilde{H}$ and this definition of social energy is facilitated by figure 3. In that figure the terms, $f(C) - v(L)$, and $(\partial f/\partial C)\dot{K}$ for each year have already been interpreted. The term $\int_t^{t_1} \lambda_L \tau L_e \, dt$ represents utility lost in the point of time t and in subsequent points of time because labor in time point t and subsequent points is not as efficient in production as it is in time t_1. This term thus represents an unrealized potential for utility creation and social satisfaction. The sum of these terms constitutes social energy, that is the capability of the *system* to do *work* and to create social satisfaction and welfare. For fuller discussion of this extended Hamiltonian, see appendix D.

   Also observe that the utility value of the quantity D of the economic good, diverted to replace used-up capital ρK, does not appear in $-H$ and is not a component of social energy. This is as it should be. The amount D

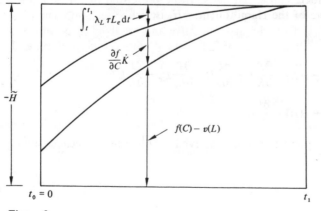

Figure 3.

is subtracted along with $\dot{K}$ from Y to leave a smaller amount C for consumption than would be the case if capital were not used up in production. Thus the $f(C)$ component of social energy is smaller, and the social capability to do work (to provide welfare) is smaller, because certain economic goods must be diverted from consumption to maintain the capital resource as a production factor.

6 Concluding remarks

We have now presented our concept of social energy. Using the analytic apparatus of classical mechanics, we have defined it precisely as the magnitude which corresponds to the Hamiltonian in any social science theory which may be propounded by an analyst. We then indicated reasonable ways in which social energy can be interpreted, especially through the association of relevant social masses, weighted by their paces (velocities), with the kinetic energy concept of physics, and associating the interaction among the units of the social system with the potential energy concept of physics. We then identified the general concept of social energy, and related concepts, with specific magnitudes of specific models of the social system: in particular with simple Ramsey-type models of growth.

Finally we have tried, both in the text and mathematical appendix, to develop the concepts and formal structure in such a way that they can be applied easily to specific models and theories of interest to a particular scholar. We, for example, have already utilized these concepts and formal structures in air pollution models for both single and multi-city (region) situations; in both industry (2-body) and residential (n-body) location models, in urban and regional growth models, and in multi-national political situations involving both *big* and *small* powers.

Perhaps most important of all are the potential contributions which the notion of social energy, and the related concepts of social momentum, social acceleration and social mass (to be presented in forthcoming papers) makes possible for studying (1) the growth processes and dynamics of social systems and (2) the agglomerative and feedback type of effects which we have already been able to attack with the help of general (relativistic) gravitational theory.

References
Allen, R. G. D., 1939, *Mathematical Analysis for Economists* (Macmillan, New York).
Goldstein, H., 1959, *Classical Mechanics* (Addison-Wesley, Reading, Mass.).
Lanczos, C., 1960, *The Variational Principles of Mechanics*, Mathematical Expositions, number 4 (University of Toronto Press, Toronto).
Landau, L. D., Lifshitz, L. M., 1960, *Mechanics* (Pergamon Press, Oxford).

APPENDICES. Mathematical Proofs

Appendix A

Suppose $q_i(t)$ minimizes the action integral

$$S = \int_{t_0}^{t_1} \mathcal{L}\,\mathrm{d}t \ .$$

By δS, the variation of S, we mean the change in S if we replace $q_i(t)$ by $q_i(t) + \delta q_i(t)$ and consequently $\dot{q}_i(t)$ by $\dot{q}_i(t) + \delta\dot{q}_i(t)$, where $\delta\dot{q}_i(t) = \mathrm{d}(\delta q_i)/\mathrm{d}t$. Thus we have:

$$\delta S = \delta \int_{t_0}^{t_1} \mathcal{L}(q_i, \dot{q}_i, t)\,\mathrm{d}t = \int_{t_0}^{t_1} [\delta\mathcal{L}(q_i, \dot{q}_i, t)]\,\mathrm{d}t$$

$$= \int_{t_0}^{t_1}\left[\frac{\partial\mathcal{L}}{\partial q_i}\delta q_i + \frac{\partial\mathcal{L}}{\partial\dot{q}_i}\delta\dot{q}_i\right]\mathrm{d}t = 0 \ . \tag{A1}$$

Now from standard operations of calculus, we have

$$\frac{\mathrm{d}}{\mathrm{d}t}\left(\frac{\partial\mathcal{L}}{\partial\dot{q}_i}\delta q_i\right) = \frac{\mathrm{d}}{\mathrm{d}t}\left(\frac{\partial\mathcal{L}}{\partial\dot{q}_i}\right)\delta q_i + \frac{\partial\mathcal{L}}{\partial\dot{q}_i}\frac{\mathrm{d}}{\mathrm{d}t}(\delta q_i) = \frac{\mathrm{d}}{\mathrm{d}t}\left(\frac{\partial\mathcal{L}}{\partial\dot{q}_i}\right)\delta q_i + \frac{\partial\mathcal{L}}{\partial\dot{q}_i}\delta\left(\frac{\mathrm{d}q_i}{\mathrm{d}t}\right)$$

$$= \frac{\mathrm{d}}{\mathrm{d}t}\left(\frac{\partial\mathcal{L}}{\partial\dot{q}_i}\right)\delta q_i + \frac{\partial\mathcal{L}}{\partial\dot{q}_i}\delta\dot{q}_i \ .$$

Hence, by transposing terms, we obtain

$$\frac{\partial\mathcal{L}}{\partial\dot{q}_i}\delta\dot{q}_i = \frac{\mathrm{d}}{\mathrm{d}t}\left(\frac{\partial\mathcal{L}}{\partial\dot{q}_i}\delta q_i\right) - \frac{\mathrm{d}}{\mathrm{d}t}\left(\frac{\partial\mathcal{L}}{\partial\dot{q}_i}\right)\delta q_i \ . \tag{A2}$$

Replacing $\dfrac{\partial\mathcal{L}}{\partial\dot{q}_i}\delta\dot{q}_i$ in equation (A1) by the right-hand side of equation (A2), we obtain:

$$\int_{t_0}^{t_1}\left[\frac{\partial\mathcal{L}}{\partial q_i}\delta q_i + \frac{\mathrm{d}}{\mathrm{d}t}\left(\frac{\partial\mathcal{L}}{\partial\dot{q}_i}\delta q_i\right) - \frac{\mathrm{d}}{\mathrm{d}t}\left(\frac{\partial\mathcal{L}}{\partial\dot{q}_i}\right)\delta q_i\right]\mathrm{d}t = 0 \tag{A3}$$

$$= \int_{t_0}^{t_1}\left[\frac{\partial\mathcal{L}}{\partial q_i} - \frac{\mathrm{d}}{\mathrm{d}t}\left(\frac{\partial\mathcal{L}}{\partial\dot{q}_i}\right)\right]\delta q_i\,\mathrm{d}t + \int_{t_0}^{t_1}\frac{\mathrm{d}}{\mathrm{d}t}\left(\frac{\partial\mathcal{L}}{\partial\dot{q}_i}\delta q_i\right)\mathrm{d}t$$

$$= \int_{t_0}^{t_1}\left[\frac{\partial\mathcal{L}}{\partial q_i} - \frac{\mathrm{d}}{\mathrm{d}t}\left(\frac{\partial\mathcal{L}}{\partial\dot{q}_i}\right)\right]\delta q_i\,\mathrm{d}t + \left(\frac{\partial\mathcal{L}}{\partial\dot{q}_i}\delta q_i\right)\Bigg|_{t=t_0}^{t=t_1} = 0 \ .$$

But $q_i(t_0) = $ constant; and $q_i(t_1) = $ constant. Hence $\delta q_i = 0$ at $t = t_0$ and $t = t_1$; and hence $\left(\dfrac{\partial\mathcal{L}}{\partial\dot{q}_i}\delta q_i\right)\Bigg|_{t=t_0}^{t=t_1} = 0$. Thus

$$\int_{t_0}^{t_1}\left[\frac{\partial\mathcal{L}}{\partial q_i} - \frac{\mathrm{d}}{\mathrm{d}t}\left(\frac{\partial\mathcal{L}}{\partial\dot{q}_i}\right)\right]\delta q_i\,\mathrm{d}t = 0 \ . \tag{A4}$$

But the δq_i, $i = 1, 2, ..., s$, may be varied arbitrarily, independent of each other, for $t \neq t_0, t_1$. Hence

$$\frac{\partial\mathcal{L}}{\partial q_i} - \frac{\mathrm{d}}{\mathrm{d}t}\left(\frac{\partial\mathcal{L}}{\partial\dot{q}_i}\right) = 0 \ . \tag{A5}$$

Appendix B

By equations (2.5) and (A3) we have:

$$\delta S = \delta \int_{t_0}^{t_1} \mathcal{L}(q_i, \dot{q}_i, t) = \int_{t_0}^{t_1} \left[\frac{\partial \mathcal{L}}{\partial q_i} - \frac{d}{dt}\left(\frac{\partial \mathcal{L}}{\partial \dot{q}_i}\right) \right] \delta q_i \, dt + \int_{t_0}^{t_1} \frac{d}{dt}\left(\frac{\partial \mathcal{L}}{\partial \dot{q}_i} \delta q_i\right) dt \ .$$

Since S is computed along a real, optimal path, the Lagrange equations are satisfied, namely, the integrand of the first term vanishes. Hence,

$$\delta S = \int_{t_0}^{t_1} \frac{d}{dt}\left(\frac{\partial \mathcal{L}}{\partial \dot{q}_i} \delta q_i\right) dt = \left(\frac{\partial \mathcal{L}}{\partial \dot{q}_i} \delta q_i\right) \Bigg|_{t = t_0}^{t = t_1} \ .$$

For $q_i(t_0) = $ constant, $\delta q_i(t_0) = 0$. So for unspecified $q_i(t_1)$, which we replace simply by q_i, we have

$$\delta S = p_i \, \delta q_i \ , \tag{B1}$$

since by definition, $p_i = \dfrac{\partial \mathcal{L}}{\partial \dot{q}_i}$.

Now since q_i, or generally speaking the end point $q_i(t_1)$, $t_1 \neq t_0$, of the actual path is unspecified, the action S for any given $q_i(t_0)$ must itself then be a function of q_i and time. That is

$$S = S(q_i, t) \ ,$$

and

$$dS = \frac{\partial S}{\partial q_i} dq_i + \frac{\partial S}{\partial t} dt \ . \tag{B2}$$

For the moment set $t = t_k$ so that $dt = 0$. Then

$$dS = \frac{\partial S}{\partial q_i} dq_i \tag{B3}$$

or, recalling equation (B1),

$$\frac{\partial S}{\partial q_i} = p_i \ . \tag{B4}$$

But

$$S = \int \mathcal{L}(q_i, \dot{q}_i, t) dt \ ,$$

so

$$\frac{dS}{dt} = \mathcal{L} \ ,$$

and from equation (B2)

$$\frac{dS}{dt} = \mathcal{L} = \frac{\partial S}{\partial q_i} \frac{dq_i}{dt} + \frac{\partial S}{\partial t} \ ,$$

which from equation (B4) yields

$$\mathcal{L} = p_i \dot{q}_i + \frac{\partial S}{\partial t} \ .$$

On transposing terms and recalling equation (2.12)

$$\frac{\partial S}{\partial t} = -(p_i \dot{q}_i - \mathcal{L}) = -H \, .$$ (B5)

Further,

$$\frac{\partial S}{\partial t} + H\left(q_i, \frac{\partial S}{\partial q_i}, t\right) = 0 \, ,$$ (B6)

the well-known Hamilton-Jacoby equation, which must be satisfied by the function $S(q_i, t)$.

Remark

$\dfrac{\partial S}{\partial q_i} = -p_i$ if S is taken along optimal paths ending at prespecified q_i^1 at $t = t_1$.

Appendix C

We now wish to show that:

$$p_i \dot{q}_i = \sum_i \sum_k A_{ik}(q_1, q_2, ..., q_s) \dot{q}_i \dot{q}_k \, .$$ (C1)

By equation (3.18)

$$\mathcal{L} = \tfrac{1}{2} \sum_{i,k} A_{ik} \dot{q}_i \dot{q}_k - V \, ,$$ (C2)

where

$$A_{ik} = A_{ik}(q_1, q_2, ..., q_s) \quad \text{and} \quad V = V(q_1, q_2, ..., q_s) \, .$$

Hence it follows that

$$\frac{\partial \mathcal{L}}{\partial \dot{q}_l} = \tfrac{1}{2} \sum_{i,k} A_{ik} \frac{\partial}{\partial \dot{q}_l}(\dot{q}_i \dot{q}_k) \, ,$$

$$= \tfrac{1}{2} \sum_{i,k} A_{ik} \left(\frac{\partial \dot{q}_i}{\partial \dot{q}_l} \dot{q}_k + \dot{q}_i \frac{\partial \dot{q}_k}{\partial \dot{q}_l} \right) \, ,$$

thus

$$\frac{\partial \mathcal{L}}{\partial \dot{q}_l} = \tfrac{1}{2} \sum_{i,k} A_{ik} (\delta_{il} \dot{q}_k + \dot{q}_i \delta_{lk}) \, ,$$ (C3)

where δ_{il} is the Kronecker delta, which is equal to 1 when $i = l$ and equal to 0 when $i \neq l$. Now the only terms in the summation $\tfrac{1}{2} \sum_{i,k} A_{ik} \delta_{il} \dot{q}_k$ which are non-zero are those for which $i = l$. Hence,

$$\tfrac{1}{2} \sum_{i,k} A_{ik} \delta_{il} \dot{q}_k = \tfrac{1}{2} \sum_k A_{lk} \dot{q}_k \, .$$ (C4)

Similarly,

$$\tfrac{1}{2} \sum_{i,k} A_{ik} \delta_{lk} \dot{q}_i = \tfrac{1}{2} \sum_i A_{il} \dot{q}_i \, .$$

Now k and i are both dummy indices and interchangeable. So the right-hand term of equation (C4) may be written

$$\tfrac{1}{2}\sum_i A_{li}\dot{q}_i ,\tag{C5}$$

and equation (C3) may be rewritten as:

$$\frac{\partial \mathcal{L}}{\partial \dot{q}_l} = \tfrac{1}{2}\sum_i [A_{li}+A_{il}]\dot{q}_i .\tag{C6}$$

Now we can take A_{ik} of equation (C1) to be symmetric, so that

$$A_{li} = A_{il} ,$$

and also k and l are both dummy indices, so we may replace l with k. Hence equation (C6) becomes

$$\frac{\partial \mathcal{L}}{\partial \dot{q}_k} = \sum_i A_{ik}\dot{q}_i ,\tag{C7}$$

and

$$\sum_k \frac{\partial \mathcal{L}}{\partial \dot{q}_k}\dot{q}_k = \sum_{k,i} A_{ik}\dot{q}_i\dot{q}_k .$$

Or since $\dfrac{\partial \mathcal{L}}{\partial \dot{q}_k} = p_k$, and k and i are interchangeable, we have

$$p_i\dot{q}_i = \sum_{i,k} A_{ik}\dot{q}_i\dot{q}_k .$$

Appendix D
We wish to set down here the procedure for defining the extended Hamiltonian for open systems[9].

From equation (2.13) we have

$$\frac{dH}{dt} = -\frac{\partial \mathcal{L}}{\partial t} .\tag{D1}$$

That is for an open system, for which $\partial \mathcal{L}/\partial t \neq 0$, the Hamiltonian is not a constant of motion; it is not conserved. From equation (D1) we write

$$\frac{d}{dt}\left(H+ \int^t \frac{\partial \mathcal{L}}{\partial t} dt \right) = 0 ,\tag{D2}$$

where $\displaystyle\int^t \frac{\partial \mathcal{L}}{\partial t}dt$ is the indefinite integral of $\dfrac{\partial \mathcal{L}}{\partial t}$. Hence, we define

$$\widetilde{H} \equiv H+ \int^t \frac{\partial \mathcal{L}}{\partial t}dt = \text{a constant} ,\tag{D3}$$

and we designate this new Hamiltonian $\widetilde{H}$ as the *extended* Hamiltonian, which is conserved. Its meaning is obtained as follows. Suppose we

[9] An excellent reference here is Lanczos (1960).

consider the path of our system in space-time in parametric form, so that both the q_i and t are functions of λ, $q_i(\lambda)$ and $t(\lambda)$. Thereby we treat t as another configuration variable, namely the variable q_{s+1}. Thus we have

$$\mathcal{L} = \mathcal{L}(q_i, q_{s+1}, \dot{q}_i) , \tag{D4}$$

and

$$H = H(q_i, q_{s+1}, p_i) . \tag{D5}$$

From the principle of least action,

$$\delta \int_{t_0}^{t_1} \mathcal{L}(q_i, \dot{q}_i, t) \, \mathrm{d}t = 0 \qquad (i = 1, ..., s) . \tag{D6}$$

Since $t = q_{s+1}(\lambda)$, it follows that

$$\dot{q}_i = \frac{\mathrm{d}q_i}{\mathrm{d}t} = \frac{\mathrm{d}q_i}{\mathrm{d}\lambda} \frac{\mathrm{d}\lambda}{\mathrm{d}t} = \frac{q_i'}{q_{s+1}'}$$

and

$$\mathrm{d}t = \frac{\mathrm{d}t}{\mathrm{d}\lambda} \mathrm{d}\lambda = q_{s+1}' \, \mathrm{d}\lambda ,$$

where the prime indicates a derivative with respect to λ. Then equation (D6) becomes

$$\delta \int_{\lambda_0}^{\lambda_1} \mathcal{L}\left(q_i, q_{s+1}, \frac{q_i'}{q_{s+1}'}\right) q_{s+1}' \, \mathrm{d}\lambda = 0 , \tag{D7}$$

and we define a new Lagrangian $\overline{\mathcal{L}}$ as:

$$\overline{\mathcal{L}}(q_1, ..., q_{s+1}, q_1', ..., q_{s+1}') = q_{s+1}' \mathcal{L}\left(q_i, q_{s+1}, \frac{q_i'}{q_{s+1}'}\right) . \tag{D8}$$

From equation (D8) we obtain the Lagrange equations:

$$\frac{\mathrm{d}}{\mathrm{d}\lambda}\left(\frac{\partial \overline{\mathcal{L}}}{\partial q_h'}\right) = \frac{\partial \overline{\mathcal{L}}}{\partial q_h} , \qquad (h = 1, 2, ..., s+1) , \tag{D9}$$

and the definition of the generalized momentum is

$$p_h = \frac{\partial \overline{\mathcal{L}}}{\partial q_h'} . \tag{D10}$$

Accordingly the corresponding Hamiltonian, $\overline{H}$, is:

$$\overline{H} = p_h q_h' - \overline{\mathcal{L}} . \tag{D11}$$

Hamilton's equations are then $2(s+1)$ in number, since we now have $(s+1)$ configuration variables, and can be stated:

$$q_h' = \frac{\mathrm{d}q_h}{\mathrm{d}\lambda} = \frac{\partial \overline{H}}{\partial p_h} , \tag{D12}$$

$$\qquad\qquad (h = 1, 2, ..., s+1)$$

$$p_h' = \frac{\mathrm{d}p_h}{\mathrm{d}\lambda} = -\frac{\partial \overline{H}}{\partial q_h} . \tag{D13}$$

Now we demonstrate that the $\overline{H}$ corresponding to $\overline{\mathcal{L}}$ can be selected to be the $\widetilde{H}$ of equation (D3). Suppose we select our parameter λ in such a way that $q'_{s+1} = dq_{s+1}/d\lambda = 1$. Then from the $(s+1)$th Lagrange equation (D9), we have

$$p'_{s+1} = \frac{\partial \overline{\mathcal{L}}}{\partial q_{s+1}} , \qquad\qquad (D14)$$

or

$$\frac{dp_{s+1}}{dt}\frac{dt}{d\lambda} = \frac{\partial \overline{\mathcal{L}}}{\partial t}\frac{dt}{d\lambda} = q'_{s+1}\frac{\partial \mathcal{L}}{\partial t}\frac{dt}{d\lambda} . \qquad\qquad (D15)$$

But since $dt/d\lambda = q'_{s+1} = 1$, we have

$$\dot{p}_{s+1} = \frac{\partial \mathcal{L}}{\partial t} . \qquad\qquad (D16)$$

Hence,

$$p_{s+1} = \int^{t}\frac{\partial \mathcal{L}}{\partial t}dt , \qquad\qquad (D17)$$

and

$$\overline{H} = p_{s+1}q'_{s+1} + p_i q'_i - q'_{s+1}\mathcal{L} ,$$

or

$$\overline{H} = p_{s+1} + p_i \dot{q}_i - \mathcal{L} = p_{s+1} + H = \widetilde{H} \qquad \text{QED.} \qquad (D18)$$

The above procedure for identifying an extended Hamiltonian, which we now employ as our relevant definition of social energy, permits us to reconceive any open system as a closed system. In this step we introduce the new variable p_{s+1} at any point t, intermediate between t_0 and t_1 (the end points of our relevant optimal process). We interpret it as the cumulative sum of small continuous changes in utility due to processes associated with time itself, such as the increasing productivity of labor with time, and for which time serves as a proxy. Thus p_{s+1} is a value (utility) to be associated with time (as a stock variable). That is

$$p_{s+1}(t) = -\int_{t}^{t_1}\frac{\partial \mathcal{L}}{\partial t}dt . \qquad\qquad (D19)$$

Further

$$\dot{p}_{s+1} = \frac{\partial \mathcal{L}}{\partial t} ,$$

which is the current value (price or cost) of the 'services' of a unit of time, comparable to p_k, the current value of the services of a unit of capital. Thus p_{s+1} is a potential (or 'virtual') utility to be realized.

Appendix E

At times it is required that the generalized coordinates q_i, $i = 1, 2, ..., s$, satisfy certain constraints; that is, are not free to vary independently. Let these constraints be:

$$f_l(q_1, q_2, ..., q_s, t) = 0 \quad \text{for} \quad l = 1, 2, ..., k .\tag{E1}$$

Under these circumstances, any variation of the q_i, that is, any set of δq_i, must satisfy the following k relations:

$$\frac{\partial f_l}{\partial q_i} \delta q_i = 0 , \qquad l = 1, 2, ..., k .\tag{E2}$$

On the other hand we have shown in equation (A4) that

$$\delta \int_{t_0}^{t_1} \mathcal{L} \, dt = \int_{t_0}^{t_1} \left[\frac{\partial \mathcal{L}}{\partial q_i} - \frac{d}{dt} \left(\frac{\partial \mathcal{L}}{\partial \dot{q}_i} \right) \right] \delta q_i \, dt = 0 .\tag{E3}$$

However, we cannot infer from equation (E3) that the integrand vanishes since δq_i are not independent, but are related by equation (E2).

In accord with the Lagrange method of finding extrema of $\int \mathcal{L} \, dt$, k parameters exist, $\lambda_1, \lambda_2, ..., \lambda_k$, the Lagrange multipliers, such that the addition to the integrand of equation (E3) of the sum of the products,

$$- \sum_{l=1}^{k} \lambda_l \frac{\partial f_l}{\partial q_i} \delta q_i ,$$

allows us to vary the δq_i arbitrarily. When this addition is effected, condition (E3) becomes:

$$\int_{t_0}^{t_1} \left[\frac{\partial \mathcal{L}}{\partial q_i} - \frac{d}{dt} \left(\frac{\partial \mathcal{L}}{\partial \dot{q}_i} \right) - \lambda_l \frac{\partial f_l}{\partial q_i} \right] \delta q_i \, dt = 0 .\tag{E4}$$

Since the δq_i can now be viewed as independent, we must have the revised Lagrange equations:

$$\frac{\partial \mathcal{L}}{\partial q_i} - \frac{d}{dt} \left(\frac{\partial \mathcal{L}}{\partial \dot{q}_i} \right) - \lambda_l \frac{\partial f_l}{\partial q_i} = 0 .\tag{E5}$$

Here f_l depend only on the generalized coordinates q_i and not the generalized velocities, $\dot{q}_i$. If we now define $\bar{\mathcal{L}}$:

$$\bar{\mathcal{L}} = \mathcal{L} - \lambda_l f_l ,\tag{E6}$$

we have

$$\frac{\partial \bar{\mathcal{L}}}{\partial q_i} = \frac{\partial \mathcal{L}}{\partial q_i} - \lambda_l \frac{\partial f_l}{\partial q_i} ,\tag{E7}$$

and

$$\frac{\partial \bar{\mathcal{L}}}{\partial \dot{q}_i} = \frac{\partial \mathcal{L}}{\partial \dot{q}_i} .\tag{E8}$$

Hence equations (E5) may be viewed as the Lagrange equations associated with the effective Lagrangian $\bar{\mathcal{L}}$.

Constraints among the coordinates, expressed through relationships of the form of equation (E1) are designated *holonomic* constraints. However, constraints may also pertain to the $\dot{q}_i$, as well as the q_i. That is,

$$g_h(q_1, ..., q_s, \dot{q}_1, ..., \dot{q}_s, t) = 0 , \qquad (h = 1, 2, ..., j) . \tag{E9}$$

These latter are designated *nonholonomic constraints.* We can easily handle a particular case of equations (E9)

$$c_{hi}\dot{q}_i = a_h , \tag{E10}$$

where c_{hi} and a_h may depend on the generalized coordinates. Writing equation (E10) as an expression among differentials, we have

$$c_{hi}\,dq_i = a_h\,dt . \tag{E11}$$

In the variational problem, however, we consider variations of q_i at a fixed point of time t such that $dt = 0$. Thus equation (E11) implies:

$$c_{hi}\,\delta q_i = 0 . \tag{E12}$$

Once again Lagrange multipliers exist, $\lambda_1, \lambda_2, ..., \lambda_j$ such that the addition to the integrand of expression (E3) of the sum of the products,

$$-\sum_{h=1}^{j} \lambda_h c_{hi}\,\delta q_i ,$$

allows us to vary the q_i arbitrarily. When this addition is effected, condition (E3) becomes

$$\int_{t_0}^{t_1} \left[\frac{\partial \mathcal{L}}{\partial q_i} - \frac{d}{dt}\left(\frac{\partial \mathcal{L}}{\partial \dot{q}_i}\right) - \lambda_h c_{hi} \right] \delta q_i\,dt = 0 . \tag{E13}$$

Unlike a situation involving only *holonomic* constraints, we cannot in general state here that there formally exists an effective Lagrangian $\overline{\mathcal{L}}$,

$$\overline{\mathcal{L}} = \mathcal{L} - \lambda_h c_{hi} q_i , \tag{E14}$$

which yields the corresponding revised Lagrange equations,

$$\frac{\partial \mathcal{L}}{\partial q_i} - \frac{d}{dt}\left(\frac{\partial \mathcal{L}}{\partial \dot{q}_i}\right) - \lambda_h c_{hi} = 0 , \tag{E15}$$

unless the c_{hi} are constants.

It should be noted that, when constraints are present, the time rate of change of the Hamiltonian,

$$\frac{dH}{dt} \neq -\frac{\partial \mathcal{L}}{\partial t} . \tag{E16}$$

However, we can find the correct expression for dH/dt as follows: Let us consider the case of holonomic constraints of the type (E1) and assume $\partial \mathcal{L}/\partial t = 0$. We then have

$$\frac{d\mathcal{L}}{dt} = \frac{\partial \mathcal{L}}{\partial q_i}\dot{q}_i + \frac{\partial \mathcal{L}}{\partial \dot{q}_i}\ddot{q}_i . \tag{E17}$$

We recall that $H = p_i \dot{q}_i - \mathcal{L}$ where $p_i = \partial \mathcal{L}/\partial \dot{q}_i$. Obtaining the expression for $\partial \mathcal{L}/\partial q_i$ from expression (E5) and substituting in equation (E17) we have

$$\frac{\mathrm{d}\mathcal{L}}{\mathrm{d}t} = \frac{\mathrm{d}}{\mathrm{d}t}(p_i)\dot{q}_i + \lambda_l \frac{\partial f_l}{\partial q_i}\dot{q}_i + \frac{\partial \mathcal{L}}{\partial \dot{q}_i}\ddot{q}_i$$

$$= \dot{p}_i \dot{q}_i + \lambda_l \frac{\partial f_l}{\partial q_i}\dot{q}_i + p_i \ddot{q}_i = \frac{\mathrm{d}}{\mathrm{d}t}(p_i \dot{q}_i) + \lambda_l \frac{\partial f_l}{\partial q_i}\dot{q}_i . \tag{E18}$$

Hence,

$$\frac{\mathrm{d}}{\mathrm{d}t}(p_i \dot{q}_i - \mathcal{L}) = -\lambda_l \frac{\partial f_l}{\partial q_i}\dot{q}_i ; \tag{E19}$$

$$\frac{\mathrm{d}H}{\mathrm{d}t} = -\lambda_l \frac{\partial f_l}{\partial q_i}\dot{q}_i . \tag{E20}$$

We may then define an extended Hamiltonian $\overline{H}$ such that

$$\frac{\mathrm{d}\overline{H}}{\mathrm{d}t} = \frac{\mathrm{d}H}{\mathrm{d}t} + \lambda_l \frac{\partial f_l}{\partial q_i}\dot{q}_i = 0 . \tag{E21}$$

If f_l do not depend on time explicitly, then it follows from equation (E1) that $\mathrm{d}f_l/\mathrm{d}t = 0$; and hence

$$-\lambda_l \frac{\partial f_l}{\partial q_i}\dot{q}_i = 0 \quad \text{since} \quad \frac{\mathrm{d}f_l}{\mathrm{d}t} = \frac{\partial f_l}{\partial q_i}\dot{q}_i . \tag{E22}$$

On the other hand, if the holonomic constraints depend on time explicitly, we have

$$\frac{\mathrm{d}f_l}{\mathrm{d}t} = \frac{\partial f_l}{\partial q_i}\dot{q}_i + \frac{\partial f_l}{\partial t} = 0 , \tag{E23}$$

and hence

$$\frac{\partial f_l}{\partial q_i}\dot{q}_i = -\frac{\partial f_l}{\partial t} , \tag{E24}$$

and equation (E20) becomes

$$\frac{\mathrm{d}H}{\mathrm{d}t} = \lambda_l \frac{\partial f_l}{\partial t} . \tag{E25}$$

Similar analysis can be carried through for the nonholonomic constraints.

An Econometric Export Base Model of Regional Growth: A Departure from Conventional Techniques

V.K.MATHUR, H.S.ROSEN
Cleveland State University,

Base theory is well known and has been discussed at length in the literature on regional economics (for example, Pfouts, 1960). Its usefulness lies in its relative simplicity as compared, for example, to the input–output technique and its provision of a theoretical framework for empirical regional multiplier studies. Isard and Czamanski (1964) have even shown the similarity and Billings (1969) the mathematical identity of aggregate multipliers derived from base models and input–output models. In this paper we develop a new technique, based upon an econometric model, of conducting regional economic base analysis. In contrast to the other traditional and popular indirect estimation methods such as the location quotient (Tiebout, 1962, p.47) and the minimum requirements (Ullman and Dacey, 1960) techniques for estimating regional export activity (non-localized or basic) and local consumption oriented activity (localized or non-basic), we present an alternate model for estimating localized and non-localized components of total regional economic activity as measured by employment with its corresponding multiplier[1], which does away with many of the shortcomings of these two commonly used techniques.

The techniques of location quotient and minimum requirements are designed to separate a region's total economic activity, for example, employment, into the localized and the non-localized components. Both methods assume that $e_{ij}^n = (E_{iO}/E_O)$, where e_{ij}^n is the proportion of localized employment in ith industry of region j; E_{iO} is the employment in ith industry of the benchmark economy, for example, nation; E_O is the total employment in the nation. Therefore, according to the location quotient method, non-localized employment in an industry is the amount by which the total employment in that industry exceeds the estimated localized employment in the corresponding industry. In the case of the minimum requirements technique, non-localized employment in a region's industry is equal to the total regional employment in that industry minus the estimated minimum amount needed to meet local needs. This

---

[1] Efforts other than location quotient and minimum requirements methods to estimate regional multiplier are based upon either educated guesses about region's propensity to consume and import, for example, Brown *et al.* (1967) and Archibald (1967) or upon unrealistic assumption of exogenously given export income (Tiebout, 1960).

minimum for each industry in a region is the smallest ratio of the industry's employment to total employment in other regions of similar size and structure multiplied by the total employment of the reference region j.

The major deficiency of these two techniques (location quotient and minimum requirements) is the use of very restrictive assumptions made in order to derive localized and non-localized employment, and hence the employment multiplier. Greytak's study (1969) is one of the most recent among the voluminous literature on the subject. Using the results of Theil's (1960) inequality proportions, he doubts the predictability of these traditional techniques. Unfortunately, Greytak does not offer any solution to the problem of delineating regional employment into localized and non-localized sectors and of obtaining a reliable employment multiplier.

Our econometric model does away with many of the unrealistic assumptions of traditional approaches, for example, the same propensity to consume, the same community preference patterns, and the same production functions, in the regional and the benchmark economies. At the same time, it retains the attributes of simplicity and good predictability. Finally, it is neither time consuming nor expensive, both of which are a matter of concern to both regional economists and regional planners.

1 The model

A region, however defined, is considered a bundle of economic activity within a system of regions. One way, and the most important one, to measure the level of economic activity of a region is by its level of employment. This particular measure is used in our model.

A region is an open economy and, therefore, it is not only affected by the economic activity of other regions, but it also affects the economic activity of other regions. This model only concentrates on the former relationship because the latter is inconsequential due to the fact that the reference region R is very small relative to the rest of the world W (all other regions combined). It is a short run model and can be presented in two steps.

Step 1
It is hypothesized that [2]:

$$E_R = E_R^n + E_R^b \tag{1}$$

where

$$E_R^n = \sum_k E_R^{nk} \quad \text{and} \quad E_R^b = \sum_k E_R^{bk} \quad k = 1, ..., m$$

$$E_R^n = \alpha_0 + \alpha_1 E_R^b . \tag{2}$$

---

[2] Since all variables are in terms of current period, the subscript t is suppressed in all definitions and equations.

By inserting equation (2) into equation (1) we obtain

$$E_R = \alpha_0 + (1 + \alpha_1)E_R^b ,\tag{3}$$

where we define:

E_R as the total employment in region R;
E_R^n as the total localized (non-basic) employment in the region;
E_R^b as the total non-localized (basic) employment in the region;
E_R^{nk} as the localized employment in kth industry in the region; and
E_R^{bk} as the non-localized employment in kth industry in the region.

Step 2

To this point the model is like any other traditional base model. The problem which confronts regional economists and planners is the estimation of localized (E_R^n) and of non-localized (E_R^b) sectors of the region. Here we depart from the traditional estimation procedures.

A priori we expect that the magnitude and the sensitivity of employment in each industry in the region will differ substantially with respect to changes in the rest of the world's (W) employment [3]. Therefore, it is desirable first to estimate the localized and non-localized employment of each industry.

It is further hypothesized that that portion of kth industry's employment in the region which is sensitive to total employment in W (E_W) is non-localized and that which is insensitive localized. In order to obtain these two components of regional employment, the following procedure is used.

Assume

$$E_R^k = \beta_0 + \beta_1 E_W + e \tag{4}$$

where E_R^k is the employment in kth industry in the region and E_W is the total employment in W. The β's are the regression coefficients and e is the stochastic disturbance term. Applying the ordinary least squares (OLS) method with its usual assumptions, we can obtain an estimated line:

$$\hat{E}_R^k = \hat{\beta}_0 + \hat{\beta}_1 E_W .\tag{4.1}$$

For those industries where equation (4.1) gives significant regression coefficients [4] we can obtain average estimated employment in kth industry of the region ($\overline{\hat{E}_R^k}$) from the following equation:

$$\overline{\hat{E}_R^k} = \hat{\beta}_0 + \hat{\beta}_1 \overline{E}_W .\tag{4.2}$$

---

[3] The rest of the world in this study is represented by the United States of America (nation). Due to the unavailability of suitable data and almost negligible international repercussions on the local economy R, the part of the world which is outside the USA can be ignored.

[4] In those cases where equation (4.1) or equation (5), as the case may be, were not significant, all the employment for such industries was classified as localized.

If we assume that the ratio of average localized to average non-localized employment in the region remains constant during the time period under consideration, a fair assumption in the short run, it follows that

$$1 = \frac{\hat{\beta}_0}{\overline{\hat{E}_R^k}} + \hat{\beta}_1 \frac{\overline{E}_W}{\overline{\hat{E}_R^k}} \tag{4.3}$$

where $\hat{\beta}_0/\overline{\hat{E}_R^k}$ and $\hat{\beta}_1(\overline{E}_W/\overline{\hat{E}_R^k})$ are the estimated proportions of localized and non-localized employment respectively. After estimating these proportions, it is then possible to obtain the amount of localized and non-localized employment in kth industry by simply multiplying its actual employment by the proportions. It is quite conceivable that the relationship between regional employment in the kth industry and the employment of the rest of the world is non-linear; a case which we found for many industries in the Cleveland Standard Metropolitan Statistical Area. In such cases, the following equation was formulated:

$$\ln E_R^k = \ln b_0 + b_1 E_W + \ln U, \qquad k = m+1, ..., n . \tag{5}$$

The coefficients (b's) can be estimated by OLS method. After taking antilogs of the estimated equation, one can obtain, following the procedure described above, the proportions of localized and non-localized employment for $m-n$ industries. These proportions could then be used to divide the actual employment of these industries of the region into the above two components. The total localized (E_R^n) and non-localized (E_R^b) employment is then obtained by summing each industry's localized and non-localized employment respectively.

Finally, it is then possible to estimate the employment multiplier α_1 by applying OLS to equation (2), and hence, the total employment in the region E_R.

2 Empirical findings

The model was applied to the Cleveland SMSA[5] for the period 1961 to 1966[6]. Table 1 lists the industries incorporated in this study. The classifications, Other durable and Other non-durable, were excluded from

[5] Since 1964 Cleveland SMSA includes Geauga, Medina, Lake, and Cuyahoga counties. In order to have uniform employment data for the period 1961–1966, employment of all the industries, prior to 1964, was adjusted according to the new definition. The adjustment factors by industries were obtained from Ohio Bureau of Unemployment Compensation (1964).

[6] 1963–1966 was used for Furniture and fixtures, and Food and kindred products. These were the only industries whose employment showed a substantial lagged relationship with net national quarterly total employment (outside world), that is, national quarterly total employment minus quarterly total employment of Cleveland SMSA. Since lags are a separate issue and need to be examined by different econometric techniques, it was considered desirable to choose the period 1963–1966 for these industries. The proportions of localized and non-localized employment generated from 1963–1966 were applied to the actual employment of these industries

the reported data by the Ohio Bureau of Unemployment Compensation (1961–1969) in the latter part of the sixties, probably due to a change in reporting procedures. Employment data for these industries could have been calculated but it would not have been comparable to earlier reported data. Hence, the decision was made to drop these industrial classifications in this study.

Quarterly average non-agricultural employment data, used in this study, were generated for the above industries of the Cleveland SMSA [Ohio Bureau of Unemployment Compensation (1961–1969) and for the nation (US Department of Labor, 1961–1969)] by utilizing the reported monthly employment data. We first experimented with a quarterly multiple linear regression model in which kth industries' employment was regressed against net national employment, net north-central region's[7] employment and net Ohio employment for the period 1961–1969. The net figures were obtained by subtracting Cleveland SMSA's total employment from the national, north-central and Ohio total employment respectively. Due to the problem of multicollinearity which was expected a priori, the regional and state employment variables were dropped from the model[8]. Similarly our efforts with a model in which Cleveland's quarterly population, estimated from annual population data, and net national employment were used as exogenous variables, were also unsuccessful, primarily because of high multicollinearity[9]. The purpose of including a population variable was to explicitly identify the localized component of the region's employment. Therefore, the decision was made to retain net national employment as the only exogenous variable in the model as specified in equation (4) and equation (5).

Equation (4) was estimated for the industries numbered 1, 6, 7, 10, and 12 and equation (5) was estimated for the rest of the industries by

[6] contd.
to obtain the localized and non-localized employment for 1961–1966. Moreover, as will be shown later on in this paper, those employment multipliers obtained with and without these industries were approximately the same.

The following observations were omitted for Transportation equipment between 1961–1966 because of unusually low or high employment.
(a) The 1961 third quarter and 1964 fourth quarter were omitted due to automobile strikes and 1965, third quarter, due to unusually large accumulation of automobiles by dealers coupled with the annual model changeover.
(b) The 1966 fourth quarter employment was abnormally high due to the Vietnam war.

[7] The north-central region includes Indiana, Illinois, Michigan, Wisconsin, and Ohio.

[8] The correlation coefficients between net national and net north-central and between net national and net Ohio quarterly employment were above 0·90.

[9] The correlation between net national employment and Cleveland's quarterly population was 0·97. It may be partly because the population variable as used in the model may be a proxy for time.

Table 1. Regression equations for quarterly non-agriculture employment for each industry in the Cleveland SMSA (1961–1966)[a].

Number	SIC Code Number	Industry	β_0 and $\ln b_0$	β_1 and $\hat{b}_1$	r^2 and $\bar{r}^2$	S_e	F	D	$\hat{\rho}$
1	25	Furniture and fixture[b]	0·05588	0·0000604396 (0·000024333) *	0·27 *	0·122903	6·16935 *	1·80608 *	0·653462
2	33	Primary metals	3·30626	0·00000629052 (0·00000209293) *	0·29 *	0·0363429	9·0337 *	1·32015 **	—
3	34	Fabricated metals	23·714	0·0000098268 (0·00000231139) *	0·46 *	0·0199562	18·075 *	1·89453 *	0·521383
4	35	Machinery (except electrical)	12·722	0·0000214664 (0·00000295815) *	0·72 *	0·0236003	52·6598 *	1·86301 *	0·572929
5	36	Electrical equipment and supplies	6·373	0·0000245127 (0·00000269576) *	0·79 *	0·0254316	82·6835 *	1·6905 *	0·460583
6	37	Transportation equipment[b]	26·644	0·000201054 (0·0000762537) *	0·28 *	1·13764	6·95191 *	1·98576 *	—
7	20	Food and kindred products[b]	5·6908	0·000129286 (0·0000628498) *	0·20 *	0·360757	4·23155 *	1·9895 *	0·552682
8	22	Textile mill products	3·3642	0·00000790018 (0·00000344781) *	0·20 *	0·0457092	5·25034 *	1·80704 *	0·189801
9	23	Apparel and other textile products	5·3373	0·00000717932 (0·00000149516) *	0·52 *	0·0153995	23·0566 *	1·43321 *	0·397392
10	26	Paper and allied products[b]	1·00737	0·0000654646 (0·0000115529) *	0·61 *	0·10325	32·1093 *	1·48698 *	0·498175
11	27	Printing and publishing	4·8671	0·00000020216 (0·0000334116) *	0·64 *	0·0315828	36·6098 *	2·10869 *	0·459458

Number	SIC Code Number	Industry	β_0 and $\ln b_0$	β_1 and b_1	r^2 and $\bar{r}^2$	S_e	F	D	$\hat{\rho}$
12	28	Chemicals and allied products[b]	6·2895	0·000142117 (0·0000550657) *	0·25 *	0·328153	6·66088 *	2·54629 *	0·755778
13	15–17	Contract construction	2·8272	0·0000106128 (0·0000699394)	0·10	0·121447	2·30257	1·73594 *	–
14	40–49	Transportation and utilities	3·34893	0·0000856196 (0·000000937532) *	0·79 *	0·0162799	83·4015 *	1·28363 **	–
15	50	Wholesale trade	27·2313	0·0000104087 (0·0000290856) *	0·38 *	0·0201767	12·8066 *	1·59663 *	0·660547
16	52–59	Retail trade	3·90448	0·0000121582 (0·00000183627) *	0·67 *	0·0318863	43·8391 *	1·83418 *	–
17	60–67	Finance, insurance, and real estate	2·99171	0·00000973352 (0·00000000709007) *	0·90 =	0·0123117	188·469 *	1·34636 **	–
18	70–89	Service and miscellaneous industries	36·8	0·00001722 (0·00000171867) *	0·83 *	0·0167266	100·411 *	1·71187 *	0·438691
19	91	Federal government	7·2916	0·0000179633 (0·00004468965) *	0·41 *	0·0327851	14·672 *	2·12543 *	0·655756
20	92,93	Local and state government[c]	3·01899	0·00190744 (0·00000166955) *	0·86 *	0·0289511	130·528 *	1·28693 **	–

[a] The regressions for all the industries except Furniture and fixtures, and Food and kindred products cover the period 1961–1966. The period 1963–1966 was used for the other two industries. The symbols r^2 and $\bar{r}^2$, S_e, D, and $\hat{\rho}$ indicate the coefficient of determination, unadjusted and adjusted for degrees of freedom, standard error of estimate, Durbin–Watson statistic, and first order estimated correlation of the estimated disturbances, respectively. The standard errors are written underneath the regression coefficients.
[b] The linear relationship of equation (4) was assumed for these industries while for the rest of the industries relationship of equation (5), log–linear, was hypothesized and the results are presented in natural logarithms.
[c] In the early sixties separate data were not available for state and local government, therefore, both classifications were combined.
* Significant at 5 percent level. ** Significant at 1 percent level.

applying the OLS method[10]. The Durbin–Watson statistic D, obtained for each industry, revealed that in all of the industries except industries 2, 6, 13, 14, 16, 17, and 20 (table 1, column 1) there was serial correlation[11]. In order to alleviate this problem, a transformation procedure was used which some econometricians call "the method of generalized differencing" (Wonnacott and Wonnacott, 1970, pp.140–144).

By using the Markov autoregressive scheme of first order (Johnston, 1963, pp.195–199), we obtain

$$E_R^{k'} = \beta_0' + \beta_1 E_W'   \tag{6}$$

where the 'prime' variables are given by equation (7); $\beta_0' = \beta_0(1-\rho)$ and $\beta_0 = \beta_0'/(1-\rho)$.

$$\left. \begin{array}{l} E_R^{k'} = E_R^k - \hat{\rho} E_{R-1}^k \\ E_W' = E_W - \hat{\rho} E_{W-1} \end{array} \right\}   \tag{7}$$

The OLS method was applied to the transformed variables of all industries except those mentioned above[12]. As indicated by the D statistics (table 1) we were successful in eliminating serial correlation in the problem industries. According to the t-test, the regression coefficients β_1's and b_1's were significant at the 5 percent level for all the industries except Contract construction (table 1). The F test shows that the r^2's were significant for all industries at 5 percent except for Contract construction and Food and kindred products. Since Food and kindred products was a border line case, not only with respect to $\bar{r}^2$ but also with respect to the significance of the regression ($F = 4 \cdot 23$, table 1), it was decided to use its equation to generate the proportions of localized and non-localized employment.

We utilized the estimated coefficients of all the industries except Contract construction to generate the proportions of localized and non-localized employment according to the procedure described in part 1 of this paper. All the employment of Contract construction was considered

[10] The decision regarding the appropriate form of the equation to be estimated was made on the basis of scatter diagrams of quarterly employment of each industry in the Cleveland SMSA against net national quarterly employment.

[11]
$$D = \frac{\sum(\Delta\hat{e}_t)^2}{\sum \hat{e}_t^2}$$

where $\hat{e}_t$'s are the least squares estimated disturbance (Theil and Nagar, 1961, p.793; Johnston, 1963, p.192). We used Theil–Nagar test (TN test) to test the significance of D statistic. This test gives us approximately the upper limit of the D statistic under Durbin–Watson test (Theil and Nagar, 1961, p.803). Significance levels of 1 and 5 percent were used.

[12] The regression coefficients obtained by applying OLS method to the transformed variables are equivalent to generalized least squares estimators (Wonnacott and Wonnacott, 1970, pp.331–332). After estimating equation (6) we can state it in terms of original variables as: $\hat{E}_R^k = \hat{\beta}_0 + \hat{\beta}_1 \hat{E}_W$.

as localized. The proportions were then used to obtain the localized and non-localized quarterly employment in each industry and hence, the totals of the two components of employment for the Cleveland SMSA. Table 2 presents the percent of localized and non-localized employment for each industry.

The estimated equation (2) for the Cleveland SMSA for 1961–1966 is[13]:

$$E_R^n = 62 \cdot 6398 + 0 \cdot 8002 E_R^b \qquad (2')$$
$$(0 \cdot 0420)$$

$$r^2 = 0 \cdot 94; \quad S_e = 4 \cdot 00; \quad F = 363 \cdot 05 .$$

Table 2. Percent of localized (non-basic) and non-localized (basic) employment by industry for Cleveland SMSA for the period 1961–1966.

Number	Industry	Non-localized (basic)	Localized (non-basic)
1	Furniture and fixtures	98·48	1·52
2	Primary metals	30·27	69·73
3	Fabricated metals	42·96	57·4
4	Machinery (except electrical)	70·9	29·1
5	Electrical equipment	75·56	24·44
6	Transportation equipment[a]	30·04	69·96
7	Food and kindred products	57·6	42·4
8	Textile mill products	35·75	64·25
9	Apparel and allied products	33·65	66·35
10	Paper and allied products	78·82	21·18
11	Printing and publishing	68·87	31·13
12	Chemical and allied products	56·83	43·17
13	Contract construction	0	100·00
14	Transportation and utilities	38·78	61·22
15	Wholesale trade	45·17	54·83
16	Retail trade	50·18	49·82
17	Finance, insurance, and real estate	42·76	57·24
18	Service and miscellaneous industries[b]	62·76	37·24
19	Federal government	64·14	35·86
20	Local and State government[c]	66·5	33·5

[a] The localized sector of this industry may look on the high side but it is conceivable that in Cleveland SMSA a substantial portion of the output of this industry becomes an input in other predominantly non-localized industries.

[b] This classification consists of services like medical and health, legal services, educational services, engineering and professional services, non-profit organizations, and so on, in which Cleveland SMSA enjoys a considerable share. Therefore it is not surprising to find its non-localized component to be higher than the localized.

[c] The upward bias in this industry towards non-localized component may be due to the inclusion of state government employment.

[13] The estimated equation without Furniture and fixtures, and Food and kindred products was: $\hat{E}_R' = 69 \cdot 3774 + 0 \cdot 7907 E_R^b$. The coefficient (0·7907) and the regression was significant at 5 percent level.

Therefore, total quarterly estimated employment in the Cleveland SMSA is [14]:

$$\hat{E}_R = 62 \cdot 6398 + (1 + 0 \cdot 8002)E_R^b \ . \tag{3'}$$

Equation (3') can be utilized to predict total quarterly employment in Cleveland SMSA. For example, if non-localized employment E_R^b in Cleveland SMSA increases by 1000 persons in a quarter, the total employment would increase by 1804 men $(1 \cdot 8044)$ (1000). The $0 \cdot 95$ confidence interval of this predicted increase would be between 1779 to 1945 men. As it is a short run model, one should be careful in using it for long run projections.

A distinctive feature of our model, besides others, is that it can relate the growth in national employment (assuming no structural changes) to the local employment (Cleveland SMSA). In order to project Cleveland SMSA's employment by national employment projections, one has to follow three steps.

(1) Apply net national quarterly employment projections to the industry equations (table 1) to obtain the estimated quarterly employment in each industry. Note that this employment increase incorporates only the direct impact of outside employment but ignores the indirect impact of non-localized employment on localized employment.

(2) Multiply the estimated quarterly employment of the kth industry to the proportions of non-localized employment for each industry (table 2) to obtain non-localized employment in the kth industry. Summing them over all industries one would get total non-localized quarterly employment for the Cleveland SMSA.

(3) Use the total non-localized employment in equation (3') to obtain the predicted increase in total quarterly employment for the SMSA.

3 Projection test

To test the predictability of our model, we forecast total quarterly Cleveland SMSA's employment for the sample period 1961–1966 and outside the sample period 1967–1969. The accuracy of both the forecasts was tested by calculating Theil's (1960, pp.28–32) inequality coefficients [15]

---

[14] The small employment multiplier $0 \cdot 80$ may be due to a number of reasons, for example, a high capital to labor ratio, a local economy which is closely integrated with the nation, a substantial amount of leakages and an inelastic labor supply, etc. Moreover, since the traditional method of location quotient usually overstates the size of the multiplier due to the understatement of the non-localized sector of the local economy (Tiebout, 1962, p.49), this multiplier for Cleveland economy is not unrealistic.

[15]
$$U = \left(\frac{\sum (P_i - A_i)^2}{\sum A_i^2} \right)^{1/2}$$

where P_i is the ith predicted value and A_i is the ith actual value. The smaller the U, the better are the predictions.

and proportions[16] of the predicted percentage changes of employment (table 3).

The coefficients in table 3 suggest that our predictions are reasonably precise. The U^c is the only error which is the largest in all cases, but as Theil put it "... we cannot be able to predict such that their points are all located on a straight line" (Theil, 1960, p.32). Predictions for outside the sample period (1967–1969) are presented in table 4. The reader can verify the accuracy of our predictions including all turning points as well (table 4).

Table 3. Theil's inequality coefficients and proportions for percentage changes of total quarterly employment predictions for the Cleveland SMSA.

	Sample period (1961–1966) percent changes	Outside the sample period (1967–1969) percent changes
U^m	0·002	0·015
U^s	0·457	0·276
U^c	0·541	0·709
U	0·348	0·385

Table 4[a]. Predicted and actual total quarterly non-agricultural employment levels (in thousands) and percent changes for the Cleveland SMSA 1967–1969[b].

Quarter	Predicted		Actual	
	levels	percent change[c]	levels	percent change[c]
1967 1	768·63		764·14	
2	775·91	0·95	773·03	1·16
3	777·00	0·14	775·73	0·35
4	787·19	1·31	782·00	0·81
1968 1	785·93	−0·16	777·90	−0·52
2	795·14	1·17	794·60	0·02
3	798·48	0·42	797·60	0·38
4	809·44	1·37	807·87	1·29
1969 1	805·97	−0·43	804·80	−0·38
2	820·10	1·75	824·90	2·50
3	823·79	0·45	828·77	0·47
4	831·88	0·98	832·23	0·42

[a] A similar table for earlier years is available upon request from the authors.
[b] Excludes Other durable goods and Other non-durable goods industries which were not part of this study.
[c] Rounded to two decimal places.

[16] Theil divides the numerator of U, that is, mean square error (MSE) into three proportions: $U^m = (\bar{P}-\bar{A})^2/\text{MSE}$; $U^s = (S_P - S_A)^2/\text{MSE}$; $U^c = 2(1-r)S_P S_A/\text{MSE}$; where $\bar{P}$ and $\bar{A}$ are the means, S_P and S_A are the standard deviations and r is the correlation coefficient of predicted and actual values. Positive values of U^m, U^s and U^c imply errors of central tendency, errors of unequal variation and errors of incomplete covariance respectively.

4 Conclusion

In this paper we have introduced an alternate simple technique for estimating localized and non-localized employment, and hence, the employment multiplier of a local economy. No attempt has been made to refute or modify economic base theory. Our new approach is a better method than the traditional techniques of location quotient and minimum requirements on several counts:

(1) It does away with many of the restrictive assumptions of the traditional approaches.

(2) The employment multiplier and, therefore, the forecasts, take into account the industrial composition of the local economy and its relationship to national economic activity.

(3) The model can be used to find the impact of national employment growth on each local industry and, therefore, on the total local employment. It also reveals how national growth may constrain local growth in spite of actions taken by local authorities to stimulate the local economy.

(4) Lastly, the model gives better predictions.

Klein (1968, pp.112–113) would argue that 'satellite' models, that is, models which are linked to national models, besides being manageable and feasible also retain the peculiar characteristics of individual regions and industries. Our model, though a unisectoral model, retains attributes of a satellite model.

Acknowledgement. The authors wish to thank the Department of Economics and T. F. Campbell, Director of the Institute of Urban Studies, Cleveland State University, for providing partial financial help. The authors benefitted from the continuous discussions with W. Naleszkiewicz who was always willing to help, and from the comments of William Hockter of Federal Reserve Bank of Cleveland and K. Prodromidis on the earlier draft of this paper. Finally the authors thank Koorosh Pirzadeh for research assistance, and Leasco Data Systems, Cleveland, Ohio, for their continuous programming help. All the computations were done by the authors on a Leasco Response Computer Terminal.

References

Archibald, G. C., 1967, "Regional multiplier effects in the UK", *Oxford Economic Papers*, **19**, 22–45.

Billings, B. R., 1969, "The mathematical identity of the multipliers derived from the economic base model and input–output model", *Journal of Regional Science*, **9**, 471–473.

Brown, A. J., Lind, H., Bowers, J., 1967, "The 'Green Paper' on the development areas", *National Institute Economic Review*, number 40, 26–33.

Greytak, D., 1969, "A statistical analysis of regional export estimating techniques", *Journal of Regional Science*, **9**, 387–395.

Isard, W., Czamanski, S., 1964, "Techniques of estimating local and regional multiplier effects of changes in the level of major government programs", *Peace Research Society (International) Papers*, **3** (Chicago Conference, 1964), 19–45.

Johnston, J., 1963, *Econometric Methods* (McGraw-Hill, New York).

Klein, L. R., 1968, "The specification of regional econometric models", *Papers of the Regional Science Association,* **23**, 105–115.

Ohio Bureau of Unemployment Compensation, 1961–1969, *Ohio Labor Market Information,* Monthly Reports (Division of Research and Statistics, Columbus, Ohio).

Pfouts, R. W., 1960, *The Techniques of Urban Economic Analysis* (Chandler–Davis, New Jersey).

Theil, H., 1960, *Applied Economic Forecasting* (Rand, McNally, New York).

Theil, H., Nagar, A. L., 1961, "Testing the independence of regression disturbances", *Journal of American Statistical Association,* **56**, 793–806.

Tiebout, C. M., 1962, *The Community Economic Base Study,* Supplementary Paper number 16 (Committee for Economic Development, New York).

Tiebout, C. M., 1960, "The community income multiplier: a case study", in *The Techniques of Urban Economic Analysis,* Ed. R. W. Pfouts (Chandler–Davis, New York).

Ullman, E. L., Dacey, M. F., 1960, "The minimum requirements approach to the urban economic base", *Papers and Proceedings of the Regional Science Association,* **6**, 175–194.

Wonnacott, R. J., Wonnacott, T. II., 1970, *Econometrics* (John Wiley, New York).

US Department of Labor, Bureau of Labor Statistics, 1961–1969, *Employment and Earnings,* Monthly Reports (Government Printing Office, Washington D.C.).

Dynamic Simulation of an Urban System †

M.BATTY
University of Reading

Introduction

The need to incorporate the concept of time into models of urban development has long been recognised as an important priority in urban research. Yet this temporal factor, which is referred to here as the dynamic element in modelling urban systems, has been largely neglected in previous work. Most urban development models have dealt with cross-sectional relationships measured at one point in time, and analysis of such models has been moulded in the tradition of comparative statics in economics. Recent developments in urban modelling in Britain have reinforced the emphasis on modelling urban phenomena in a static way and, although these modelling efforts have mainly revolved around the model first proposed by Lowry (1964), there has resulted from these applications a fairly critical assessment of the static equilibrium approach (Goldner, 1971).

Despite the many practical advantages of modelling urban systems in a macro-static way, two major directions for improving urban models have been proposed, and both strategies essentially involve attempts at improving the model's descriptive power. First, there is the attempt to disaggregate the variables of the model in the quest to link more macro-models of urban phenomena with micro-economic models of the land market. In particular this approach is being pursued by Cripps and Cater (1972), who are constructing a disaggregated residential location model along lines suggested by Wilson (1970a). It appears that the major difficulty of this kind of disaggregation is statistical in that problems of sample size can confound the analysis. The second approach to improving urban models is concerned with replacing the concept of static equilibrium with dynamic disequilibrium, in short with constructing models which explicitly simulate the processes of urban change. In this paper, a preliminary design for a dynamic model of urban development will be explored and some applications of the model in an experimental context will be outlined.

The rationale for designing an urban dynamic model is based on many factors. Perhaps the most important concept leading to the dynamic approach revolves around the idea that urban structure is an inevitable reflection of several complex processes of change in the urban system (Batty, 1971a). To understand structure, it is therefore essential to explore the processes, past and present, which have generated that structure. One of the central problems of the static equilibrium approach

† This research is financed by the Centre for Environmental Studies, London.

to modelling echoes this argument over process and structure; of critical importance to static models are variables which attempt to measure locational attraction, and the difficulties of finding suitable indices of attraction reflecting the locational history of the system are paramount. Furthermore there are severe difficulties of building constraints on location into static models, and also in interpreting the real meaning of such constraint procedures. Although Harris (1970) has argued that static equilibrium models are preferable for generating the consequences of long term forecasts in a planning context, there is an argument for the use of dynamic models in shorter term forecasting where interest is centred around marginal changes in the distribution of urban activity. From a research viewpoint, however, there is little doubt that a model of urban dynamics adds a new dimension to hypothesis formulation and testing, and provides a considerably richer tool for exploring the structure of urban systems.

The design for a macrodynamic model to be outlined here is the result of many compromises. Although the model may appear a little rough around the edges, and over complex in some parts, the preliminary design appears to provide a promising approach to simulation in urban systems. In essence the model is quite simple, for it builds upon the ideas of spatial interaction described by Wilson (1970b) and upon an interpretation of the dynamic multiplier in macroeconomic theory (Allen, 1967). Before the model is outlined, it is important to clarify its position in the context of other research. To this end, Paelinck (1970) has suggested that model-building research can be organised under three classes; first, research based upon empirical analysis; second, research based upon mathematical analysis; and third, research based upon simulation. It is this third approach—the approach to model-building through simulation—which forms the method described in this paper.

Concepts of simulation

Although the term simulation is frequently used in a general context to refer to any process of modelling artifacts such as economic or city systems, the term has a more specific and somewhat more technical meaning in this paper. In this sense, simulation is a process of modelling in which solutions to complex situations are reached without recourse to deductive mathematics. Solutions to models having many variables which interact simultaneously and sequentially may be intractable to analytic methods, and in such cases the technique of simulation may be appropriate. A good example of the use of simulation in the social sciences is provided by the work of Orcutt et al. (1961); these researchers show that although deductive solutions to their demographic model are theoretically possible, the practical difficulties of obtaining solutions in this way are so great that simulation is the only feasible method of modelling.

This discussion raises an important point concerning the suitability of the system being modelled for simulation. Although most models of urban development have some part of their solution reached by simulation, the central feature of simulation concerns the repeated application of the model's equations in a sequence leading to a solution. It is immediately apparent why dynamic models are well suited to the technique of simulation, for the sequential nature of time forms the basic module on which the simulation can be based. Indeed many of the classic simulation models, such as the industrial models of Forrester (1961) and the household sector models of Orcutt et al. (1961), are based on dynamic factors.

Apart from the fundamental advantages which simulation techniques have in dealing with complexity, the concept of simulation is deeply embedded in the experimental approach to understanding natural and artificial phenomena. In the social sciences simulation has been identified with computer modelling, and the ease with which different hypotheses can be tested experimentally using computer simulation is obvious. The experimental approach has also been adopted in previous applications of urban models but the techniques of simulation provide a greater flexibility in the design of such experiments.

Perhaps the most important feature of simulation concerns the new insights into the behaviour of the system under study which can be gained from experiments. If the structure of the model is difficult to interpret a priori, simulation can lead to useful appraisals of the validity of the model, and the process of model design can be much improved using the results of simulation. The value of simulation in handling complexity and in revealing solutions and predictions which are impossible to obtain deductively is the main argument adopted by Forrester (1969), who maintains that simulation is the only method of modelling capable of revealing that the behaviour of social systems may in many instances be counter intuitive. Another important feature of simulation is described by Simon (1969), who argues that simulation is essential in the behavioural sciences for generating new knowledge about how the system works and how it is likely to work under foreseeable conditions. Therefore, with these arguments in mind, the simulation approach to urban research is seen as a fundamental method for setting and testing hypotheses about the workings of the urban system.

The treatment of time in urban models

The most formidable problem of modelling dynamic behaviour in urban systems appears to revolve around the paucity of real data available. Where time-series data do exist, however, problems such as the lack of independence between successive observations, multicollinearity and related difficulties, and the aggregative nature of such series, tend to make the data highly unsuitable for purposes of testing. It now appears that 'perfect' time-series may never be available, and therefore the lack of data should not be regarded as a barrier to progress. Too often, in the recent past, modelling efforts have been narrowed and pruned according to data availability, and sometimes halted due to the lack of data. Clearly, little progress will be made if data availability becomes the central issue. Yet despite these problems there have been several different attempts to embody the concept of time in urban models. As some of these models have had a strong influence on the design of the model to be outlined here, a brief summary of three of the most important dynamic models is warranted.

The three models are very different in their design, and provide a comprehensive view of the spectrum of approaches to urban dynamics. One of these models—the Time Oriented Metropolitan Model (TOMM)—was originally based on Lowry's *Model of Metropolis* and provides an interesting attempt at improving the macrostatic model. This model was developed by Crecine (1964) for the Pittsburgh Community Renewal Program; the first version attempted to model changes in the stock of activity over 5 year time intervals using the same mechanisms as Lowry's model, and an important distinction was made in the model between new locators and relocators. The TOMM model has been improved in several ways since the first attempt, and three major versions of the model, including the first, now exist. The second version—TOMM II—was developed for the METRO gaming project at the University of Michigan and fitted to data from the town of Lansing (Crecine, 1967). In this second version a more realistic formulation of the measures of locational attraction, incorporating site rent, amenity, and transport cost, was provided, although the simulation procedure is still similar to that used in Lowry's model (Crecine, 1968). TOMM III is the model at present under development at Michigan (Crecine, 1969) and it appears that research is centred on questions of dynamics and mover behaviour in the model. A time interval of 2 years is now being used in the model.

A limitation of the TOMM effort concerns the rather elementary approach to modelling dynamics. In all versions of the model, the processes for modelling changes in activity, whether new locators or relocators, are similar to the processes used in the Lowry model for allocating the total stock. The model is essentially a set of difference equations, mainly of the first-order, which are solved sequentially, and iteratively. The most appealing characteristic of the model, however, concerns the way in which it simulates spatial behaviour; the model is built around the concept of spatial interaction, which is regarded as fundamental to a model of urban structure.

The EMPIRIC model is also based on a system of first-order difference equations, which are organised more formally than TOMM. This model was designed by Hill for the Boston Regional Planning Project and has since been revised through several versions (Irwin and Brand, 1965).

Unlike TOMM, the EMPIRIC model treats the concept of spatial interaction implicitly. Furthermore the solution method adopted by EMPIRIC recognises the simultaneous nature of urban interrelationships, and formal solution methods, such as those based on two-stage least squares, have been used. The time interval adopted is 10 years, and consequently the emphasis upon dynamics is implicit rather than explicit in the model. The EMPIRIC model has an interesting parallel in the POLIMETRIC model developed by Dieter at about the same time. In essence the POLIMETRIC model is the differential equation form of the EMPIRIC, but is somewhat more elegant in detail (Irwin and Brand, 1965). The EMPIRIC model has been well explored by its original authors, and Harris (1966) has undertaken a revealing analysis of the model's equilibrium properties.

This model suffers from the same limitation as TOMM: the emphasis on dynamics is elementary, although it must be noted that both TOMM and EMPIRIC do not set out to model the intricate and detailed repercussions of urban processes in time. A model, or what is rapidly becoming a set of models, which attempts to simulate the detail of dynamics, is the collection of models based on Forrester's concepts of Industrial Dynamics. In his book *Urban Dynamics*, Forrester (1969) has applied to the city ideas built up in the study of dynamics in industrial and economic processes. His approach to modelling is an attempt to represent the urban system as a large system of difference equations relating a host of variables in complex loops. The concepts of both negative and positive feedback are well exploited, and the simulation period must be divided into many intervals of time for the results of the model to be meaningful. In fact Forrester demonstrates his model for an hypothetical city using a 5 year time module over a 250 year period. The ideas of industrial dynamics have also been applied in an economic model of water resource development in the Susquehana River Basin (Hamilton *et al.,* 1969) and in a demographic model for Kent County, Michigan (Swanson and Waldmann, 1970).

There are many criticisms which can and have been levelled at the application of industrial dynamics in the sphere of urban modelling. Yet the simulation technique and its emphasis on modelling dynamic behaviour is certainly relevant. The major difficulty in applying these techniques seems to arise from the presumption that such techniques can be applied untempered to any system whether it be a firm, a city, or a world. Perhaps the most ardent criticism which can be levelled against Forrester's urban model, and indeed the Susquehana and Kent County models, is their virtual neglect of the spatial dimension and the factors which differentiate activity in space. In the light of existing research into locational behaviour these are glaring omissions, but the techniques of simulation pioneered by Forrester do provide a useful entry point into dynamic simulation in urban systems.

The models described above are all peculiarly one-sided. The TOMM and EMPIRIC models use space as their basic module and the simulation period is highly aggregated. On the other hand, the Forrester models ignore space as a basic organising principle for model design, and adopt a highly disaggregate simulation period. One goal of this research was to design a model which gave roughly equal weight to spatial and temporal interaction, in short to organise the model about both concepts of space and time. Another guiding principle for dynamic model design has been suggested by Harris (1970). Harris argues that as urban systems are usually tending to move to equilibrium, "... for well constructed models a set of equilibrium solutions will be available for most inputs of policies and environmental conditions". This principle suggests that although disequilibrium may be the usual condition of a dynamic model, such a model should always be tending to equilibrium and in the absence of further stimuli, should reach this state.

A model of urban dynamics
The design principles for a model of spatial and temporal interactions need further clarification. In previous attempts at macrostatic modelling, and in particular in the Lowry model, the interactions or flows of activity between different areas have been central to the way in which different patterns of location develop. Activities have been modelled as summations of spatial interactions or flows (Cordey-Hayes and Wilson, 1971). It is also obvious that, at any point in time, the distribution of activity represents the summation of changes in activity in previous time periods. Such a concept of temporal interaction is well developed in macroeconomic theory, where the stock of activity at any instant is a function of previous stocks. In particular the concept of the distributed lag has been developed to deal with the effects which different levels of activity have in time. Distributed lags are also a central feature of Forrester's model, where the difference equations describing change are to a high order.

Just as spatial interaction declines as distance or spatial cost increases from a point, the effect of activity on other activities declines as time increases from a particular instant. In dealing with changes in activity, dynamic modelling has considerably more potential for incorporating aspects of population growth and migration, which have been hitherto ignored in urban development models. Furthermore an important component of change is due to the relocation of existing activities. This internal migration is dealt with in TOMM and in Forrester's model but only net change is dealt with by EMPIRIC. It appears to be important to model the behaviour of relocators, which is referred to here as the mover pool.

In the model, at any point in time, a configuration of activities called stocks can be derived by summing interactions over time and space. In economic parlance the activities generated in any period of time are called

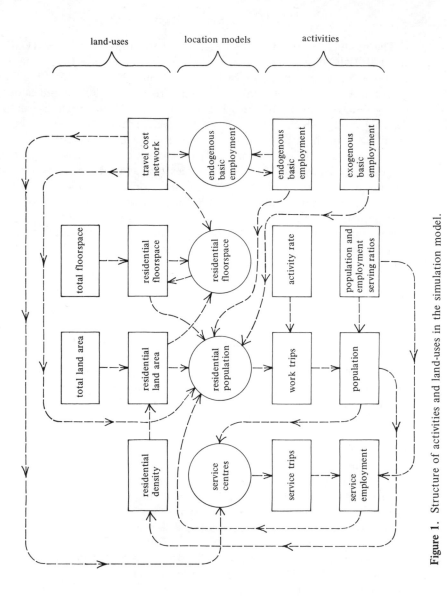

Figure 1. Structure of activities and land-uses in the simulation model.

flows, but to distinguish such flows from spatial interaction, they are referred to here as changes. The repercussions of activity in time are generated using a dynamic interpretation of the multiplier effect. As in other urban models the prime input to the model, which starts the process, is basic employment; in the dynamic case the repercussions from basic employment are generated through time. The spatial interactions derived in the model are oriented around the location of activities. Activities are divided into three major types: residential population, services, and basic employment. Services are subdivided into consumer and producer oriented groups, and basic employment is broken down into employment dependent on existing employment, and unique locators whose location cannot be forecast by the model.

The unique locators provide the external stimuli to the model for, although the total level of basic employment is exogenous, the other category of basic employment is distributed spatially using a linear model. Both population and service employment are allocated using production and attraction constrained gravity models of the type derived by Wilson (1970b). These models attempt to stimulate, albeit very coarsely, an equilibrium between demand and supply of activities although, in the case of the residential location model, a further submodel has been designed to deal with the supply of residential land and floorspace. Figure 1 illustrates a schematic form for the model and the main relationships between the sectors. Both new locators and relocators, in terms of different activities, are allocated using these models. Although basic employment is exogenous to the model, other inputs include the transport system, various density limits on activity location, and the set of model parameters. The model begins with a complete configuration of existing activities and spatial interactions.

The way in which dynamics are modelled is somewhat different in this model, and two dynamic effects can be recognised. Firstly, there is the influence of previous stocks and changes in activity on the future distribution of activities: this is an effect which all of the models described earlier incorporate. Secondly, there are the repercussions from previous changes in activity which are still working through the system: this is an effect which is not explicitly embodied in the models described above. To describe the detailed methods by which these processes are simulated, each part of the model will first be described separately, and then these parts will be assembled into the system of equations used in the model.

Modelling the distribution of activities in time

The approach to dynamics adopted in this model is through the concept of the multiplier and the economic base hypothesis. This concept has formed a basis for several models of urban development, in particular Lowry's model, and can be stated succinctly in four equations (Batty, 1970).

Without suggesting any dynamic interpretation, these four equations are written as follows:

$$P = \alpha E , \qquad \alpha > 1 , \tag{1}$$

$$S_1 = \beta_1 P , \qquad 0 < \beta_1 < 1 , \tag{2}$$

$$S_2 = \beta_2 E , \qquad 0 < \beta_2 < 1 , \tag{3}$$

$$E = E^B + S_1 + S_2 . \tag{4}$$

P is total population and E is total employment; S_1 are consumer oriented services and S_2 are producer oriented services; E^B is basic employment; α is an inverse activity rate, β_1 can be called a population-serving ratio, and β_2 an employment-serving ratio. The multiplier connecting total population to basic employment is derived as follows. First, it is necessary to express E in terms of E^B.

$$E - (\alpha\beta_1 + \beta_2)E = E^B . \tag{5}$$

Note that $0 < (\alpha\beta_1 + \beta_2) < 1$. Then by setting

$$\mu = \alpha\beta_1 + \beta_2 , \tag{6}$$

and

$$\gamma = 1 - \mu , \tag{7}$$

equation (5) can be rewritten as

$$E = \frac{E^B}{\gamma} . \tag{8}$$

Then it is obvious that the equation linking population to basic employment is

$$P = \alpha\frac{E^B}{\gamma} . \tag{9}$$

$1/\gamma$ is the multiplier which features so strongly in macroeconomic theory.

Equations (1) to (9) provide a static approach to urban activity analysis, and it is interesting to note ways in which this kind of analysis can be made dynamic. The classical method of macroeconomic theory is largely concerned with tracing the growth paths of variables linked together by multipliers. For example, classical analysis could proceed by formulating equation (5) as a first-order difference equation (Allen, 1967).

$$E_t - \mu E_{t-1} = E^B . \tag{10}$$

Note that the subscripts t and $t-1$ denote time. The solution to equation (10) in terms of an initial level of employment E_0 is found by recursion to be

$$E_t = \frac{E^B}{\gamma} + \left(E_0 - \frac{E^B}{\gamma}\right)(1 - \gamma)^t . \tag{11}$$

In the context of urban modelling Paelinck (1970) has pursued this type of analysis in some depth, examining the equilibrium properties of a series of dynamic models. A similar analysis with a more empirical bias has been made by Czamanski (1965). Using equations (1) to (4) as the basis of his model, Czamanski has built an econometric model of Baltimore incorporating a second-order lag in equation (1), and a first-order lag in equation (2). Like Paelinck, Czamanski uses classical economic analysis to derive solutions to the model.

A different interpretation of the multiplier is suggested in this model, which can be regarded as a more disaggregated approach than that implied above. It is well known that under most conditions the multiplier can be expanded in the following way (Artle, 1961):

$$\frac{1}{\gamma} = \frac{1}{1-\mu} = 1 + \mu + \mu^2 + \ldots + \mu^n \ . \tag{12}$$

Given an increment of employment ΔE_t^B, where the difference operator Δ defines $\Delta E_t^B = E_{t+1}^B - E_t^B$, the total population P generated from this increment is

$$P = \alpha \Delta E_t^B (1 + \mu + \mu^2 + \ldots + \mu^n) \ . \tag{13}$$

Economic analysis tends to treat the multiplier itself as a rate of change, because activity is often multiplied up to its true level quite quickly. In other words the repercussions associated with the multiplier quickly work themselves through the economy. From equation (13), however, each increment of activity generated from ΔE_t^B is associated with a term in the series, and each term could be associated with a particular time period. This of course depends upon the length of the time period, but the hypothesis adopted here states that the repercussions traced by equation (13) are sufficiently large and take sufficiently long in urban systems to form a suitable basis for dynamic modelling.

Assuming a constant parameter μ and that each increment of activity is generated in successive time periods, any particular increment of population ΔP_t is derived from an equation of the following form:

$$\Delta P_t = \alpha (\Delta E_t^B + \Delta E_{t-1}^B \mu + \Delta E_{t-2}^B \mu^2 + \ldots + \Delta E_{t-n}^B \mu^n) \ . \tag{14}$$

Equation (14) shows that the lag is distributed over $n+1$ time periods, and this equation has similarities with the geometric distributed lag equation defined by Allen (1967). Each increment of activity generated by equation (13) need not be associated with a particular time period, for it is possible to combine two or more terms of equation (13) into a particular time period. The time period has to be sufficiently short to detect the geometric series of equation (13) in a discrete fashion, and furthermore it is likely that, after a given number of time periods, the multiplier effects will become insignificant. These considerations have lead to the adoption of a 1 year time interval within which two successive increments of activity are generated. It is also assumed that after 10 time periods, the multiplier effects are small enough to ignore; in other words, in equation (13) n is never greater than 20. Table 1 shows the amounts of employment and population generated using this scheme.

From table 1, the distributed lag equations for employment and population can be written as follows:

$$\Delta E_t = \Delta E_t^{B} + (1+\mu)(\Delta E_t^{B}\mu + \Delta E_{t-1}^{B}\mu^3 + ... + \Delta E_{t-n}^{B}\mu^{2n+1}) , \tag{15}$$

$$\Delta P_t = \alpha(1+\mu)(\Delta E_t^{B}\mu + \Delta E_{t-1}^{B}\mu^2 + ... + \Delta E_{t-n}^{B}\mu^{2n}) . \tag{16}$$

Equations (15) and (16) summarise the way in which activities are generated in time although, in the simulation model, employment and population are not formally generated in this manner, for each time period is modelled separately. In the above equations the ratios are shown as constants which do not vary through time. Although it is probable that such ratios do vary, it would be difficult to detect such variation from data. Therefore, in the case of μ, it is assumed that

$$\mu = \frac{1}{n+1}\sum_{t=0}^{n}\mu_t . \tag{17}$$

Although equation (17) implies a strong assumption, it is possible to vary μ in the simulation model over longer periods of time incorporating about 5 time periods.

Table 1. Generation of activity in successive time periods from ΔE_t^{B}.

Time period	Employment activity		Population activity	
1st period	$\Delta E_t^{B}(1+\mu+\mu^2)$	$= \Delta E_t^{B} + \Delta E_t^{B}\mu(1+\mu)$	$\alpha\Delta E_t^{B}(1+\mu)$	$= \alpha\Delta E_t^{B}\mu^0(1+\mu)$
2nd period	$\Delta E_t^{B}(\mu^3+\mu^4)$	$= \Delta E_t^{B}\mu^3(1+\mu)$	$\alpha\Delta E_t^{B}(\mu^2+\mu^3)$	$= \alpha\Delta E_t^{B}\mu^2(1+\mu)$
3rd period	$\Delta E_t^{B}(\mu^5+\mu^6)$	$= \Delta E_t^{B}\mu^5(1+\mu)$	$\alpha\Delta E_t^{B}(\mu^4+\mu^5)$	$= \alpha\Delta E_t^{B}\mu^4(1+\mu)$
.	.	.	.	.
.	.			.
.	.			.
nth period	$\Delta E_t^{B}(\mu^{2n-1}+\mu^{2n})$	$= \Delta E_t^{B}\mu^{2n-1}(1+\mu)$	$\alpha\Delta E_t^{B}(\mu^{2n-2}+\mu^{2n-1})$	$= \alpha\Delta E_t^{B}\mu^{2(n-1)}(1+\mu)$

Modelling the distribution of activities in space

The simulation model has been designed initially for application at the subregional scale, and is operated mainly through the location of activities rather than land uses. Figure 1 shows that three submodels exist to allocate activity to zones of the spatial system; basic employment endogenous to the simulation, population, and service employment are the three categories of activity which are modelled in spatial terms, and these activities can be treated in turn.

The basic employment location model attempts to predict the location of the growth in basic employment which depends upon previous levels of activity in the system. Declines in such employment are not simulated using this model, which is appropriate only to a growth situation.

Successful models of this sector have been built elsewhere using linear equations (see for example Putnam, 1970), and it was decided to model this activity in a similar way. The model was built outside the main framework of the simulation by Cheshire (1970) and was fitted using stepwise regression analysis. The change in endogenous basic employment $\Delta Y_i(t)$, where $\Delta Y_i(t) = Y_i(t+1) - Y_i(t)$, is allocated as follows (note that the i, j subscripts define zones and that the index of time is now placed in brackets after the variable):

$$\Delta Y_i(t) = \sum_k a_k Z_{i_k}(t) + \sum_m b_m \Delta Z_{i_m}(t-1) + c . \tag{18}$$

$Z_{i_k}(t)$ is the stock of activity k in zone i at t, and $\Delta Z_{i_m}(t-1)$ is the change in activity m in i between t and $t-1$. a_k, b_m, and c are parameters of the equation. At each time period the total change in endogenous basic employment is input to the model, and equation (18) is normalised before this activity is allocated.

The residential location model is perhaps the most complex of all the spatial submodels, for a crude attempt has been made to model both the demand and supply of residential space. The model is based on some theoretical work by Schneider (1967), who argues that the attraction of an area to residential locators must be some function of both the land available and the existing residential floorspace. Schneider has proceeded to devise a model for the allocation of floorspace, and he has further extended his research by fitting the model to data from Chicago (Schneider, 1969). A variant of Schneider's model has been adopted here as a simple model of the supply of floorspace which is, in turn, an input to the residential location model. The actual form of this model is similar to the potential model used by Lowry (1964) to allocate population. At each time period, total floorspace $\Delta F(t)$, which is exogenous to the model, is allocated to zones as follows:

$$\Delta^* F_i(t) = \Delta F(t) K_i(t) X_i(t) , \tag{19}$$

$$X_i(t) = \sum_j [F_j(t+1) + L_j(t-1)] f_1[c_{ij}(t-1)] , \tag{20}$$

$$K_i(t) = \frac{1}{\sum_j X_j(t)} . \tag{21}$$

Note that, in the following discussion, a difference operator of the type Δ^* shows that a change in a time period is *not* the net change between t and $t+1$. In the above equations, $\Delta^* F_i(t)$ is the expected rather than the actual change in the supply of floorspace in i, $F_i(t+1)$ is the expected supply of floorspace in j at $t+1$, $L_i(t-1)$ is the amount of land available for residential development in i at the end of the previous time period $t-1$, and $f_1[c_{ij}(t-1)]$ is some function of travel cost between i and j at $t-1$. On starting with $F_j(t)$ as a first approximation to $F_j(t+1)$, equations

(19) to (21) are iterated until convergence, with the new level of expected floorspace at time $t+1$ being computed at each iteration from

$$F_j(t+1) = F_j(t) + \Delta^* F_j(t) . \tag{22}$$

There are several problems connected with the development of this model and among those requiring further research are questions of overlap between the 'supply' of residential space predicted by this model and the 'demand' for such space, which is simulated by the residential location model described below. Although floorspace and land in this supply model are measured in the same units, there are also problems of combining such variables as appear in equation (20) which need further investigation.

Floorspace from equation (22) and available land form the critical variables measuring the locational attraction of zone j for residential purposes between t and $t+1$. Residential attraction $D_j(t)$ is calculated as follows:

$$D_j(t) = \delta_j[\sigma F_j(t+1) + (1-\sigma)L_j(t-1)] , \qquad 0 \leqslant \sigma \leqslant 1 , \tag{23}$$

$$\delta_j \begin{cases} = 0, \text{ if } P_j(t) \geqslant C_j(t) , \\ = 1, \text{ otherwise} , \end{cases}$$

where σ is a parameter controlling the relative influence of land and floorspace on residential attraction. δ_j controls the overall level of residential attraction. $P_j(t)$ is population in j at t, and $C_j(t)$ is the population limit in zone j at t.

The residential location model is based on a production-constrained gravity model of the type outlined by Wilson (1970b). The model allocates a change in employment $\Delta E_i(t)$ located in i to place of residence in j.

$$\Delta T_{ij}(t) = A_i(t)\Delta E_i(t)D_j(t)f_2[c_{ij}(t-1)] , \tag{24}$$

$$A_i(t) = \frac{1}{\sum_j D_j(t)f_2[c_{ij}(t-1)]} , \tag{25}$$

where $\Delta T_{ij}(t)$ is the change in work trips between i and j, and $f_2[c_{ij}(t-1)]$ is some function of travel cost between i and j at $t-1$. This model satisfies the constraint

$$\sum_j \Delta T_{ij}(t) = \Delta E_i(t) , \tag{26}$$

and the change in population $\Delta P_j(t)$ in j can be found by summing equation (24) over i, and scaling the result by α, the inverse activity rate.

$$\Delta P_j(t) = \alpha \sum_i \Delta T_{ij}(t) = \alpha D_j(t) \sum_i A_i(t)\Delta E_i(t)f_2[c_{ij}(t-1)] . \tag{27}$$

The land available for residential purposes at the end of the time period can be calculated by converting $\Delta P_j(t)$ to land area, using a population density ratio g_j.

$$L_j(t+1) = L_j(t) - g_j \Delta P_j(t) . \tag{28}$$

The third submodel allocates the demand for service employment in j to service centres in i, and is formulated as an attraction-constrained gravity model. Service centre attraction in i is assumed to be a function of the previous demands for service employment in i, and at present this attraction $V_i(t)$ has the following form:

$$V_i(t) = p\Delta S_i(t-1) + p^2 \Delta S_i(t-2) + ... + p^n \Delta S_i(t-n) , \qquad 0 < p < 1. \tag{29}$$

The change in demand for consumer services in i by the population living at j, called $\Delta S_{ij}(t)$, is computed from the following equations:

$$\Delta S_{ij}(t) = V_i(t)R_j(t)\beta_1 \Delta P_j(t) f_3[c_{ij}(t-1)] , \tag{30}$$

$$R_j(t) = \frac{1}{\sum_i V_i(t) f_3[c_{ij}(t-1)]} , \tag{31}$$

where $f_3[c_{ij}(t-1)]$ is some function of travel cost between i and j at $t-1$. The model presented in equations (30) and (31) is subject to the constraint

$$\sum_i \Delta S_{ij}(t) = \beta_1 \Delta P_j(t) . \tag{32}$$

The total change in service employment at i is calculated by summing equation (30) over j and adding the producer services generated from the change in employment at i;

$$\Delta S_i(t) = \sum_j \Delta S_{ij}(t) + \beta_2 \Delta E_i(t) . \tag{33}$$

As this completes the description of the spatial submodels, it is now necessary to outline the factors which affect the relocation of activity in the system. The previous equations are valid for the generation and location of new activities in the system but some slight modifications are needed to model the relocation of existing activities.

Modelling the relocation of existing activities
In the model, only existing population and service employments are allowed to relocate in each time period. This is consistent with the structure of the model, in which basic employment is largely exogenous to the simulation. Yet the structure of the model poses many problems with regard to relocation, and the following discussion must be seen only as a first approach to the problem. As with the modelling of external changes in activity, the mechanism for relocating the existing population and

associated services must be operated from the basic employment on which these relocators initially depend. In other words it is necessary to identify basic employment associated with population and services and to relocate these activities from this point.

A further complicating feature of the model, but one which makes the simulation much easier to execute, concerns the relocation of activities in time. As with external changes in activities the relocation of activity is lagged according to the multiplier effects. If we revert to the previous notation of subscripting variables to indicate time, the relocation of service employment between $t+1$ and t, called ΔS_t^m, and of population, called ΔP_t^m, is as follows:

$$\Delta S_t^m = \lambda(1+\mu)(E_t^B \mu + E_{t-1}^B \mu^3 + ... + E_{t-n}^B \mu^{2n+1}) ,$$ (34)

$$\Delta P_t^m = \alpha\lambda(1+\mu)(E_t^B \mu^0 + E_{t-1}^B \mu^2 + ... + E_{t-n}^B \mu^{2n}) .$$ (35)

λ is referred to as the mover pool ratio and $0 \leqslant \lambda \leqslant 1$. This ratio indicates the proportion of the existing stock in previous time periods which is gradually working its way through the mover pool. Although λ is likely to vary in time, it is assumed here that λ is an average over the simulation period.

The most complex feature of the mover pool arises from a need to simplify the simulation. When the simulation is begun at $t = 0$ the ratios α, β_1, and β_2 are likely to be very different in the initial configuration of activities from the ratios used in the simulation period. It is extremely difficult, if not impossible, to take account of these differences for, at each time period, new activity, generated using the new ratios, is being added to the existing configuration thus changing the actual ratios. Furthermore new activities generated in previous time periods are also eligible for relocation in later time periods. These factors mean that, for each activity, the ratio λ must be modulated at each time period to ensure that the right amount of activity is reallocated. If we take the example of population, at each time period a new ratio λ_t is computed from

$$\lambda_t = \lambda \frac{P_0(1/\alpha - \beta_2/\alpha - \beta_1) + \sum_{t=0}^{N} \Delta E_t^B}{E_0^B + \sum_{t=0}^{N} \Delta E_t^B} .$$ (36)

Note that the summation of ΔE_t^B is from $t = 0$ to $t = N$, where N is the previous time period. As the calculation of λ_t is complex, it is necessary to explain the terms in equation (36) in more detail. The term $P_0(1/\alpha - \beta_2/\alpha - \beta_1)$ converts total population in the system at the beginning of the simulation ($t = 0$) into a hypothetical amount of basic employment, which is consistent with the ratios α, β_1, and β_2. This basic employment is likely to be different from actual basic employment E_0^B because the ratios α, β_1, and β_2 are averages pertaining to changes in activity over the simulation period, not to the structure of activities at the start of the simulation. At each time t, total basic employment consistent with these ratios is divided by actual basic employment, and this proportion is used to weight the mover pool ratio λ. This mechanism is purely a device to enable movers in the system to be reallocated according to the same ratios used to allocate changes in activity, and has been introduced solely to minimise computer time. In applying the weighted mover pool ratio λ_t, equation (35) now becomes

$$\Delta P_t^m = \alpha(1+\mu)(\lambda_t E_t^B \mu^0 + \lambda_{t-1} E_{t-1}^B \mu^2 + \dots + \lambda_{t-n} E_{t-n}^B \mu^{2n}) \,. \tag{37}$$

The rather unrealistic nature of the relocation procedure is seen quite clearly when space is considered. The ratio λ_t is constant in each time period and for the whole system; therefore the numbers of trips which are affected by relocation are a constant proportion λ_t of each i–j pair. This seems highly unrealistic since it is likely that λ_t varies spatially. As yet no efficient way of incorporating a spatial mover pool ratio has been found, but if a feasible method exists, it may be possible to make λ_t endogenous to the model. At present, changes in travel costs and measures of locational attraction are the key determinants of relocation. A fairly elaborate accounting procedure, which is dealt with in more detail later, is used to ensure that no double counting of activities occurs; relocation is essentially internal migration which is largely independent of the absolute growth of the system, and in each time period the following equation is always satisfied:

$$\sum_j \Delta P_j^m(t) = \sum_i \Delta S_i^m(t) = 0 \,. \tag{38}$$

At this stage the major components of the simulation model have been described and now the task is to assemble these components into the basic model. The equation system is outlined below in two parts: the equations concerned with generating and allocating activity in each time period are discussed first, and then the relationships used in accounting for net changes and total stocks of activity are outlined.

The equation system 1: generation and allocation
At the start of the simulation an initial configuration of activities and trips in the system is required. Although activities must be available, trip distributions are often difficult to obtain and therefore an option is built into the program to generate such distributions using production–attraction-constrained gravity models. When $t = 0$, the distribution of work trips is generated as follows:

$$T_{ij}(t) = A_i(t)B_j(t)E_i(t)P_j(t)f_4[c_{ij}(t)] \,, \tag{39}$$

$$A_i(t) = \frac{1}{\sum_j B_j(t)P_j(t)f_4[c_{ij}(t)]} \,, \tag{40}$$

and

$$B_j(t) = \frac{1}{\sum_i A_i(t)E_i(t)f_4[c_{ij}(t)]} \,. \tag{41}$$

A distribution for $S_{ij}(t)$ is obtained using a similar model with $\beta_1 P_i(t)$ replacing $E_i(t)$, and $S_j(t)$ replacing $P_j(t)$ in equations (39) and (40). The parameters of the function $f_4[c_{ij}(t)]$ are approximated using formulae and numerical procedures derived by Hyman (1969).

The constant ratios—the inverse activity, population-serving, and employment-serving ratios—are calculated at this stage for the simulation period

$$\alpha = \frac{\sum_t \Delta P_t}{\sum_t \Delta E_t} \,, \tag{42}$$

$$\beta_1 = \frac{\sum_t \Delta S_{1t}}{\sum_t \Delta P_t} \,, \tag{43}$$

and

$$\beta_2 = \frac{\sum_t \Delta S_{2t}}{\sum_t \Delta P_t} \,. \tag{44}$$

The summations in equations (42) to (44) are from $t = 0$ to $t = n$, where n is the end of the simulation period. At this point, the model begins to simulate changes in activity in each time period. The network of travel costs or distances is updated using a shortest routes program, and the equation modulating the mover pool ratio λ is worked out;

$$\lambda(t) = \lambda \frac{P_0(1/\alpha - \beta_2/\alpha - \beta_1) + \sum_t \Delta E^B(t)}{E_0^B + \sum_t \Delta E^B(t)} \,. \tag{45}$$

Next, endogenous basic employment $\Delta Y(t)$ is allocated to zones of the system, using the basic employment location model;

$$\Delta Y_i(t) = \Delta Y(t) \frac{\sum_k a_k Z_{i_k}(t) + \sum_m b_m \Delta Z_{i_m}(t-1) + c}{\sum_i \left[\sum_k a_k Z_{i_k}(t) + \sum_m b_m \Delta Z_{i_m}(t-1) + c \right]} \,. \tag{46}$$

The measures of locational attraction for this time period are now calculated; first, the Schneider model, which allocates the total change in floorspace $\Delta F(t)$ to zones, is run. Accessibilities $X_i(t)$ are derived:

$$X_i(t) = \sum_j [F_j(t+1) + L_j(t-1)]f_1[c_{ij}(t-1)] \,, \tag{47}$$

$$\Delta^* F_i(t) = \Delta F(t) \frac{X_i(t)}{\sum_i X_i(t)} \ , \tag{48}$$

$$F_j(t+1) = F_j(t) + \Delta^* F_j(t) \ . \tag{49}$$

As $F_i(t) = f[F_i(t)]$, equations (47) to (49) are reiterated until convergence. At the present time Schneider's original model is being investigated in a separate program. With certain starting values and parameters Schneider's model does not converge, and therefore the variant described in equations (47) to (49) was adopted until further work has been done on the structure of Schneider's model. Next, residential attraction in each zone j is computed,

$$D_j(t) = \delta_j [\sigma F_j(t+1) + (1-\sigma) L_j(t-1)] \ , \tag{50}$$

and then the measures of service centre attraction are calculated,

$$V_i(t) = \sum_{r=1}^{n'} p^r \Delta S_i(t-r) \ . \tag{51}$$

The total basic employment to be allocated, including the basic employment associated with relocation, is found from

$$\Delta^* E_i^B(t) = \Delta H_i(t) + \Delta Y_i(t) + \lambda(t) E_i^B(t) \ . \tag{52}$$

$\Delta H_i(t)$ is the change in exogenous basic employment. The model now moves into an inner loop which is concerned with allocating and generating two increments of employment and population. This inner loop is referred to by an index m. The first increment of employment includes the change in service employment from the previous time period t to $t-1$, which has not yet worked its way through the system;

$$\Delta^* E_i(t,m) = \Delta^* E_i^B(t) + \Delta^* S_i(t-1) \ . \tag{53}$$

Employment is first allocated to areas of residence, and scaled to population; then service employment demanded is derived and allocated to service centres using the following equations:

$$\Delta^* T_{ij}(t,m) = \Delta^* E_i(t,m) \frac{D_j(t) f_2 [c_{ij}(t-1)]}{\sum_j D_j(t) f_2 [c_{ij}(t-1)]} \ , \tag{54}$$

$$\Delta^* P_j(t,m) = \alpha \sum_i \Delta^* T_{ij}(t,m) \ , \tag{55}$$

$$\Delta^* S_{ij}(t,m) = \beta_1 \Delta^* P_j(t,m) \frac{V_i(t) f_3 [c_{ij}(t-1)]}{\sum_i V_i(t) f_3 [c_{ij}(t-1)]} \ , \tag{56}$$

$$\Delta^* S_i(t,m) = \sum_j \Delta^* S_{ij}(t,m) + \beta_2 \Delta^* E_i(t,m) \ . \tag{57}$$

If m is less than the required number of iterations then

$$\Delta^* E_i(t,m+1) = \Delta^* S_i(t,m) , \tag{58}$$

and $\Delta^* E_i(t,m+1)$ is substituted for $\Delta^* E_i(t,m)$ in equation (54). Equations (54) to (57) are reiterated until the condition is met: in the simulation here, two iterations are required. The process of generation and allocation is now complete for this time period and the model moves into the accounting framework.

The equation system 2: accounting

First, the gross changes in activities and trips are easily calculated from the earlier equations: these changes are listed below:

$$\Delta^* P_j(t) = \sum_m \Delta^* P_j(t,m) , \tag{59}$$

$$\Delta^* S_i(t) = \sum_m \Delta^* S_i(t,m) , \tag{60}$$

$$\Delta^* E_i(t) = \Delta^* S_i(t) + \Delta^* E_i^B(t) + \Delta^* S_i(t-1) , \tag{61}$$

$$\Delta^* T_{ij}(t) = \sum_m \Delta^* T_{ij}(t,m) , \tag{62}$$

$$\Delta^* S_{ij}(t) = \sum_m \Delta^* S_{ij}(t,m) . \tag{63}$$

Equations (59) to (63) are gross changes, in that they include activity which is relocating in the system. To avoid double counting, this activity must be subtracted. Furthermore to obtain the net changes the complex

Table 2. Proportions of population and service employment allocated at each time period.

Time period	Population or service employment[a]			
1st period	$\dfrac{\mu^0(1+\mu)}{(1-\mu)^{-1}}$	$= (1-\mu^2)$		$= \theta(1)$
2nd period	$\dfrac{\mu^2(1+\mu)}{(1-\mu)^{-1}}$	$= \mu^2(1-\mu^2)$	$=$	$= \theta(2)$
3rd period	$\dfrac{\mu^4(1+\mu)}{(1-\mu)^{-1}}$	$= \mu^4(1-\mu^2)$	$= \mu^2\theta(2)$	$= \theta(3)$
.	.	.	.	.
.	.	.	.	.
.	.	.	.	.
nth period	$\dfrac{\mu^{2(n-1)}(1+\mu)}{(1-\mu)^{-1}}$	$= \mu^{2(n-1)}(1-\mu^2)$	$= \mu^2\theta(n-1)$	$= \theta(n)$

[a] It can easily be shown that the proportions for service employment are the same as those for population.

modulations of the mover pool ratio through time must be taken into account. The proportions of activity relocating at different periods from any point in time are easily calculated as in table 2, and these proportions are also given below:

$$\left.\begin{aligned}
\theta(1) &= 1 - \mu^2 \\
\theta(2) &= \mu^2\theta(1) \\
\theta(3) &= \mu^2\theta(2) \\
&\cdot \quad \cdot \quad \cdot \\
&\cdot \quad \cdot \quad \cdot \\
&\cdot \quad \cdot \quad \cdot \\
\theta(n) &= \mu^2\theta(n-1) \, .
\end{aligned}\right\} \tag{64}$$

These proportions are relevant to the relocation of population but must be modulated for service employment, work trips and service trips in the following way (the subscripts R, T, and S denote service employment, work trips, and service trips respectively):

$$\theta_R(t) = \theta(t)\frac{P(t)(\beta_1 + \beta_2/\alpha)}{S(t)} \, , \tag{65}$$

$$\theta_T(t) = \theta(t)\frac{P(t)}{\alpha E(t)} \, , \tag{66}$$

$$\theta_S(t) = \theta(t)\frac{\beta_1 P(t)}{S(t) - \beta_2 E(t)} \, . \tag{67}$$

The main calculations for deriving net changes are given below; total stocks of activity at time $t+1$ need not be shown explicitly, for their calculation is obvious.

$$P_j(t+1) - P_j(t) = \Delta^* P_j(t) - \lambda \sum_{z=1}^{N} \theta(z)P_j(z) \, , \tag{68}$$

$$S_i(t+1) - S_i(t) = \Delta^* S_i(t) - \lambda \sum_{z=1}^{N} \theta_R(z)S_i(z) \, , \tag{69}$$

$$T_{ij}(t+1) - T_{ij}(t) = \Delta^* T_{ij}(t) - \lambda \sum_{z=1}^{N} \theta_T(z)T_{ij}(z) \, , \tag{70}$$

$$S_{ij}(t+1) - S_{ij}(t) = \Delta^* S_{ij}(t) - \lambda \sum_{z=1}^{N} \theta_S(z)S_{ij}(z) \, , \tag{71}$$

$$E_i(t+1) - E_i(t) = S_i(t+1) - S_i(t) + \Delta H_i(t) + \Delta Y_i(t) \, . \tag{72}$$

(Note that $N = 10$.)

Total quantities of activity in the system can be calculated by summing over i, or j, or both. There are also several other outputs from the model at each time period such as zonal activity rates, trip lengths, and residential densities. Before the model goes on to simulating changes in the following

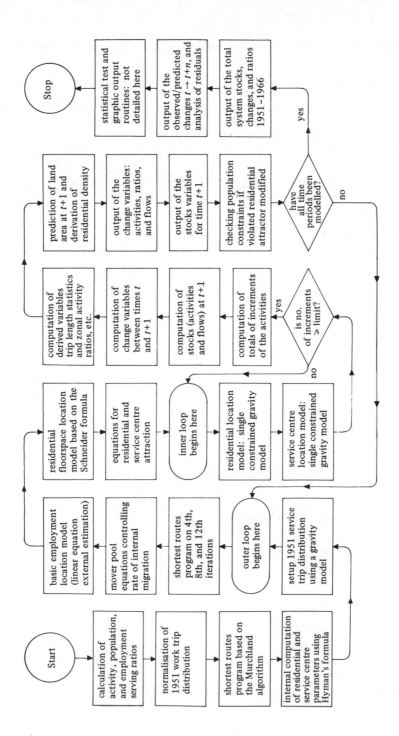

Figure 2. Dynamic model of the Reading subregion: generalised flow chart.

time period, the land available for future residential development is calculated,

$$L_j(t+1) = L_j(t) - g_j[P_j(t+1) - P_j(t)] \ . \tag{73}$$

A new measure of actual floorspace in residential uses is also derived from

$$F_j(t+1) = F_j(t) + \Delta F(t) \frac{P_j(t+1) - P_j(t)}{\sum_j P_j(t+1) - \sum_j P_j(t)} \ . \tag{74}$$

A test is made to assess whether the constraints on population in each zone have been violated. The term δ_j is set as follows for the next time period:

$$\delta_j \begin{cases} = 0 \quad \text{if} \quad P_j(t+1) \geqslant C_j(t+1) \ , \\ = 1, \text{otherwise} \ . \end{cases} \tag{75}$$

If $t < n$, t is increased to $t+1$ and the simulation begins again at equation (45). Equations (45) to (75) are reiterated until all time periods in the simulation period have been modelled. A flow diagram of the main operations in the model is presented in figure 2.

Restrictive assumptions of the simulation

Although the equation system describes the various feedback loops which operate in the model within and between time periods, a more direct presentation of these linkages is provided in figure 3. At any point in time the model is in disequilibrium in the sense that previous changes in the level of activity are generating further changes. These repercussions due to multiplier effects are assumed small enough to be ignored ten time periods after the initial stimulus, and this means that, in any time period, changes originally generated in the nine previous time periods are part of the total change in activity. Furthermore when the simulation is terminated there are still repercussions to work themselves out; there is also the problem of starting the simulation, for to preserve consistency the model should begin in disequilibrium. This could easily be achieved by adding the potential activity, not yet generated at the end of the simulation, to the starting position. As yet this problem has not been dealt with although, in absolute terms, there is little effect on the system.

The subdivision of the simulation period and the spatial system into discrete units is an important factor in detecting variance. Broadbent (1969) has argued that spatial systems should be zoned to maximise the ratio of interzonal to intrazonal interaction. A similar rule is necessary for fixing the length of the time period: the ratio of activity generated in the first time period to repercussions from that activity generated in later time periods should be minimised. As the length of the time period increases, more of the multiplier effects from a change in activity are

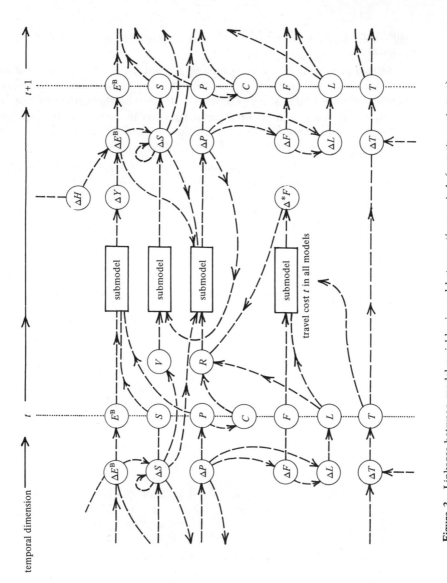

Figure 3. Linkages between model variables in and between time periods (notation as in text).

generated within that time period, and a time interval of one year is considered most appropriate here.

Although the activity parameters, α, β_1, and β_2, are taken as constant over the simulation period, it is possible to vary these parameters over periods of time longer than two years. Because of the nature of the multiplier, it is difficult to vary the parameters in each time period, for this would change the form of the economic base relationship. This problem is largely one of estimating the parameters from data, and of accounting for different values of the parameters in the simulation. In future research it may be possible to assume a trend in these parameters over the simulation period, thus implicitly recognising that the parameters vary. With regard to the mover pool ratio, this parameter can be varied over time, but it is much more difficult to vary the parameter spatially. This ratio should be partly endogenous to the simulation in that changes in the age-sex-household structure of the population are important determinants of internal migration. In future work, these relationships will be explored in more detail.

It is also necessary to comment on the recursive structure of the simulation model, and to assess its validity. In designing such a model, what appear to be simultaneous relationships, in reality, must be approximated by a sequence of relationships; this embodies certain assumptions as to the order of operations in the sequence. For example, the relationship between the supply and demand for floorspace is approximated in the following way The expected supply of floorspace is derived using Schneider's model, and this becomes an input to the measure of locational attraction used in the demand model locating population. Population is then converted into actual floorspace, which is likely to be different from expected floorspace. No iteration is used to establish consistency between the expected and actual supply of floorspace. This sequence of operations could easily be ordered so that the expected and actual demand for, rather than supply of, floorspace were computed. Such decisions with regard to ordering abound in the model, and it is assumed that the time period is short enough to make little difference to the order of operations.

Application and preliminary calibration

The simulation model is being run with data from the Reading area in central Berkshire. This subregion has been divided into 18 zones, and the simulation is from 1951 to 1966 in one year time periods. There is an immediate problem in collecting data for this model; although good cross-sections of activity and work trips exist for 1951, 1961, and 1966 from the Population Census, very little data exists in yearly periods between these dates. Data on total employment by Standard Industrial Classification (SIC) is available for each year from the Employment Exchange Areas, and this provides the only time-series to guide the simulation. Consequently many of the model's hypotheses cannot be validated in any strict sense. It is clear that the model cannot be calibrated in the usual way, for gaps exist in the set of data which have been filled by assumption, or by outputs from other models.

The zoning of the subregion and the route network in 1966 are shown in figure 4. Changes in the network and data on land use have been

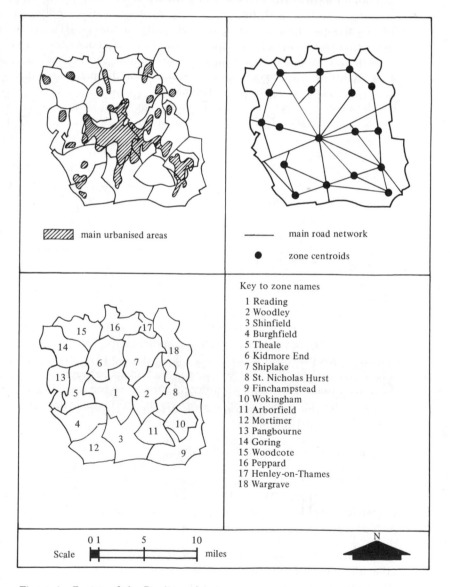

Figure 4. Zoning of the Reading subregion.

provided by the Local Authorities in the area, and at present the model is being run using a hypothetical time-series for basic employment. In general terms the mathematical methods developed for fitting and analysing time-series are quite unsuitable for such a hybrid model as this. Furthermore at present this model is regarded as an exploratory tool for setting up experiments concerning urban growth processes, and for refining and developing existing theories of urban structure. The experimental approach is quite consistent with the form of the model, and the emphasis in the rest of this paper is on testing the sensitivity of the model's parameters and variables to change. In this way the key determinants of urban growth and structure, as simulated by the model, can be revealed. As a first step in this approach reasonable values for the parameters need to be estimated using some short cut techniques.

The basic employment location model was fitted to data from 1961 1966 using stepwise linear regression analysis (Cheshire, 1970). Although there are more accurate and less biased methods of fitting such a linear equation to data consistent with a one year time module (Rogers, 1968), the equations presented below are appropriate for experimental purposes. The variables $X_i(t)$ and $\Delta X_i(t)$ are now superscripted for clarity. These equations now become

$$X_i^s(t) = \sum_j \frac{S_j(t)}{d_{ij}(t)} , \qquad (76)$$

$$\Delta X_i^p(t) = \sum_j \frac{P_j(t)}{d_{ij}(t)} - \sum_j \frac{P_j(t-1)}{d_{ij}(t-1)} , \qquad (77)$$

$$\Delta Y_i(t) = -0 \cdot 7307 + 0 \cdot 1215 B_i(t) + 0 \cdot 0200 \Delta X_i^p(t) - 0 \cdot 0119 P_i(t)$$
$$- 0 \cdot 0264 S_i(t) - 0 \cdot 0581 X_i^s(t) . \qquad (78)$$

$d_{ij}(t)$ and $d_{ij}(t-1)$ are distances between i and j in miles at t and $t-1$. Equation (78) is normalised in the simulation, and total endogenous employment $\Delta Y(t)$ is allocated to zones. The coefficient of multiple correlation, R^2, is $0 \cdot 98993$ for equation (78). Despite the apparent goodness of this fit, equation (78) is determined empirically and has no theoretical underpinnings.

The following functions of travel time were assumed for the simulation, and parameters were approximated using a method of Hyman (1969).

$$\left. \begin{array}{l} f_1[c_{ij}(t-1)] \\ f_2[c_{ij}(t-1)] \\ f_4[c_{ij}(t-1)] \end{array} \right\} = \exp[-\phi_1 t_{ij}(t-1)] , \qquad (79)$$

$$f_3[c_{ij}(t-1)] = \exp[-\phi_2 t_{ij}(t-1)] . \qquad (80)$$

Travel time t_{ij} is used as a proxy for travel cost in the model. Note also that the service centre trip distribution model, necessary to set up the distribution of service trips in 1951, uses parameter ϕ_2. The parameters ϕ_1

and ϕ_2 are functions of the associated mean trip lengths, and Hyman's method generates an approximation from given means. The activity ratios α, β_1, and β_2 are estimated from data at the start of the simulation, and this presents no difficulties. A very approximate value of the mover pool ratio has been taken from data on internal migration in Berkshire, recorded by the 1966 Census between 1961 and 1966; the value of this ratio is 0·020.

A critical assumption has been made with regard to the form of the basic employment time-series between 1951 and 1966. The change in basic employment in each zone in each year over the simulation period has been guided by the total change in basic employment in each year, available from the Employment Exchange Areas. The model has been run with the above assumptions, and the results in the following section demonstrate the main features of the simulation. A summary of the model's performance in terms of various statistics is useful at this stage, bearing in mind the approximate and crude nature of the calibration. In table 3, statistics measuring the fit between the predicted and observed zonal distributions of changes in activity between 1951 and 1966, and stocks of activity at 1966, are presented. Although the statistics measuring the fit of the stocks are heavily biased towards a good fit, the statistics associated with the changes in activity reveal that the performance of the model is fair in the light of the major assumptions.

Table 3. A statistical summary of the model's performance.

Statistics[a]	Stocks 1966		Changes 1951–1966	
	service employment	population	service employment	population
Means ratio	0·006	0·006	0·023	0·023
Standard deviation ratio	0·007	−0·042	0·030	0·280
Mode ratio	0·000	0·027	0·033	−0·949
Mean absolute deviations ratio	0·008	0·072	0·083	0·375
Root mean square error ratio	0·071	0·197	0·262	0·735
R^2	0·999	0·999	0·983	0·380
Slope	0·991	1·008	0·949	0·434
Intercept	9·917	−210·576	29·774	2168·047

[a] Notes: The ratios are formed by subtracting the predicted from the observed statistic and dividing by the observed statistic. The slope and intercept statistics are measures of the regression line of predicted on observed values of each activity.

Experiments in urban simulation
At the end of each time period, the model output gives a new configuration of the stock, and new patterns of interaction; also, changes in the stock

and in the interaction patterns, computed in the previous time period, are produced. Therefore, during each simulation run, a large volume of data needs to be digested quickly and, to facilitate presentation, a graph-plotting subroutine has been developed. Changes and stocks of activity in each zone are plotted through the simulation period, and some of the following figures show this facility. With regard to future research it is hoped that other means of graphic presentation such as computer mapping can be developed, for at present a large part of the output is being ignored on each run.

The trajectories of change in the whole subregion are shown in figure 5. The important point to note from this graph concerns the sensitivity of endogenous variables, such as population and service employment, to

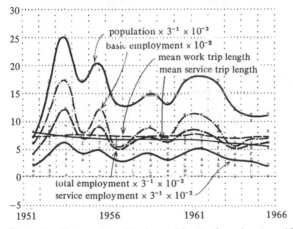

Figure 5. Changes in critical variables in the subregion, 1951–1966.

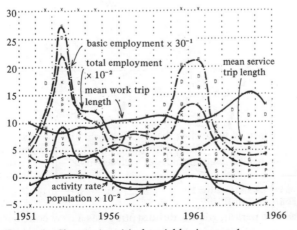

Figure 6. Changes in critical variables in zone 1.

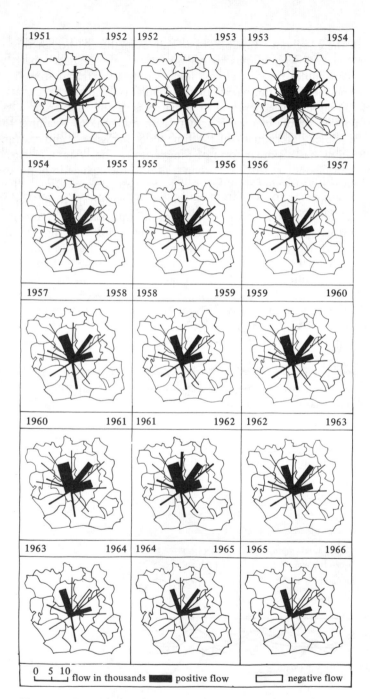

Figure 7. Distribution of work trips from Reading 1951–1966.

changes in the exogenous variable, basic employment. Although this
graph and the following graphs are not to scale, figure 5 shows that the
endogenous variables respond almost immediately to external stimuli; this
is to be expected from the nature of the simulation and the fact that
much of the lag in the generation of activities is of the first order. As a
large proportion of the change in activity is in the zone of Reading, this
zone is the major determinant of the time-series in figure 5 and, as figure 6
shows, Reading has a similar form of time-series to the system as a whole.
An important characteristic of this zone relates to the change in population,
which is both positive and negative during the simulation period. The
behaviour of this zone shows features typical of decentralisation and
suburbanisation in that the ratio of changes in population to changes in
employment is close to zero throughout the simulation. In figure 7 the
pattern of work trips generated by persons working in Reading and living
in other zones of the system is shown for each time period of the
simulation. It is interesting that the changes in activity in figure 6 are
also reflected in figure 7: the two peaks in activity in 1953–1954 and in
1961–1962 are apparent in a peaking of the work trip distribution at
those dates.

Two other zones in the subregion, Wokingham and Henley, show
behaviour similar to that of Reading. In both these cases the change in
the inverse activity rate is close to zero, which indicates that population
generated in these zones is being largely located outside of them. In the
case of Wokingham, shown in figure 8, the change in basic employment is
similar to the system as a whole. In figure 9, which shows changes in the
case of Henley, marked peaking of the mean service trip length is due to
the fact that service employment increases in these years.

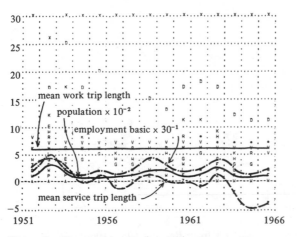

Figure 8. Changes in critical variables in zone 10.

The experimental approach to urban simulation is clearly illustrated by figures 10 and 11, which show changes in the zones of Kidmore End and Shiplake respectively. Both these zones reveal behaviour patterns opposite but complementary to zones such as Reading, for the changes in the inverse activity rates are high, showing that these areas are growing from an incoming population which has its place of work elsewhere. In the case of Shiplake (figure 11), changes in activity reveal the essential purpose of simulation in that it provides new insights into the structure of urban systems. The peculiar oscillatory behaviour which starts in Shiplake towards the end of the simulation can be accounted for as follows. In terms of the performance of the model, Shiplake's population is growing too rapidly, and in 1962–1963 reaches the population constraint limit

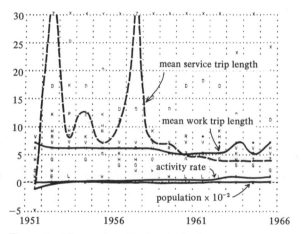

Figure 9. Changes in critical variables in zone 17.

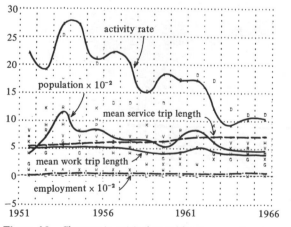

Figure 10. Changes in critical variables in zone 6.

$C_j(t)$. When this limit is reached, the term δ_j is set equal to zero and the residential attraction in the following time period is also zero. Besides allocating new activity, the residential location model *reallocates* activity in the mover pool. In Shiplake the attraction is zero, and persons in the mover pool will not relocate in Shiplake although this may be their place of residence in the previous time period. Hence there is a net outmigration from Shiplake; this lowers the population, which falls below $C_j(t)$, the residential attraction becomes positive and, in the next time period, population flows back in.

In the simulation these oscillations, although in absolute terms not large, may continue indefinitely. This may or may not be realistic of urban systems, but such behaviour was not anticipated *a priori* and is certainly

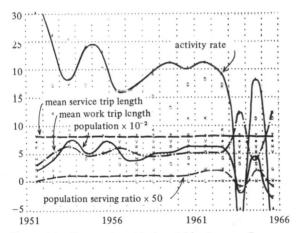

Figure 11. Changes in critical variables in zone 7.

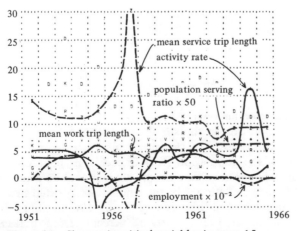

Figure 12. Changes in critical variables in zone 15.

cause for further testing of the realism of this particular mechanism in the model. Figure 12, which illustrates changes in Woodcote, demonstrates the way in which lags are distributed in the system. A decline in basic employment is reflected in declines in service employment in later time periods. This decline in services also has an effect in damping the measure of service centre attraction in later time periods. Such effects can be seen easily in figure 12, where the major effect on the mean service trip length follows two periods after the decline in employment.

Changes in the zone of Rotherfield Peppard, shown in figure 13, demonstrate the sensitivity of various ratios to changes in employment. As an example, when the inverse activity rate declines, the mean work trip length increases. Several different hypotheses can be advanced for this behaviour, but it seems that a more rigorous analysis of the model's structure and further experiments in sensitivity analysis are necessary before such relationships can be clarified. Already, in the case of Shiplake, the importance of relocator behaviour has been discussed. The experimental approach to relocation can be taken further and, in the following section, some migration analysis based on the simulation is presented.

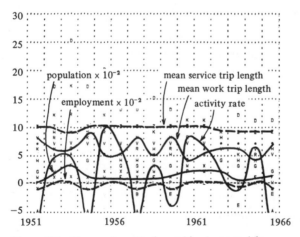

Figure 13. Changes in critical variables in zone 16.

An approach to migration analysis

The importance of relocation in the simulation cannot be overstressed. As an example, consider those runs of the model in which the mover pool ratio is set at $0 \cdot 02$ of the population stock in each time period. During 15 such periods in a situation of no growth, there would be a turnover of about one-third of the population. In the simulation reported here, where the growth in population between 1951 and 1966 is about 36 percent of the population in 1951, nearly 50 percent of the total change in location is due to relocation. This is a very high percentage, and it is certain that the mover pool ratio is the most sensitive parameter in the model. A large proportion of relocation, however, remains undetected, for most relocation occurs within a zone, even though migration across zonal boundaries is quite high in absolute terms.

In reality the whole population never completely relocates, for the propensity to migrate varies widely between different social, economic, and age groups. The model, however, is too 'macro' to account for this kind of detail; if a disaggregation of the population was to be considered in future research it appears, in the light of the above example, that such disaggregation would need to be closely related to relocator behaviour rather than to travel behaviour.

The sensitivity of the mover pool ratio is demonstrated by figure 14, where changes in the population of Reading are compared when the ratio is equal to $0 \cdot 0$ and $0 \cdot 02$. Changes in the value of this parameter are reflected in most of the spatial distributions predicted by the model, and in most of the statistical tests which are computed. Net migration into and out of each zone for population and service activities can easily be computed by running the model with the mover pool ratio equal to $0 \cdot 0$, and subtracting these predictions from the results produced with the positive ratio. The amounts of migration at each time period are fairly constant: this is to be expected from the theory, for the critical variables which alter the rate of internal migration are those which affect location— the measures of locational attraction and travel cost. Such variables are not likely to vary very much from time period to time period. In figure 14 the amount of net outmigration of population and services is shown for Reading. In the case of population, outmigration is constant whereas in the case of services, the level of outmigration gradually increases with time.

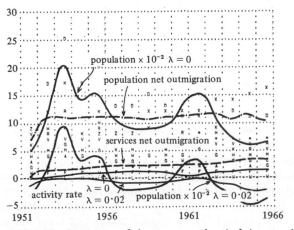

Figure 14. Sensitivity of the mover pool ratio λ in zone 1.

The initial build up in these rates is due to the fact that the simulation is not started in disequilibrium.

Spatial analysis of the pattern of net internal migration shows that in this model the mover pool ratio appears to be the critical parameter affecting the decentralisation of activity. This is apparent from figure 14, and figure 15 shows the net flow of population across different partitions of the subregion. Analysis of this type was originally developed for projections with cross-sectional land use models (Batty, 1970), but it is obviously relevant to dynamic modelling. The net outmigration from Reading, Wokingham, and Henley demonstrates that the existing population is decentralising due to changes in the relative attraction of zones in the system. Areas of greatest net inmigration are typically suburban areas or rural areas with enclaves of exurban growth.

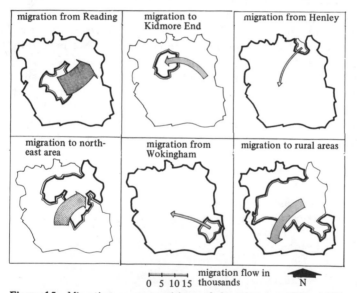

Figure 15. Migration across partitions of the subregion 1951–1966.

Conclusions and further research

The approach to simulation outlined in this paper represents some first steps in modelling the dynamics of urban systems. There are many mechanisms in the model which are unrealistic simulators of urban activity, and future research will be devoted to clarifying and modifying the structure of the model in an experimental fashion. In particular, four research areas can be defined; these are labelled calibration, dynamics, structure, and application, and are now discussed in turn.

The calibration described above is approximate in several respects. The degree to which such a model can be 'calibrated' in the traditional sense is an important area for research and, as yet, there are several sensitivity analyses of the model's variables still to be undertaken. Some calibration methods, based on the theory of search, and on numerical–iterative processes, have been developed recently by the author (Batty, 1971b, 1971c) specifically for cross-sectional models of spatial interaction, and these methods will be adapted to the dynamic model in future research. With regard to research into the model's dynamics, two major directions for study can be delineated. Firstly, the specification of the model using a system of difference equations is worthy of further research possibly in terms of a more theoretical approach such as that used by Paelinck (1970). Secondly, the concept of time as a one dimensional continuum needs some exploration. In urban modelling the temporal element is complicated by concepts such as expectation and uncertainty as in economics (Shackle, 1957); already such concepts have been introduced, as in the case of the floorspace location model, and it is probable that other mechanisms in the model can be made more realistic in this way.

Questions of structure are partly related to dynamics for the temporal as well as spatial relationships in the model produce what is called structure. These relationships need to be explored in much more detail with a view to altering the sequential order of certain operations in the model, and modifying the balance between endogenous and exogenous variables. Finally, applications of the model are to be extended in two ways. Firstly, the model can be used to make short term predictions of changes in urban activity, and in particular the model is probably sensitive enough to forecast the impact of the new motorway system already planned for the Reading subregion. The second type of application is much more interesting, for the model can also be used in an historical context; as the simulation is initially fitted to a previous span of time, it is possible to compare the present with predictions generated during the history of the simulation. This type of retrospective analysis could, for example, be used to compare the present with what might have happened if the course of recent spatial history had been slightly different.

This summary of future research reads rather like a catalogue, but many of these areas can be explored in a straightforward manner. Taking the 'fourth dimension' into consideration in modelling certainly opens up new vistas of research, which have hitherto remained largely unexplored, and it appears that many of the problems of cross-sectional modelling can *only* be resolved in a dynamic context. The dynamic simulation outlined here offers a promising approach to urban research and should eventually lead to more realistic methods of spatial forecasting.

Acknowledgement. The author wishes to thank Alison Cheshire, of South Hampshire Plan Technical Unit, for her work on the basic employment location model.

References

Allen, R. G. D., 1967, *Macro-Economic Theory* (Macmillan, London).

Artle, R., 1961, "On some methods and problems in the study of metropolitan economics", *Papers and Proceedings of the Regional Science Association,* **8**, 71-87.

Batty, M., 1970, "Models and projections of the space-economy", *Town Planning Review,* **41**, 121-147.

Batty, M., 1971a, "Modelling cities as dynamic systems", *Nature,* **231**, 425-428.

Batty, M., 1971b, "Exploratory calibration of a retail location model using search by Golden Section", *Environment and Planning,* **3**, 411-432.

Batty, M., 1971c, "A note on the calibration of a retail location model using Hyman's method", Working Note, Urban Systems Research Unit, University of Reading.

Broadbent, T. A., 1969, "Zone size and spatial interaction in operational models", CES-WN-106, Centre for Environmental Studies, London.

Cheshire, Alison, 1970, "The development of a basic employment generation and allocation model", Working Note, Urban Systems Research Unit, University of Reading.

Cordey-Hayes, M., Wilson, A. G., 1971, "Spatial interaction", *Socio-Economic Planning Sciences,* **5**, 73-95.

Crecine, J. P., 1964, "TOMM: Time oriented metropolitan model", CRP Technical Bulletin No.6, CONSAD Research Corporation, Pittsburgh.

Crecine, J. P., 1967, "Computer simulation in urban research", P-3734, Rand Corporation, Santa Monica.

Crecine, J. P., 1968, "A dynamic model of urban structure", P-3803, Rand Corporation, Santa Monica.

Crecine, J. P., 1969, "Spatial location decisions and urban structure: a time-oriented model", Discussion Paper No.4, Institute of Public Policy Studies, University of Michigan.

Cripps, E. L., Cater, E. A., 1972, "The empirical development of a disaggregated residential location model: some preliminary results", in *London Papers in Regional Science,* Volume 3, Ed. A. G. Wilson (Pion, London).

Czamanski, S., 1965, "A method of forecasting metropolitan growth by means of distributed lags analysis", *Journal of Regional Science,* **6**, 35-49.

Forrester, J., 1961, *Industrial Dynamics* (John Wiley, New York).

Forrester, J., 1969, *Urban Dynamics* (MIT Press, Cambridge, Mass.).

Goldner, W., 1971, "The Lowry model heritage", *Journal of American Institute of Planners,* **37**, 100-110.

Hamilton, H. R., Goldstone, S. E., Milliman, J. W., Pugh, A. L., Roberts, E. B., Zellner, A., 1969, *Systems Simulation for Regional Analysis: An Application to River-Basin Planning* (MIT Press, Cambridge, Mass.).

Harris, B., 1966, "Preliminary note on aspects of equilibrium in urban growth models", Institute for Environmental Studies, University of Pennsylvania.

Harris, B., 1970, "Change and equilibrium in the urban system", Institute for Environmental Studies, University of Pennsylvania.

Hyman, G. M., 1969, "The calibration of trip distribution models", *Environment and Planning,* **1**, 105-112.

Irwin, N. A., Brand, D., 1965, "Planning and forecasting metropolitan development", *Traffic Quarterly,* **19**, 520-540.

Lowry, I. S., 1964, *Model of Metropolis,* RM-4035-RC, Rand Corporation, Santa Monica.

Orcutt, G. H., Greenberger, M., Korbel, J., Rivlin, A. M., 1961, *Microanalysis of Socio-economic Systems: A Simulation Study* (Harper and Row, New York).

Paelinck, J., 1970, "Dynamic urban growth models", *Papers of the Regional Science Association,* **24**, 25-37.

Putnam, S. H., 1970, "Developing and testing an intra-regional model", *Regional Studies,* **4**, 473-490.

Rogers, A., 1968, *Matrix Analysis of Inter-Regional Population Growth and Distribution* (University of California Press, Berkeley).

Schneider, M., 1967, "Access and land development", in *Urban Development Models,* Ed. G. C. Hemmens, Special Report 97, Highway Research Board, Washington D.C.

Schneider, M., 1969, "Transportation and land development—a unified theory and prototype model", Creighton-Hamburg Inc. and US Department of Commerce, Springfield, Virginia.

Shackle, G. L. S., 1957, *Time in Economics* (North Holland, Amsterdam).

Simon, H. A., 1969, *The Sciences of the Artificial* (MIT Press, Cambridge, Mass.).

Swanson, C. V., Waldmann, R. J., 1970, "A simulation model of economic growth dynamics", *Journal of American Institute of Planners,* **36**, 314-322.

Wilson, A. G., 1970a, "Disaggregating elementary residential location models", *Papers of the Regional Science Association,* **24**, 103-125.

Wilson, A. G., 1970b, *Entropy in Urban and Regional Modelling* (Pion, London).

Appendix. Notation.

i, j	are subscripts referring to zones of the bounded subregion;
k, m	are subscripts referring to types of activity;
$0, t, t-1, t+1$	are subscripts and bracketed indices referring to instants of time;
n, n', N	are indices referring to the final instants in a period of time;
r, z	are generalised indices referring to several successive instants of time;
Δ	is the difference operator defining net changes in activity between t and $t+1$;
Δ^*	is the difference operator defining gross changes in activity between t and $t+1$;
(m)	is the index describing iteration of the inner loop of the model;
M	is a superscript defining relocating activity;
P	is the total population;
E	is the total employment;
S_1	is the consumer oriented service employment;
S_2	is the producer oriented service employment;
E^B	is the total basic employment;
H	is the exogenous basic employment (unique locators);
Y	is the endogenous basic employment;
T	are the work trips;
S	are the trips to service centres or total service employment;
Z	are unspecified activities;
F	is the residential floorspace;
L	is the land available for residential development;

X	is the index of accessibility or potential;
D	is residential attraction;
V	is service centre attraction;
C	is the constraint limit on population;
A, B, R, K	are balancing factors or normalising constants;
c_{ij}	is the generalised travel cost between i and j;
t_{ij}	is the travel time between i and j;
d_{ij}	is the over-the-road distance between i and j;
g_j	is the residential density of j, that is the ratio of land to population;
α	is the inverse activity rate;
β_1	is the population serving ratio;
β_2	is the employment serving ratio;
μ	is the ratio of service to total employment or $\alpha\beta_1 + \beta_2$;
γ	is the ratio of basic to total employment or $1 - \mu$;
δ_j	is the term controlling residential attraction in j;
σ	is a parameter controlling relative influence of available land over floorspace or vice versa;
p	is a parameter describing lagged effect of services on service centre attraction;
λ	is the mover pool ratio;
θ	is the proportion of population in mover pool;
θ_R	is the proportion of services in mover pool;
θ_S	is the proportion of service trips in mover pool;
θ_T	is the proportion of work trips in mover pool;
ϕ_1, ϕ_2	are the respective parameters of residential and service trip distributions;
a, b, c	are parameters of the linear basic employment location model.

Static and Dynamic Characteristics of the Negative Exponential Model of Urban Population Distributions

R.BUSSIÈRE
Centre de Recherche d'Urbanisme, Paris

1 Introduction

The object of this paper is to review the main static and dynamic features of the negative exponential model of urban population distribution. For some reason, many of the most interesting and potentially useful properties of the static model have been widely ignored in previous work on this subject. And in the case of modern growing cities, very little attention has been given to the remarkable adaptability of the model to a dynamic situation.

In the author's opinion, one of the main reasons why some of the important characteristics of the negative exponential model have been so long neglected is that most researchers interested in the question have chosen, in their experiments, to work directly with Clark's (1951) original formulation of the model:

$$D(r) = A \exp(-br) \tag{1}$$

or its logarithmic equivalent:

$$\ln D(r) = \ln A - br , \tag{2}$$

where $D(r)$ is the mean surface population density at a distance r from the urban centre; A is the extrapolated density at the centre; b is the exponential rate of decline of density with distance from the centre.

The simplicity of these expressions is, of course, appealing, and equation (2), which plots as a straight line on semi-log paper, would seem to offer considerable convenience in performing empirical tests of the model.

The convenience of the negative exponential model in its 'density' formulation, however, is more apparent than real, as has been shown in a previous study (Bussière, 1968).

It was pointed out in that study that the calibration of the model was bound to be unreliable if based on direct observations of surface densities in thin concentric rings, since the results are highly sensitive to the choice —necessarily arbitrary—of the ring 'thickness', Δr.

Fortunately it is possible to obtain precise and reliable calibrations, in a manner consistent with scientific standards of experimental replicability, by working with the model in its 'population' form. If we assume the existence of a density function $D(r)$, then the total population contained

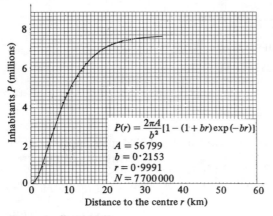

Figure 1. Paris 1962.

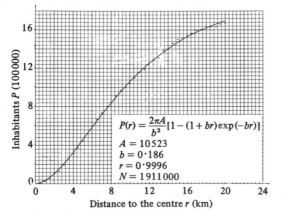

Figure 2. Toronto 1961.

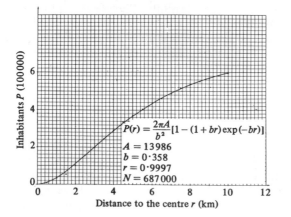

Figure 3. Zürich 1968.

within any concentric circle of radius r is

$$P(r) = 2\pi \int_0^r D(r)r\,dr \tag{3}$$

or, in the case of the negative exponential model,

$$P(r) = \frac{2\pi A}{b^2}[1 - (1+br)\exp(-br)] . \tag{4}$$

Offhand, this well-known version of the model may appear less convenient to work with than the 'density' version. Adjustments of $P(r)$ are best made by having recourse to some iterative method of curve-fitting, but the work can easily be done on a computer, with consistently meaningful results.

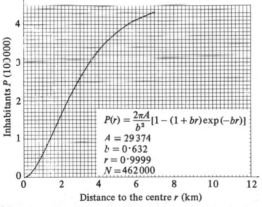

Figure 4. Bordeaux 1962.

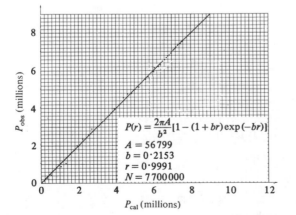

Figure 5. Paris 1962.

Figures 1, 2, 3, and 4 are typical examples of adjustments of model (4) to existing population distributions, as determined from census statistics, in the cities of Paris, Toronto, Zürich, and Bordeaux. The dots represent actual population counts within concentric circles of radius r, while the solid curves represent the 'theoretical' distributions $P(r)$ according to equation (4), into which the adjusted values of the parameters A and b have been inserted.

Figures 5, 6, 7, and 8 are plots, for the same cities, of the 'observed' values of $P(r)$ versus the values predicted by the model. The correlation coefficients cited in the legends are applicable, in each case, to the cloud of points extending to the radius within which is contained 80% of the total population of the urban agglomeration. To date, similar adjustments of the model have been made to the observed population distributions of some 15 European and North American cities. In several cases, this was done on sets of census data covering extended historical periods. The 'fidelity' of the model seems to be consistently high, and is considerably higher than previous tests based directly on density distribution have (or could have) indicated.

The population distributions studied so far make up a limited sample in which only West European and Canadian cities are represented. There has been no opportunity as yet to study population distributions in the cities of countries with planned economies, or in those of the 'third world', or, for that matter, in American cities with their special administrative, fiscal, and racial problems.

At this time, therefore, it would be rash to project upon such cities the population distribution patterns that have been observed in the sample cities.

What one may safely infer from the sample is that there are many cities whose population distribution patterns are in remarkably close agreement

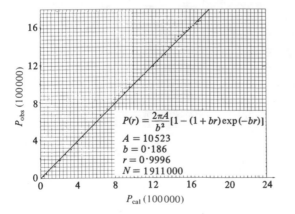

$$P(r) = \frac{2\pi A}{b^2}[1 - (1 + br)\exp(-br)]$$

$A = 10523$
$b = 0{\cdot}186$
$r = 0{\cdot}9996$
$N = 1911000$

Figure 6. Toronto 1961.

with the negative exponential model. In the case of these 'conforming' cities, mathematical properties of the formal static model are also properties of the actual population distributions—properties that may be of considerable interest to practising planners.

But this paper is also concerned with the dynamic or time-dependent negative exponential model. In this connexion, empirical evidence is building up that the population distributions of modern growing cities evolve in time in a manner that is also subject to mathematical analysis, within the context of the negative exponential model.

These preliminary remarks having been made, the discussion that follows can be couched in fairly formal terms. The mathematical development will be presented in a straightforward manner, without any further stress on the fact that there exists, in fact, a very close relationship between the formal implications of the model and 'objective reality' in the case of 'conforming cities'.

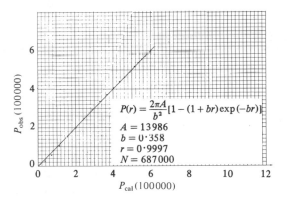

$$P(r) = \frac{2\pi A}{b^2}[1 - (1 + br)\exp(-br)]$$

$A = 13986$
$b = 0\cdot358$
$r = 0\cdot9997$
$N = 687000$

Figure 7. Zürich 1968.

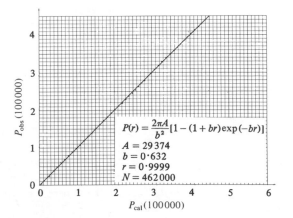

$$P(r) = \frac{2\pi A}{b^2}[1 - (1 + br)\exp(-br)]$$

$A = 29374$
$b = 0\cdot632$
$r = 0\cdot9999$
$N = 462000$

Figure 8. Bordeaux 1962.

It has become apparent that 'conforming cities', at least in the author's part of the world, are not the exception but the general rule. It is with such cities that the present paper is concerned. In what follows reference will occasionally be made, for convenience, to 'all cities'. This will merely mean all cities having population distributions closely matched by the population version of the negative exponential model.

2 Theoretical background
In the light of the empirical evidence available, there can be little doubt that the spatial distribution of the residential populations of many, if not most, cities is, at any given time, in very close agreement with model (4). In practice, therefore, planners should be able to use the model, as well as its formal characteristics, with confidence.

Theoreticians, however, are bound to ask themselves how it is that city dwellers, in choosing a place of residence, collectively behave in a manner so closely described by a simple mathematical model. Indeed, many researchers have tackled this problem, and papers on the subject are often adorned with very extensive bibliographies. A very short list drawn up today would typically include Clark (1951, 1967), Muth (1961, 1969), Stewart and Warntz (1958), Chapin and Weiss (1962), Chapin (1965), Alonso (1964), Mills (1970), Berry *et al.* (1963) and others—of whom not all have actually dealt with the negative exponential model as such.

Such research has generally been based on sophisticated techniques, bringing into consideration numerous economic, sociological, and psychological factors and systems. The use of such heavy artillery in the assault may prove necessary in order to list and weight all the factors determining the *values* of the two parameters of the model; it may well be unnecessarily powerful in attempting merely to show that the model is formally sound.

In its 'density' version, $D(r) = A \exp(-br)$, the static model (1) has only the two parameters, A and b, and is maximally aggregated: there is no breakdown of the population, the spatial distribution of which is described solely in terms of distance from the urban centre, without any zonal, sectoral, or azimuthal disaggregation. In view of this, Bussière and Snickars (1970) showed the formal plausibility of the negative exponential model by 'deriving' it directly on the basis of the broadest possible probabilistic considerations. The procedure followed consisted of applying to an urban area, considered as a spatial continuum, the entropy maximising techniques developed by Wilson (1969a, 1969b, 1970) for the construction of spatially discrete urban models.

When this approach is followed, an urban system is considered in which the choices of residential location are made under the influence of diverse motivational factors, including a propensity to visit the centre, creating a biasing centripetal field.

An attempt has been made formally to assess the probable effect of this field on the overall pattern of residential locations in the city.

The N inhabitants of a city are assumed to be spatially distributed in accordance with

$$d(r) = \frac{D(r)}{N} , \tag{5}$$

where $D(r)$ is a stochastic variable representing the mean surface density at a distance r from the centre. Then

$$\int_0^\infty 2\pi r d(r) \, dr = 1 \tag{6}$$

constitutes a normalisation constraint on the system.

Next, if the generalised cost to an individual of overcoming a distance r to the centre is defined by a cost function, $c(r)$, a cost constraint is imposed:

$$\int_0^\infty 2\pi r d(r) c(r) \, dr = \bar{c} , \tag{7}$$

where $\bar{c}$ may be considered as the average cost of overcoming distance to the centre in the city being modelled.

The most likely form of the probability density function $d(r)$ is then found by maximising the entropy S of the system defined as

$$S[d] = -\int_0^\infty 2\pi d(r) [\ln d(r)] r \, dr \tag{8}$$

subject to constraints (6) and (7).

The model obtained in this way is

$$d(r) = \frac{\exp[-bc(r)]}{\int_0^\infty 2\pi \exp[-bc(r)] r \, dr} . \tag{9}$$

In this expression, if it is assumed that $c(r)$ and r are proportional to each other, then the distance r to the centre may itself serve as a proxy for the distance cost function $c(r)$, and equation (9) then becomes

$$d(r) = \frac{b^2}{2\pi} \exp(-br) . \tag{10}$$

Multiplying equation (10) by the total number, N, of inhabitants of the city, substitution in equation (5) gives

$$D(r) = \frac{b^2 N}{2\pi} \exp(-br) , \tag{11}$$

or

$$D(r) = A \exp(-br) , \tag{1}$$

where

$$A = \frac{b^2 N}{2\pi} . \tag{12}$$

The use of distance itself as a proxy for the distance cost function is justified by the fact that, as noted above, the negative exponential model so obtained does provide—in its 'population' formulation—a remarkably good fit to the observed population distributions of many different cities.

However, this only provides a theoretical justification for the *form* of the model; no conceptual basis has yet been found for the values of its parameters.

Fortunately, as will be seen in section 4 of this paper, some empirical knowledge has been gained of the behaviour of the model as it is continuously adjusted, in time, to the shifting distribution of a city's growing population. The implications of this as regards the possibility of historical study, as well as of short and medium term forecasting, will be discussed later.

3 The static model
When

$$P(r) = \frac{2\pi A}{b^2}[1 - (1 + br)\exp(-br)] \tag{4}$$

is found to provide a good fit to an observed population distribution, the parametric values A and b obtained in the calibration may be used in a number of easy calculations or estimates, thus providing useful insights into various aspects of the distribution being modelled. This is possible because the basic model lends itself so readily to elementary mathematical operations. For example, rewriting equation (12)

$$N = \frac{2\pi A}{b^2} , \tag{13}$$

and dividing equation (4) by equation (13), we obtain

$$p(r) = 1 - (1 + br)\exp(-br) , \tag{14}$$

which is the fraction of the total population contained within any circular zone of radius r around the urban centre. But from equation (1) it is obvious that b is, dimensionally, the reciprocal of distance. It is therefore possible to express distance in units of $1/b$.

Substituting $r = \dfrac{x}{b}$ in equation (14), we obtain

$$p\left(\frac{x}{b}\right) = 1 - (1 + x)\exp(-x) , \tag{15}$$

which is the fraction of the total population contained within any circle of radius x/b around the urban centre. For any value of x, this fraction is the same for all cities. Figure 9 is the graph of $p(x/b)$, applicable to all cities, independent of their size.

Consider next the slope of $P(r)$. We define a function

$$\Phi(r) = \frac{dP(r)}{dr} \tag{16}$$

or

$$\Phi(r) = 2\pi A r \exp(-br) . \tag{17}$$

$$\frac{d\Phi(r)}{dr} = \frac{d^2 P(r)}{dr^2} , \tag{18}$$

or

$$\frac{d\Phi(r)}{dr} = 2\pi A(1 - br)\exp(-br) . \tag{19}$$

Since $\Phi(r)$ is the rate of change of $P(r)$ with r, it is a linear density: inhabitants per unit radial distance at radial distance r from the centre.

It is noted from equation (17) that $\Phi(r) = 0$ for $r = 0$ and $r = \infty$. Putting $d\Phi(r)/dr = 0$, a maximum value of $\Phi(r)$ is found at a distance of $r = 1/b$.

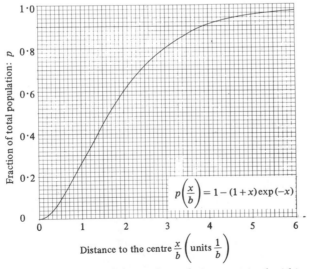

Figure 9. Fraction of the total population contained within a radius of x/b around the urban centre.

If, therefore, we consider thin concentric rings of equal thickness around the centre, the most populated such ring will be found at a distance of $1/b$ from the centre for all cities. Figure 10 is a graph of $\Phi(r)$ for Greater Paris in 1962.

Dividing equation (17) by

$$N = \frac{2\pi A}{b^2} \; , \tag{13}$$

a normalized probability density function is obtained:

$$\varphi(r) = b^2 r \exp(-br) \; . \tag{20}$$

Of course,

$$\int_0^r \varphi(r)\,\mathrm{d}r = p(r) \tag{21}$$

and

$$\int_0^\infty \varphi(r)\,\mathrm{d}r = 1 \; . \tag{22}$$

From $\varphi(r)$ we calculate the mean distance $\bar{r}$ from the centre at which residents are located:

$$\bar{r} = \int_0^\infty \varphi(r) r \,\mathrm{d}r \; , \tag{23}$$

$$\bar{r} = \int_0^\infty b^2 r^2 \exp(-br)\,\mathrm{d}r \; , \tag{24}$$

$$\bar{r} = \frac{2}{b} \; . \tag{25}$$

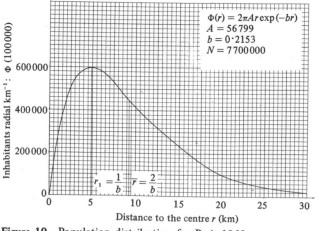

Figure 10. Population distribution for Paris 1962.

Thus the mean distance of residential locations from the urban centre is equal to $2/b$ in all cities. Figure 11 is a graph of $\varphi(r)$ for Paris in 1962.

It has been seen from equation (16) that $\Phi(r)$ is the slope of $P(r)$ and from equation (17) that its value is zero at the centre. Thus, in the small central zone, the rate of accumulation of population is low, even in the presence of high central surface densities. Consequently the $P(r)$ function, which is used in calibrating the model, is very insensitive to the existence or non-existence of a so-called density 'crater' in the immediate neighbourhood of the centre; the values obtained in fitting the curve for the parameters A and b are practically unaffected by this factor. Regardless of the 'crater' effect therefore, the simple two-parameter negative exponential model may be considered as representing accurately the following aspects of the spatial distribution of a city's population about its centre.

1. $$p(r) = 1 - (1 + br)\exp(-br) \tag{14}$$

provides a close estimate of the fraction of the total population of an urban agglomeration that is contained within a circular zone of radius r around the urban centre. Only one parameter, b, is involved in this calculation.

2. $$p\left(\frac{x}{b}\right) = 1 - (1 + x)\exp(-x) \tag{15}$$

provides the same estimate as above within a distance of x units of $1/b$ around the centre. This relationship holds for all cities.

3. $$D(r) = A\exp(-br) \tag{1}$$

gives the expected value of the stochastic variable representing the mean

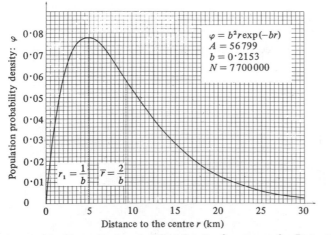

Figure 11. Normalised probability density function φ for Paris, 1962.

surface density at a distance r from the centre. Surface density might be loosely associated with characteristic *types* of housing that may be found at different distances from the centre.

4. $\Phi(r) = 2\pi A r \exp(-br)$ (17)

is the expression for linear density (inhabitants per unit radial distance) at a distance r from the centre, $\Phi(r)$ being directly related to the *amount* of housing at that distance. In all cities it is maximum at the central distance of $1/b$.

5. $\varphi(r) = b^2 r \exp(-br)$ (20)

is the equation for the probability density of one of the N inhabitants of the city being located at a distance r from the centre. This function directly illustrates the distribution of the population with respect to central distance. Its maximum value, of course, also occurs at a distance of $1/b$.

6.   In all cities the population is located at an average distance from the centre of

$$\bar{r} = \frac{2}{b} \ .$$ (25)

7. $N = \dfrac{2\pi A}{b^2}$ (13)

is an easy and useful formula for estimating the total population of an urban agglomeration.

4 The dynamic model
4.1 Empirical findings
It is widely recognized that, as a modern city grows, its central density tends to diminish, as does also the rate of decrease of surface density from the centre to the periphery. Under these conditions, if the negative exponential model is continuously adjusted to the actual distribution of population densities about the centre, it will take on the time dependent form

$$D(r,t) = A(t)\exp[-b(t)r] \ ,$$ (26)

in which the parameters $A(t)$ and $b(t)$ are decreasing functions of time. That is,

$$\frac{\mathrm{d}A(t)}{\mathrm{d}t} < 0$$ (27)

and

$$\frac{\mathrm{d}b(t)}{\mathrm{d}t} < 0 \ .$$ (28)

In a growing city the total population of the agglomeration is an increasing function of time, $N(t)$, and therefore,

$$\frac{dN(t)}{dt} > 0 . \tag{29}$$

It follows that, for a growing city, A and b may just as well be regarded as functions of N as of t, and that equations (26), (27), and (28) may be rewritten as

$$D(r,N) = A(N)\exp[-b(N)r] , \tag{30}$$

$$\frac{dA(N)}{dN} < 0 , \tag{31}$$

and

$$\frac{db(N)}{dN} < 0 \tag{32}$$

From equations (31) and (32) it follows that

$$\frac{dA}{dN} \bigg/ \frac{db}{dN} = \frac{dA}{db} > 0 .^{(1)} \tag{33}$$

Following a historical review of the evolving population distribution patterns in a number of European and Canadian cities, it has been observed that, in all cases studied, not only was the rate of change of A positive with respect to b, as shown in equation (33), but that it tended strongly to remain constant in time:

$$\frac{dA}{db} = K > 0 . \tag{34}$$

As examples, figures 12 to 18 are plots of A versus b, as these parameters varied in time, in the cities of Paris, Montreal, Toronto, Winnipeg, Stockholm, Malmö, and Hälsingborg. The points on these graphs are plots of A and b as determined from calibrations of the model based on census data for the years indicated. The straight lines are the theoretical linear regressions based on each cloud of points. The deviations of individual points from the regression lines are usually only a fraction of one percent. Correlation coefficients have been calculated and are given in the legend of each of the graphs.

This observation is, as yet, purely empirical. We cannot even speculate at this time on the reason why our cities, in their modern phase of growth,

----

(1) In the interest of simplicity in notation, the N-dependency of A and b, and the time-dependency of N will not, in the remainder of this discussion, be made explicit by the use of parentheses as in $A(N)$, $b(N)$, or $N(t)$; these dependencies will be understood.

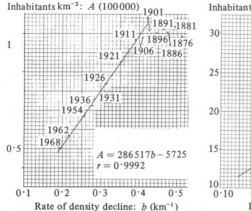

Inhabitants km⁻²: A (100000)

$A = 286517b - 5725$
$r = 0.9992$

Rate of density decline: b (km⁻¹)

Figure 12. Plot of values of A versus b for Paris, 1876–1968.

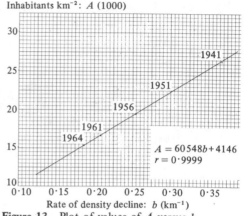

Inhabitants km⁻²: A (1000)

$A = 60548b + 4146$
$r = 0.9999$

Rate of density decline: b (km⁻¹)

Figure 13. Plot of values of A versus b for Montreal, 1941–1964.

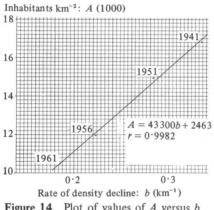

Inhabitants km⁻²: A (1000)

$A = 43300b + 2463$
$r = 0.9982$

Rate of density decline: b (km⁻¹)

Figure 14. Plot of values of A versus b for Toronto, 1941–1961.

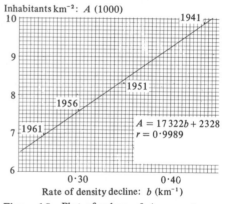

Inhabitants km⁻²: A (1000)

$A = 17322b + 2328$
$r = 0.9989$

Rate of density decline: b (km⁻¹)

Figure 15. Plot of values of A versus b for Winnipeg, 1941–1961.

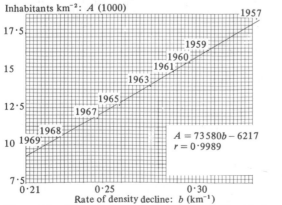

Inhabitants km⁻²: A (1000)

$A = 73580b - 6217$
$r = 0.9989$

Rate of density decline: b (km⁻¹)

Figure 16. Plot of values of A versus b for Stockholm, 1957–1969.

have undergone an evolution in their population distributions reflected by a linear variation of A with b in the continuously adjusted model.

It is to be noted that the linear relationship of A with b seems to be observed only in the 'modern' phase of a city's growth. Thus, as may be seen in figure 12, $A(b)$ for Paris was not linear prior to 1911. In the case of Hälsingborg there is a strong linear tendency, but with a sudden change in slope occurring in 1963–1964. It is a moot question whether the new planning policies introduced at that time in Hälsingborg have been instrumental in bringing about this change of slope.

For as long as it persists, the straight line variation of A with b provides a handy means of following the past history of a city's population distribution about its centre. To the extent that demographic projections are themselves reliable, it may also provide the most reliable means presently available for short and perhaps medium-term forecasts of population distribution patterns.

The growth of a city is practically a continuous process. It is to be expected that the function $A(b)$ should be continuous, single valued, and analytical; by a fortunate circumstance, for most contemporary cities this function also seems to be linear. This makes it possible to picture the evolution in time of a growing city's population distribution as a veritable succession of centrifugal 'waves', representing such variables as the linear density $\Phi(r)$, the linear density probability density function $\varphi(r)$, the surface density $D(r)$, the population function $P(r)$, etc., as well as the partial derivatives of these variables with respect either to N (or, equivalently, to time) or to r, the distance to the centre. This results directly from the fact that, of all the pairs (A, b) that correspond to a given value of N in

$$N = \frac{2\pi A}{b^2}, \tag{13}$$

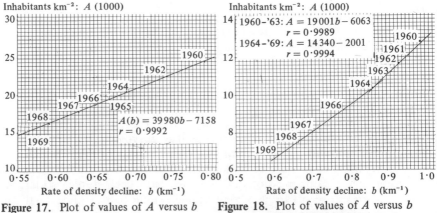

Figure 17. Plot of values of A versus b for Malmö, 1960–1969.

Figure 18. Plot of values of A versus b for Hälsingborg, 1960–1969.

only one such pair is 'permitted' for a given city: the one that lies on the regression line $A(b)$ of that city's model.

The degree of accuracy, with which the shifting and expanding population distributions of growing cities can be represented by the abstraction of a continuously evolving two-parameter negative exponential model, has thus made it possible to give quantitative expression to expanding wave theories of metropolitan growth such as those of Blumenfeld (1949, 1954, 1959) and Korcelli (1970). The growth of Greater Paris between the years 1911 and 1968 will be used as an example to illustrate this point.

It has been seen in figure 12 that eight different adjustments of the model, between 1911 and 1968, yielded values of A and b such that the variation of A with respect to b in this interval could be accurately represented by the regression line

$$A = 286517b - 5725 , \tag{35}$$

with a correlation coefficient of $0 \cdot 9992$.

The percentage deviations of individual points from the regression line are extremely small. Any error introduced by using parametric values obtained directly from equation (35) would therefore seem to be negligible.

We shall now examine families of curves describing the evolution of the continuously calibrated model for Paris in the period 1911–1968, based on values of A and b taken from equation (35), with the total population N being at all times determined by

$$N = \frac{2\pi A}{b^2} . \tag{13}$$

During this time interval the population of Greater Paris grew from some $4 \cdot 4$ million inhabitants in 1911 to about $8 \cdot 4$ million in 1968.

There is no doubt that the following families of curves are quite accurate for the historical period covered. Beyond 1968 they have been projected, on the basis of the parametric values predicted by equation (35), for a future growth reaching a total population of more than 12 million. The reliability of such extrapolations—necessarily diminishing as the time projection increases—is left to the good judgment of individual urbanists. One word of caution, however, is in order. The established trends summarized in equations (31), (32), (33), and (34) seem to be firmly established in the sample cities; but these trends cannot persist indefinitely. For real cities, parameters A and b must both have finite positive values; neither parameter may approach zero (let alone become negative) without absurd implications. Sooner or later, therefore, these 'recent' trends must be broken; it would be difficult to say how soon or how late. For most of the cities that have been studied so far, however, there still seems to be a comfortable margin for further growth along established lines.

4.2 Linear density: the functions $\Phi(r, N)$ and $\varphi(r, N)$ for Paris

Figure 19 is a family of curves $\Phi(r, N)$ with total population N as the parameter and covering the historical period 1911 to 1968. Beyond this, and assuming continued growth, extrapolations have been made, in accordance with equation (35), for larger populations yet to be reached.

Any one of the curves of this family represents the instantaneous distribution of the population with respect to distance from the centre at any time when the population reaches a selected value $N = N^*$. While the surface density function $D(r, N)$, which will be discussed below, indicates average conditions of crowding at a specified distance to the centre and total population, it is this linear density function $\Phi(r, N)$ that shows, at a glance, 'where the people are' in terms of central distance at a particular time.

Thus while surface densities may be highest in the central zone, it is not there that a numerically important proportion of the population is to be found. In fact, at any time the highest numerical concentration of residents (the most populated of a set of concentric rings of equal 'thickness') occurs at the maximum point on the appropriate Φ curve. And this maximum, in terms of the instantaneous value of the parameter b of the model, always occurs at a distance from the centre of $1/b$. It is to be noted that, in the case of Paris, the maximum linear densities diminish constantly as the city grows.

The family of curves in figure 20 represents the probability density functions corresponding to the linear densities of figure 19. The

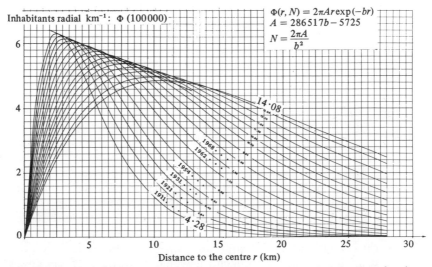

Figure 19. Linear density curves for Paris, 1911–1968. Population values for the curves drawn are respectively (in millions) 4·28, 4·84, 5·40, 5·93, 6·56, 7·33, 7·96, 8·69, 9·34, 10·08, 10·64, 11·26, 11·94, 12·70, 13·54, 14·08.

curves of figure 19 divided by the applicable values of N, transform into those of figure 20. Their maximum points, of course, also occur at the distance $1/b$. For future reference, we shall call this important distance r_1,

$$r_1 = \frac{1}{b} . \tag{36}$$

The dotted line in the graph is the locus of maximum points. It clearly shows the wave-like centrifugal propagation of the maximum linear densities.

Also it has been shown that the mean distance of all the residents from the centre is given by

$$\bar{r} = \frac{2}{b} . \tag{25}$$

This mean distance $\bar{r}$, therefore, also progresses centrifugally in a wave-like manner, but at twice the velocity of r_1.

Figure 21 is a family of curves of $\Phi(r, N)$ in which the central distance r has been taken as the generating parameter. It shows at a glance the 'history' of the linear density at any chosen fixed distance to the centre. For example, it is shown that at distances ranging up to 2 km, linear densities have been steadily falling since 1911, and are continuing to fall. At 6 km from the centre, it is seen that the linear density increased

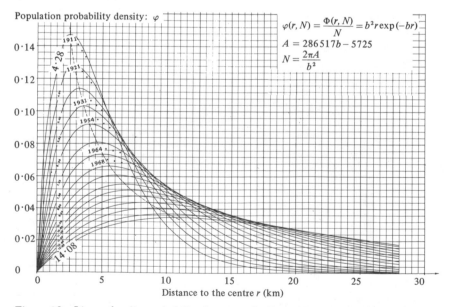

Figure 20. Linear density probability functions for Paris, 1911–1968. Population values for the curves drawn are respectively (in millions) 4·28, 4·84, 5·40, 5·93, 6·56, 7·33, 7·96, 8·69, 9·34, 10·08, 10·64, 11·26, 11·94, 12·70, 13·54, 14·08.

steadily from 1911 to the time, around 1965, when the population reached about 8 million inhabitants; it is now declining and, at this distance of 6 km from the centre, it will continue to do so. At a distance of 8 km from the centre, however, the linear density is still increasing, and it is not expected to reach its peak value until the population has reached a figure of some 10 million inhabitants. The 'local' linear density at $r = 8$ km will then be almost 550000 inhabitants per radial kilometer.

For any given total population in the time interval under study, figure 21 shows that there is a radius at which the linear density passes through a maximum, reaching an all time high from which it will thereafter decline. The locus of maximum points on the curves of figure 21 would represent the relationship of this important radius with N.

It is worth noting the mathematical conditions under which $\Phi(r, N)$ reaches such a maximum.

Operating on

$$\Phi(r, N) = 2\pi r A \exp(-br) ,$$

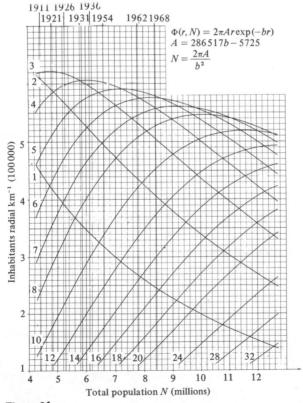

Figure 21.

in which, of course, A and b are functions of N, we obtain

$$\frac{\partial \Phi}{\partial N} = 2\pi r \frac{db}{dN} A \exp(-br) \left[\frac{dA}{db} \frac{1}{A} - r \right].$$ (37)

Now, providing the conditions

$$\frac{db}{dn} < 0$$ (32)

and

$$\frac{dA}{db} > 0$$ (33)

are satisfied,

$$\frac{\partial \Phi}{\partial N} = 0$$ (38)

is the condition for Φ to be maximum. But, of course, throughout this discussion it is assumed that equations (32) and (33) are satisfied, as well as

$$\frac{dA}{dN} < 0$$ (31)

and

$$\frac{dA}{db} = K > 0 .$$ (34)

Equating $\frac{\partial \Phi}{\partial N}$ to zero in equation (37), we obtain another important distance from the centre:

$$r_2 = \frac{dA}{db} \frac{1}{A} ,$$ (39)

the distance at which, for a given N, Φ is at its maximum and the rate of change of Φ with N (that is, with time) is momentarily zero.

4.3 Surface density: the function $D(r, N)$

The negative exponential model derives its name from its first and simplest formulation:

$$D(r) = A \exp(-br) .$$ (1)

Among the many equivalent statements that can be made regarding the basic manner in which urban populations tend to distribute themselves about the city centre, this one is perhaps, in a planning sense, the least interesting.

But many urbanists continue to be primarily concerned with the $D(r)$ aspect of population distributions, and to theoretically oriented researchers and model-builders formulation (1) is an essential element in the logical development of the overall model.

By using values of A and b consistent with

$$A = 286517b - 5725 , \tag{35}$$

the $A(b)$ regression line for Paris (cf.figure 12), and values of N consistent with

$$N = \frac{2\pi A}{b^2} , \tag{13}$$

surface densities have been computed from

$$D(r,N) = A(N)\exp[-b(N)r] , \tag{30}$$

first as functions of r with a generating parameter N (figure 22) and then as functions of N with a generating parameter r (figure 23).

The curves of figure 22, drawn on semi-log paper, are familiar plots of the exponential decline of surface density with increasing distance from the centre. In terms of population the historical period covered is that of 1911 to 1968, with extrapolations extending into the realm of expected further growth. One can see at a glance that density at the centre fell steadily in the historical period covered, from more than 100000

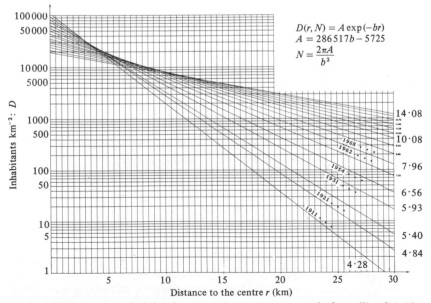

Figure 22. Population values for the curves drawn are respectively (in millions) 4·28, 4·84, 5·40, 5·93, 6·56, 7·33, 7·96, 8·69, 9·34, 10·08, 10·64, 11·26, 11·94, 12·70, 13·54, 14·08.

inhabitants km^{-2} in 1911, to about 47000 in 1968. The slopes of the
lines have also steadily diminished as the city grew. This is only another
illustration of the fact that, in its 'modern' phase of growth, the
parameters A and b have both been falling in value in accordance with the
$A(b)$ regression expressed in equation (35) and illustrated in figure 12.

From these curves one may see at a glance what the mean surface
density was, at any distance from the centre, at any chosen moment
(represented by a value of N) in the city's recent history from 1911 to
1968. Use of the extrapolated curves is, of course, subject to caution. It
may be noted, however, that the extrapolations are based on a trend,
shown in figure 12, that, once established around 1911, never deviated
appreciably in the course of the following 57 years.

From figure 23 it is seen that, up to a distance of almost 3 km from the
centre of Paris, densities have been steadily falling since 1911, and may be
expected to continue doing so. At greater distances maximums have been,
or will be, reached. Thus at 6 km from the centre the average surface
density reached its all-time high value of 15250 inhabitants km^{-2} at the
time, around 1967, when the total Paris population reached, and passed,

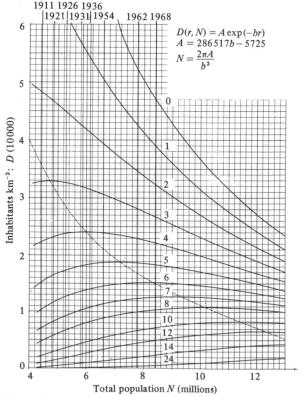

Figure 23.

the mark of 8 300 000 inhabitants. And, if one were to venture a forecast concerning densities at 10 km from the centre, say, figure 23 would show that the mean density is currently on the increase at this distance and that it is likely to continue to increase until it reaches about 8 300 inhabitants km^{-2} at the time when the total population of the city will have reached 11 400 000 inhabitants. Thereafter, surface densities will decline at $r = 10$ km. As to *when*, in chronological time, N will reach the 11 400 000 mark, that is a question that can be best answered by the specialists in such matters: the demographers.

The dotted line in figure 23 is the locus of the maximum densities ever reached at each of the central distances shown for which such a maximum exists. It is obvious that under the same conditions as those specified in section 4.2 above, the condition for $D(r, N)$ to pass through a maximum is

$$\frac{\partial D}{\partial N} = 0 . \tag{40}$$

Now

$$\frac{\partial D}{\partial N} = \frac{\mathrm{d}b}{\mathrm{d}N} A \exp(-br) \left[\frac{\mathrm{d}A}{\mathrm{d}b} \frac{1}{A} - r \right] . \tag{41}$$

Equating expression (41) to zero, we obtain the same distance that was found for a maximum of $\Phi(r, N)$ in the preceding section 4.2, namely:

$$r_2 = \frac{\mathrm{d}A}{\mathrm{d}b} \frac{1}{A} . \tag{39}$$

For a given N, then, it is at the same distance, r_2, that both the surface density D and the linear density Φ pass through their maximum values.

If we return to the dotted line in figure 23, it clearly pictures the outward progression of the 'crest' of a circular 'wave', the height of which represents, at any radial distance from the centre, the highest surface density ever attained there; the time (expressed in terms of N) at which this crest passes a given radius r (momentarily, $r = r_2$) is also clearly shown. Since r_2 is the same for Φ as it is for D, the propagation of r_2, as illustrated in figure 23, applies to the outward progression of the 'crest' of the 'wave' of linear densities.

4.4 Population distribution: the functions $P(r, N)$ and $p(r, N)$

Still using the growth of Paris between 1911 and 1968 as an example, we have drawn families of $P(r, N)$ and $p(r, N)$ curves, illustrating the evolution and the spatial propagation of the cumulative population functions $P(r, N)$ and $p(r, N)$. As in the case of the linear and surface density functions, provision has been made for some measure of extrapolation corresponding to the expected future growth of the Metropolis.

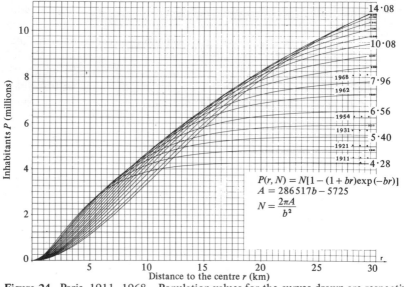

Figure 24. Paris, 1911–1968. Population values for the curves drawn are respectively (in millions) 4·28, 4·84, 5·40, 5·93, 6·56, 7·33, 7·96, 8·69, 9·34, 10·08, 10·64, 11·26, 11·94, 12·70, 13·54, 14·08.

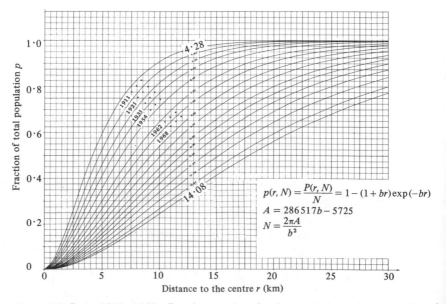

Figure 25. Paris, 1911–1968. Population values for the curves drawn are respectively (in millions) 4·28, 4·84, 5·40, 5·93, 6·56, 7·33, 7·96, 8·69, 9·34, 10·08, 10·64, 11·26, 11·94, 12·70, 13·54, 14·08.

The curves of figure 24 are plots of

$$P(r,N) = \frac{2\pi A(N)}{b^2(N)}\{1 - [1 + b(N)r]\exp[-b(N)r]\} \tag{42}$$

with the generating parameter N. Those of figure 25 are plots of

$$p(r,N) = 1 - [1 + b(N)r]\exp[-b(N)r], \tag{43}$$

also with the generating parameter N. Any one of the $P(r,N)$ curves shows, for a selected value of N, the number of inhabitants that were, are, or presumably will be, included within a circular zone of any radius r around the city's centre. Any one of the $p(r,N)$ curves shows, also for a selected value of N, the fraction of that N that is contained within a similar circular zone of any radius r.

Each P curve of figure 24 is, of course, asymptotic to its own value of N. It is readily seen that as the city grows and N increases, the points at which the curves begin to 'flatten out' and approach their asymptotes recede from the centre. This progression marks the spatial growth of the

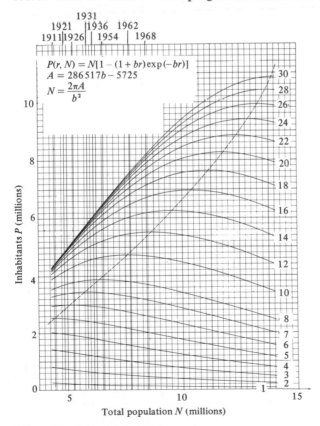

Figure 26. Paris, 1911–1968.

city, though this is perhaps even better visualised by studying the p curves of figure 25, which all have an asymptote of one (or 100%). If we consider, for example, the radius of the circular zone within which 95% of the total population is to be found, we observe that in 1911 this radius was close to 12 km, while in 1954 it was 19 km, and in 1968 it had passed 25 km.

Since N in the same interval passed from about 4·4 to about 8·4 million inhabitants, it is seen that the average surface population density of the circular zone containing 95% of the population (which zone meanwhile doubled in radius) became in 1968 less than half of what it had been in 1911. These curves can thus also serve to estimate past and future city sprawl.

The curves in figure 26 represent, as functions of N, the populations contained within concentric circular zones of radii ranging from 1 km to 30 km.

Reading these curves we see that, since 1911, inner circular zones of 5 km radius or less have all steadily been losing population, while the city's total population was continuously growing. The 5 km zone itself, for example, had a population of 2·53 million residents in 1911, but only 2 million in 1968. In 1911, a circular zone having a radius of, say, 10 km around the centre, had a population of 3·75 million residents; this was then due to increase, and it did, until it reached an all time high figure of 4·74 million, around 1961, when the total population of Greater Paris was 7·4 million. At that moment, the population within the 10 km radius zone was shifting internally but was numerically at a standstill: from that time onwards, its own population would decline and all the city's population growth would take place outside of it.

The dotted line in figure 26, the locus of maximum points in time of the P function at fixed central distances, shows the centrifugal expansion of the ever larger 'central' zones within which population growth has not only stopped, but has, in fact, reversed itself. In this paper, these central distances have been given the label: r_6. It will be shown in the next section that r_6 can be readily computed as an implicit function of r_1 and r_2.

4.5 Waves of growth
4.5.1 r_1: Φ_{max} along the $r-axis$
It has been shown in section 4.2 that the maximum of $\Phi(r, N)$ along the r-axis occurred at

$$r_1 = \frac{1}{b} . \tag{36}$$

This could have been independently derived by taking

$$\frac{\partial \Phi}{\partial r} = 2\pi A(N)\exp[-b(N)r][1 - b(N)r] \tag{44}$$

and equating it to zero, in order to find the r value at which Φ was maximum for a given value of N.

The wave-like centrifugal propagation of r_1 has already been noted, and illustrated in figures 19 and 20; r_1 increases with N (with time).

4.5.2 r_2: Φ_{max} and D_{max} along the N-axis

For any given population N, the maxima of the curves of figures 21 and 23 occur at the same radius, r_2.

This radius r_2 is determined either by equating $\partial\Phi/\partial N$ to zero in equation (37) or by equating $\partial D/\partial N$ to zero in equation (41). In both cases, we obtain the same result. Thus, if

$$\frac{\partial\Phi}{\partial N} = 0 \, ,$$

then

$$\frac{\partial D}{\partial N} = 0 \, ,$$

both at a radius

$$r_2 = \frac{dA}{db}\frac{1}{A} \, . \tag{39}$$

It should be remembered that

$$\frac{dA}{db} = K > 0 \, . \tag{34}$$

In equation (39) therefore, it is the value of the parameter A that determines r_2. It is readily seen that, since A decreases with time (or as N increases), r_2 must increase with time: the 'wave' of r_2—as that of r_1—is propagated centrifugally.

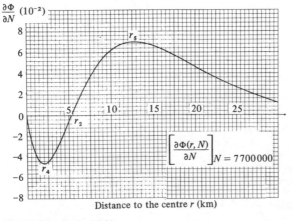

Figure 27. Paris 1962.

Figures 27 and 28 are graphs of $\partial\Phi/\partial N$ and $\partial D/\partial N$ respectively, for Paris in 1962, in accordance with equations (37) and (41). Both graphs, of course, pass through zero at $r = r_2$. It is seen that both functions are negative for $r < r_2$, and positive for $r > r_2$.

The graphs show that $\partial D/\partial N$ passes through a maximum at $r = r_3$, while $\partial\Phi/\partial N$ has both a minimum (negative) at a central distance r_4, and a maximum (positive) at r_5. These radii: r_3, r_4, and r_5 will be discussed below.

4.5.3 r_3: $\left(\dfrac{\partial D}{\partial N}\right)_{max}$ along the r-axis

The rate at which, at a given moment and distance from the centre, the residential surface density is increasing or decreasing should be of interest to planners, since it may be associated with demand (positive or negative) for particular types of residential accommodation. In particular the distance, at which the rate of increase is at its maximum at a given time, would appear important.

In order to find the maximum of $\partial D/\partial N$ in the radial direction at a given moment (with its corresponding value of N), we need only solve for r in

$$\frac{\partial^2 D}{\partial N \partial r} = 0 . \tag{45}$$

The solution obtained is

$$r_3 = r_1 + r_2 , \tag{46}$$

a convenient result since r_1 and r_2 are so easily determined.

4.5.4 r_4: $\left(\dfrac{\partial\Phi}{\partial N}\right)_{min}$ and r_5: $\left(\dfrac{\partial\Phi}{\partial N}\right)_{max}$ along the r-axis

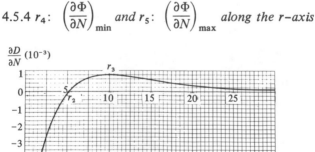

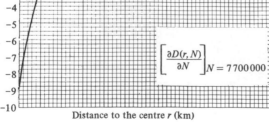

Figure 28. Paris 1962.

As has been noted previously, the linear density Φ may be associated with the *quantity* of residential accommodation required at every distance from the city centre. The rate $\partial\Phi/\partial N$ therefore may be associated with the distribution along the r-axis of total *demand* for housing accommodation; hence this function's particular interest from the standpoint of planning.

In order to find the maximum and minimum values of $\partial\Phi/\partial N$ in the radial direction at a given moment, we must take an approach similar to that of the preceding section, and solve for r in

$$\frac{\partial^2\Phi}{\partial N\partial r} = 0 . \tag{47}$$

This yields a quadratic equation in r, with two real positive roots. These roots are

$$r_4 = r_1+\tfrac{1}{2}r_2-[r_1^2+(\tfrac{1}{2}r_2)^2]^{\frac{1}{2}} , \tag{48}$$

and

$$r_5 = r_1+\tfrac{1}{2}r_2+[r_1^2+(\tfrac{1}{2}r_2)^2]^{\frac{1}{2}} . \tag{49}$$

Thus two more radii of particular urbanistic interest are seen to be expressible in terms of the convenient radii, r_1 and r_2.

Again, since r_1 and r_2 both increase with time (with N) it follows that r_4 and r_5 must behave similarly.

4.5.5 r_6: $P_{\max}$ *along the N-axis*
In section 4.4, the properties of the family of curves in figure 26 were examined. These curves represent, as functions of N, the total populations contained within concentric circular zones of radii ranging from 1 km to 30 km, based on the evolving distribution of the Parisian population in the period 1911–1968.

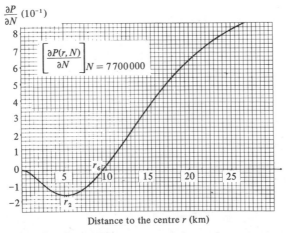

Figure 29. Paris 1962.

The curves were seen generally to pass through a maximum value of P at different times (different values of N) for different radii. These maxima are important in two respects:

1 At the time that a maximum value of P is reached for a zone of given radius, the total population within that zone is momentarily stable. All the growth of the city is taking place outside the zone's boundaries.

2 From that time on, the population of the zone in question is due to decline.

The radius r_6 of the circular zone that, at a given moment, has a higher population than it has ever had or will ever have again, would seem to be a matter of considerable interest. This radius can be read from a family of curves like those of figure 26, if such curves have been drawn. If we lack such a graph, r_6 can be calculated directly from the model.

By definition, when any zone of radius r has reached its maximum value in time,

$$\frac{\partial P}{\partial N} = 0 . \tag{50}$$

The expression for $\partial P/\partial N$ is rather cumbersome and is omitted from this text. Any one interested may easily derive it from the N-dependent $P(r, N)$ function defined in equation (42). It will then be found that equating the partial derivative to zero, as in equation (50), provides a means of finding r_6 by solving for r in

$$1 + \frac{r}{r_1} + \frac{r^2}{r_1(2r_1 - r_2)} = \exp\left(\frac{r}{r_1}\right) . \tag{51}$$

This calculation is not as direct as those proposed for r_3, r_4, and r_5. It does still have the advantage, however, of being based only on the prior knowledge of the easily determined values of r_1 and r_2.

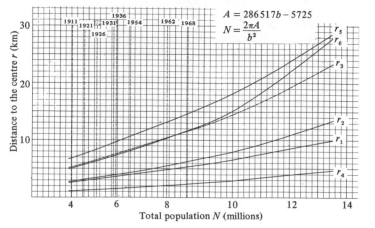

Figure 30. Propagation of characteristic waves: Paris, 1911–1968.

Figure 29 is a graph of $\partial P/\partial N$, as a function of r, for Paris in 1962. It is seen that, inboard of r_6, all inner zones were losing population. The population of the zone of radius r_6 was momentarily stable, but shifts of population distribution within the zone were clearly occurring. The entire population growth of the city was taking place beyond the zone of radius r_6.

4.5.6 *Propagation of six 'waves'*
Figure 30 is a plot of the six radii of special interest discussed above. Distance to the centre is plotted along the y ordinate, while N, the total population, is plotted along the x abscissa.

The manner in which these radii all increase as the city grows is quite apparent.

References
Alonso, W., 1964, *Location and Land Use* (Harvard University Press, Cambridge, Mass.).
Berry, B. J. L., Simmons, J. W., Tennant, R. J., 1963, "Urban population densities: structures and change", *Geographic Review,* **53,** 389-405.
Blumenfeld, H., 1949, "The concentric theory of urban growth", *Land Economics,* **25,** 209-212.
Blumenfeld, H., 1954, "The tidal wave of metropolitan expansion", *Journal of the American Institute of Planners,* **20,** 3-14.
Blumenfeld, H., 1959, "Are land use patterns predictable?", *Journal of the American Institute of Planners,* **25,** 61-66.
Bussière, R., 1968, "Morphologie urbaine, répartition de la population", Centre de Recherche d'urbanisme, Paris, France. English translation: "The spatial distribution of urban populations" (International Federation for Housing and Planning, The Hague, Holland).
Bussière, R., Snickars, F., 1970, "Derivation of the negative exponential model by an entropy maximising method", *Environment and Planning,* **2,** 295-301.
Chapin, F. S., 1965, *Urban Land Use Planning,* second edition (University of Illinois Press, Urbana).
Chapin, F. S., Weiss, Shirley F. (Eds.), 1962, *Urban Growth Dynamics in a Regional Cluster of Cities* (John Wiley, New York).
Clark, C., 1951, "Urban population densities", *Journal of the Royal Statistical Society, Series A,* 114, 490-496.
Clark, C., 1967, *Population Growth and Land Use* (Macmillan, London).
Korcelli, P., 1970, "A wave-like model of metropolitan spatial growth", *Papers of the Regional Science Association,* **24,** 127-138.
Mills, E. S., 1970, "Urban density functions", *Urban Studies,* **7,** 5-20.
Muth, R., 1961, "The spatial structure of the housing market", *Papers and Proceedings of the Regional Science Association,* **7,** 207-220.
Muth, R., 1969, *Cities and Housing* (University of Chicago Press, Chicago).
Stewart, J. Q., Warntz, W., 1958, "Physics of population distribution", *Journal of Regional Science,* **1,** 99-123.
Wilson, A. G., 1969a, "Development of some elementary residential location models", *Journal of Regional Science,* **9,** 377-385.
Wilson, A. G., 1969b, "Dissaggregating elementary residential location models", CES-WP-37, Centre for Environmental Studies, London.
Wilson, A. G., 1970, *Entropy in Urban and Regional Modelling* (Pion, London).

The Empirical Development of a Disaggregated Residential Location Model: Some Preliminary Results

E.L.CRIPPS‡, ERLET A.CATER
University of Reading

1 Introduction
In recent years, a number of attempts have been made to build operational models to predict the location of households in cities and sub-regions. These have often been incorporated in wider modelling frameworks which deal with the location of other activities (the retail sector, for example) in addition to residential location. Frequently the form of the residential location model used in such cases has been either that of a potential model or of a gravity model. It will usually be found, and particularly insofar as British experience is concerned, that the more general framework within which such models are embedded is some variant of that proposed by Lowry (1964). A fairly exhaustive review of applications of this model can be found in Goldner's (1971) recent article.

For the most part, the only theory contained in such sub-models of residential location is that the location of households in the city region will be a function of the attraction of the residential area, however that may be defined, and of the cost of travel from job locations to the residential area.

Evidence from the experience of a number of recent experiments with the kinds of model referred to above suggests that such models are adequate for the purpose of describing static macro-distributions of activities in cities and for predicting associated travel patterns. But the evidence also suggests that they offer few insights, on the one hand, into economic or other theories of residential location, or of the spatial organisation of housing markets; and on the other hand into many of the problems which urban policy makers, and particularly urban planners, need to solve. A need can be established, therefore, for a model which takes greater cognisance of micro-theories of residential location, but which at the same time will eventually lead to a tool which can be fairly readily put into operation within an urban planning context.

The locational equilibrium of households at the micro-scale is dealt with by the more theoretical models of Alonso (1964), Wingo (1961), and by Muth (1969). The two former theories deal with the determination of location rents and the consumption of residential space (sites) by individual households, whereas the latter is more concerned with the consumption of housing services and thus with the spatial organisation of the housing market.

† This research is financed by the Centre for Environmental Studies, London.
‡ Present address: Department of Geography, University of Leeds.

Typically, however, such micro-economic theory maximises household utility, subject to a budget constraint which exhausts household income by expenditure on transport and either housing or residential space, and by expenditures on a composite good which represents household expenditure on all other goods and services, except housing or residential space and transport.

Expenditure on housing or residential space is a function of the quantity of space or housing consumed and its price which varies with location. Similarly, transport expenditures vary with location. Thus micro-theory defines an equilibrium not only in terms of the quantity of housing or residential land consumed, but also in terms of location. It is able to explain differentiation in locational choices by households due to variation in the income level of households, variation in the prices of housing or land, and in transport costs.

The micro-theories of residential location, however, tend to be limited by a set of restrictive assumptions, and thus a level of abstraction, which inhibits their direct utilization within a policy making context, although they may infer some insights into the effects of policy.

The more common of the limiting assumptions in these theories are that the city is regarded as a featureless plain, in which all land or housing services can be regarded as homogeneous, and that all job opportunities are located in the central business district.

Clearly a more operational model needs to relax some of these assumptions, so that it is at least possible to deal with a city which has multiple job locations, and also to begin to recognise that urban housing and land are not homogeneous and that this will affect locational decisions.

The model will thus need to take into account the fact that housing, for example, varies not only in size and quality, but also that there are a number of sectors in the urban housing market, both public and private, which can be further sub-divided into owner-occupied and rented housing. These additional dimensions define a set of housing sub-markets some of which, because of various market imperfections, may not be able to satisfy the housing needs of different households in the city, for income or other reasons.

From the point of view of both short term housing policy and longer term strategic planning policy, it is important to be able to assess the demands for housing in each of these markets. An aspatial assessment of demand as the micro-theory suggests could, however, be as limited in value as the more or less total reliance placed on notions of simple accessibility to jobs by the more elementary potential or gravity concepts.

Demand in each housing market for the majority of households, clearly has to be seen in part as a function of the spatial distribution of jobs and of transportation.

In this paper, we describe our first and preliminary results of the empirical development of an operational model designed to meet some of these requirements.

2 An outline of the model

An effective proposal for an operational model which compromises between the explanatory power of the micro-models and the needs of urban planners and policy makers has been put forward by Wilson (1970). Wilson, in fact, suggests an extensive scheme for disaggregating the more elementary residential location models which rely on the gravity concept, and this gives rise to a considerable variety of models incorporating a number of determinants and aspects of residential location.

These models deal with the need to incorporate different types of locational behaviour, and in addition with the need to disaggregate elementary location models to allow for at least

1 different income groups,
2 different wage levels by location,
3 different types of houses, and
4 variation in the price of houses by location.

These are the kinds of variables which to some extent are important in theories of land rent and the spatial organisation of the housing market.

The major attraction of Wilson's proposal from an operational standpoint is that it retains but extends the gravity model framework which, in spite of the criticisms levelled at it, has seen more operational success (i.e. use in plan making contexts) than many of the more elaborate alternatives. The expectation could be held, therefore, that the extended version of the gravity concept could meet with equal operational success, and perhaps a greater success than other attempts to operationalise micro-theories of residential location. (See, for example, Herbert and Stevens, 1960; Harris *et al.*, 1966.)

In this paper, we develop and make preliminary tests on one variant of the many models which Wilson has outlined, and in particular, we incorporate an income (or proxy) and house type disaggregation. Following Wilson [1], we define:

T_{ij}^{wk} is the number of workers of income group w who work in i and live in residential zone j in a house type k.

H_j^k is the number of houses in zone j of type k.

E_i^w is the number of jobs in zone i offering income w.

k is a size/age/condition index of housing.

c_{ij} is the costs of travel from workplace to residential zone.

p_j^k is the price of a type k house in zone j.

q^w is the average percentage of income after transportation costs have been deducted which a member of income group w spends on housing.

c_{ij}' is that component of the usual generalised journey-to-work cost, which is the actual money paid.

C^w is total expenditure on transport by each income group w.

[1] Throughout this paper the definitions of i and j used by the authors are opposite to those used by Wilson (1970).

Then, assuming that there is one worker only per household, that earnings are the only source of income, and if T_{ij}^{kw} satisfies the following constraints

$$\sum_j \sum_k T_{ij}^{wk} = E_i^w , \tag{1}$$

$$\sum_i \sum_j \sum_k T_{ij}^{wk} c_{ij} = C^w , \tag{2}$$

$$\sum_i \sum_j \sum_k T_{ij}^{wk} [p_j^k - q^w(w - c_{ij}')]^2 = \sigma^{w2} , \tag{3}$$

then we can derive a set of interlinked gravity models of the form given below in equation (4) using entropy maximising methods (Wilson, 1970).

$$T_{ij}^{wk} = A_i^w E_i^w H_j^k \exp(-\beta^w c_{ij}) \exp\{-\mu^w [p_j^k - q^w(w - c_{ij}')]^2\} , \tag{4}$$

where

$$A_i^w = \frac{1}{\sum_j \sum_k H_j^k \exp(-\beta^w c_{ij}) \exp\{-\mu^w [p_j^k - q^w(w - c_{ij}')]^2\}} . \tag{5}$$

Equation (3) provides a way of relating the two variables p_j^k and q^w by incorporating a distribution which shows the spread of expenditure on housing by each income group around the mean and relating this to the price of houses. The assumption is made that the distribution of expenditure on housing by each income group is normal and σ^{w2} is defined as the variance of the normal distribution for income group w. In addition, equation (3) compares expenditure on housing with out-of-pocket costs on transport on the journey to work.

As Wilson points out, if the last term on the right hand side of equation (4), which results from equation (3), were to be dropped, then the model (in our case here) would simply be a disaggregated singly-constrained residential location model of the familiar gravity type. He argues further, however, that the final term makes the disaggregation worthwhile and effective.

"... if $q^w(w - c_{ij}')$, the average available housing expenditure (note how this varies with c_{ij}', out of pocket costs of transport on the journey to work) [2], is very different (either way) from p_j^k, then very few wage w people working in i would be allocated to a type k house in j. It is obviously the sort of device we need to build appropriate income effects into a residential (location) model."

In other words, the model will tend only to allocate people to housing, and thus locations they can afford. As Wilson suggests:

"In a purely spatial interaction kind of model, this would not happen, and could lead to misleading results which might look all right in aggregate, but which may hide some severe planning problems."

---

[2] The parentheses are the authors'.

Two further items of notation need to be defined; β^w is the usual transport parameter which controls trip length and μ^w is clearly a parameter which controls the shape of the distribution of expenditure on housing. Further discussion of these parameters will arise when we describe calibration of the model later in the paper.

In part three of our paper, discussion is centred on measurement and classification problems associated with the development of the model discussed thus far. Before we tackle these problems at length, it is worth identifying those which lead directly to modifications in the formulation of the model outlined in equations (1) to (5), or at least to the relaxation of some of the assumptions made.

Firstly, it is important to note that unlike most of the disaggregated models proposed by Wilson (1970) the system described above is a production-constrained model and not a production–attraction-constrained model. We have in fact relaxed a fourth constraint frequently included in interaction models, namely that

$$\sum_i \sum_w T_{ij}^{wk} = H_j^k \ . \tag{6}$$

By relaxing this constraint we can perhaps use the identity described by equation (6) to predict the number of type k houses demanded at j as an outcome of the allocation of workers of wage w from zones i.

In an urban planning context, this enables us to forecast the location of demand for quantities of housing of different types from a given distribution of jobs paying wages w, from a given configuration of the transport network, and from knowledge of the prevailing market prices in each housing sub-market.

However, a complication arises due partly to the inadequacy of data sources in providing good estimates of the wages earned in job locations, and partly because of the restricting assumption of only one worker per household which is used in the foregoing description of the model. Clearly, in any real world observations of interactions between job locations and residential locations, a situation of more than one worker per household will arise, but it is easier, and more appropriate, to measure the budget term $q^w(w - c_{ij}')$ from household income data rather than from the earnings of individual workers. Therefore, in developing the model empirically, it becomes important to assume more than one worker per household.

We can therefore restate equation (6) as follows:

$$\frac{\sum_i \sum_w T_{ij}^{wk}}{r} = H_j^{k*} \ , \tag{7}$$

where r denotes a system ratio of workers per dwelling and $*$ that this equation (7) is an identity established by the model rather than *a priori* information which the model has to satisfy. Equation (7) does, however, impose the assumption that in the system to be modelled there is only one household per type k house and this will be seen to conveniently fit with the census measurements of the variables we shall use. The fact that r is constant for the whole system of T_{ij}^{wk}'s makes its incorporation in equations (4) and (5) superfluous, the more so since we are using H_j^k as a measure of the attraction of residential zones. The measurement of $q^w(w - c_{ij}')$ in terms of household income, however, does point up a weakness in this preliminary development of the model. Since in equation (4) we are allocating aggregations of individual workers of wage w in i to houses of type k in j as a function of their average household income, some information about the probability of an earner of wage w being in a household of income w ought to be incorporated (Wilson, 1970), and the assumption made that all working members of the household contribute to household income.

Thus far, we have not been able to overcome this particular problem, empirically at least, and the way in which we have measured workers in jobs in workplace locations, although it possibly lessens the problem, does not overcome it entirely.

3 Empirical classification and measurement of variables in the model
The classification of E_i^w
In the preliminary runs of the model reported here, E_i^w jobs of type w in i have been classified into three broad groups, namely professional and managerial jobs, white collar jobs, and blue collar jobs. In this case, therefore, the index w when attached to jobs, describes an aggregation of the standard socioeconomic groups (SEG) into which workers in job locations fall rather than by wage levels. This avoids the problem for the time being of generating small area distributions of income or wages by workplace. From various national series [3], average income levels can be attached to

Table 1. Average earnings by job type—1966[a].

Type of job	Weekly average earnings
Professional and managerial	£32.50
White collar	£21.10
Blue collar	£19.10

[a] All data used throughout the paper are as at 1966 or will be adjusted to a 1966 base date. Data in table 1 are taken from the Family Expenditure Survey (1966) and relate to full time adult employees in selected occupations but for all industries.

[3] See for example the Family Expenditure Surveys (Ministry of Labour, 1967) and the Department of Employment and Productivity (1969) Earnings Surveys which provide national, and in some cases, regional statistics on earnings by different occupations. Difficulties can arise, however, in relating classifications of occupations and socioeconomic groups from these different series.

this particular classification of workers, but since any variation in income in a small area would vary solely with the spatial distribution of professional and managerial, white collar, and blue collar jobs, it is perfectly reasonable to use these distributions as proxies for earnings by workplace location.

An indication of the average difference in earnings levels measured by a professional/blue collar/white collar type of job split, is given in table 1.

The classification of jobs at workplace locations into the groups specified above and the avoidance of a wages index, perhaps makes less contentious the use of average household income in the budget term. The worst assumption we are now making is that households will tend to be homogeneous with respect to occupation status; white collar fathers will have white collar sons and wives, if employed, which is clearly much less damaging that assuming that all will have very similar incomes.

The classification of H_j^k

H_j^k measures the number and types of houses in residential locations in a bounded sub-region. As mentioned earlier, j denotes a residential zone and k is an index of the house type. In developing the model, we have attempted to classify housing into a number of housing sub-markets characterised by tenure, the size, and the quality of housing. Ideally a quality index should include some measure of age and condition, and perhaps some assessment of the amenity afforded by site and neighbourhood characteristics, while a size index should account for the floorspace available. In the model described here, a condition index has been constructed which merely defines housing as being poor or good, and the size index merely describes whether housing is large or small. Tenure, on the other hand, classifies three housing market sectors, namely owner-occupied housing, public rented housing, and private rented housing. In all, these classifications categorize housing into $3 \times 2 \times 2 = 12$ housing sub-markets which are described in table 2.

Combined with the three employment types described in the previous section, this particular classification of housing sub-markets would give rise to 36 inter-linked sub-models of the form given by equation (4). A more elaborate description of the data base and the particular data sources from which these classification schemes are derived, is given later but some definition of the dimensions of our k index described in table 2 is appropriate here. Most of the measurements of variables used in the model are derived from the 10% Sample Census of 1966 and rely therefore on the Census classifications of variables.

Insofar as tenure is concerned, the definition of the owner-occupied sector is self-evident. The public rented sector comprises both local authority and new town corporation housing, while the private rented sector embraces both unfurnished and furnished lettings. The distinction currently drawn in our model between large and small housing is quite arbitrary and based on the assumption that a dwelling with 6 or less census rooms is small (our argument is that a house of 6 census rooms was probably equivalent to the average 3 bedroomed semi-detached house). No systematic check has yet been made of this assumption.

Our condition index is again a fairly arbitrary one. Good housing is represented by that housing which is recorded in the census as having exclusive use of a fixed bath. Any household (worker) in the census who did not live in a house with a fixed bath, or shared the use of a bath, was considered to live in poor housing. The lack or availability of other standard amenities recorded in the census was assumed to co-vary with the presence or lack of a fixed bath and again further systematic analysis will be required to improve our classification of the various housing sub-markets. Work by Caulfield (1970) has shown, however, that the presence or lack of a fixed bath provides as reasonable an indicator of housing condition as any, at least insofar as the use of census data is concerned. We shall, however, return to this and other problems in a later general comment on the difficulties of classification associated with building a model of this kind.

One further point on the classification of housing in the model, is pertinent at this juncture, however, and leads to a revision of the classification set out in table 2.

Given only a 10% sample, or even larger samples, of the interaction variable T_{ij}^{wk}, it is reasonable to expect that many, if not all, of the cells in some of the T_{ij}^{wk} matrices will be zero. For example, it would be most unlikely that local housing authorities would build housing which lacked the standard amenities and was poor in quality, when public housing policy exists to remedy these very deficiencies. Similarly, it would be unusual to find many, if any, higher income professional and managerial workers in

Table 2. First preliminary scheme for classification of housing markets.

	Tenure	Size	Condition
1	owner-occupied	small	poor
2	owner-occupied	small	good
3	owner-occupied	large	poor
4	owner-occupied	large	good
5	public rented	small	poor
6	public rented	small	good
7	public rented	large	poor
8	public rented	large	good
9	private rented	small	poor
10	private rented	small	good
11	private rented	large	poor
12	private rented	large	good

public rented housing, when again public housing policy ostensibly provides shelter for lower income groups who cannot compete in the private housing markets.

Clearly, calibration of the series of models described by equation (4) requires that each of the separate matrices of T_{ij}^{wk} should contain adequate observations of the variable. To achieve this it became necessary to reduce the dimensions of our classification of housing as set out in table 2, and to amalgamate some of the classes to stress only those dimensions of the k type index which were significant in each housing sub-market, while at the same time implicitly incorporating those dimensions which had been suppressed.

These considerations led to a second, yet we would stress, still preliminary classification which is described in table 3. Nevertheless, this is the scheme adopted for the first tests of the model reported in this paper.

Thus from table 2, house types 1 and 2 have been amalgamated to produce type 1 in table 3, types 3 and 4 to produce type 2, types 5, 6, 7, and 8 to produce type 3, types 9 and 11 to produce type 4, and types 10 and 12 to produce type 5.

Examination of the first 36 T_{ij}^{wk} interaction matrices to be produced from the data suggested, much as might be expected, that in the owner-occupied sector only size was significant in distinguishing sub-markets. The housing stock could be considered homogeneous (though not entirely so) in our chosen criteria of condition. In the public rented sector housing was homogeneous both with respect to size and condition. Thus public authority housing is generally small and in good condition. Private rented housing on the other hand proved to be capable of separation into poor and good sub-markets.

Therefore, the revision of the classification of housing sub-markets reduces the number of sub-models to be calibrated from 36 to 15, while implicitly retaining, and in some cases making explicit, all the categories included in the original 36.

In table 4 and figure 1, an analysis is given of the extent to which each of our groups of workers are represented in each of the five housing sub-markets. In both table 4 and figure 1 the number of workers in each of

Table 3. Second preliminary scheme for classification of housing sub-markets.

	Tenure	Size	Condition
1	owner-occupied	small	–
2	owner-occupied	large	–
3	public rented	–	–
4	private rented	–	poor
5	private rented	–	good

the classes within each housing sub-market is expressed as a percentage of the total number of workers in the sub-region illustrated in figure 2. So that from observations of T_{ij}^{wk} for the region defined in figure 2, the

Table 4. Distribution of workers by type in housing sub-markets.

Worker classes	Housing sub-markets					
	owner-occupied housing		public rented housing	private rented housing		all housing markets
	small	large		poor	good	
Professional and managerial workers as % of total workers	9·25	3·50	1·00	0·90	3·25	17·90
White collar workers as % of total workers	23·00	4·00	10·25	4·50	7·60	49·35
Blue collar workers as % of total workers	14·00	1·90	8·25	3·50	5·10	32·75

Source: Special Analysis of Usual Workplace and Residence Data 1966 Sample Census. (A more detailed description of the data base from which this analysis is made is given later in the paper.)

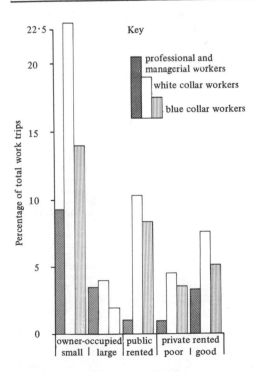

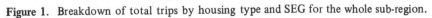

Figure 1. Breakdown of total trips by housing type and SEG for the whole sub-region.

percentage of workers in each of the three job type classes in each housing sub-market is equal to

$$\frac{\sum_i \sum_j T_{ij}^{wk}}{\sum_i \sum_j \sum_k \sum_w T_{ij}^{wk}} \times 100 \ .$$

It is readily apparent from table 4 that about half of the workers in our area of study have white collar jobs, some 33% have blue collar jobs, and about 18% may be classified as having professional and managerial jobs. Other features of note are the relatively similar profiles of white and blue collar workers with respect to their representation in the different housing sub-markets, and the greater proportion of white collar workers in each market (solely due to their relatively greater number). Perhaps blue collar workers have a relatively greater share of public rented housing, and white collar workers a relatively greater share of the small owner-occupied housing market, but generally speaking, the two profiles parallel each other quite closely. In view of the similarity of average earnings by each of these two groups illustrated in table 1, this is not surprising.

Of greater significance is the quite different profile of professional and managerial workers, and as might be expected, only relatively small proportions of these higher income workers are to be found in public rented and the poorer private rented housing.

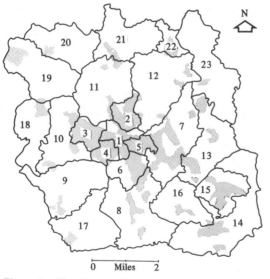

Key to zones

1 Abbey
2 Caversham
3 Norcot
4 Minster
5 Redlands
6 Christchurch
7 Woodley
8 Shinfield
9 Burghfield
10 Tilehurst
11 Kidmore End
12 Shiplake
13 St Nicholas Hurst
14 Finchampstead
15 Wokingham
16 Arborfield
17 Mortimer
18 Pangbourne
19 Goring
20 Woodcote
21 Peppard
22 Henley
23 Wargrave

Figure 2. The 23 zone Reading sub-region.

Measurement of c_{ij} and c'_{ij}

In the model described by equation (4) two quite separate variables both of which describe the costs of travel between workplace and residential zones are used, one in the usual cost deterrence function, $\exp(-\beta^w c_{ij})$, and the other in the budget term, $\exp[-\mu^w[p_j^k - q^w(w - c'_{ij})]^2]$. In both cases the journey to work cost is measured on the minimum time path between each workplace origin and each residential destination. It is important, however, to note the distinction between the two measures of travel cost used. c_{ij} in this model should, as Wilson (1970) points out, be measured as the usual generalised cost of travel. In most traffic distribution models, this is usually taken to be a linear combination of time and cost, where cost includes the opportunity cost of time spent travelling as well as the out-of-pocket expenses of travel, additions for congestion, and terminal costs such as parking. c'_{ij} on the other hand represents the actual out-of-pocket expenses of travel, which is the only element of travel cost which can realistically be set against disposable household income in computing the household budget.

In this our initial development of the model, we have not developed an appropriate measure of generalised cost as the usual deterrence function, but have relied on a simple measure of travel time in minutes to index c_{ij}. c'_{ij} is then measured as λc_{ij} where λ is a constant measure of the out-of-pocket costs of travel per minute of travel time. λ is in fact expressed as a weekly equivalent of the cost of travel per minute of the journey to work in order to make c'_{ij} comparable with weekly measures of household income used in the budget term. The value of λ used in the model is equal to £0·097 [4] per minute of travel time. In our interpretation of the working of the model, it matters little that we have not used a measure of generalised cost in the $\exp(-\beta^w c_{ij})$ term, but it is clearly important to have deducted the appropriate amount of travel cost from the budget term $\exp\{-\mu^w[p_j^k - q^w(w - c'_{ij})]^2\}$.

The measurement of p_j^k

p_j^k as defined earlier is the price of a k type house in j. The main problem of measurement in this variable is to provide some monetary measure of prices in residential locations j for a set of house types which are described in only a very general way. We have already referred to our use of census data to classify house types and to the kind of broad indication of condition and size which aggregation problems make necessary. The first difficulty occurs therefore in the fact that these very general classifications of house types are not readily recognisable in real world housing markets, or at least at a detailed enough level of description which permits prices to be attached to them.

[4] Estimates of out-of-pocket costs of travel used here were derived from 1965 survey data obtained by the Road Research Laboratory. See Dawson (1968).

Our sources of data for house prices varied with each of the housing sectors dealt with in the model. In the owner occupied sector, a survey of prices was conducted with estate agents. Similarly in the private rented sector a survey was carried out with those agents who particularly specialised in letting accommodation. In the public rented sector, reliance has been placed entirely on the very detailed statistics of council house rents published in the Housing Statistics (England and Wales) by the Institute for Municipal Treasurers and Accountants (1968)[5].

A second difficulty is occasioned by the different spatial units on which house prices may be measured from these different sources. While it was by and large possible for agents in the private markets to differentiate house prices by the areas in which we were interested (wards and parishes and their aggregations to zones in our study area), in the public sector prices are only differentiated by local authority areas. Since our study area contains a number of local authority areas (and our proposed considerable extension of the area described in this paper will contain quite a large number), some spatial variation in local authority housing rents is accounted for in the model, but much less than in the private housing sector.

A further difficulty in measuring house prices arises from differences between the census attributes of housing and those attributes of housing to which both the public and private sectors of the market find it easy to relate variations in house price. The Population Census classifies household accommodation according to the number of rooms available to the household, tenure, and the presence, lack, or sharing of the so-called standard amenities of hot water, internal or external water closet, and fixed bath, or shower, or both. In the owner-occupied sector these attributes of housing are no longer useful in reflecting variations in the market price of housing. The presence or lack of a fixed bath proved of marginal use, but it was found that for this sector, it was necessary to classify housing according to whether the accommodation had central heating or not, a garage or space for a garage, the number of bedrooms rather than the total number of rooms, and according to whether housing was detached, semi-detached, or terraced, or was comprised of flats or maisonettes. Similar attributes are also to be found in published statistics on public housing referred to earlier.

It was only in the private rented sector that the attributes of housing defined by the census had any relevance at all. Since a great deal of private rented accommodation occurs in subdivided housing units, or in a flat of some kind or another, the number of rooms rather than bedrooms

[5] These reports provide a detailed breakdown of rents for all local authority housing, for housing of different sizes, measured by the number of bedrooms in each house, for each local authority in England and Wales. Rents are also classified according to whether housing is in flats, maisonettes, semi-detached or other house types. Rents are measured weekly and statistics are available for each year from 1964 onwards.

is usually taken as an indicator of size and it is in the private rented sector that shared accommodation and the sharing or sheer lack of basic standard amenities, still exists. For this reason we were able to retain our census based classification to measure the variation of prices in this sector.

Our survey of prices of housing in each sector by location was therefore carried out on the basis of two different classification schemes for house types, and at a very much more disaggregated level than that required for the model. In the process of aggregation to estimate average prices for each type k house in each residential zone j, therefore, some of the dimensions in attributes of housing had to be ignored. In the owner occupied sector, for example, if a house had a fixed bath, it would be classified as good, whether or not it had central heating. A three bedroomed house was regarded as equivalent to a six roomed census house, and it was not possible to account for whether the house was detached or semi-detached. Fairly major assumptions of these kinds and the extensive averaging of data over differing classes made possible the assignment of average prices to type k houses described by the model.

Finally, one further complication needs to be dealt with. Prices of houses in the owner-occupied sector were measured as the current (1971) capital value of the house in the market, and those in the private rented sector as prevailing weekly rents. In the public sector, weekly rents for our base year 1966 were available directly from published sources. Since household income and all other variables in the model are measured as at 1966, current prices had to be discounted to 1966 values. Our survey, therefore, asked for estimates of increases in house prices and rents by area since 1966, and these were used to adjust current 1971 values. In addition, since in the model, household incomes are measured as weekly incomes, capital values obtained for the owner-occupied sector had to be converted to weekly rents. The usual valuation procedures were adopted for this purpose.

The measurement of q^w

As defined earlier q^w is a measure of the average percentage of income (after transport costs have been deducted) which a member of income group w spends on housing. It has already been stated that in developing the model it has been appropriate to use a classification of professional and managerial, white collar, and blue collar groups of workers as a proxy for income groups, and also convenient to use household income in the budget term. In this case, it is appropriate to measure q^w as the average percentage of household income which professional and managerial, white collar, and blue collar households spend on housing, again after transport costs have been deducted. It is worth noting in passing that since q relates only to the proportion of household income spent on housing, the model assumes, like micro-theories, a fixed amount of expenditure in the housing budget on all other goods and services.

The source of data used for the measurement of q^w was the 1966 Family Expenditure Survey. The Survey provides a detailed breakdown for a national sample of households of expenditure on housing, and all other goods and services, including transport. From this data it is possible to estimate the proportion of disposable household income, net of transport expenditure, which on average is spent on housing by groups approximating to our professional/white collar/blue collar split.

The proportions derived from the Survey were respectively 11%, 11·8%, and 9·3%. It is interesting to note that on the basis of our classification of households, white collar households spend on average a higher proportion of their income on housing than the professional and managerial group, and blue collar households significantly less.

The measurement of w

It will be apparent from our preceding account of the measurement of variables included in the models that for reasons of data problems, the measurement of w has varied. It will have been evident from equation (4) that strictly speaking it is necessary that w, as a measure of both earnings in job locations and of disposable household income, should, particularly if the assumption of one worker per household is retained, and that earnings are the sole source of income, be measured in terms which are directly comparable. The convenience of available data, it has been argued, makes it more expedient, as with q, to measure w in the budget term $q^w(w - c'_{ij})$ as the disposable household income of professional, white collar, and blue collar households respectively. As with q, the w variable in the term $(w - c'_{ij})$ was obtained from the Family Expenditure Survey of 1966 and represents the total disposable household income of each occupational or SEG group from which transport costs, c'_{ij}, are deducted.

As at 1966, average household income for professional, white collar, and blue collar households respectively was £38.66, £27.59, and £25.59.

4 A summary of the empirical version of the model

It is convenient at this point to summarise the net effect that the considerable variety of problems encountered in measuring variables included in the model has had in reshaping the hypothesis which is put forward by equation (4). It is evident to some extent that some modifications at least in interpretation are effected by the solutions adopted to these problems. These modifications can probably best be illustrated by re-writing equations (1) to (4) in the terms given in equations (8) to (12) below.

$$T_{ij}^{sk} = A_i^s E_i^s H_j^k \exp(-\beta^s c_{ij}) \exp\{-\mu^s [p_j^k - q^s(w^s - c'_{ij})]^2\}, \tag{8}$$

$$A_i^s = \frac{1}{\sum_j \sum_k H_j^k \exp(-\beta^s c_{ij}) \exp\{-\mu[p_j^k - q^s(w^s - c'_{ij})]^2\}}, \tag{9}$$

and where equation (7) satisfies the constraints,

$$\sum_j \sum_k T_{ij}^{sk} = E_i^s ,$$ (10)

$$\sum_i \sum_j \sum_k T_{ij}^{sk} c_{ij} = C^s ,$$ (11)

$$\sum_i \sum_j \sum_k T_{ij}^{sk} [p_j^k - q^s(w^s - c'_{ij})]^2 = \sigma^{s2} .$$ (12)

In equation (8) T_{ij}^{sk} now refers to the number of workers in professional and managerial, white collar, and blue collar jobs, denoted by s, who work in workplace zones i and live in a k type house in j and where s type jobs are classified from aggregation of the standard socioeconomic group classifications. There are five k type housing sub-markets as defined in table 3. E_i^s clearly represents the distribution of workers in s type jobs in workplace locations i, and H_j^k the distribution of k type houses in residential zones j. It is also clear that separate values of the β and μ parameters need to be found for s type workers. p_j^k remains unchanged in definition, but q^s now refers to the average percentage expenditure on housing, after transport costs have been deducted by s type households. Income is now defined as the disposable household income, and will thus be different for each s type household. Accordingly, it is written as w^s. c'_{ij} means exactly the same as it did before.

The hypothesis represented by equation (8) is a modification of equation (4) and verbally stated argues that workers in s type jobs in job locations i will be allocated to type k housing in residential zones j
1) in direct proportion to the number of type k houses in j
2) inversely in proportion to the cost of travelling from i to j (measured in minutes) and
3) as a function of the degree to which the average available expenditure on housing of s type households varies from the price of a k type house in each residential zone j, after transport costs have been accounted for.

5 General comment and caveat on the classification schemes adopted in this preliminary development of the model

It will be evident to the reader that many of the classifications and measurements of variables used in this first development of the model are to a large extent forced by data availability, and lead to at least some of the difficulties in interpretation. They may not at this stage provide a taxonomy which would adequately test the hypothesis put forward, either by Wilson's original proposals or any modifications which have been introduced here.

Our development of three simple classes of professional and managerial, white collar, and blue collar workers, for example, represents an arbitrary grouping of SEG's observed in census data and may not differentiate workers or households sufficiently to provide an adequate test of the budget term on the location of households in the sub-region depicted by figure 2. A greater difference, for example, between the average income earned by blue collar and white collar workers would have proved more satisfactory.

Similarly, the classification of housing sub-markets was to a large extent intuitive and would bear further and more systematic analysis. Much of the averaging of data, for example, in estimating the prices of k type houses by location, also raises doubts about how successfully this preliminary development of the model might perform.

These kinds of considerations should be borne very much in mind when interpreting the results reported in the later sections of this paper. Our continuing work on this model will be examining much more closely and systematically the taxonomical and measurement problems raised in this paper, and our *caveat* is that these could clearly lead to different results from those reported here.

6 Note on the data base

The degree to which measurement and taxonomical problems raised in a model of this kind can be solved is obviously a function of the kind of data base which can be assembled to empirically test the model. Reference has already been made to the sources of data, mostly national series, from which measurements of household budget variables can be obtained. We have also referred to the surveys of house prices and rents which provide the data for these variables.

Perhaps the most formidable data problem, and one to which Wilson referred in proposing the development of disaggregated models of this form, is the collection of observations of T_{ij}^{wk} and including any further disaggregations of T_{ij} (such as transport mode, for example), which we might find desirable. As Wilson (1970, p.85) put the problem,

"with the variable T_{ij}^{wkn}, if there are 50 zones, 5 house types, 5 income groups, and 4(n) types of locational behaviour, there are

$50^2 \times 5 \times 5 \times 4 = 250000$ cells or population categories",

for which we need observations. Apart from the fact that sample surveys cannot provide this number of observations with adequate statistical properties, the doubt is raised as to whether public planning agencies would be prepared to finance and undertake the kind of survey necessary to collect the data.

An essential part of our experimental work has, therefore, been to examine the extent to which an appropriate data base can be established from readily available sources of data collected for other purposes.

The most appropriate source of data to measure T_{ij}^{wk} has proved to be the 10% sample data on usual workplace and residence of people in employment collected in the 1966 Sample Census. This data provided observations of the numbers of persons in employment by place of residence at the enumeration district level, and by workplace at the local authority level, classified by age, sex, marital condition, mode of transport on the journey to work, employment status, occupation order, SEG of the chief economic supporter of the household, and by industry (Standard Industrial Classification, SIC).

To fulfil the requirements established by the model, two modifications proved necessary to this set of data. Firstly we needed the workplace of each person in employment coded to a spatial unit smaller than the local authority area (preferably to the enumeration district level), and secondly we needed to incorporate a classification of persons in employment by the housing variables of tenure, size, and standard amenities, collected in the census. Both of these requirements meant that the Census Office had to recover the individual census returns to add in the additional codes to the usual workplace and residence record.

The incorporation of these additional attributes of persons in employment unfortunately raised problems of confidentiality under the Census rules, and to overcome these it was necessary to accept aggregation of our basic spatial unit from the enumeration district level to the ward and parish level. The file of data we have containing the information described above covers a geographical area comprising much of the western sector of the Outer Metropolitan Area of the South East, and figure 2 defines only a small part of that area.

The essential feature of the file is that it permits the exploration of a variety of classifications of T_{ij}^{sk}, but for sample reasons, and for reasons of developing a computationally feasible model, a need is imposed for aggregations of spatial and other dimensions of T_{ij}^{sk}.

A systematic examination of this aggregation problem still lies before us.

The test sub-region

Initial experiments in developing the model are being conducted on a small sub-region centred on Reading County Borough, as illustrated in figure 2. The sub-region defines the commuter hinterland around Reading, and is self-contained to the extent that in excess of 80% of worktrips have origins and destinations within the area. In our first trials of the model, we have in any event extracted from our data file a closed system of T_{ij}'s which have origins and destinations only in that area. Reading itself is comprised of zones 1–6, and all zones in the rest of the sub-region are aggregations of wards and parishes.

Table 5 illustrates the observed distribution of persons in employment in each of our s type jobs. All totals are calculated from observed values of T_{ij}^{sk} and are equal to $\sum_{j} \sum_{k} T_{ij}^{sk}$. The locations of jobs within the zones, as with other variables, are defined by a weighted centroid in each zone. A feature of the distribution of jobs within the sub-region is the heavy concentration of jobs for all occupation groups in the central wards of Reading (zone 1).

Since the model is to allocate workers distributed as shown in table 5 to k type houses in j, or more strictly, in our terms, to estimate the demand by this distribution of workers for k type houses in residential zones j, it will also be useful to examine the observed distribution of H_j^k. This, again, is estimated as $\sum_i \sum_s T_{ij}^{sk}$, but now divided by r where r, as defined earlier, is a sub-region-wide ratio of workers per dwelling[6]. Table 6, therefore, illustrates the number of houses by type of zone in the sub-region shown in figure 2.

The reader will readily be able to interpret the spatial distributions shown in table 6 against the map of the region given in figure 2. Perhaps attention should be drawn, however, to the relatively heavy concentration of private rented housing in the older and central wards of Reading (zone 1) compared with concentration of public rented housing in the more suburban zones of Reading (zones, 3, 4, and 6). This feature of the

Table 5. Total employment by SEG group by workplace.

Zone	Professional and managerial number of jobs	White collar number of jobs	Blue collar number of jobs
1	6020	21630	11180
2	400	1660	1050
3	670	1670	1420
4	500	1090	660
5	1670	2520	670
6	650	1910	2040
7	1390	2730	2710
8	500	660	760
9	190	410	630
10	360	840	840
11	180	280	110
12	210	430	350
13	250	710	490
14	180	320	350
15	890	2180	2040
16	100	530	770
17	20	190	180
18	160	510	260
19	370	390	310
20	130	130	260
21	150	240	190
22	600	1700	870
23	120	520	530

[6] This ratio is computed from data given in the Ward and Parish Library of the Sample Census, 1966.

localisation of the public and private rented sectors of housing in a town like Reading is perhaps to be expected. It is worth noting, however, when we come to compare the relative trip lengths of different types of workers on the journey to work. We shall find that the mean trip length for blue collar workers is a little longer than that for white collar workers, and their relatively higher share of the public rented sector of the housing market could well account for this.

Table 6. Number of houses by type by residential zone.

Zone	Owner-occupied housing		Public rented housing	Private rented housing	
	small	large		poor	good
1	3096	875	139	2381	1548
2	2624	701	410	243	541
3	8422	340	1784	222	764
4	1360	139	1833	257	250
5	2200	694	42	1131	916
6	2089	146	2728	83	430
7	4526	576	770	62	736
8	791	215	396	56	416
9	271	83	361	49	333
10	1777	229	486	35	389
11	958	174	236	35	285
12	500	76	76	49	285
13	902	153	208	153	229
14	729	139	174	62	125
15	1006	354	646	111	423
16	271	7	90	28	347
17	208	111	146	14	264
18	167	83	970	42	236
19	271	201	139	49	201
20	160	42	62	14	97
21	97	62	69	7	194
22	541	201	673	236	548
23	167	118	333	21	180

7 Calibration of the model

The calibration procedure in the case of the model presented here involves finding estimates of β^s and μ^s which achieve the best fit between values of T_{ij}^{sk} predicted by the model, and those observed in the data. For two reasons, however, it is more convenient to measure the fit between aggregations of T_{ij}^{sk}, namely $\sum_k T_{ij}^{sk}$. Firstly, β and μ both refer only to the behaviour of our s type workers, professional and managerial, white collar, and blue collar, and secondly, because of the problems of obtaining sufficient observations of T_{ij}^{sk} in each cell of the array. Even more conveniently, measures of observed and predicted trip lengths for each group can be obtained, and Hyman (1969) has suggested a systematic procedure which uses the mean trip length statistic for calibrating spatial interaction models. Batty (1971) has developed a number of search procedures in applying Hyman's method, but in addition points to the need for the use of a calibration statistic for each parameter in a two parameter model. The two statistics appropriate to use in the case described here were the mean trip length for each s type group of employees which can be shown to be related to β^s, and a normalised measure of the variance σ^{s2}, defined earlier in the paper, which is related to μ^s. These were respectively

$$\overline{C^s} = \frac{\sum_i \sum_j \sum_k T_{ij}^{sk} c_{ij}}{\sum_i \sum_j \sum_k T_{ij}^{sk}} \, , \tag{13}$$

and

$$\sigma^{s2} = \frac{\sum_i \sum_j \sum_k T_{ij}^{sk} [p_j^k - q^s(w - c'_{ij})]^2}{\sum_i \sum_j \sum_k T_{ij}^{sk}} \, . \tag{14}$$

In calibration it is required to minimise the differences between the observed and predicted values of $\overline{C^s}$ and σ^{s2} as defined above. Observed and predicted values for each of these statistics should therefore be equal.

Table 7 reports the values of β and μ estimated for each of our socioeconomic groups.

The values of β estimated for each group are consistent with both observed and predicted mean trip lengths (measured in minutes of travel time). These were, for professional and managerial workers, 8·08 minutes (measured over the whole system of T_{ij}^{sk}'s); 6·82 minutes for white collar workers; and 7·36 for blue collar workers. Surprisingly, blue collar workers travel further on average than white collar workers, though only slightly further, and this, as suggested earlier, may have much to do with the location of public rented housing. In general, however, the values obtained for β are consistent with the theory that the lower the value of β the greater the separation of workplace and residence.

What is surprising and disturbing, however, is the fact that the values of μ obtained for professional and managerial groups and white collar groups are negative. These values are quite inconsistent with the hypothesis

Table 7. Calibrated values for β and μ.

SEG group	β	μ
Professional and managerial	0·156845	−0·032470
White collar	0·208760	−0·000861
Blue collar	0·195283	0·011185

suggested by the budget term. They suggest that the greater the difference between the price of a type k house in a residential zone j and the average available expenditure of an s type household, the more attractive is the k type house and the residential zone j to this household. Only in the case of blue collar workers is the original hypothesis supported.

These results, however, being preliminary, cannot be taken as refuting the original hypothesis or the value of the budget term in the equation. There are a number of reasons why the negative values obtained could be spurious.

Firstly, there is some evidence in our data that the distribution of prices around the values of average expenditure on housing by each household group is not normal. What evidence we have is not yet conclusive, but these distributions all appear positively skewed and platykurtic. The assumption of normality is not essential, and in further work alternative forms for the budget term will be tested.

Secondly, there were problems in measuring the variables which may have contributed to the result. These included the spatial units adopted, the classification schemes adopted, and the considerable amount of averaging necessary for some of the data described earlier.

Finally, we have as yet no evaluation of the effect of running the model as a singly constrained model as opposed to the double constrained model proposed by Wilson (1970) and again this could have had some effect.

All of these problems remain to be investigated.

8 Some indications of the performance of the model

The danger of spurious values for the μ parameters, and the uncertainty attached to the effect of the budget term in the model, do not in themselves invalidate further analysis of the performance of the model. It could well be, for example, that the travel deterrence function $[\exp(-\beta^s c_{ij})]$, together with the attraction of H_j^k, accounts for most of the variance in the distributions of T_{ij}^{sk}.

In figures 3, 4, and 5, illustrations are given of how well the model has predicted values of $\sum_k T_{ij}^{sk}$, the arrays which provided the main observations for calibration purposes. Figure 3 shows a log–log plot of the fit achieved between the model predictions of $\sum_k T_{ij}^{sk}$ and observations of this variable from the census. Data refers to the trips made by professional and managerial workers. r^2 is used to give an indication of the goodness of fit between observed and predicted values and was $0 \cdot 7751$. A similar pattern can be observed for the white collar workers in figure 4, although the model can be judged to have predicted rather better on this occasion, producing a value for r^2 of $0 \cdot 8518$. The best prediction of all is that for the blue collar workers, and in this case r^2 is $0 \cdot 8950$ (see figure 5). It is clearly a matter of some speculation as to whether the improvements in the value of r^2, and thus the rather closer estimates of observed and

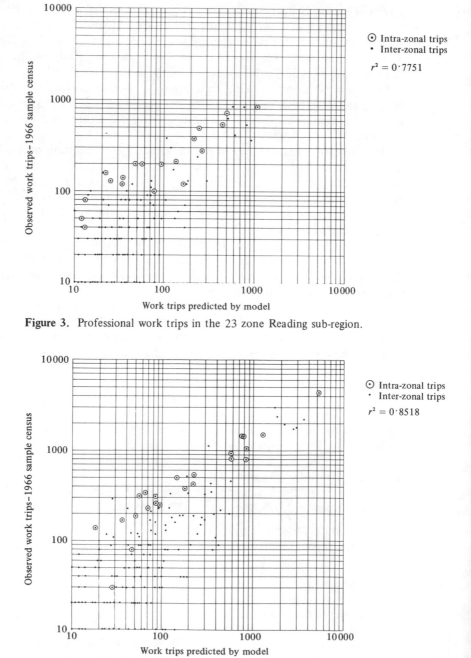

Figure 3. Professional work trips in the 23 zone Reading sub-region.

Figure 4. White collar work trips in the 23 zone Reading sub-region.

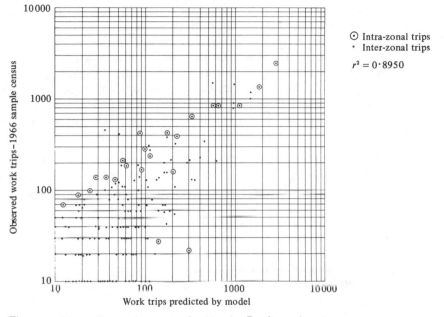

Figure 5. Blue collar work trips in the 23 zone Reading sub-region.

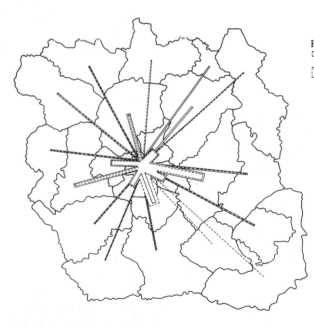

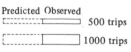

Figure 6. Observed and predicted flows from Abbey zone to zones of residence (Professional).

predicted values of the journey from work to home, evident in the
progression from professional, through white collar to blue collar workers,
are due to the effect of the budget term and the values obtained for μ. It
should be noted, however, that the best predictions are obtained when the
budget term in the model performs in the manner expected.

Figures 3, 4, and 5, as stated above, measure the degree to which the
model has been able to reproduce the whole system of flows of workers
from a multi-nodal system of job locations to residential locations where
the flows were defined as $\sum_{k} T_{ij}^{sk}$. In figures 6, 7, and 8, illustrations are

provided of the pattern of flows from a single job location, the central
wards of Reading (zone 1) which as indicated earlier, contained by far the
greatest number of jobs in each of our occupation or SEG groups.
Figure 6 compares the actual and predicted flows of professional and
managerial workers from workplace zone 1 to their various residential
zones. Observed flows measured from the Census data of usual workplace
and residence are shown by solid lines, and predicted flows by a pecked
line. In cases where the predicted flow of workers is greater than the
observed flow the pecked line appears outside the solid line, and *vice versa*.
It is left to the reader to judge how well observed flows are reproduced by
the model flows.

Similar comparisons are made for white collar workers in figure 7 and
for blue collar workers in figure 8.

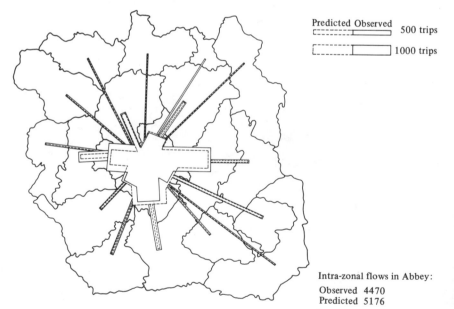

Predicted Observed
500 trips
1000 trips

Intra-zonal flows in Abbey:
Observed 4470
Predicted 5176

Figure 7. Observed and predicted flows from Abbey zone to zones of residence (white
collar workers).

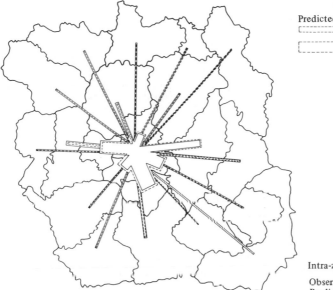

Predicted Observed

500 trips

1000 trips

Intra-zonal flows in Abbey:

Observed 2570
Predicted 2795

Figure 8. Observed and predicted flows from Abbey zone to zones of residence (blue collar workers).

Some aspects of locational behaviour

In figures 9, 10, and 11, a somewhat different representation is given of the locational behaviour of the different occupational groups depicted in the model. In the examples presented, we examine the distributions of workers in intervals of time spent travelling on the journey to work for each occupation group. In this case we are looking at the flow from the zone of residence to all workplace zones. Three residential zones are chosen to illustrate the quite different distributions brought about by increasing distance of the residential zone from the main employment centre. In table 5 we showed this to be the central wards of Reading (zone 1). The zones chosen represent a 'downtown' residential location (zone 1) and two suburban-cum-rural zones beyond the boundary of Reading County Borough.

Figure 9 compares both the predicted and observed proportions of professional, white collar, and blue collar workers who live in zone 1 in increasing intervals of minutes spent travelling to work. Observed and predicted mean travel times are also given. In view of the heavy concentration of jobs for each occupational group in zone 1, as expected, the average time spent travelling by each group is quite short, and each of the distributions tails off very steeply with increasing distance. Some reference needs to be made to the fact that the observed mean trip length for blue collar workers is greater than for other groups. This could be

Zone 1: Abbey (urban)

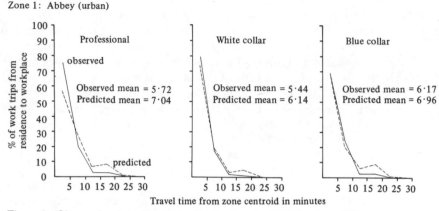

Figure 9. Observed and predicted trip distributions by SEG for three different zones.

Zone 9: Burghfield (suburban/rural)

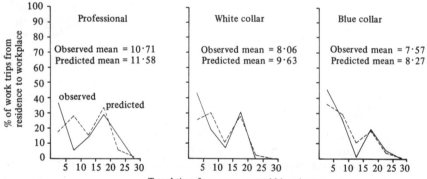

Figure 10. Observed and predicted trip distributions by SEG for three different zones.

Zone 17: Mortimer (rural/suburban)

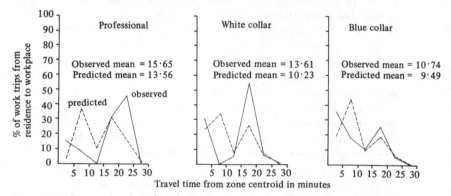

Figure 11. Observed and predicted trip distributions by SEG for three different zones.

due to the fact that blue collar jobs are more widely dispersed throughout the sub-region, and this can be checked against table 5 and figure 2. Another feature of note is that the predictions by the model are rather better for the white collar and blue collar workers than for the professional and managerial groups. This, however, is consistent with the results of calibration described earlier in the paper.

Figure 10 illustrates equivalent data for a suburban–rural zone, and clearly, quite different distributions can be expected. Both observed and predicted travel behaviour by each occupational group are more consistent with expectations than in the case of zone 1, however. Greater proportions of all groups travel further to work, but in this case the professional and white collar groups on average travel further to work than blue collar groups. Significantly, the average travel time for blue collar workers is not much greater than in the downtown case, but this can again probably be explained by the greater accessibility of blue collar workers to jobs in the suburban–rural zone chosen.

Figure 11 shows a similar pattern of behaviour for the three groups resident in a zone (17) still more distant from central Reading. Mean trip lengths are higher, as is to be expected, and the differences between occupational groups are similar. Blue collar workers, in this case, however, do have to travel somewhat further to work.

Of note is the fact that for the suburban–rural zones the model predicts less well than for the central Reading case illustrated in figure 9. This is almost certainly due to the smaller populations which obtain in the more rural locations.

The allocation of occupational groups to housing sub-markets
The greater part of our foregoing analysis of the performance of the model has concerned itself with the examination of the distributions of the variable $\sum_k T_{ij}^{sk}$. In one sense this is reasonable, since the calibration statistics used to estimate the parameters β^s and μ^s avoid the explicit incorporation of the dimension k, which defines our housing sub-markets. On the other hand, as stated at the outset of our paper, our purpose is not merely to model the residential locations of different occupational groups, but primarily their allocation to, or demand for, specific kinds of housing in residential locations. Before concluding the paper, it behoves us to illustrate how well the model developed has performed in allocating each occupational group employed in all job locations in the sub-region to each k type house.

Figures 12, 13, and 14, therefore, compare model predictions and values observed from the census data of the allocation of professional and managerial, white collar, and blue collar workers respectively, to each housing sub-market. These were earlier defined as owner-occupied small housing, owner-occupied large housing, public rented housing, private rented poor housing, and private rented good housing. Comparisons are made for each of the 23 zones in the sub-region.

Each histogram in each zone represents a comparison of the predicted and observed values of

$$\frac{\sum_i T_{ij}^{sk}}{\sum_i \sum_k T_{ij}^{sk}} \times 100 \ .$$

Thus, in figure 12, each column of the histogram in each zone represents the number of professional and managerial workers allocated to each house type in that zone as a percentage of the total number of professional and managerial workers residing in each zone. Once again, the solid line represents values observed in the sample census data, and the pecked line the model predictions of those values. A pecked line appearing above a solid line indicates that the model is over-predicting the allocation of professional and managerial workers to each house type, and *vice versa*. The gap between the pecked and solid lines represents the percentage error between predicted and observed values. Equivalent results are presented in figure 13 for white collar workers, and in figure 14 for blue collar workers.

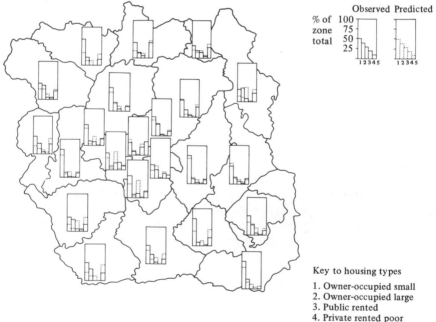

Figure 12. Allocation of professional workers to house types in each zone.

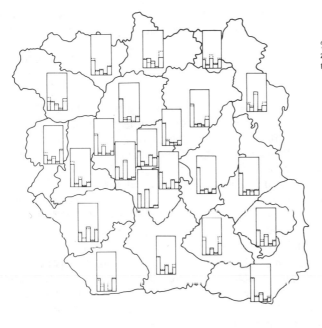

Figure 13. Allocation of white collar workers to house types in each zone.

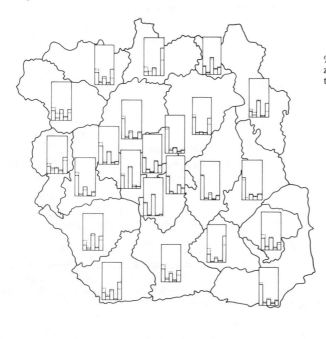

Figure 14. Allocation of blue collar workers to house types in each zone.

The detailed analysis of how well the model has performed in this respect in each of 23 zones would lengthen this paper beyond the endurance of both the reader and the writers. The detailed examination of figure 12, 13, and 14 by the reader will enable him to judge this for himself.

9 Some conclusions

The sub-title of this paper is "Some preliminary results" and this is of considerable relevance to the kind of conclusions one can draw at this stage of the work. Interpretation of the performance of the model reported here is bedevilled by many of the taxonomical and measurement problems discussed at many points in the paper, and since the results given here are the outcome of our preliminary runs of the model it would be premature to even attempt sound judgements of its merits. As suggested earlier, some of the results achieved, particularly with regard to the value of the μ parameter, could be quite spurious for these reasons.

Much work remains to be done in our own research in at least two directions. Firstly, an adequate statistical analysis of the properties of the data we are dealing with needs to be completed. Various multivariate procedures are being pursued to achieve a better taxonomy with the set of data available to us of both worker groups and housing sub-markets. This alone could improve the performance of the model.

Secondly, alternative forms of a residential location model also capable of handling in an operational sense the spatial structure of housing markets, may need to be pursued.

For urban and regional science, two prospects are opened up by the successful conclusion of the kind of experiment reported here:
1) the incorporation of better operational models of residential location in more extensive models of the city and region; and
2) a better understanding of the spatial organisation of housing markets, incorporating an explicit recognition of multiple centres in sub-regions.

As to whether a truly operational tool, from the urban planner's and policy maker's point of view, is likely to emerge, is not yet clear. Our first impressions are that much will depend on whether the data base most readily available to him will permit the kind of differentiation of households required to isolate the most pressing problems in the spatial organisation of housing markets. No doubt we cannot solve his problems, but we may be able to say more about whether he has enough information to ask the questions.

Acknowledgements. The authors would like to acknowledge the invaluable help of Miss Jane Sugden on many aspects of the work reported in this paper, namely in data collection and the preparation of diagrams. They would also like to thank Michael Batty for his help in calibration of the model.

References

Alonso, W., 1964, *Location and Land Use—Towards a General Theory of Land Rent* (Harvard University Press, Cambridge, Massachusetts).

Batty, M., 1971, "A note on the calibration of a retail location model using Hyman's method", Working Note, Urban Systems Research Unit, Department of Geography, University of Reading (mimeo).

Caulfield, I. G., 1970, "The development of the house condition models", *Journal of the Town Planning Institute*, **56**, 220-224.

Dawson, R. F. F., 1968, *The Economic Assessment of Road Improvement Schemes*, Road Research Laboratory, Tech. Paper No.75 (HMSO, London).

Department of Employment and Productivity, 1969, "The distribution of earnings by occupation, September 1968", *Employment and Productivity Gazette* (HMSO, London).

Goldner, W., 1971, "The Lowry model heritage", *Journal of the American Institute of Planners*, **37**, 100-110.

Harris, B., Nathanson, J., Rosenburg, L., 1966, "Research on an equilibrium model of metropolitan housing and locational choice", Interim Report, Institute for Environmental Studies, Graduate School of Fine Arts, University of Pennsylvania.

Herbert, J. D., Stevens, B., 1960, "A model for the distribution of residential activity in urban areas", *Journal of Regional Science*, **2**, 21-36.

Hyman, G. M., 1969, "The calibration of trip distribution models", *Environment and Planning*, **1**, 105-112.

Institute for Municipal Treasurers and Accountants, 1968, *Housing Statistics (England and Wales) 1966-1967*, London.

Lowry, I. S., 1964, *A Model of Metropolis*, Rand Corporation, RM-403-RC, Santa Monica.

Ministry of Labour, 1967, *Family Expenditure Survey* (HMSO, London).

Muth, R., 1969, "Equilibrium of the household", in *Cities in Housing* (University of Chicago Press, Chicago).

Wilson, A. G., 1970, *Entropy in Urban and Regional Modelling*, Chapter 4 "Location models" (Pion, London), pp.63-86.

Wingo, L., 1961, "An economic model of the utilisation of urban land for residential purposes", *Papers, Regional Science Association*, **7**, 191-205.

A Comparative Study of Transportation in Major Cities: Some Preliminary Results [†]

SANDRA KENDALL, B.G.REDDING, R.B.SMYTH
Planning and Transportation Department, Greater London Council

Introduction

This paper presents the preliminary findings of two projects currently underway in the Planning and Transportation Department of the Greater London Council (GLC). The first is a comparative study of the transport-related urban characteristics of the world's largest cities, with the object of comparing the London transportation situation with the experience and range of alternatives offered by different places. The second project involves the detailed study of traffic generation by individual developments, and a comparison of facts and figures from various cities.

The selection of cities for the comparative study is based on criteria dictated in part by the aim of comparing the GLC with other urban areas. The first criterion, that the selection should include cities with a regional population of at least one million, was generally adhered to with some special exceptions; this is because the study is not intended to be an analysis in which population size plays a significant role. The second criterion deals with the stage of developments: places with very low car ownership, and therefore different types of transportation congestion, are excluded. Thirdly, while the availability of information should not ideally play an important role in the selection process, it nevertheless becomes one of the chief constraints.

The areal definition of cities plays an all-important role in a comparative study of this type, for the factors that affect transportation patterns and decisions are closely related to the structure of cities and to the implied distribution of population and employment. Therefore, wherever possible, population and employment data were collected for the 'central city' and 'urban region', after careful definition of these areas, so that a meaningful comparison with the GLC area could be made. The non-availability of census information limited the definition of some cities to one areal unit, as in the case of Australian and German cities studied, and similar lack of suitable transportation data also limited the definition of most cities. It should be noted that, for many cities, data for the 'extended urban region' were also used for comparative purposes; this areal unit is particularly important where the urban region is tightly defined (e.g. London), and further data are needed to show the degree of growth taking place beyond the contiguous built-up area.

[†] The views reported in this paper are attributable only to the authors and not to the Greater London Council by whom they are, or were, employed.

The figures in tables 1 and 2 show that it has been impossible to achieve a complete comparison for all countries. Generally, 30–50% of the population is concentrated in the central city area which includes 10–30% of the total land area of the urban region. There are a few extreme variations in Tokyo, Dallas, and Houston, which have much higher proportions of the urban population in the city centre. For Dallas and Houston, however, as for most of the cities, the relation of the percentages to one another is fairly consistent, that is 20–30% more population than area, with the two outstanding exceptions being Tokyo and Los Angeles. Density figures for both the central city and urban region show enormous but not unexpected variations. Paris has the greatest density of residents in the central city at 67000 people per square mile, followed by Tokyo and Osaka with 40000, and London, New York, and Montreal with between 20000 and 26000. However, these densities are sustained over land areas that vary greatly in size. It is difficult to know what proportion of the observed variations, e.g. in density, is attributable to errors in the area definition and what is due to intrinsically different characteristics of the cities themselves. Therefore it is important to bear in mind these points of definition, for they provide an insight into the structure of the cities and are an essential background for valid comparisons.

Some comparisons among cities
Tables 1–7 (at the end of this article) show some of the data collected for this study. Since the analysis of this and other data is not complete, the following comments are limited to some of the salient points indicated so far. One of the most uniform facts is the trend towards a decrease in the population of the city centre and an increase in the population of that part of the urban region outside the central city. Almost every city centre that did not have a boundary change between 1950 and 1966 has lost population; the major exception is Tokyo which increased in population by 70%. Over a similar period a slight decrease in the number of jobs in the city centre has also been reported. Here again Tokyo is the exception.

These trends have very important and conflicting implications for transportation planning. Firstly, the employment imbalance is growing as the population is moving out faster than the jobs, creating an even greater demand for radially orientated transport routes. Secondly, as employment tends to move out to the suburban areas, the demand for non-radial transport routes will grow. Unless the balance of employment concentration is accurately predicted, investment in radial routes for the short term may be misplaced since long-term considerations suggest that other routes will become more important.

While employment location tends to be similar for Europe and North America, the mode of journey to work shows sharp differences. With the exception of New York, only 35% of the total work trips in any city are made by public transport in North America (even in cities with extensive

rapid transit systems such as Boston and Chicago) compared with a
European average of 60%, the difference being caused mainly by
considerable variations in the level of car ownership. The data indicate
that for most cities these percentages have decreased over the past ten
years, and in many cases the actual numbers have decreased. This trend
seems to be caused by two factors: increasing car ownership and the
effect of trends in employment discussed earlier; these have resulted in a
fall in demand along the radial routes where public transport facilities are
concentrated.

Although there are data to show that population density patterns within
urban regions can be related to car ownership, the relationship is weak
when the regions are compared with one another. The reason for this is
partly because of the difficulty in defining the urban area and partly
because of differences in years for which car ownership figures are
available. However, the percentages of households with no car compared
for the city centre and the urban region differ by a ratio of about 2 : 1
between Europe and North America, based on appropriate national
figures.

A comparison between Paris and London of the percentages of
households with a car is interesting.

	Central city	Inner suburban ring	Outer metropolitan area
Paris	39	49	57
London	31	49	49

It can thus be seen that the high residential densities of central Paris do
not significantly affect car ownership, although the known relatively higher
incomes of residents in Central Paris may counteract density effects. In
all cities car ownership has grown substantially over the past 20 years, and
whilst it has not been possible to collect consistent data on recent growth
for most cities, it has been established that growth rates of 10% per
annum are common in several European and American cities.

One of the strongest relationships to have emerged from the study is the
connection between car ownership and public transport usage. The
figures vary from the one extreme of Seattle, Los Angeles, Dallas, and
Houston, with car ownership at about $0 \cdot 4$ cars per head and public
transport usage at 1–5%, to Glasgow and Tokyo, with car ownership less
than $0 \cdot 1$ cars per head and public transport usage at over 70%.

Traffic generation
We now become more specific and consider traffic generation; this topic
is a part of the comparative study project where more detailed work is
being carried out. The transportation studies that have now become
almost standard include, in their analysis stage, a section where 'traffic
generation by zone' is calculated for each zone in the 'study area'. Zones
may include a mixture of land uses, and the analysis techniques employed

recognise this fact. However, relatively little detailed study on traffic generation by individual development has been reported. Obviously unless a reasonable estimate is made of traffic generated by a major development before it is constructed, it is possible that its location and size may be quite inappropriate in terms of central city redevelopment. For this reason a number of studies of traffic generation by specified land use are currently under way and progress on these is reviewed below.

There are many factors that affect trips generated by any single land use; but these can be conveniently grouped into three categories. The first is the type of use to which the land is put; by its very nature, retail development will attract a far greater number of trips than, say, a comparable area of residential development. But within each broad land use category it is easily seen that the generation of trips will vary considerably, suggesting that the intensity of the development will have considerable importance; this is the second factor. Indeed, not only will some establishments use land area more intensely or efficiently than others, but management and organisational styles will vary in levels of sophistication. These comments may be illustrated by reference to the results of a recent study of two industries in London (Redding, 1971). Establishments in the clothing industry were found to generate three times as many trips in a week per unit floor area as establishments in the electrical engineering industry ($10 \cdot 5$ trips per 1000 square feet floor area compared with $3 \cdot 7$); furthermore, there was a greater tendency for clothing firms to devote their floor area to manufacturing uses and to have high ratios of floor area per employee.

The third category of factors affecting trip generation is the location of the development within the urban area, and its accessibility to road and public transport networks and to complementary activities. For example, premises located in the centre of London were found to generate far more trips than the average for all parts of London; where premises were concentrated in central area locations a high proportion of trips were made by foot. Similar features were identified in a study of industrial activity in Manchester (Millar, 1970). In a recent study of hotel traffic in London the relationship between pedestrian flows and accessibility to public transport was investigated (Redding, 1970). An index of relative accessibility to bus stops and underground stations[1] was derived for each hotel studied and was found to be highly related to pedestrian flows at those hotels.

From a traffic generation viewpoint the central area of the city, with its concentration of many diverse activities, is of critical concern. If we turn attention to this part of the city it is interesting to note how similar the

---

[1] This index was expressed as a function of the square of the number of routes and the frequency of service incorporating a 'decay' factor to simulate lessening accessibility with increasing distance.

trip rates for the central business district of Pittsburgh, a typical expansive city in the USA, are to those for the central area of London, which is typical of the intensively developed city (see table 8). With regard to retail and manufacturing land uses the differences between the two cities may be explained by the relatively new intensive retail developments in the Pittsburgh central district, and the complex and highly diverse system of manufacturing activities established over a considerable time period in the London central area.

A particular problem in London's central area has been the mushrooming hotel development. Large hotels present two distinct traffic situations; first, the normal daily trips associated with the hotel as a place of residence for visitors, and second, the traffic associated with the increasingly more frequent convention or functional activity. This latter type of activity causes the highest fluctuations in traffic flows, and these often occur during periods of the day when road traffic is at its peak. If we consider simply the residential type of traffic, expressed in terms of daily car or taxi trips per 1000 square feet floor area (excluding functional area), a range of $1 \cdot 3$ to $3 \cdot 2$ was found to exist in London, which gave an average of about $2 \cdot 3$ vehicle trips per 1000 square feet in a day. The comparable range for traffic generated by hotels in the USA is larger— between $1 \cdot 2$ and $5 \cdot 0$ daily vehicle trips per 1000 square feet floor area— giving a mid point of $3 \cdot 1$. This higher traffic generation rate is not surprising given the differences in car use and availability of public transport.

The problem of goods vehicle trip generation by retail land uses has recently been receiving some attention in London. Two surveys conducted in London at Wembley and Hammersmith shopping centres provide information on the volume, pattern, and type of generation by commercial vehicles delivering to the different types of shops comprising these two major suburban shopping centres (Metra Consulting Group Ltd., 1970). Hammersmith is a traditional 'high street' type of centre, with deliveries mainly taking place on-street outside the shop frontages; retail turnover remains steady. In contrast, Wembley has the highest rate of increase in

Table 8. Trip generation rates for the central areas of Pittsburgh and London expressed as daily person journeys (destination) per 1000 square feet floor area.

Land use	Pittsburgh[a]	London[b]
Retail	$8 \cdot 1$	$6 \cdot 4$
Manufacturing	$1 \cdot 0$	$5 \cdot 5$
Warehousing	$1 \cdot 2$	$1 \cdot 1$
Offices	$5 \cdot 2$	$4 \cdot 9$
Public buildings	$3 \cdot 9$	$3 \cdot 5$

[a] Source: Wilbur Smith and Associates, 1966, p.27.
[b] Source: London County Council, 1964.

retail turnover for any London shopping centre and incorporates some new traffic-free pedestrian precinct development, which includes vehicles delivering to rear service areas.

The study indicated that the 442000 square feet of shops surveyed at Hammersmith generated an average of 276 deliveries per day, whereas the 463000 square feet of shops in Wembley generated an average of only 218 deliveries per day. Thus Hammersmith averaged 0·62 deliveries per square foot of gross shop floor space per day, where the equivalent average for Wembley was 0·47. This difference was mainly attributable to the presence of larger and newer shops at Wembley, particularly supermarkets, which, because of their requirement for larger orders of goods often placed with fewer wholesalers, made more economical use of delivery vehicles. The average weight of drop per load delivered to Wembley was 1007 lbs compared to only 389 lbs at Hammersmith.

The inference here is that as shops get larger, and perhaps place orders with fewer wholesalers, the loads delivered by each vehicle will be greater and a more economic use of vehicles will be made. Thus the actual number of freight vehicles generated will diminish for a given retail floor area. Some support for this assumption may be derived from traffic generation figures for similar sized American regional shopping centres where larger stores tend to predominate and only about 120 deliveries per day might be expected (Wilbur Smith and Associates, 1965). These differences in the volume of servicing traffic generated by the different types of shopping centres may be accounted for only partly by differences in design and scale of operation. They may also reflect style of management in terms of modern methods of retailing, and policies of ordering goods.

Some conclusions
As already stated, the object of the studies described above is to allow the compilation of facts about transportation in London, and thus to allow a comparison of London with the experience and range of alternatives offered by other major cities. In turn this allows a check on the London situation. So far, the major comparative study project has been most rewarding. The information collected has allowed the establishment of a 'typology' for the various cities, and this provides a base or sifting device prior to more detailed study in specific areas. In the more general work completed so far detailed relationships are cloudy, obscured by the data and definition problems.

The general relationships so established are insufficient for rigorous model building, but do suggest the directions that could be taken in the next stage of the more detailed work. For example, a very positive indication is given that the situation in cities today results as much from historical development as from the interaction of forces currently at play. That is, one element of 'time', 'age', or 'historical development' should be allowed for in urban modelling work.

In the tables which follow, the areal definitions described below are employed.

Australia

Sydney ⎱
Melbourne ⎰   Urban region: Census statistical metropolitan area

Austria

Vienna   Urban region: Census statistical region

Belgium

Brussels   Urban region: Census metropolitan area

Canada

Montreal ⎫
Toronto ⎬   Central city: Census central city
Vancouver ⎭   Urban region: Census metropolitan area

France

Paris   Central city: 'Ville' de Paris
                 Urban region: Census statistical region [agglomeration as defined
                                by the Institute National de le Statistique et les
                                Etudes Economiques (INSEE)]
                 Extended region: Région Parisienne

Germany

Hamburg ⎱
Munich ⎰   Urban region: Census statistical region

Italy

Milan ⎱
Rome ⎰   Urban region: Commune

Japan

Tokyo ⎫
Osaka ⎬   Central city: Central city wards (census)
Nagoya ⎭   Urban region: Prefecture (metropolitan area of census)

Tokyo   Extended region: Prefectures of Tokyo, Karagowa, Saitama, Chiba

Netherlands

Amsterdam   Central city: Census city
Amsterdam   Urban region: Amsterdam region
Rotterdam   Urban region: Census city

Spain

Barcelona ⎱
Madrid   ⎰   Urban region: Municipality

Sweden

Stockholm   Central city: 'Inre' and 'Yttre' Strad
                 Urban region: 'Inre' and 'Yttre' Strad and suburban communes

United Kingdom

London   Central city: 15 London Boroughs: City, Camden, Greenwich,
                                Hackney, Hammersmith, Haringey, Islington,
                                Kensington and Chelsea, Lambeth, Lewisham,
                                Newtham, Southwark, Tower Hamlets, Wandsworth,
                                Westminster
                 Urban region: Greater London Council
                 Extended region: Metropolitan region (GLC and Outer Metropolitan
                                Area)

United Kingdom (contd.)

Birmingham ⎫
Manchester ⎟
Liverpool ⎬ Central city: County Borough
Leeds ⎟ Urban region: Conurbation
Newcastle ⎟
Glasgow ⎭

United States

New York Central city: NY City—5 Boroughs
Urban region: Census urbanised area 1960
Extended region: 23 county metropolitan areas

All other US cities Central city: Census and political central city
Urban region: Census urbanised area 1960
Extended region: Standard Metropolitan Statistical Area

USSR

Moscow Urban region: City of Moscow
Extended region: Moscow region

Table 1. Population statistics for major cities (years given in brackets apply to all cities within the country unless another year is shown).

	Central city		Urban region		% Population in central city
	Population (10^3)	Area $(mile^2)$	Population (10^3)	Area $(mile^2)$	
Sydney			2541 (66)	974	
Melbourne			2231	1933	
Vienna			1642 (68)	159	
Brussels			1077 (68)	63	
Montreal	1222 (66)	58	2436	520	50
Toronto	665	35	2158	799	31
Vancouver	410	43	892	499	46
Paris	2753 (62)	41	7261	560	38
Hamburg			1847 (66)	288	
Munich			1244	120	
Milan			1683 (67)	70	
Rome			2631	582	
Tokyo	8893 (65)	221	10869	783	82
Osaka	3156	78	6657	710	47
Nagoya	1935	125	4799	1953	40
Amsterdam	867 (63)	67	1945	628	46
Rotterdam			900	78	
Barcelona			1761 (67)	154	
Madrid			2765	234	
Stockholm	779 (66)	72	1207	523	64
London	3610 (66)	144	7863	616	46
Birmingham	1064	81	2374	270	45
Manchester	599	43	2404	380	25
Liverpool	691	44	1338	150	52
Leeds	505	64	1708	485	30
Newcastle	249	17	832	90	30
Glasgow	977	61	1766	300	55
New York	7782 (60)	315	14115	1892	55
Los Angeles	2479	455	6489	1370	38
Chicago	3550	222	5959	960	60
Philadelphia	2003	129	3635	597	55
Detroit	1670	138	2528	732	47
San Francisco	740	45	2431	572	31
Boston	697	46	2413	516	29
Washington	764	61	1808	341	42
Pittsburgh	604	55	1804	525	34
Cleveland	876	76	1785	587	49
St Louis	750	61	1668	323	45
Baltimore	939	78	1419	220	66
Houston	938	321	1140	431	82
Buffalo	533	41	1054	160	51
Dallas	680	254	932	647	73
Seattle	557	88	864	238	65
Milwaukee	741	90	1150	392	65
Minneapolis-St.Paul	483	53	1377	657	35
Moscow			6364 (63)	338	

Table 1 (contd.)

% land area in central city	Extended region Population (10^3)	Area (mile^2)	Density Central city	Urban region
				2610
				1156
				10310
				17090
11			21095	4687
4			19009	2700
9			9470	1786
7	8470	4660	67140	13000
				6440
				9850
				24000
				4570
28	15511	2383	40239	13880
11			40400	9376
6			15500	2457
11			12900	3110
				11510
				11436
				11810
14			10819	2300
23	12603	4412	25069	12760
30			13135	8792
11			13930	6326
29			15704	8920
13			7890	3520
19			14647	9244
20			16015	5880
16	17760 (65)	23 counties	25950	7462
33	6789 (66)	4069	5447	4736
23	6732	3720	16014	6209
22	4690	3553	15584	6092
19	4060	1952	12103	4834
8	2958	1300	15553	4253
9	3201	1769	15157	4679
18	2615	2352	12442	5308
10	2376	3049	10968	3437
13	2004	1519	11542	3042
19	2284	4118	12255	5160
35	1980	2259	12520	6441
76	1740	6286	2923	2647
24	1323	1591	12869	6582
43	1352	4564	2676	1441
38	1214	4229	6810	3626
23	1331	1456	8255	2934
17	1629	2107	9043	2095
	9077 (59)	5666		18800

Table 2. Employment in major cities (dates correspond to those given in table 1).

	Employment in urban region	Percent employment in city centre	Percent urban region employment in manufacturing industry
Sydney	1113		34
Melbourne	947		38
Vienna	821		35
Brussels	441		26
Montreal	807		33
Toronto	790		31
Vancouver	295		21
Paris	3491	56	36
Hamburg	1006		31
Munich	656		33
Milan	754		45
Rome	830		20
Tokyo	5309	90	33
Osaka	1634		38
Nagoya	972		36
Amsterdam			
Rotterdam	280		27
Barcelona	657		38
Madrid	906		23
Stockholm	523		22
London	4429	61	32
Birmingham	1261	50	57
Manchester	1204	32	48
Liverpool	609	61	33
Leeds	829	31	49
Newcastle	400	42	37
Glasgow	816	57	40
New York	6059	55	29
Los Angeles	2685	38	31
Chicago	2519	59	35
Philadelphia	1470	54	35
Detroit	1365	45	41
San Francisco	1012	33	21
Boston	approx. 1000	50	29
Washington	753	45	8
Pittsburgh	689	32	36
Cleveland	731	46	39
St Louis	660	45	32
Baltimore	594	63	26
Houston	454	80	21
Buffalo	418	47	38
Dallas	398	36	22
Seattle	358	64	27
Milwaukee	473	38	41
Minneapolis-St.Paul	562	40	26
Moscow			

Table 3. Car ownership and transit rides in major cities.

	Surface transit rides *per capita* in one year	Cars *per capita*[a]
Sydney	99	0·23
Melbourne	80	0·24
Vienna	238	0·13
Brussels	248	0·14
Montreal	148	0·24
Toronto	134	0·34
Vancouver		0·34
Paris	97	0·20
Hamburg	93	0·20
Munich	219	0·16
Milan	327	0·19
Rome	302	0·18
Tokyo	76	0·06
Osaka	213	0·02
Nagoya	289	0·04
Amsterdam	166	0·12
Rotterdam	160	0·10
Barcelona	155	0·12
Madrid	179	0·14
Stockholm	125	0·20
London	173	0·14
Birmingham	336	0·14
Manchester	285	0·14
Liverpool	278	0·12
Leeds	342	0·14
Newcastle		
Glasgow	233	0·09
New York	59	0·23
Los Angeles	21	0·39
Chicago	65	0·26
Philadelphia	59	0·27
Detroit	37	0·28
San Francisco	91 (underestimated)	0·34
Boston	(74)	0·26
Washington	96	0·29
Pittsburgh	50	0·27
Cleveland	45	0·34
St Louis	43	0·35
Baltimore	69	0·27
Houston	28	0·37
Buffalo	48	0·25
Dallas	34	0·40
Seattle	41	0·38
Milwaukee		0·32
Minneapolis-St.Paul		0·32
Moscow	344	

[a] These apply to Transportation Study Areas and years where these areas are quoted in other tables. Otherwise they apply to approx. 1964.

Table 4. Rapid transit, data for 1968 or nearest year available.

	Route (miles approx.)	Route (miles in tunnel)	Average distance between stations (miles)	Number of stations served	Number of cars operated	Average speed including stops (mph)
New York	237	137[a]	0·5	486	7287	20
Chicago	85	9	0·5	136	1159	22
Philadelphia	29	18	0·5	61	548	17
San Francisco	74		2·2	38		45
Boston	23	11	0·6	41	280	19
Cleveland	15	0	1·1	14	88	30
London	257	90	0·8	231	4000	20
Glasgow	6·5	all	0·4	15	46	14
Stockholm	39	16	0·5	68	658	20
Brussels	2·5[b]	all		6		
Paris	127	most	0·3	368	3415	14
Moscow	87		1·0	86		25
Hamburg	52	15	0·7	73		18
Barcelona	18	most	0·4	44	114	
Madrid	25	all	0·3	69	554	
Tokyo	63	most	0·6	86	1000	
Osaka	29	24	0·7	44	438	
Nagoya	10	all	0·5	17		20
Rotterdam	5					
Montreal	16	all	0·5	26	369	20[d]
Toronto	21	17	0·5	45	334	19
Vienna	16·6		0·6	25		
Rome	6·8	3·7	0·6	11	40	25
Milan	8·8	all	0·4	24	138	19

Other cities with plans for rapid transit systems are: Los Angeles, Detroit, Washington, Pittsburgh, St Louis, Baltimore, and Seattle in USA, and Munich and Amsterdam in Europe.

Table 4 (contd.)

Average trip length (miles)	Lane miles (per 10^6 population)	Number of passengers carried (10^6 pa)	Vehicle miles (10^6 pa)	Rides *per capita* for 1 year	Plans projection of route (miles)	Comments on plans
6·5		1360	328	97		extensions planned
5·9	22	120	45	20	+15	
7·5	15	77	-	21	+12	
	28	96		40	+30	by 1990
	17	18		10	+4	
4·5	31	655	216	63 (LTB)[e] 83 (GLC)		extensions planned
2·0	6	19		11		
3·6	42	180	25	149		some under construction, further plans
					+23	trams at first, then Metro system using same track
3·3	37	1087	112	150	+29?	
4·3	18	1502		236		some under construction, further plans
4·4	19	173	30	94	+11?	
3·1	6·2	197[c]		122	+32	
2·2	13	408	26	147	+20	
4·0		910		90	+36	8 miles under construction
2·5		454	21	76	+42	
		120		30	+40	
						some under construction
		125	33	51		
		136	16	63	+4	under construction
	10	76		46		
4·2	3	19		7	+9	under construction
		57		34	+5	

[a] Also 80 miles elevated track. [b] Trams. [c] Estimated for 3 out of 4 lines.
[d] Express = 30 mph. [e] LTB = London Transport Board.

Table 5. Transportation study areas: population and area.

	Year of study	Popn	Area (miles^2)	Percent popn change ('50-'60)	Popn density study year	Popn fore-cast	Year of projection
Toronto	1964	2730	3190	50[a]	856	4200	1980
Paris	1962	8469	3109	20[a]	2724	11600	1985
Rome	1966	2631	582	33[a]	4520	3780	1985
Tokyo	1965	27000		42[b]		33100	1975
London	1962	8506	941	7[c]	9039	7800	1981
Birmingham	1964	2529	376	~0[a]	6726	2671	1981
Manchester	1965	2596	413	~0[a]	6286	2707	1981
Liverpool	1966	1419	158	~0[a]	8981		
Leeds	1966	2099	1000		2099	2700	2001
Glasgow	1964	1929	454		4249		1990
New York	1963	16287	3660	12[d]	4450	21000	1985
Los Angeles	1960	8000	9000	54	842	14000	1980
Chicago	1956	5170	1237	20	4179	8053	1980
Philadelphia	1960	3936	1175	18	3350	5361	1985
Detroit	1953	2969	709	25	4180	5986	1980
San Francisco	1965	4336	7000	24	6194	5471	1990
Boston	1963	3524	2369	7	1513	3924	1975
Washington	1955	1569	2353	37	667	4032	1980
Pittsburgh	1958	1470	420	9	3500	1902	1980
Cleveland	1963	2200	1450	23	1517	3562	1990
St Louis	1965	2169	1673	20	1290	3620	1990
Baltimore	1962	1608	860	23	1869	2161	1980
Houston	1953	1159	612	54	1892	2225	1980
Buffalo	1962	1263	810	20	1557	1811	1985
Dallas	1964	1156	908	46	1273	2566	1985
Seattle	1961	1322	986	31	1341	2384	1985
Milwaukee	1963	1674	2628	25	609	2678	1990
Minneapolis-St.Paul	1958	1377	890	29	1547	2675	1980

[a] Study Area.
[b] Urban region.
[c] Metropolitan region.
[d] Standard Metropolitan Statistical Area.

Table 6. Analysis of trip purpose over 24 hours in Study Area.

	Home (%)	Work (%)	Shop (%)	School (%)	Social recreational (%)	Other (%)
Toronto	43	24			9	24
Paris	44	30	5		4	10
Rome	47	31	4	7		10
Tokyo	41	27	12	9	11	
London	42	28	11		7	9
Birmingham						
Manchester	40	35	5	4	10	6
Liverpool	40	26	5	5	9	16
Glasgow						
New York	38	21	8	5	6	21
Los Angeles						
Chicago	44	21	6	2	13	15
Philadelphia	38	20	9	3	13	18
Detroit	40	24	8	3	12	13
San Francisco	40	17	10	4	5	24
Boston	36	18	11	5	10	20
Washington	42	23	8	4	7	
Pittsburgh	43	21	8	6	8	
Cleveland						
St Louis	41	21	11	3	12	
Baltimore						
Houston	40	19	10	5	11	
Buffalo	42	18	12	5	16	7
Dallas	38	15	12	5	11	19
Seattle	41	18	11	5	10	15
Milwaukee	39	17	11	3		30
Minneapolis-St.Paul	40	18	11	4	9	18

Table 7. Trip generation, car ownership, and modal split (internal trips over 24 hours).

	Total trips	Trips *per capita*	Car ownership *per capita* forecast	Growth 196 – 8 (% pa)
		Study year		
Toronto	3962	1·5	a	
Paris	10963	1·3	0·42	5·2
Rome	3093	1·2	0·38	7·0
Tokyo	48000	1·7		
London	11332	1·3	0·28	4·7
Birmingham	3229	1·3	0·31	7·1
Manchester	4175	1·6	0·24	4·4
Liverpool	1745	1·2	0·21	5·1
Leeds			0·22	3·8
Glasgow	2442	1·3		
New York	29570	1·8	0·34	2·2
Los Angeles	18199	2·3	0·46	0·9
Chicago	9590	1·8	0·33	1·1
Philadelphia	8013	2·0	0·29	
Detroit	6277	2·1	0·31	
San Francisco	9886	2·3		
Boston	7477	2·1	0·34	2·6
Washington	2397	1·5		
Pittsburgh	2400	1·6	0·34	1·2
Cleveland	4777	2·2	0·44	1·1
St Louis	3557	1·7		
Baltimore	2604	1·6	0·34	1·4
Houston	2457	2·1	0·49	1·6
Buffalo	2755	2·2	0·37	1·4
Dallas	3291	2·8	0·53	1·6
Seattle	2956	2·2	0·47	1·0
Milwaukee	3611	2·2		
Minneapolis-St.Paul	3366	2·4		

[a] Forecasts for Toronto, Chicago, Philadelphia and Detroit already show evidence of under-estimation.
[b] In some cases the percentages do not add up to 100. This is because 'other' trips such as motorcycle trips have been separately categorized.

Percent in central city + no car	Percent in urbanized area + no car	Study year		Public transport (%)
		auto driver (%)	auto passenger (%)	
	27	67		33
61	51	35		48[b]
		44		56
69	58	32	11	51
	57	36	14	47
	64	33	16	46
	61	29	14	53
	65			
		20	8	72
58	41	45	19	34
22	16	67	32	1
40	30	48	28	25
44	31	54	27	16
28	18	57	26	17
47	25	63	27	10
47	28	57	25	19
47	27			
39	26			
32	20	62	27	11
39	26			
41	31	56	27	18
19	17	61	34	5
34	24	58	31	8
18	15	64	32	4
26	20	63	33	4
28	22	60	27	9
27	18	58	29	13

References

Articles which have actually been cited in the text are marked ●

Automobile Manufacturers' Association, 1969, "Automobile facts and figures",
Detroit, Michigan.

Automotive Safety Foundation, 1968, "Urban transit development in 20 major cities",
Washington, D.C.

Bottiny, W. H., 1965, "Trends in automobile ownership and indicators of saturation",
Highway Research Record, Number 106, pp.1-21.

Colin Buchanan and Partners, 1969, "The conurbations", British Road Federation,
London.

Bureau of Public Roads, 1969, "Urban transportation planning data", Washington, D.C.

Dallimore, D. C., Robertson, J., Bagnall, S., 1970, "Freight deliveries to shops in
Wembley, an analysis of duration and delays", RM 248, GLC Department of
Planning and Transportation, London.

Davis, K., 1959, *The World's Metropolitan Areas* (California University Press,
California).

Ganz, A., 1968, *Emerging Patterns of Urban Growth and Travel* (MIT Press,
Cambridge, Mass.).

Greater London Council, 1968, "The generation of business traffic in central
London", GLC Department of Planning and Transportation, London.

Hall, P., 1966, *The World Cities* (Weidenfeld and Nicholson, London).

Institute of Traffic Engineering, 1965, "Traffic engineering handbook", Washington
D.C.

International Statistical Institute, 1968, *International Statistical Yearbook of Large
Towns,* The Hague, Holland.

Jane's World Railways 1969-1970, 1969, 12th edition (S. Low, London).

Kanwit, E. L., Eckartt, A. F., 1966, "Transportation implications of employment
trends in central cities and suburbs", *Highway Research Record,* Number 187,
pp.1-14.

London County Council, 1964., *London Traffic Survey,* volume 1.

●Metra Consulting Group Ltd., 1970, *Study of Generation of Goods Vehicles
Movements in Selected Town Centres, Volumes 1-4,* London.

Meyer, J. R., Kain, J. F., Wohl, M., 1965, *The Urban Transportation Problem* (MIT
Press, Cambridge, Mass.).

●Millar, J. S., 1970, *Industry and Wholesale Distribution in Manchester,* Manchester
City Planning Department. See also *Journal Town Planning Institute,* **56** (9),
384-388.

Pickard, J. P., 1967, "Dimensions of metropolitanism", Urban Land Institute,
Washington, D.C.

●Redding, B. G., 1970, "Traffic generation of hotels in central London", RM 234,
GLC Department of Planning and Transportation, London.

●Redding, B. G., 1971, "A study of industrial traffic generation in London", RM 292,
GLC Department of Planning and Transportation, London.

Robson, W. A., 1969, "Second report on Tokyo metropolitan government", London
School of Economics, London.

Thomas, R., 1968, "Journeys to work", *Political Economic Planning,* **34,** Number 504
Planning.

A. M. Voorhees and Associates Inc., 1969, "Factors and trends in trip lengths",
National Cooperative Highway Research Project 7-4, Washington, D.C.

●Wilbur Smith and Associates, 1965, an unpublished design document on servicing
traffic generation at regional shopping centres in the USA, New Haven, Conn.

●Wilbur Smith and Associates, 1966, "Transportation and parking for tomorrow's
cities", New Haven, Conn.

The Distribution of Social Groups within Cities: Models and Accounts

P.H.REES
University of Leeds

Introduction

Work on the spatial distribution of social groups in cities has been very largely descriptive of pattern, or concerned with the modelling of group distributions at a point in time. Much of the work in social area analysis (Shevky and Williams, 1949), factorial ecology (Rees, 1970), and residential location modelling (Wilson, 1971a, 1971b) might be described as cross-sectional in orientation. The time oriented work on social patterns has consisted of comparing cross-sectional pictures at different points in time, or in simple pattern analyses of changes (Murdie, 1969; Brown and Horton, 1970). Most authors of cross-sectional or cross-temporal studies of social group distribution are concerned with interpreting their pattern results in terms of the dynamic processes that go on in the city (residential choice, city growth, neighbourhood change, and so on). This work has provided some valuable insights into the nature of the social geographies of contemporary Western cities, but pattern tests of processes at work are unlikely to be conclusive because of the problem of equifinality. The same pattern may have resulted from more than one process.

It is the intention of this paper to speculate about ways in which our social group distribution models can be made more dynamic in content, and can incorporate devices which will measure the kind of processes that everyday observation tells us are going on in the city. To make these speculations the paper draws heavily from previous work on dynamic models—in particular, the work of Forrester (1969) and his associates on the *Urban Dynamics* model, the work of Wilson (1971a and 1971b) on demographic and migration models, and the work of Stone (1971) on demographic accounting and modelling.

Forrester's urban dynamics model

Though at first reading the model developed by Forrester (1969) does not look like a model of social group distribution, it does contain features which would valuably be incorporated into a dynamic version of a social group model. It can be regarded as a species of social group model in that it attempts to predict, albeit for one zone, the size of some three social groups—professionals and managers, labour, and the underemployed (the underemployed include people who are unemployed and workers in poorly paid dead-end jobs).

The valuable features of the *Urban Dynamics* model are several.
1. It links together the principal sectors of the urban system—people, housing, and economic activity—in a series of equations which transmit changes in one sector through to the other sectors over a period of time.
2. It attempts to describe how migration takes place into and out of the urban system for the three social groups considered (managerial-professional, labour, and the underemployed).
3. It describes how workers move from one category to another. In other words it incorporates the mechanism of social mobility into a model of the urban system.
4. It incorporates the process of business and structure aging which lies behind many urban problems. The aging of housing structures and associated condition changes are the basis for the process of filtering in the housing market.
5. It includes a sub-model for the generation of new businesses and jobs in the city upon which the ultimate social health of the urban system must depend.

At the heart of the Forrester model are sets of equations which express the numbers in a social group or housing type at a point in time (the stock) as the sum of the stock at a previous point in time plus the flows into and out of that stock over the intervening period. For example, the size of the underemployed group is given by the following equation (Forrester's equation 16,L)

$$U.K = U.J + (DT)(UA.JK + UB.JK + LTU.JK - UD.JK - UTL.JK) , \qquad (1)$$

where
U.K is the number of underemployed (men) at time K;
U.J is the number of underemployed (men) at time J;
DT is the time interval (in years);
UA.JK is the number of underemployed arrivals (men/year) rate in the period from J to K;
UB.JK is the number of underemployed 'births' (really births less deaths) (men/year) rate in the period J to K;
LTU.JK is the labour to underemployed mobility rate (men/year) in period J to K;
UD.JK is the number of underemployed departures (men/year) rate in the period J to K;
UTL.JK is the underemployed to labour mobility rate (men/year) in period J to K.

All the *Urban Dynamics* model equations are expressed in the DYNAMO programming language. It would be useful to examine what they would look like in more standard mathematical notation, and thus to demonstrate the links between Forrester's equations and those of the demographic models discussed later in the paper. We can express the first equation as follows;

for the population of persons in the underemployed category W_u:

$$W_u^I(t+T) = W_u^I(t) + \left(\frac{T}{\tau}\right)[m_{uu}^{RI}(t,t+T,\tau) + g_u^I(t,t+T,\tau) + s_{lu}^{II}(t,t+T,\tau)$$

$$- m_{uu}^{IR}(t,t+T,\tau) - s_{ul}^{II}(t,t+T,\tau)] . \qquad (2)$$

The term $W_u^I(t+T)$ refers to the number of underemployed in zone I (Forrester's urban area—the inner central city of the American metropolis) at time $t+T$, the end point of the period under consideration. The corresponding number at the beginning of the period is $W_u^I(t)$, and to this is added the net change in the number of underemployed over the period $(t, t+T)$. The net change part of equation (2) is made up of a length of time, T, expressed in integral numbers of years by dividing by τ, a length of time equal to one year, multiplied by a set of five time-dependent flow-rates [1]. The first of these, $m_{uu}^{RI}(t, t+T, \tau)$, represents the flow-rate of migration of persons from category u (the underemployed) in zone R (the rest of the world, or the environment as Forrester calls it) into category u in zone I per time period τ. This period τ is a year in the Forrester model but could be any length in principle, being linked to the T period by the simple relationship $n\tau = T$. This migration flow-rate is characteristic of the historical or future time period $(t, t+T)$.

The term $g_u^I(t, t+T, \tau)$ corresponds to the 'births' term of equation (1) and is the flow-rate of natural increase (or decrease) of persons in category u in zone I per time period τ, a rate which is characteristic of the period $(t, t+T)$. The flow-rate of natural increase g is, in fact, made up of the birth flow-rate less the death flow-rate:

$$g_u^I(t, t+T, \tau) = b_u^I(t, t+T, \tau) - d_u^I(t, t+T, \tau) , \qquad (3)$$

where $b_u^I(t, t+T, \tau)$ is the birth flow-rate of persons into category u, the underemployed in zone I per time period τ, a rate which is characteristic of the period $(t, t+T)$. These births are not births in the obstetric sense but rather are additions to the labour force from states outside the labour force, mainly from persons in full-time education or inactive in the labour market. Births in this sense may also be migrations from a non-labour force state in the rest of the world to the underemployed state in the urban area. The $d_u^I(t, t+T, \tau)$ component is the death flow-rate of persons in category u in zone I per time period. This flow-rate is characteristic of the period $(t, t+T)$. The deaths referred to in the death flow-rate may be deaths in the ordinary sense, or they may be either retirements from the labour force at a specific retirement age or drop-outs to the inactive category (women getting married and becoming housewives and mothers).

[1] Forrester uses the term 'rate' for his variables, but they are in the nature of flows of persons per unit time rather than rates expressed in relation to base populations.

Downward social mobility is captured in the $s_{lu}^{II}(t, t+T, \tau)$ term of equation (2): this is the flow-rate per time period τ of persons who 'survive' the transition from the labour class to the underemployed class, accomplishing the transition within zone I. The flow-rate is characteristic of the period $(t, t+T)$. Upward social mobility is represented in the other survival flow-rate term, $s_{ul}^{II}(t, t+T, \tau)$, in which the order of the labour and underemployed subscripts is reversed. Finally, the flow-rate of persons out-migrating from the urban area is given by the component term $m_{uu}^{IR}(t, t+T, \tau)$, which is defined in the same way as the first migration flow-rate term except that the urban area and environment superscripts have been reversed.

Equations (1) and (2) are model equations in the sense that the flow-rates incorporated in the net change portions of the right-hand side are the predicted outcomes of other equations. However, before examining the nature of these equations in the underemployed case, it would be useful to spell out what equation (2) would look like in an accounting form, that is with the flows themselves explicitly represented. We can define the flow-rates in the following way:

$$m_{uu}^{RI}(t, t+T, \tau) = \frac{M_{uu}^{RI}(t, t+T)}{T/\tau} , \tag{4}$$

$$g_u^I(t, t+T, \tau) = \frac{G_u^I(t, t+T)}{T/\tau} , \tag{5}$$

$$s_{lu}^{II}(t, t+T, \tau) = \frac{S_{lu}^{II}(t, t+T)}{T/\tau} , \tag{6}$$

$$m_{uu}^{IR}(t, t+T, \tau) = \frac{M_{uu}^{IR}(t, t+T)}{T/\tau} , \tag{7}$$

$$s_{ul}^{II}(t, t+T, \tau) = \frac{S_{ul}^{II}(t, t+T)}{T/\tau} . \tag{8}$$

The upper case variables on the right hand side of equations (4) to (8) are the flow equivalents of each of the flow-rates defined above. In Forrester's *Urban Dynamics* such flows do not appear because the simulation is a purely hypothetical one—there is no attempt to link the model with a real city, in order to calibrate and test it. But, if we are to build a satisfactory model of the distribution of social groups within cities, this must be done. A first and essential step would be to produce the information needed in the following accounting version of equation (2):

$$W_u^I(t+T) = W_u^I(t) + M_{uu}^{RI}(t, t+T) + G_u^I(t, t+T) + S_{lu}^{II}(t, t+T)$$
$$- M_{uu}^{IR}(t, t+T) - S_{ul}^{II}(t, t+T) . \tag{9}$$

One may note, at this juncture, that this equation is an identity only under certain special conditions (for example, no flow from the underemployed category to the managerial–professional category, and no flow in the opposite direction). Later in the paper a more complete and general specification of the social class accounting equation is made.

Each of the terms in parentheses in equation (1) in Forrester's work is dependent on further model equations. Here we will just examine the underemployed arrivals flow-rate (the in-migration flow rate), a crucial variable in a model of the changing distribution of a population group in a city.

The underemployed arrivals flow-rate is given by Forrester's equation 1,R:

$$UA.KL = (U.K + L.K)(UAN)(AMMP.K) , \qquad (10)$$

where

U.K is the number of underemployed (men) at time K:
L.K is the amount of labour (men) at time K;
UAN is the underemployed arrivals normal (fraction per year);
AMMP.K is the attractiveness-for-migration multiplier perceived (dimensionless).

What this equation says is that the number of in-migrants to the urban area is a product of the stock levels of persons in the underemployed *and* labour categories, the normal propensity to in-migrate, and a factor which measures the attractiveness of the urban area to underemployed persons in the environment.

We can re-express the equation in our revised notation and examine the nature of the relationships proposed in the equation in more detail:

$$M_{uu}^{RI}(t, t+T, \tau) = [W_u^I(t) + W_l^I(t)][m_{uu}^{RI}(\tau)][AMMP_u^I(t)] , \qquad (11)$$

where $W_l^I(t)$ is the number of men in the labour class in the urban area (zone I) at time t, and $AMMP_u^I(t)$ is the attractiveness-for-migration multiplier perceived at time t. This variable measures the attractiveness of zone I for group u and is given a value in another model equation. The $m_{uu}^{RI}(\tau)$ refers to the propensity of persons in the underemployed category, u, to migrate from the environment, zone R, to the urban area, zone I, in a time period τ in length (one year in Forrester's case). The propensity is defined as the fraction or multiple of some population exposed to the possibility of migration. In the *Urban Dynamics* model this base population is defined as the population of the destination zone, the urban area, and the $m_{uu}^{RI}(\tau)$ can therefore be defined in the situation where one is concerned with empirical verification of the model as

$$m_{uu}^{RI}(\tau) = \frac{M_{uu}^{RI}(t, t+\tau)}{W_u^I(t) + W_l^I(t)} . \qquad (12)$$

The observed migration flow M_{uu}^{RI} takes place over a particular time period $(t, t+\tau)$ of length τ (one year in the *Urban Dynamics* model). The flow-rate defined in equation (4) is linked, in the empirical case, to the propensity to in-migrate by the following relation,

$$m_{uu}^{RI}(t, t+T, \tau) = \frac{1}{T/\tau} \sum_{v=t}^{T-\tau} \{[W_u^I(v) + W_1^I(v)]m_{uu}^{RI}(v, v+\tau, \tau)\}, \tag{13}$$

where we use v rather than t to indicate points in time on the right hand side of the equation, in order to be able to sum up the separate periods that make up the longer $(t, t+T)$ period.

The attractiveness-for-migration multiplier in equations (10) and (11) is dependent on further variables (Forrester's equation 2,L):

$$\text{AMMP.K} = \text{AMMP.J} + \frac{\text{DT}}{\text{AMMP.J}}(\text{AMM.J} - \text{AMMP.J}), \tag{14}$$

where

AMMP.K is the attractiveness-for-migration multiplier perceived (dimensionless) at time K;

AMMP.J is the attractiveness-for-migration multiplier perceived (dimensionless) at time J;

AMMPT is the attractiveness-for-migration multiplier perception time (years);

AMM.J is the attractiveness-for-migration multiplier (dimensionless) at time J.

In our revised notation this becomes

$$\text{AMMP}_u^I(t+T) = \text{AMMP}_u^I(t) + \frac{T/\tau}{\text{AMMPT}}[\text{AMM}_u^I(t) - \text{AMMP}_u^I(t)]. \tag{15}$$

The attractiveness of zone I for underemployed in-migrants at time $t+T$ is equal to its old attractiveness at time t, plus the change in attractiveness over the period represented by people's perceptions catching up with the 'reality' of the situation. The 'reality' of the situation—the attractiveness of the urban area, zone I, for migrants—is a function of the housing available in the zone for underemployed, of the amount being spent from public funds on the underemployed, of the number of jobs available there, of the size of any program of public housing in the urban area, and finally of the attractiveness of the area accruing from other factors (its image, for example). In the DYNAMO language, the attractiveness of the urban area is expressed thus (Forrester's equation 3,A):

$$\text{AMM.K} = (\text{UAMM.K})(\text{UHM.K})(\text{PEM.K})(\text{UJM.K})(\text{UHPM.K})(\text{AMF}) \tag{16}$$

where

AMM.K is the attractiveness-for-migration multiplier (dimensionless) at time K;

UAMM.K is the underemployed-arrivals-mobility multiplier (dimensionless) at time K;

UHM.K is the underemployed/housing multiplier (dimensionless) at time K;

PEM.K is the public-expenditure multiplier (dimensionless) at time K;
UJM.K is the underemployed/job multiplier (dimensionless) at time K;
UHPM.K is the underemployed-housing-program multiplier
    (dimensionless) at time K;
AMF is the attractiveness-for-migration factor (dimensionless).
Expressed in revised notation equation (16) reads

$$AMM_u^I(t) = [UAMM^I(t)][UHM^I(t)][PEM^I(t)][UJM^I(t)][UHPM^I(t)](AMF^I)$$
(17)

We simply append the zone I superscript to each multiplier. If the
intention of the paper were to completely revise the Forrester notation,
then many further modifications would be suggested. Here we are
concerned only with the basic approach and a few of the equations as
illustrations.

The multipliers used in this equation range around $1 \cdot 0$; when below
that figure the normal migration rate is suppressed, when above $1 \cdot 0$ it is
inflated. The multipliers link the in-migration of the underemployed to
conditions in the urban area's housing and job market and to the public
policies at work in the city. Thus the in-migration of a particular
population group is made a function of the prior size of the group and of
conditions in the other sectors of the urban system, housing and business.
The strength of the *Urban Dynamics* model is in building in these
relationships and in capturing the feedbacks (largely negative) that occur in
the system over time.

Criticisms of the Urban Dynamics model

Many criticisms have been made of the *Urban Dynamics* model, and
Forrester suggests the most useful answer to these criticisms in the book
itself: if you do not like the model, revise it. Later in the paper we
describe how this can be done at a very simple level for some of the
equations discussed above.

The two major criticisms that may be levelled at the model are that it is
spatially naïve, and that it has not been tested empirically. It is never
quite clear to what part of the city the term 'urban area' applies; the
spatial extent of the 'environment' within the functional city is obscure.
If the urban area being modelled is the inner central city of an American
central city, as many remarks in the text imply, then this area is simply
the innermost zone of a multi-zonal metropolis. It is not useful in that
context to assume that the urban area has no effect on its 'environment',
since the level of interaction between the inner city and the rest of the
metropolis is considerable. On the other hand, if by urban area is meant the
whole functional metropolis, then the model fails to incorporate a crucial
feature of the real city, namely that it grows in total area, population,
employment, and housing stock over time.

Several researchers (Hester, 1969; Babcock, 1970; Burdekin, 1971, personal communication and others) have modified the *Urban Dynamics* model so as to give it multi-zonal properties. These efforts have been directed essentially at modifying the existing model rather than at replacing it with something else. These approaches retain the valuable comprehensive and feedback properties of the model, but do not make possible a detailed empirical test.

The modifications suggested here are more fundamental, in that they involve changing the nature of some of the most basic model equations. However, work to date has not proceeded beyond the first tier of the relationships captured in the *Urban Dynamics* model. A fully satisfactory dynamic model will have to include these complex relationships.

A simple accounting system for aggregate populations
Before specifying a model for social groups equivalent to equation (2), we need to describe the kind of basic accounting framework envisaged and the kinds of population equations that can be built from it. We do this for an aggregate undifferentiated population at first, and then introduce an ordered series of disaggregations.

We define a simple two-zone world, similar to Forrester's, but one which can be broken down very easily into a large number of regions for analysis of detailed intra-city changes. The zone of interest is called zone i, and all other zones are included in a rest of the world, zone R, which is made up of n zones j $(= 1, ..., n)$ where $j \neq i$. There are some n zones in our system in all. Some 16 population flows can be said to be taking place in this world over any particular time period $(t, t + T)$. These population flows are bundles of individual life-lines that experience the same history in relation to the available measurement system (population censuses, vital events records, and large social surveys). These flows are set out in figure 1 in a diagrammatic form.

(1) Flow 1 consists of people who survive in zone i over the period $(t, t + T)$. They enter the period living in zone i, and leave the period living in zone i. This group consists, for the purposes of population accounting, of persons who may have moved to another zone j in R in the period, but who returned to zone i before the end of the period.

(2) Flow 2 is made up of people who enter period $t + T$ living in zone i and die there during the period. This flow may again include out- and return-migrants.

(3) Flow 3 is composed of persons born in zone i in the period and who survive through to the end of the period. Again some of them may leave and then come back.

(4) Flow 4 consists of persons born in zone i in the period and who die in the period in zone i. Babies in this flow make up the infant mortality statistics. These people could again have left the zone and later returned before dying.

These four flows are repeated in zone R (in each of its component j zones) as flows 13, 14, 15, and 16. They are also repeated in flows 5, 6, 7, and 8 by persons whose life-lines are punctuated by a migration event—they all migrate *out from* zone i to zone R. There are also the corresponding population flows for persons who migrate *into* zone i from zone R in the period (9, 10, 11, and 12). These migrations may represent the net result of a number of moves between zone i and the rest of the world.

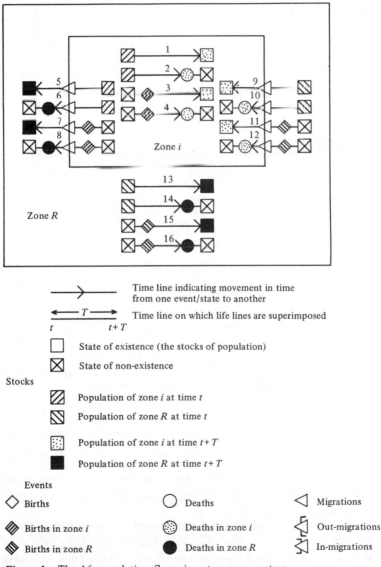

Figure 1. The 16 population flows in a two-zone system.

Table 1. A closed demographic matrix for a single period based on opening and closing stocks for a two-zone case.

Location at time t	State at time t	Location at time $t+T$				Totals
		zone i	zone i'	zone R	zone R'	
		State at time $t+T$				
		Survival (e)[a]	Death (ne)[b]	Survival (e)	Death (ne)	
Zone i	survival (e)	1 $S^{ii}(t,t+T)$	2 $D^{ii'}(t,t+T)$	5 $M^{iR}(t,t+T)$	6 $D^{iR'}(t,t+T)$	$W^i(t)$
Zone i'	birth (ne)	3 $B^{i'i}(t,t+T)$	4 $\mathcal{B}^{i'i'}(t,t+T)$	7 $B^{i'R}(t,t+T)$	8 $\mathcal{B}^{i'R'}(t,t+T)$	$B^{i'\bullet}(t,t+T)$
Zone R	survival (e)	9 $M^{Ri}(t,t+T)$	10 $D^{Ri'}(t,t+T)$	13 $S^{RR}(t,t+T)$	14 $D^{RR'}(t,t+T)$	$W^R(t)$
Zone R'	birth (ne)	11 $B^{R'i}(t,t+T)$	12 $\mathcal{B}^{R'i'}(t,t+T)$	15 $B^{R'R}(t,t+T)$	16 $\mathcal{B}^{R'R'}(t,t+T)$	$B^{R'\bullet}(t,t+T)$
Totals		$W^i(t+T)$	$D^{\bullet i'}(t,t+T)$	$W^R(t+T)$	$D^{\bullet R'}(t,t+T)$	$F^{\bullet\bullet}(t,t+T)$

[a] (e) is existence. [b] (ne) is non-existence.

The symbols in this table have the following definitions. The figures refer to the numbers of the timelines in figure 1.

$S^{ii}(t,t+T)$	Persons who *survive* in zone i over period $(t,t+T)$.
$S^{RR}(t,t+T)$	Persons who *survive* in the rest of the world in the period $(t,t+T)$.
$M^{iR}(t,t+T)$	Persons who *migrate and survive* over the period $(t,t+T)$, moving from zone i to zone R.
$M^{Ri}(t,t+T)$	Persons who *migrate and survive* over the period $(t,t+T)$, moving from zone R to zone i.

All these groups of persons are present at the beginning of the period (members of the opening stock of population) and at the end of the period (members of the closing stock).

$B^{i'i}(t,t+T)$	Persons *born* in zone i in period $(t,t+T)$ who *survive* through to the end of the period in zone i.
$B^{R'R}(t,t+T)$	Persons *born* in zone R in period $(t,t+T)$ who *survive* through to the end of the period in zone R.
$B^{i'R}(t,t+T)$	Persons *born* in zone i in period $(t,t+T)$ who *migrate* to zone R in the period *and survive* there at the end of the period.
$B^{R'i}(t,t+T)$	Persons *born* in zone R in period $(t,t+T)$ who *migrate* to zone i in the period *and survive* there at the end of the period.

All these groups of persons are present at the end of the period and are therefore members of the closing stock. They are not present at the beginning of the period.

$D^{ii'}(t,t+T)$	Persons *present* in zone i at time t who *die* in zone i at sometime during the period $(t,t+T)$.
$D^{RR'}(t,t+T)$	Persons *present* in the rest of the world at time t who *die* in zone R at sometime during the period $(t+T)$.
$D^{iR'}(t,t+T)$	Persons *present* in zone i at time t who *migrate* to zone R *and die* there during the period $(t,t+T)$.
$D^{Ri'}(t,t+T)$	Persons *present* in zone R at time t who *migrate* to zone i *and die* there during the period $(t,t+T)$.

All these groups of persons are present at the beginning of the period, but are not present at the end of the period. They are members of the opening stock but are absent from the closing stock of population.

$\mathcal{B}^{i'i'}(t,t+T)$	Persons *born* in zone i in period $(t,t+T)$ who *die* in zone i during the period.
$\mathcal{B}^{R'R'}(t,t+T)$	Persons *born* in zone R in period $(t,t+T)$ who *die* in zone R during the period.

Table 1 (contd.)

$B^{i'R'}(t, t+T)$	Persons *born* in zone i in period $(t, t+T)$ who *migrate* to zone R *and die* there during the period.
$B^{R'i'}(t, t+T)$	Persons *born* in zone R in period $(t, t+T)$ who *migrate* to zone i *and die* there during the period.
	These groups do not appear in either the opening stock of population or in the closing stock. They do, however, appear in the vital events records.
$W^i(t)$	The population of zone i at time t.
$W^R(t)$	The population of zone R at time t.
$W^i(t+T)$	The population of zone i at time $t+T$.
$W^R(t+T)$	The population of zone R at time $t+T$.
$W^*(t)$	The population of all zones at time t.
$W^*(t+T)$	The population of all zones at time $t+T$.
	These are the opening (time t) stocks of population and the closing (time $t+T$) stocks of population.
$B^{i'*}(t, t+T)$	The total number of live-births recorded in zone i during the period $(t, t+T)$, irrespective of the location or situation of such persons at the end of the period.
$B^{R'*}(t, t+T)$	The total number of live-births recorded in zone R during the period $(t, t+T)$, irrespective of the location or situation of such persons at the end of the period.
$D^{*i'}(t, t+T)$	The total number of deaths recorded in zone i during the period $(t, t+T)$ irrespective of the location or situation of such persons at the beginning of the period.
$D^{*R'}(t, t+T)$	The total number of deaths recorded in zone R during the period $(t, t+T)$ irrespective of the location or situation of such persons at the beginning of the period.
$B^{**}(t, t+T)$	The total number of live births recorded in all zones in the period.
$D^{**}(t, t+T)$	The total number of deaths recorded in all zones in the period.
$F^{**}(t, t+T)$	$= W^*(t) + B^{**}(t, t+T) = W^*(t+T) + D^{**}(t, t+T)$
	$=$ All the people involved in the opening and closing stocks together with those born and dying within the period.

Location and state

The unprimed location superscripts refer to the place of residence of persons at time t (the first superscript) and at time $t+T$ (the second superscript). These persons are members of the opening and closing stocks of population. Members of the opening and closing stocks are in a state of existence at the beginning and end of the period under consideration respectively.

Primed location superscripts refer to the place of residence of a person at the time at which the event took place that resulted in transition from a state of non-existence into a state of existence as a person or vice versa. The zone i' can be regarded for some purposes as equivalent to zone i, for other purposes it will be regarded as equivalent to another and separate zone.

These conventions differ from those adopted by Stone (1971) who labels the 'non-existence locations' as 'the outside world', because he was essentially concerned with only the national educational system (one zone) and a rest of the world category. A third way of dealing with this notational problem would be to create three locational superscripts, the end two referring to location and state at time t and $t+T$ respectively, the middle one referring to location at birth or death. This is unwieldy and has its own associated difficulties.

These flows can be represented symbolically in an accounting matrix which Stone (1971) has characterised as "the closed demographic matrix for a single period based on opening and closing stocks". Such an accounting matrix for our two-zone system and aggregate population is set out in table 1, where a number of accounting identity equations are represented. The populations of the two zones at the beginning of the period are given by the *forward accounting equations*:

$$W^i(t) = S^{ii}(t, t+T) + D^{ii'}(t, t+T) + M^{Ri}(t, t+T) + D^{Ri'}(t, t+T), \qquad (18)$$

and

$$W^R(t) = S^{RR}(t, t+T) + D^{RR'}(t, t+T) + M^{iR}(t, t+T) + D^{iR'}(t, t+T). \quad (19)$$

Populations at the end of the period are given by the *backward accounting equations*:

$$W^i(t+T) = S^{ii}(t, t+T) + B^{i'i}(t, t+T) + M^{Ri}(t, t+T) + B^{R'i}(t, t+T), \quad (20)$$

and

$$W^R(t+T) = S^{RR}(t, t+T) + B^{R'R}(t, t+T) + M^{iR}(t, t+T) + B^{i'R}(t, t+T). \tag{21}$$

The forward accounting equations inform us about *what happened* to the opening stock over the time period; the backward accounting equations tell us about where the population composing the closing stock *comes from*. In a forward looking analysis that attempts to predict future populations both the backward *and* forward accounting equations are used. The reason that both are used is that an estimate of the term $S^{ii}(t, t+T)$ is not usually available directly (except as the product of a sophisticated information system based on a population register and unique identification of individuals). It is usually estimated indirectly using a rearrangement of the forward accounting equation

$$S^{ii}(t, t+T) = W^i(t) - D^{ii'}(t, t+T) - M^{iR}(t, t+T) - D^{iR'}(t, t+T), \qquad (22)$$

and

$$S^{RR}(t, t+T) = W^R(t) - D^{RR'}(t, t+T) - M^{Ri}(t, t+T) - D^{Ri'}(t, t+T). \quad (23)$$

Of the other terms making up equations (20) and (21), the $M^{Ri}(t, t+T)$ and $M^{iR}(t, t+T)$ terms are usually available directly from the census of population. The $B^{R'i}(t, t+T)$ and $B^{R'R}(t, t+T)$ may be available from the census of population as migration terms, or via estimation from other migration figures (Rees, 1971b). The $B^{i'i}(t, t+T)$ and $B^{R'R}(t, t+T)$ terms, however, must be estimated by subtracting birth losses from the observed births in the zone:

$$B^{i'i}(t, t+T) = B^{i'*}(t, t+T) - \mathcal{B}^{i'i'}(t, t+T) - B^{i'R}(t, t+T) - \mathcal{B}^{i'R'}(t, t+T). \tag{24}$$

Methods employing birth record data and census migration information must be used to estimate the three negative terms of equation (24) (Rees, 1971a). In order not to overcomplicate the analysis at this stage we consider only the normal substitution equation for survival.

Equations (22) and (23) are substituted in (20) and (21) respectively to yield

$$W^i(t+T) = W^i(t) - D^{ii'}(t,t+T) - M^{iR}(t,t+T) - D^{iR'}(t,t+T)$$
$$+ B^{i'i}(t,t+T) + M^{Ri}(t,t+T) + B^{R'i}(t,t+T), \qquad (25)$$

and

$$W^R(t+T) = W^R(t) - D^{RR'}(t,t+T) - M^{Ri}(t,t+T) - D^{Ri'}(t,t+T)$$
$$+ B^{R'R}(t,t+T) + M^{iR}(t,t+T) + B^{i'R}(t,t+T). \qquad (26)$$

The equations can be rearranged to yield expressions for the three sets of net changes involved

$$W^i(t+T) = W^i(t) + [B^{i'i}(t,t+T) - D^{ii'}(t,t+T)]$$
$$+ [M^{Ri}(t,t+T) - M^{iR}(t,t+T)]$$
$$+ [B^{R'i}(t,t+T) - D^{iR'}(t,t+T)], \qquad (27)$$

and

$$W^R(t+T) = W^R(t) + [B^{R'R}(t,t+T) - D^{RR'}(t,t+T)]$$
$$+ [M^{iR}(t,t+T) - M^{Ri}(t,t+T)]$$
$$+ [B^{i'R}(t,t+T) - D^{Ri'}(t,t+T)]. \qquad (28)$$

The population at the end of the period is equal to the population at beginning of the period plus net natural increase of persons remaining within the zone, net migration into the zone, and net natural increase of persons moving between zones. Equations (27) and (28) bear a strong resemblance to equation (9), which was our accounting version of Forrester's basic model equation for the underemployed. We shall later compare equation (9) with a version of (27) and (28) disaggregated by social class, but it is already apparent that equation (9) assumes terms like $[B^{R'i}(t,t+T) - D^{iR'}(t,t+T)]$ to be zero.

The two-zone division of the world adopted in table 1, and the equations associated with it, can very easily be converted into a multizone system by breaking zone R into its component j zones. Terms $S^{RR}(t,t+T)$, $D^{RR'}(t,t+T)$, $B^{R'R}(t,t+T)$, and $B^{R'R'}(t,t+T)$ in table 1 then become matrices; terms $M^{iR}(t,t+T)$, $D^{iR'}(t,t+T)$, $B^{i'R}(t,t+T)$, and $B^{i'R'}(t,t+T)$ become $1 \times n$ row vectors; terms $M^{Ri}(t,t+T)$, $D^{Ri'}(t,t+T)$, $B^{R'i}(t,t+T)$, and $B^{R'i'}(t,t+T)$ become $n \times 1$ column vectors. The two equations (20) and (21), which yield end of period populations, can be replaced by a general equation in which the expanded terms are represented explicitly:

$$W^i(t+T) = S^{ii}(t,t+T) + B^{i'i}(t,t+T) + \sum_{\substack{j=1 \\ j \neq i}}^{n} M^{ji}(t,t+T) + \sum_{\substack{j'=1' \\ j' \neq i'}}^{n'} B^{i'i}(t,t+T),$$
$$(29)$$

and the equation for survivors becomes

$$S^{ii}(t,t+T) = W^i(t) - D^{ii'}(t,t+T) - \sum_{\substack{j=1 \\ j \neq i}}^{n} M^{ij}(t,t+T) - \sum_{\substack{j'=1' \\ j' \neq i'}}^{n'} D^{ij'}(t,t+T) . \tag{30}$$

Following the notation of figure 1 and table 1, we can recognise some $2n$ origins for the population surviving in zone i at time $t+T$; that is, survival from zones $j = 1, ..., n$, and birth and survival from zones $j' = 1', ..., n'$. If we represent any population flow in table 1 by the term F, then the end of period population can be generalised as

$$W^i(t+T) = \sum_{j=1}^{n} F^{ji}(t,t+T) + \sum_{j'=1'}^{n'} F^{j'i}(t,t+T) , \tag{31}$$

or

$$W^i(t+T) = \sum_{k} F^{ki}(t,t+T) , \tag{32}$$

where k is a superscript covering all zones of origin, $k = 1, ..., n, 1', ..., n'$. Similarly, if we recognise some $2n$ destinations for population starting out in zone i at time t, we can represent time t population as

$$W^i(t) = \sum_{k} F^{ik}(t,t+T) , \tag{33}$$

and generalise equation (30) as

$$S^{ii}(t,t+T) = W^i(t) - \sum_{\substack{k=1 \\ k \neq i}} F^{ik}(t,t+T) . \tag{34}$$

A simple model for aggregate populations

Equations (18) through (34) are accounting equations. It is of historical interest to discover the relative size of the right hand side terms in a given city, having specified the population groups of interest and the spatial scale at which the flows will be measured. Such a historical study will be of vital importance in any projection by providing information on trends in births, deaths, and migrations. But to make use of such information we have to convert the accounting equations into model equations.

To do this we convert the flows into propensities by dividing by the appropriate population from which the flows can be said to have emanated. These propensities have been called rates (Wilson, 1971a, 1971b) or outflow coefficients (Stone, 1971); we use the terms interchangeably. The population of a zone i within a city at a time $t+T$ is given, in the model form, by:

$$W^i(t+T) = s^{ii}(t,t+T)W^i(t) + b^{i'i}(t,t+T)W^i(t) + \sum_{\substack{j=1 \\ j \neq i}}^{n} m^{ji}(t,t+T)W^j(t)$$

$$+ \sum_{\substack{j'=1' \\ j' \neq i'}}^{n'} b^{j'i}(t,t+T)W^j(t) , \tag{35}$$

where

$s^{ii}(t, t+T)$ is the survival propensity of persons in zone i over $(t, t+T)$;

$b^{i'i}(t, t+T)$ is the propensity of persons in zone i to give birth to persons who survive in zone i over the period;

$m^{ji}(t, t+T)$ is the propensity of persons in zone j to migrate to zone i over the period $(t, t+T)$;

$b^{j'i}(t, t+T)$ is the propensity of persons in zone j to give birth to persons who migrate into zone i and survive there over the period $(t, t+T)$.

These propensities are explicitly defined thus:

$$s^{ii}(t, t+T) = \frac{S^{ii}(t, t+T)}{W^i(t)}$$

$$= \left[W^i(t) - D^{ii'}(t, t+T) - \sum_{\substack{j=1 \\ j \neq i}}^{n} M^{ij}(t, t+T) \right.$$

$$\left. - \sum_{\substack{j'=1' \\ j' \neq i'}}^{n'} D^{ij'}(t, t+T) \right] \bigg/ W^i(t) , \tag{36}$$

$$b^{i'i}(t, t+T) = \frac{B^{i'i}(t, t+T)}{W^i(t)} , \tag{37}$$

$$m^{ji}(t, t+T) = \frac{M^{ji}(t, t+T)}{W^j(t)} , \tag{38}$$

and

$$b^{j'i}(t, t+T) = \frac{B^{j'i}(t, t+T)}{W^j(t)} . \tag{39}$$

The birth propensities incorporated in equation (35) are equivalent to the demographer's crude birth rates. These are frequently replaced by fertility rates, which express births as a proportion of women in the fertile age group. We consider the sex and age disaggregation of the population in a later section of the paper, and retain the total population denominator in the aggregate equations. Although only women can give birth to babies, both men and women are necessary for reproduction, and the number of births is a function of the number of male–female pairs rather than of the number of women alone (neglecting harem or rape-by-conqueror situations). The number of pairs will be influenced by whichever is smaller—the number of men or the number of women in reproductive age groups.

For any historical period for which both the numerator and denominator of the propensity or rate equation are known, equations (28) and (35) are equivalent since we can equate their right hand sides after substituting the propensity definitions into equation (35):

$$S^{ii}(t,t+T)+B^{i'i}(t,t+T)+\sum_{\substack{j=1\\j\neq i}}^{n}M^{ji}(t,t+T)+\sum_{\substack{j'=1'\\j'\neq i'}}^{n'}B^{j'i}(t,t+T)$$

$$=\frac{S^{ii}(t+T)}{W^i(t)}W^i(t)+\frac{B^{i'i}(t,t+T)}{W^i(t)}W^i(t)+\sum_{\substack{j=1\\j\neq i}}^{n}\frac{M^{ji}(t,t+T)}{W^j(t)}W^j(t)$$

$$+\sum_{\substack{j'=1'\\j'\neq i'}}^{n'}\frac{B^{j'i}(t,t+T)}{W^j(t)}W^j(t). \qquad (40)$$

However, in using the propensities measured historically for projection purposes, some difficulties become evident when we examine the concept "appropriate population from which the flows can be said to have emanated". With respect to migration and survival the appropriate population can only be the population of zone j or zone i at the beginning of the period under consideration. No-one else can be included in these flows because the accounting framework recognises only the 'net' relocation at the end of the period resulting from a series of inter-zone moves.

Births, however, are in a somewhat different category in that the parents of children born in a zone during the time period may have been living outside the zone at the start of the period. Table 2 shows how the 8 birth-associated terms in table 1 can be expanded to 16 when parental location at time t is taken into account [2].

The symbols in table 2 have the same meaning as those in table 1, except that an additional subscript has been added to indicate the location at time t of the parents of the person whose birth or birth and death is represented in the table. In-migrants can be the parents of persons born in zone i, and should be represented in the appropriate population denominator.

Table 2. The parental origin of zonal births (expansion of the birth terms of table 1).

Location at time of birth	Location of parents at time t	Location at time $t+T$				Totals
		Zone i Survival (e)[a]	Zone i' Death (ne)[b]	Zone R Survival (e)	Zone R' Death (ne)	
Zone i'	Zone i	$B_i^{i'i}(t,t+T)$	$B_i^{i'i'}(t,t+T)$	$B_i^{i'R}(t,t+T)$	$B_i^{i'R'}(t,t+T)$	$B_i^{i'\bullet}(t,t+T)$
	Zone R	$B_R^{i'i}(t,t+T)$	$B_R^{i'i'}(t,t+T)$	$B_R^{i'R}(t,t+T)$	$B_R^{i'R'}(t,t+T)$	$B_R^{i'\bullet}(t,t+T)$
Zone R'	Zone i	$B_i^{R'i}(t,t+T)$	$B_i^{R'i'}(t,t+T)$	$B_i^{R'R}(t,t+T)$	$B_i^{R'R'}(t,t+T)$	$B_i^{R'\bullet}(t,t+T)$
	Zone R	$B_R^{R'i}(t,t+T)$	$B_R^{R'i'}(t,t+T)$	$B_R^{R'R}(t,t+T)$	$B_R^{R'R'}(t,t+T)$	$B_R^{R'\bullet}(t,t+T)$
Totals		$B_{\bullet}^{\bullet i}(t,t+T)$	$B_{\bullet}^{\bullet i'}(t,t+T)$	$B_{\bullet}^{\bullet R}(t,t+T)$	$B_{\bullet}^{\bullet R'}(t,t+T)$	$B_{\bullet}^{\bullet\bullet}(t,t+T)$

[a] (e) is existence.   [b] (ne) is non-existence.

[2] In the aggregate model we have to assume that both parents have the same zonal location at time t. This assumption can be relaxed if the model is disaggregated by sex.

However, the risk that they face of producing an offspring will be less than that of people who live in zone i throughout the period. In-migrants will move into zone i at points in time intermediate between t and $t+T$. Similarly some of the population present in zone i at time t (the opening stock) will migrate out of the zone, most of them permanently, some of them temporarily. Some of the opening stock will die, and so will not be available for reproduction. If all these factors are taken into account the correct denominator for the birth propensity, $b^{i\,i}(t,t+T)$, will be

$$f[W^i(t)] = \sum_{k_1}\sum_{k_2} \frac{\overline{\theta}_i(F^{k_1 k_2})}{T} F^{k_1 k_2}(t,t+T), \qquad (41)$$

where

$f[W^i(t)]$ is the population available in zone i to give birth to persons in
 zone i;

$\overline{\theta}_i(F^{k_1,k_2})$ is the average length of time a given demographic flow spends in
 zone i in period $(t,t+T)$;

$F^{k_1 k_2}(t,t+T)$ is the demographic flow of persons from zone k_1 to zone k_2
 in $(t,t+T)$.

The F terms are meant to represent the 16 terms in table 1 generally.

Each population flow in table 1 spends some time in zone i during period $(t,t+T)$, or rather, some members of each population flow may spend some time in zone i. During this time they will be available in the parental 'pool'. The average time spent in zone i is divided by the length of the period, T, to yield a coefficient that may vary from zero to one. In any of the applications of the demographic model envisaged in this paper the contribution of the death flows and birth flows to the reproductive population will be negligible, because the vast majority of persons in those flows will be outside the reproductive age groups. We can regard the $S^{RR}(t,t+T)$ flow as making a negligible contribution to the reproductive population of zone i, and the coefficient modifying the $S^{ii}(t,t+T)$ term will generally approximate to one. So that the divisor of the birth propensity equation may be estimated as

$$f[W^i(t)] = S^{ii}(t,t+T)+ \sum_{\substack{j=1 \\ j\ne i}}^{n} \frac{\overline{\theta}_i(M^{ji})}{T} M^{ji}(t,t+T) - \sum_{\substack{j=1 \\ j\ne i}}^{n} \frac{\overline{\theta}_i(M^{ij})}{T} M^{ij}(t,t+T). \qquad (42)$$

If migration into and out of zone i is in balance, this will be approximately equal to $S^{ii}(t,t+T)$ or to $W^i(t)$ if we consider the reproductive age groups only.

Is it worth substituting the expression on the right hand side of equation (42) for $W^i(t)$ in equation (37), and an equivalent expression in equation (39)? If net migration patterns remain stable between zones then it should make little difference but, if they are changing, use of the simple opening stock population may lead to incorrect projection of the births terms. On the other hand it is simpler to employ time t population as the base population, since this avoids difficult problems of recycling the projection procedure several times before satisfactory projections are achieved. Where estimation of most of the terms in table 1 is fairly easy there is probably a case for using the more complicated births denominator; for harder estimation problems the simplicity of using the opening stock population may be an advantage.

Use of the simple model for projection purposes

Models, such as that represented in equation (35), have often been used to examine the future growth of population under the assumption that the propensity coefficients remain stable. These studies show that the population distribution will change until a state of stationary equilibrium is reached at some time in the future. However, in practice it is not reasonable to suppose that the coefficients remain stable over time. One of the key tasks that needs to be addressed in population projection is the determination of the future path of these coefficients.

To generalise equation (35) for any number of time periods we adopt a slightly different time notation from the one specified there. Periods are given their own subscipt rather than being defined in terms of beginning and end points in time. They run $1, 2, ..., \lambda - 1, \lambda$, where lambda is the notation for the last period before the projection date, and are assumed to be equal in length of time, all of T time units. The base-point in time is designated t, the projection-point in time is $t + \lambda T$. Equation (35) can then be generalised using the devices employed by Stone [1971, pp.92–93, particularly equations (IX.20) and (IX.21)] as follows:

$$
\begin{aligned}
W^i(t + \lambda T) = & \left[\prod_{\beta = \lambda}^{0} s^{ii}(\beta) \right] W^i(t) + b^{i\,'i}(\lambda) W^i[t + (\lambda - 1)T] \\
& + \sum_{\theta = 1}^{\lambda - 1} \left[\prod_{\beta = \lambda}^{\lambda + 1 - \theta} s^{ii}(\beta) \right] b^{i\,'i}(\lambda - \theta) W^i[t + (\lambda - 1 - \theta)T] \\
& + \sum_{\substack{j = 1 \\ j \neq i}}^{n} m^{ji}(\lambda) W^j[t + (\lambda - 1)T] \\
& + \sum_{\substack{j = 1 \\ j \neq i}}^{n} \sum_{\theta = 1}^{\lambda - 1} \left[\prod_{\beta = \lambda}^{\lambda + 1 - \theta} s^{ii}(\beta) \right] m^{ji}(\lambda - \theta) W^j[t + (\lambda - 1 - \theta)T] \\
& + \sum_{\substack{j = 1 \\ j \neq i}}^{n} b^{j\,'i}(\lambda) W^j[t + (\lambda - 1)T] \\
& + \sum_{\substack{j = 1 \\ j \neq i}}^{n} \sum_{\theta = 1}^{\lambda - 1} \left[\prod_{\beta = \lambda}^{\lambda + 1 - \theta} s^{ii}(\beta) \right] b^{j\,'i}(\lambda - \theta) W^j[t + (\lambda - 1 - \theta)T] .
\end{aligned}
\tag{43}
$$

The Π sign refers to product multiplication and means "multiply together the terms that follow from the first value of the subscript index through to the last". These are arranged in order from the period furthest in the future through to the period furthest in the past. This is done in order that the propensities be correctly pre-multiplied when they are expanded to whole transition matrices in later sections. Thus,

$$\prod_{\beta=\lambda}^{0} s^{ii}(\beta) = s^{ii}(\lambda) \times s^{ii}(\lambda-1) \times ... \times s^{ii}(2) \times s^{ii}(1) \times s^{ii}(0) , \qquad (44)$$

where $s^{ii}(0)$ is assumed to be one. Similarly $b^{ii}(0)$, $m^{ji}(0)$, and $b^{ji}(0)$ are assumed to be zero.

This is merely a formal definition in one equation of an operation that would be programmed as a loop through equation (35), shifting the relevant time period into the future at the end of each cycle until the required future population had been projected. All intermediate $(t + \alpha T)$ populations, where $\alpha = 1, ..., \lambda$, have to be generated to project a $(t + \lambda T)$ population.

A hierarchy of disaggregated demographic models
So far we have talked only of population in the aggregate. To begin to match our dynamic models with the degree of social detail captured in the cross-section pattern studies mentioned in the introduction to the paper, we have to break the population down into its component social groups. The typology of social groups is shown in figure 2 and follows the very useful triad of dimensions proposed over twenty years ago by Shevky and Williams (1949).

The two decades of work in the social area and factorial ecology tradition have basically established that the social geography of the American Metropolis is characterized by three socio-spatial patterns (Rees, 1972).
1. The first is a pattern of *socioeconomic status* which describes how the subareas of the city differ in terms of the social rank characteristics of their populations. This pattern ranges from complete sectorality to complete concentricity in different cities, with a bias toward the former pattern.
2. The second is a pattern of *family status* which describes how the subareas of the city differ in terms of the type of household occupying those areas, and the stage in the family life cycle which those households have reached. This pattern is dominantly concentric and always independent of the socioeconomic status pattern.
3. Thirdly there are as many patterns of *ethnic status* as there are distinctive ethnic groupings. In particular, Negro Americans are found to be residentially segregated to a very high degree from non-Negroes. Because of the socioeconomic disadvantage of black Americans the racial status pattern may not be independent of the socioeconomic status pattern.

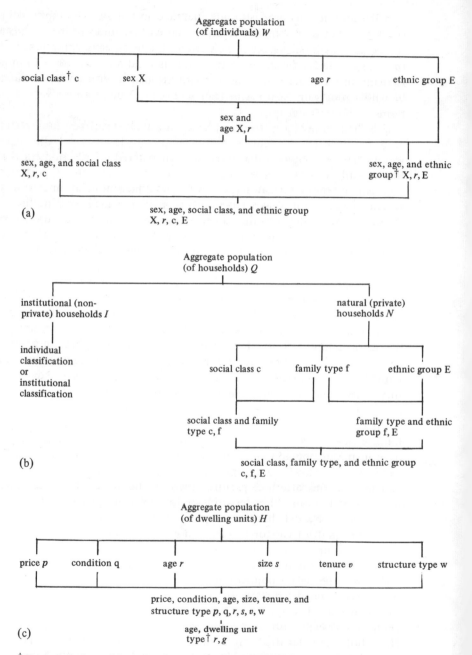

† These particular models are described in some detail in the paper.

Figure 2. A typology of social groups and housing types. (a) The individual as population unit; (b) the household as population unit; (c) the dwelling unit as population unit.

When housing characteristics are included in the analyses (Rees, 1972) two sets of housing attributes emerge: those associated with socioeconomic status, such as home value, or home rental, and housing condition, and those associated with family status, such as type of unit, tenure, and age. Housing size and occupancy density are associated with both population dimensions. Again Negro Americans are seen to be at a disadvantage in terms of housing occupied.

In British cities the patterns of socioeconomic status and family status have usually been distinguished (Robson, 1969; Herbert, 1970). The various immigrant groups have distinctive clustered distributions in the British cities in which they appear in more than negligible proportions, but their socioeconomic disadvantage vis-à-vis the host population means that their spatial pattern is associated with that of socioeconomic status. Housing characteristics do not align themselves in joint population and housing analyses in as neat a fashion as in American studies, and often a separate housing characteristics dimension emerges which distinguishes areas of overcrowding and poor condition housing from areas of sound, standard housing occupied at lower densities. This dimension is not correlated with that of socioeconomic status, because sound standard housing is available to the working class in the council sector of the market.

The classifications to be explored in the models proposed in this paper, set out in figure 2, follow the distinctions which have been found empirically useful. Population is firstly regarded as an aggregation of individuals who can be described separately in terms of their sex, age, social class, and ethnic group membership. More usually these characteristics are considered in combination: the sex and age combination is the one normally employed in cohort survival and population projection models (Keyfitz and Flieger, 1971; Rogers, 1968), and is the classification used in the demographic models described by Wilson (1971a, 1971b) in this volume. These models may be disaggregated further in terms of social class or in terms of ethnic groups. Finally, the model can be disaggregated in terms of all four characteristics—only then will the variety of the city's social geography that has been documented empirically be replicated.

An alternative basis for disaggregation is to regard the population as being made up of households. Households are of two kinds: institutional (non-private) or natural (private) [3]. Institutional populations can be regarded as aggregate populations of individuals which experience 'migration' to and from the set of natural households. Natural households can be broken down in three ways, paralleling the socio-spatial patterns found empirically, into social classes, family types, or ethnic groups. Households are classified into a particular social class, family type, or ethnic group category according to the characteristics of their individual members as classified in the preceding individual typology. Some difficult

[3] The terms are from Stone (1971) and the population census (in parentheses).

classification problems will have to be faced when the demographic model is specified for households. We are justified in making the attempt, however, for the simple reason that the household rather than the individual is the important decision agent on the demand side of the housing market.

To model the supply side of the housing market realistically, we need to break the aggregate population of dwelling units down into a number of disaggregated categories. Some note should be taken of the price of a dwelling, its condition, age, size, tenure, and structure type, either separately or collectively. If a collective typology is to be used then a very parsimonious shifting of categories and variables would probably have to be made. Otherwise the disaggregation becomes unmanageable.

The models to be developed and the processes to be incorporated
A selection of the population models corresponding to the typology outlined in figure 2 will be developed. The social class model will be analysed in some detail because of its links with the *Urban Dynamics* model of Forrester discussed earlier. The sex, age, and ethnic group model will be specified, being of particular interest in a dynamic intra-urban context, and will be related to previous work (Morrill, 1965). The main outlines of only these models will be sketched, and an attempt to spell out the social class, family type, and ethnic group models for households will be deferred to a later paper.

In these models we should aim to capture some of the social processes at work within the city.

Empirical applications of the model should make possible:
(a) the tracing through time of the evolution of the population characteristics of the zones making up an urban area; and
(b) the tracing through time–space and a series of social states of the paths taken by any particular social group.
To do this we will have to specify the necessary transition and migration propensities. The transition propensities should be linked with changes being generated by the business sector of the urban system in the social structure of the city's population through changes in the number of jobs and job mix. The migration propensities should be linked with changes in the housing structure of the city, these changes being generated in the housing sector of the urban system (cf.Forrester, 1969).

After considering the social group models, we shall tackle a demographic model for the housing market, classifying housing by age and by a composite typology g, made up of the remaining characteristics listed in figure 2(c). The rates of housing obsolescence, of housing conversions, of demolition, and of building will all have to be incorporated in the model.

Finally some suggestions will be made about the links needed between the social group and housing models. A full analysis, not carried out in this paper, would demand a careful consideration of the migration models used, and the construction of an accounting system that links household and housing unit characteristics. Such an accounting system should make possible the measurement of the degree of fit between the population and the housing stock of a given intra-urban zone.

A social class model

The accounting system of table 1 is expanded in table 3 to take account of a population disaggregated by social class. Social classes are represented by the subscript c. In the table the flows out of and into a particular social class c from all other social classes D are represented. This is merely a convenience that enables a manageable table to be drawn up. In practice we shall be concerned with social groups $c = 1, 2, ..., m$ defined in terms of education, occupation, or income.

Table 3. A closed demographic matrix for a single period for a population disaggregated by social class.

Category		4	Zone i		Zone i'	Zone R		Zone R'		Totals
		5	Survival (e)[a]		Deaths (ne)[b]	Survival (e)		Deaths (ne)		
		6	c	D	c D	c	D	c	D	
1	2	3								
Zone i Survival	c		S_{cc}^{ii}	S_{cD}^{ii}	$D_{cc}^{ii'}$ $D_{cD}^{ii'}$ M_{cc}^{iR}	M_{cD}^{iR}		$D_{cc}^{iR'}$ $D_{cD}^{iR'}$		$W_c^i(t)$
(e)	D		S_{Dc}^{ii}	S_{DD}^{ii}	$D_{Dc}^{ii'}$ $D_{DD}^{ii'}$ M_{Dc}^{iR}	M_{DD}^{iR}		$D_{Dc}^{iR'}$ $D_{DD}^{iR'}$		$W_D^i(t)$
Zone i' Births	c		$B_{cc}^{i'i}$	$B_{cD}^{i'i}$	$B_{cc}^{i'i'}$ $B_{cD}^{i'i'}$ $B_{cc}^{i'R}$	$B_{cD}^{i'R}$		$B_{cc}^{i'R'}$ $B_{cD}^{i'R'}$		$B_{c\bullet}^{i'*}(t, t+T)$
(ne)	D		$B_{Dc}^{i'i}$	$B_{DD}^{i'i}$	$B_{Dc}^{i'i'}$ $B_{DD}^{i'i'}$ $B_{Dc}^{i'R}$	$B_{DD}^{i'R}$		$B_{Dc}^{i'R'}$ $B_{DD}^{i'R'}$		$B_{D\bullet}^{i'*}(t, t+T)$
Zone R Survival	c		M_{cc}^{Ri}	M_{cD}^{Ri}	$D_{cc}^{Ri'}$ $D_{cD}^{Ri'}$ S_{cc}^{RR}	S_{cD}^{RR}		$D_{cc}^{RR'}$ $D_{cD}^{RR'}$		$W_c^R(t)$
(e)	D		M_{Dc}^{Ri}	M_{DD}^{Ri}	$D_{Dc}^{Ri'}$ $D_{DD}^{Ri'}$ S_{Dc}^{RR}	S_{DD}^{RR}		$D_{Dc}^{RR'}$ $D_{DD}^{RR'}$		$W_D^R(t)$
Zone R' Births	c		$B_{cc}^{R'i}$	$B_{cD}^{R'i}$	$B_{cc}^{R'i'}$ $B_{cD}^{R'i'}$ $B_{cc}^{R'R}$	$B_{cD}^{R'R}$		$B_{cc}^{R'R'}$ $B_{cD}^{R'R'}$		$B_{c\bullet}^{R'*}(t, t+T)$
(ne)	D		$B_{Dc}^{R'i}$	$B_{Dc}^{R'i}$	$B_{Dc}^{R'i'}$ $B_{DD}^{R'i'}$ $B_{Dc}^{R'R}$	$B_{DD}^{R'R}$		$B_{Dc}^{R'R'}$ $B_{DD}^{R'Rp}$		$B_{D\bullet}^{R'*}(t, t+T)$
Totals			$W_c^i(t+T)$ $W_D^i(t+T)$ $D_{\bullet c}^{*i'}$ $D_{\bullet D}^{*i'}$		$W_c^{R*}(t+T)$ $W_D^R(t+T)$ $D_{\bullet c}^{*R'}$ $D_{\bullet D}^{*R'}$					$F_{\bullet\bullet}^{**}(t, t+T)$

[a] (e) is existence. [b] (ne) is non-existence.

The categories in the table refer to the row and column headings, and are defined as follows:
1 location at time t, or at first existence
2 state at time t
3 social class category at time t, or at time of birth
4 location at time $t+T$, or at last existence
5 state at time $t+T$
6 social class at time $t+T$, or at time of death.
The symbols are defined in the same way as those in table 1 with modifications.
(1) Subscripts for social class have been added. The subscript c refers to any social group.
 D refers to the remainder of the population.
(2) The time period notation $(t, t+T)$ has been dropped in order to keep the table compact.
 Every flow listed in the table should be understood to refer to the period $(t, t+T)$.
(3) $F_{\bullet\bullet}^{**}(t, t+T)$ represents the total number of lifelines involved in the period $(t, t+T)$.

Before discussing in detail the structure of the table and the equations generated from it, we need to establish fairly carefully what we mean by social class, and whether all of the population can be assigned to a social class. In studies of social stratification and social mobility (Lipset and Bendix, 1962; Blau and Duncan, 1967), occupation is the principle criterion used to classify persons in the labour force (active or unemployed) into social classes. Persons outside the labour force, and usually women inside it, are ignored. Bogue (1969, Chapter 14) has argued that occupation is no longer as useful a stratification measure as it used to be and that the education attained and income received by a person should also be taken into account.

Let us assume initially that the population represented in table 1 is the labour force, male and female, that births under that definition represent the transition of persons from full-time education to employment, and that deaths can occur through entry into the inactive category, the retired category, or through mortality in the medical sense. This is roughly the set of definitions employed in the *Urban Dynamics* model, and makes the connection of population and business sectors fairly straightforward. However, in principle it should be possible to assign all members of the population including children, students in higher education, housewives, the disabled, and the retired to a social class. This assignment would involve, in many cases, the attribution of the social class of a labour force member to a dependent member of the same household. Consideration of the social class of the whole population is postponed to a later paper, where we shall specify demographic models based on households.

So, to return to table 3, we can see that the number in a social class at a future point in time is given basically by

$$W_c^i(t+T) = S_{cc}^{ii}(t,t+T) \quad + S_{Dc}^{ii}(t,t+T)$$
$$+ B_{cc}^{i'i}(t,t+T) \quad + B_{Dc}^{i'i}(t,t+T)$$
$$+ M_{cc}^{Ri}(t,t+T) \quad + M_{Dc}^{ii}(t,t+T)$$
$$+ B_{cc}^{R'i}(t,t+T) + B_{Dc}^{R'i}(t,t+T). \tag{45}$$

The first column of terms on the right hand side of the equation represents population flows within the social class; the second column of terms represents flows from other social classes into the particular social class c. Each of the survival and birth terms in equation (45) would probably have to be estimated by the residual method: subtraction of the row outflows from the appropriate row totals. For example, within-zone and within-class survivors are given by

$$S_{cc}^{ii}(t,t+T) = W_c^i(t) - S_{cD}^{ii}(t,t+T) - D_{cc}^{ii'}(t,t+T) - D_{cD}^{ii'}(t,t+T)$$
$$- M_{cc}^{iR}(t,t+T) - M_{cD}^{iR}(t,t+T) - D_{cc}^{iR'}(t,t+T) - D_{cD}^{iR'}(t,t+T)$$
$$\tag{46}$$

Substituting equation (46) in equation (45), we obtain

$$
\begin{aligned}
W_c^i(t+T) = {} & W_c^i(t) - S_{cD}^{ii}(t,t+T) - D_{cc}^{ii'}(t,t+T) - D_{cD}^{ii'}(t,t+T) \\
& - M_{cc}^{iR}(t,t+T) - M_{cD}^{iR}(t,t+T) - D_{cc}^{iR'}(t,t+T) - D_{cD}^{iR'}(t,t+T) \\
& + S_{Dc}^{ii}(t,t+T) + B_{cc}^{i'i}(t,t+T) + B_{Dc}^{i'i}(t,t+T) \\
& + M_{cc}^{Ri}(t,t+T) + M_{Dc}^{Ri}(t,t+T) + B_{cc}^{R'i}(t,t+T) + B_{Dc}^{R'i}(t,t+T) \, .
\end{aligned}
$$

$$(47)$$

Now this equation is directly comparable with the accounting version of the level equation for the underemployed in the *Urban Dynamics* model, equation (9) in our notation. We can see immediately that equation (9) is incompletely specified or, in other words, that many of the terms in equation (47) were assumed to be zero when equation (9) was stated. The equivalence of terms in the two equations is traced term by term in table 4. Terms involving transitions between social classes in which persons do not survive at time $t+T$ in the zone of interest are assumed to be zero in equation (9). Some of them may be small in reality but the migration terms $M_{cD}^{iR}(t,t+T)$ and $M_{Dc}^{Ri}(t,t+T)$ are probably quite large, given that migration and upward social mobility have been shown to be connected (Blau and Duncan, 1967).

Table 4. The equivalence of terms in equations (9) and (47).

Equation (9) terms (the accounting version of Forrester's equation 16,L)	Relationship	Equation (7) terms (social class model accounting equation)
$W_u^I(t+T)$	$=$	$W_c^i(t+T)$
$W_u^I(t)$	$=$	$W_c^i(t)$
$M_{uu}^{RI}(t,t+T)$	$=$	$M_{cc}^{Ri}(t,t+T)$
$G_u^I(t,t+T)$	$\subset$	$[B_{cc}^{i'i}(t,t+T) - D_{cc}^{ii'}(t,t+T)]$
$S_{Iu}^{II}(t,t+T)$	$\supset$	$S_{Dc}^{ii}(t,t+T)$
$M_{uu}^{IR}(t,t+T)$	$=$	$M_{cc}^{iR}(t,t+T)$
$S_{uI}^{II}(t,t+T)$	$\supset$	$S_{cD}^{ii}(t,t+T)$
Not specified or assumed to be zero		$D_{cD}^{ii'}(t,t+T)$
ditto		$M_{cD}^{iR}(t,t+T)$
ditto		$D_{cc}^{iR'}(t,t+T)$
ditto		$D_{cD}^{iR'}(t,t+T)$
ditto		$B_{Dc}^{i'i}(t,t+T)$
ditto		$M_{Dc}^{Ri}(t,t+T)$
ditto		$B_{cc}^{R'i}(t,t+T)$
ditto		$B_{Dc}^{R'i}(t,t+T)$

Equation (47) can be rearranged to yield a series of expressions for net changes [cf.equations (27) and (28) for the aggregate population]:

$$W_c^i(t+T) = W_c^i(t) + [S_{Dc}^{ii}(t,t+T) - S_{cD}^{ii}(t,t+T)]$$
$$+ [B_{cc}^{i'i}(t,t+T) - D_{cc}^{ii'}(t,t+T)]$$
$$+ [B_{Dc}^{i'i}(t,t+T) - D_{cD}^{ii'}(t,t+T)]$$
$$+ [M_{cc}^{Ri}(t,t+T) - M_{cc}^{iR}(t,t+T)]$$
$$+ [M_{Dc}^{Ri}(t,t+T) - M_{cD}^{iR}(t,t+T)]$$
$$+ [B_{cc}^{R'i}(t,t+T) - D_{cc}^{iR'}(t,t+T)]$$
$$+ [B_{Dc}^{R'i}(t,t+T) - D_{cD}^{iR'}(t,t+T)] . \tag{48}$$

The pairs of terms in parentheses represent respectively net social movement into class c within zone i, net natural increase within zone i, the net natural increase *and* social movement into class c within zone i, the net migration within class c into zone i, the net migration *and* social movement into class c in zone i, the net natural increase through migration within class c, and the net natural increase associated with migration and social movement into social class c. The simple concepts of net migration, net social mobility, and net natural increase break down into a set of more complex, interacting net flows. If we transpose the matrix of population flows represented in table 3, and subtract the result from the original matrix (Leicester, 1967; Stone, 1971), we obtain a matrix of net flows:

$$\mathbf{N} = \mathbf{F} - \mathbf{F}' , \tag{49}$$

where
$\mathbf{N}$ represents the matrix of net flows ($N_{cD}^{k_1 k_2}$);
$\mathbf{F}$ represents the matrix of population flows ($F_{cD}^{k_1 k_2}$);
$\mathbf{F}'$ is the transpose of F; and
k_1 and k_2 are general locational superscripts.
Table 5 lists the elements of the matrix N for our two-zone, two-class case. Construction of such a matrix for an urban zone system would make possible answers to some very simple questions about the development of the city's social class geography over time. Questions such as the relative contribution of social mobility or migration or both to the changes in the social status of the suburban and inner city portions of the metropolis could be tackled directly [4].

---

[4] A considerable task of information system development and data estimation will be necessary to make the theoretical propositions of this paper operational. However, it has been demonstrated (Rees, 1971b) that such a task can be done at a grosser spatial scale, and it should be possible to use some of the same techniques to make the intra-urban demographic models proposed here operational.

Equation (47) can be expanded from the special two-zone, two-class case to a full multi-zone, multi-social class equation:

$$W_c^i(t+T) = W_c^i(t) - \sum_{\substack{d=1 \\ d \neq c}}^{m} S_{cd}^{ii}(t,t+T) - D_{cc}^{ii'}(t,t+T) - \sum_{\substack{d=1 \\ d \neq c}}^{m} D_{cd}^{ii'}(t,t+T)$$

$$- \sum_{\substack{j=1 \\ j \neq i}}^{n} M_{cc}^{ij}(t,t+T) - \sum_{\substack{j=1 \\ j \neq i}}^{n} \sum_{\substack{d=1 \\ d \neq c}}^{m} M_{cd}^{ij}(t,t+T) - \sum_{\substack{j'=1' \\ j' \neq i'}}^{n'} D_{cc}^{ij'}(t,t+T)$$

$$- \sum_{\substack{j'=1' \\ j' \neq i'}}^{n'} \sum_{\substack{d=1 \\ d \neq c}}^{m} D_{cd}^{ij'}(t,t+T) + \sum_{\substack{d=1 \\ d \neq c}}^{m} S_{dc}^{ii}(t,t+T) + B_{cc}^{i'i}(t,t+T)$$

$$+ \sum_{\substack{d=1 \\ d \neq c}}^{m} B_{dc}^{i'i}(t,t+T) + \sum_{\substack{j=1 \\ j \neq i}}^{n} M_{cc}^{ji}(t,t+T) + \sum_{\substack{j=1 \\ j \neq i}}^{n} \sum_{\substack{d=1 \\ d \neq c}}^{m} M_{dc}^{ji}(t,t+T)$$

$$+ \sum_{\substack{j'=1' \\ j' \neq i'}}^{n'} B_{cc}^{j'i}(t,t+T) + \sum_{\substack{j'=1' \\ j' \neq i'}}^{n'} \sum_{\substack{d=1 \\ d \neq c}}^{m} B_{dc}^{j'i}(t,t+T) . \tag{50}$$

This equation can then be converted to a projection equation by formulating it in rate rather than flow terms. Simplifying equation (50) by using a survival term explicitly, we get

$$W_c^i(t+T) = s_{dc}^{ii}(t,t+T)W_c^i(t) + \sum_{\substack{d=1 \\ d \neq c}}^{m} s_{dc}^{ii}(t,t+T)\,W_d^i(t) + b_{cc}^{i'i}(t,t+T)W_c^i(t)$$

$$+ \sum_{\substack{d=1 \\ d \neq c}}^{m} b_{dc}^{i'i}(t,t+T)W_d^i(t) + \sum_{\substack{j=1 \\ j \neq i}}^{n} m_{cc}^{ji}(t,t+T)W_c^j(t)$$

$$+ \sum_{\substack{j=1 \\ j \neq i}}^{n} \sum_{\substack{d=1 \\ d \neq c}}^{m} m_{dc}^{ji}(t,t+T)W_d^j(t) + \sum_{\substack{j'=1' \\ j' \neq i'}}^{n'} b_{cc}^{j'i}(t,t+T)W_c^j(t)$$

$$+ \sum_{\substack{j'=1'd=1 \\ j' \neq i' d \neq c}}^{n' \quad m} b_{cc}^{j'i}(t,t+T)W_d^j(t) . \tag{51}$$

This can be generalised as

$$W_c^i(t+T) = \sum_{k=1}^{n'} \sum_d f_{dc}^{ki}(t,t+T)W_d^k(t) , \tag{52}$$

where

$$f_{dc}^{ki}(t,t+T) = \frac{F_{dc}^{ki}(t,t+T)}{W_d^k(t)} , \tag{53}$$

and k refers to any zone $1,...,n$ or $1',...,n'$. We can either define $W_d^k(t)$ in the case of the primed zones to be the opening stock population of zone

k, or the total births that occur in zone k, $B_{d*}^{k'*}(t, t+T)$. In the latter case what we need is a subsidiary equation to relate births to population

$$B_{d*}^{k'*}(t, t+T) = b_{d*}^{k'*}(t, t+T) W_d^k(t),\tag{54}$$

where historically

$$b_{d*}^{k'*}(t, t+T) = \frac{B_{d*}^{k'*}(t, t+T)}{W_d^i(t)}.$$

The rates would be projected into the future for population forecasts. In many respects it is very convenient to have the births model outside the main projection equation. We can separately explore different definitions of the parental population[5].

Table 5. A matrix of net flows for the two-zone, two-class case.

Category 4			Zone i Survival (e)[a]		Zone i' Deaths (ne)[b]		Zone R Survival (e)		Zone R' Deaths (ne)		Totals
5			c	D	c	D	c	D	c	D	
Zone i' Survival (e)	c		$-$ $-S_{Dc}^{ii}$	S_{cD}^{ii}	$D_{cc}^{ii'}$ $-B_{cc}^{i'i}$	$D_{cD}^{ii'}$ $-B_{Dc}^{i'i}$	M_{cc}^{iR} $-M_{cc}^{Ri}$	M_{cD}^{iR} $-M_{cc}^{Ri}$	$D_{cc}^{iR'}$ $-B_{cc}^{R'i}$	$D_{cD}^{iR'}$ $-B_{cc}^{R'i}$	$W_c^i(t)$ $-W_c^i(t+T)$
	D	S_{Dc}^{ii} $-S_{cD}^{ii}$	$-$	$D_{Dc}^{ii'}$ $-B_{cD}^{i'i}$	$D_{DD}^{ii'}$ $-B_{DD}^{i'i}$	M_{Dc}^{iR} $-M_{cD}^{Ri}$	M_{DD}^{iR} $-M_{cD}^{Ri}$	$D_{Dc}^{iR'}$ $-B_{cD}^{R'i}$	$D_{DD}^{iR'}$ $-B_{cD}^{R'i}$	$W_D^i(t)$ $-W_D^i(t+T)$
Zone i Births (ne)	c	$B_{cc}^{i'i}$ $-D_{cc}^{ii'}$	$B_{cD}^{i'i}$ $-D_{Dc}^{ii'}$	$-$ $-\not{B}_{cc}^{i'i'}$	$\not{B}_{cc}^{i'i'}$	$B_{cc}^{i'R}$ $-D_{cc}^{Ri'}$	$B_{cD}^{i'R}$ $-D_{cc}^{Ri'}$	$\not{B}_{cc}^{i'R'}$ $-\not{B}_{cc}^{R'i'}$	$\not{B}_{cD}^{i'R'}$ $-\not{B}_{cc}^{R'i'}$	$B_{c\bullet}^{i'\bullet}$ $-D_{\bullet c}^{\bullet i'}$
	D	$B_{Dc}^{i'i}$ $-D_{cD}^{ii'}$	$B_{DD}^{i'i}$ $-D_{DD}^{ii'}$	$\not{B}_{Dc}^{i'i'}$ $-\not{B}_{cD}^{i'i'}$	$-$	$B_{Dc}^{i'R}$ $-D_{cD}^{Ri'}$	$B_{DD}^{i'R}$ $-D_{cD}^{Ri'}$	$\not{B}_{Dc}^{i'R'}$ $-\not{B}_{cD}^{R'i'}$	$\not{B}_{DD}^{i'R'}$ $-\not{B}_{cD}^{R'i'}$	$B_{D\bullet}^{i'\bullet}$ $-D_{\bullet D}^{\bullet i'}$
Zone R Survival (e)	c	M_{cc}^{Ri} $-M_{cc}^{iR}$	M_{cD}^{Ri} $-M_{cc}^{iR}$	$D_{cc}^{Ri'}$ $-B_{cc}^{i'R}$	$D_{cD}^{Ri'}$ $-B_{cc}^{i'R}$	$-$ $-S_{Dc}^{RR}$	S_{cD}^{RR}	$D_{cc}^{RR'}$ $-B_{cc}^{R'R}$	$D_{cD}^{RR'}$ $-B_{cc}^{R'R}$	$W_c^R(t)$ $-W_c^R(t+T)$
	D	M_{Dc}^{Ri} $-M_{cD}^{iR}$	M_{DD}^{Ri} $-M_{DD}^{iR}$	$D_{Dc}^{Ri'}$ $-B_{cD}^{i'R}$	$D_{DD}^{Ri'}$ $-B_{DD}^{i'R}$	S_{Dc}^{RR} $-S_{cD}^{RR}$	$-$	$D_{Dc}^{RR'}$ $-B_{cD}^{R'R}$	$D_{DD}^{RR'}$ $-B_{DD}^{R'R}$	$W_D^R(t)$ $-W_D^R(t+T)$
Zone R' Births (ne)	c	$B_{cc}^{R'i}$ $-D_{cc}^{iR'}$	$B_{cD}^{R'i}$ $-D_{Dc}^{iR'}$	$\not{B}_{cc}^{R'i'}$ $-\not{B}_{cc}^{i'R'}$	$\not{B}_{cD}^{R'i'}$ $-\not{B}_{Dc}^{i'R'}$	$B_{cc}^{R'R}$ $-D_{cc}^{RR'}$	$B_{cD}^{R'R}$	$-$	$\not{B}_{cD}^{R'R'}$ $-\not{B}_{Dc}^{R'R'}$	$B_{c\bullet}^{R'\bullet}$ $-D_{\bullet c}^{\bullet R'}$
	D	$B_{Dc}^{R'i}$ $-D_{cD}^{iR'}$	$B_{DD}^{R'i}$ $-D_{DD}^{iR'}$	$\not{B}_{Dc}^{R'i'}$ $-\not{B}_{cD}^{i'R'}$	$\not{B}_{DD}^{R'i'}$ $-\not{B}_{DD}^{i'R'}$	$B_{Dc}^{R'R}$ $-D_{cD}^{RR'}$	$B_{DD}^{R'R}$	$\not{B}_{Dc}^{R'R'}$	$-$ $-\not{B}_{cD}^{R'R'}$	$B_{D\bullet}^{R'\bullet}$ $-D_{\bullet D}^{\bullet R'}$
Totals		$W_c^i(t+T)$ $-W_c^i(t)$	$W_D^i(t+T)$ $-W_D^i(t)$	$D_{\bullet c}^{\bullet i'}$ $-B_{c\bullet}^{i'\bullet}$	$D_{\bullet D}^{\bullet i'}$ $-B_{D\bullet}^{i'\bullet}$	$W_c^R(t+T)$ $-W_c^R(t)$	$W_D^R(t+T)$ $-W_D^R(t)$	$D_{\bullet c}^{\bullet R'}$ $-B_{c\bullet}^{R'\bullet}$	$D_{\bullet D}^{\bullet R'}$ $-B_{D\bullet}^{R'\bullet}$	$-$

[a] (e) is existence. [b] (ne) is non-existence.

The symbols are as defined in table 3.

[5] One might note that in Forrester's *Urban Dynamics* model the underemployed birth rate UBR is merely set to a constant of $0\cdot015$ of the underemployed population per year.

Rogers (1966, 1967), Wilson (1971a, 1971b), and Stone (1971) have expressed their demographic models in matrix form. Equation (51) can be usefully expressed in matrix notation:

$$\mathbf{w}(t+T) = \mathbf{G}\mathbf{w}(t) , \tag{55}$$

where
$\mathbf{w}(t+T)$ is a column vector with $2nm$ rows applying to time $t+T$;
$\mathbf{G}$ is a growth matrix of rates; and
$\mathbf{w}(t)$ is a column vector of $2nm$ rows applying to time t.
$\mathbf{w}(t+T)$ consists of a set of zonal population vectors:

$$\mathbf{w}(t+T) = \begin{matrix} \mathbf{w}^1(t+T) \\ \mathbf{w}^2(t+T) \\ \cdot \\ \cdot \\ \mathbf{w}^i(t+T) \\ \cdot \\ \mathbf{w}^n(t \mid T) \end{matrix} . \tag{56}$$

Each of these zonal population vectors consists of the populations of the social classes and the total of deaths in those social classes over the period;

$$\mathbf{w}^i(t+T) = \begin{matrix} W^i_1(t) \\ W^i_2(t+T) \\ \cdot \\ W^i_c(t+T) \\ \cdot \\ \cdot \\ W^i_m(t+T) \\ D^{*i'}_{*1}(t,t+T) \\ D^{*i'}_{*2}(t,t+T) \\ \cdot \\ \cdot \\ D^{*i'}_{*c}(t,t+T) \\ \cdot \\ D^{*i'}_{*m}(t,t+T) \end{matrix} . \tag{57}$$

If there are n zones and m social classes there will be $2nm$ rows to this vector.

The $\mathbf{w}(t)$ vector consists of a similarly structured set of zonal population vectors:

$$\mathbf{w}(t) = \begin{array}{l} \mathbf{w}^1(t) \\ \mathbf{w}^2(t) \\ \cdot \\ \cdot \\ \mathbf{w}^i(t) \\ \cdot \\ \cdot \\ \mathbf{w}^n(t) \, . \end{array} \qquad (58)$$

Each $\mathbf{w}^i(t)$ is made up of the populations of the social classes at the beginning of the period together with the projected number of births in each social class:

$$\mathbf{w}^i(t) = \begin{array}{l} W^i_1(t) \\ W^i_2(t) \\ \cdot \\ \cdot \\ W^i_c(t) \\ \cdot \\ \cdot \\ W^i_m(t) \\ B^{i\,*}_{1*}(t, t+T) \\ B^{i\,*}_{2*}(t, t+T) \\ \cdot \\ \cdot \\ B^{i'\,*}_{c*}(t, t+T) \\ \cdot \\ \cdot \\ B^{i'\,*}_{m*}(t, t+T) \, . \end{array} \qquad (59)$$

The growth matrix consists of the rates matrix corresponding to table 3 (the flows in table 3 divided by the row totals) transposed. It is made up of a set of submatrices

$$G = \begin{array}{cccccccccc}
S^{11} & B^{11} & M^{12} & B^{12} & M^{13} & B^{13} & . & . & M^{1n} & B^{1n} \\
D^{11} & \mathcal{B}^{11} & D^{12} & \mathcal{B}^{12} & D^{13} & \mathcal{B}^{13} & . & . & D^{1n} & \mathcal{B}^{1n} \\
M^{21} & B^{21} & S^{22} & B^{22} & M^{23} & B^{23} & . & . & M^{2n} & B^{2n} \\
D^{21} & \mathcal{B}^{21} & D^{22} & \mathcal{B}^{22} & D^{23} & \mathcal{B}^{23} & . & . & D^{2n} & \mathcal{B}^{2n} \\
M^{31} & B^{31} & M^{32} & B^{32} & S^{33} & B^{33} & . & . & M^{3n} & B^{3n} \\
D^{31} & \mathcal{B}^{31} & D^{32} & \mathcal{B}^{32} & D^{33} & \mathcal{B}^{33} & . & . & D^{3n} & \mathcal{B}^{3n} \cdot \\
\cdot & \cdot & \cdot & \cdot & \cdot & \cdot & . & . & \cdot & \cdot \\
\cdot & \cdot & \cdot & \cdot & \cdot & \cdot & . & . & \cdot & \cdot \\
M^{n1} & B^{n1} & M^{n2} & B^{n2} & M^{n3} & B^{n3} & . & . & S^{nn} & B^{nn} \\
D^{n1} & \mathcal{B}^{n1} & D^{n2} & \mathcal{B}^{n2} & D^{n3} & \mathcal{B}^{n3} & . & . & D^{nn} & \mathcal{B}^{nn} \\
\end{array}$$

$$(60)$$

Each of these submatrices consists of the rates of transition between one social class and another via the particular kind of population flow represented. For example, a typical survivorship sub-matrix looks like this

$$
S^{ii} = \begin{matrix}
s^{ii}_{11} & s^{ii}_{12} & s^{ii}_{13} & . & . & s^{ii}_{1m} \\
s^{ii}_{21} & s^{ii}_{22} & s^{ii}_{23} & . & . & s^{ii}_{2m} \\
s^{ii}_{31} & s^{ii}_{32} & s^{ii}_{33} & . & . & s^{ii}_{3m} \\
. & . & . & . \cdot . & . \\
. & . & . & . & . \\
s^{ii}_{m1} & s^{ii}_{m2} & s^{ii}_{m3} & & & s^{ii}_{mm} \; .
\end{matrix}
\tag{61}
$$

Each of the rates in the matrix applies to the period $(t, t+T)$, and measures the rate at which the original population of zone i in a particular social class survives within the zone in that class or moves within the zone to another class. Because of the transposition the rate s^{ii}_{cd} in equation (61) refers to a movement from social class d to social class c.

Before turning to a rather different disaggregation of the population, that involving sex, age, and ethnic group, we need to comment on how rates can be firstly measured and secondly projected for intra-urban zones.

We are unlikely to meet the demands of the accounting and modelling system presented without a great deal of ingenuity in estimation and a good deal of calculated guesswork. Many of the historical time series data needed for extrapolating rates, or variables influencing rates, into the future are available only at much higher spatial scales than the intra-urban zone. To estimate the rates at ward or enumeration district level, for example, use will have to be made of a body of estimation techniques that might be termed compositional analysis. For example, if deaths were classified by socioeconomic group (an occupational classification) at the national level, and we knew the breakdown of the zonal population by socioeconomic group, we could estimate the number of 'deaths' in a particular social class in a particular zone by

$$
D^{*i'}_{*c}(t, t+T) = \sum_{s \in c} d^{*N}_{*S}(t, t+T) W^i_s(t) + \Delta^{i'}_c(t, t+T) ,
\tag{62}
$$

where we have defined our social class c to be made up of a combination of several of the socioeconomic groups s used by the Registrar General. The $d^{*N}_{*S}(t, t+T)$ would be the national 'death' rate (say in England and Wales) for socioeconomic groups. It would be feasible to project this rate into the future using national time-series information. The population in groups at the beginning of the period is represented by $W^i_s(t)$, and the $\Delta^{i'}_c(t, t+T)$ term represents the difference between the compositional estimate and actual deaths in zone i. This local effect might be the product of particular environmental features (air pollution, climate, water quality) or cultural features (variation in propensity to smoke, for example). We should need some local information on death rates to check whether the $\Delta^{i'}_c$'s were small and random or large and systematic in their distribution.

One obvious extension of the social class model outlined here would be to break each class down into its component age groups. This would make the task of rate estimation and projection a good deal easier.

A sex, age, and ethnic group model

The sex and age models are not described in detail here. They have been described and developed extensively by Wilson (1971a, 1971b). His models are employed here in combination with an ethnic group classification. Ethnic groups behave in this model in much the same way as the sexes do in the general cohort survival model, except that we must allow for the possibility of births of mixed ethnicity. In other words both the sexes and ethnic groups behave like separate populations, replications of the aggregate population, except in relation to the reproduction and birth process, where interaction takes place!

Ethnic groups are often difficult to define in terms of published population characteristics, although the identity of such groups in the city may be quite clear to the city's inhabitants. Ethnic groups can be defined on the basis of race, language, religion, place of birth, or other particular characteristics that are largely inherited from family of origin rather than acquired during life. Very often the basis of ethnic differentiation will change through time, as some of these distinctive attributes are lost in later generations. Races may become mixed; groups may cease to speak distinctive languages; individuals may change religions; place of birth may become less relevant as it becomes place of birth of mother or grandmother.

Assuming that we have arrived at an operational ethnic classification (for applications of the model in British cities it would have to be based on place of birth), we have to decide how to deal with the offspring of marriages of mixed ethnicity. If we recognise every possible combination of ethnicity, then with succeeding generations of population an unmanageable number of groups will be created. In many societies the offspring of mixed marriages are regarded as members of the minority group by the host population. This is particularly true of offspring of marriages of mixed race in societies where racial prejudice is strong, and residential segregation based on racial prejudice is extreme.

It is more useful from the point of view of research to recognise the existence of persons of mixed ethnicity and to follow the fortunes of these persons as a separate group to be compared with the groups of pure ethnicity.

Table 6 demonstrates how a simple mixed race classification might be achieved for a British city: some seven categories would result if a simple three group classification were adopted to begin with—UK born, New Commonwealth born, and other. There would be three pure groups (the diagonal elements), three groups consisting of mixtures of two of three original groups (the off-diagonal elements, not distinguishing between the two possibilities in any combination), and a final group consisting of a

Table 6. An ethnic group classification for studies in British cities.

(a) Initial ethnic groups recognised

Place of birth	Major group	Label
United Kingdom	Native British	A
Republic of Ireland Australia, Canada, New Zealand Foreign	Other European	B
India Africa West Indies Malta, Gibraltar, Cyprus Remainder, New Commonwealth	New Commonwealth	C
Not stated	To be assigned to other groups by appropriate estimation methods	

(b) Ethnic groups resulting from the interaction of the first generation

Births by ethnic group of parent		Ethnic group of mother		
		A	B	C
Ethnic group of father	A	B_{AA}	B_{AB}	B_{AC}
	B	B_{BA}	B_{BB}	B_{BC}
	C	B_{CA}	B_{BC}	B_{CC}

B_{AB} —births to fathers in ethnic group A and mothers in ethnic group B

(c) Assignment of births to a new ethnic group classification

Ethnic group of father	mother	New ethnic group classification							
		A	B	C	BB	CC	AB	AC	BC
A	A	+							
A	B						+		
A	C							+	
B	A						+		
B	B		+		+				
B	C								+
C	A							+	
C	B								+
C	C			+		+			

Table 6 (contd.)

(d) Ethnic groups resulting from the second generation of interaction

Ethnic group to which offspring is assigned		Ethnic group of mother							
		A	B	C	BB	CC	AB	AC	BC
	A	A	AB	AC	AB	AC	AB	AC	ABC
	B	AB	B,BB	BC	BB	BC	AB	ABC	BC
	C	AC	BC	C,CC	BC	CC	ABC	AC	ABC
Ethnic group	BB	AB	BB	BC	BB	BC	AB	ABC	BC
of father	CC	AC	BC	CC	BC	CC	ABC	AC	BC
	AB	AB	AB	ABC	AB	ABC	AB	ABC	ABC
	AC	AC	ABC	AC	ABC	AC	ABC	AC	ABC
	BC	ABC	BC	BC	BC	BC	ABC	ABC	BC

(e) A 'stable' ethnic group classification

Label	Description
A	Persons with 'native British' genes only
B	Persons with genes of one 'other European' group only
C	Persons with genes of one 'New Commonwealth' group only
BB	Persons with genes of at least two 'other European' groups
CC	Persons with genes of at least two 'New Commonwealth' groups
AB	Persons with genes of 'native British' and at least one 'other European' group
AC	Persons with genes of 'native British' and at least one 'New Commonwealth' group
BC	Persons with genes of at least one 'other European' and at least one 'New Commonwealth' group
ABC	Persons with genes from 'native British' group, at least one 'other European' group and at least one 'New Commonwealth' group

(f) Ethnicity of children born in England and Wales 1969-1970

Place of birth of father	Place of birth of mother						Totals	
	United Kingdom		Elsewhere in Europe and foreign		New Commonwealth			
United Kingdom	610113	0·965	18303	0·029	3821	0·006	632237	1·000
	0·957	0·843	0·425	0·025	0·088	0·005	0·873	
Elsewhere in Europe and foreign	19784	0·456	21984	0·507	727	0·017	43389	1·000
			894	0·021				
	0·031	0·027	0·511	0·030	0·017	0·001	0·060	
			0·021	0·001				
New Commonwealth	7489	0·155	1867	0·039	37052	0·766	48398	1·000
					1990	0·041		
	0·012	0·010	0·043	0·003	0·850	0·051	0·067	
					0·046	0·003		
Totals	637386	0·880	43048	0·059	43590	0·060	724024	1·000
			1·000		1·000		1·000	1·000

Key

Number of children born	18303	0·029	Proportion of row total (total in ethnic group of father)
Proportions of column total (total in ethnic group of mother)	0·425	0·025	Proportion of grand total (all live-births)

Table 6 (contd.)
(g) Breakdown of ethnicity of children

	A	B	C	BB	CC	AB	AC	BC
Proportion	0·843	0·030	0·051	0·001	0·003	0·052	0·015	0·004
		0·925				0·075		

Source: Calculated from data on the live birth occurrences by country of birth of father and mother, April 1969 to March 1970 in England and Wales (HMSO, 1971, appendix C).

mixture of all three primary groups. Further mixtures in subsequent generations can be redefined in terms of these seven groups. If we wished to maintain more detailed distinctions within the diagonal elements, then more groups would have to be recognised. For example, offspring of parents from two different New Commonwealth groups labelled CC are distinguished from those whose parents belong to one New Commonwealth group only. These children are labelled C in the third section of table 6. When these children marry and themselves produce children their offspring can be reassigned to the original ethnic groups, applying the rule [section (d) of table 6] that anyone with genes from groups A and B, in no matter what proportion, gets assigned to group AB, anyone with genes from groups A and C, in no matter what proportion, is assigned to group AC, and so on. One further group must be recognised under these conventions —that in which the genes of all three groups are mixed, group ABC. The ethnic group classification which results [section (e) of table 6] is then stable over subsequent generations. The last section of table 6 reveals the degree of intermixture of ethnic groups that is proceeding in England and Wales today. Some 15·7% of births recorded over the year April 1969 to March 1970 were to couples at least one of whom was not born in the UK. Of this number nearly half (7·5% of the total births) were children of mixed ethnicity as we have defined it, though probably more were of mixed ethnicity given the broadness of the initial groups distinguished [table 6, section (a)].

Having made some operational decisions with respect to ethnic group classification, we can turn to the set of demographic accounts associated with the sex, age, and ethnic group model. For each sex–ethnic group combination, XE, we have a table of population flows (table 7) disaggregated by age. In principle we could specify the model derived from this set of accounts in the same way as the social class model was specified in matrix form. However, Wilson (1971a, 1971b) has pointed out that, in practice, most of the age-group to age-group transitions will be zero (no 'de-aging' process exists, for example). Expression of the model in algebraic form is more efficient in computational terms and is more general. We adapt his equations here for the ethnic group case.

For age groups r, into which people born over the study or projection period cannot survive, that is, for $r > m$ (Wilson, 1971a, 1971b), the basic accounting equation is

$$W_r^{iXE}(t+T) = \sum_{k=0}^{n_r} S_{r-kr}^{iiXE}(t,t+T) + \sum_{\substack{j=1 \\ j \neq i}}^{n} \sum_{k=0}^{n_r} M_{r-kr}^{jiXE}(t,t+T), \tag{63}$$

where

$W_r^{iXE}(t+T)$ is the population age r in zone i of sex X and ethnic group E at time $(t+T)$;

$S_{r-kr}^{iiXE}(t,t+T)$ is the number of survivors of sex X and ethnic group E into age group r at time $t+T$ from age group $r-k$ at time t;

$M_{r-kr}^{jiXE}(t,t+T)$ is the number of migrants of sex X and ethnic group E who have migrated from age group $r-k$ in zone j at time t to age group r in zone i at time $t+T$.

The function of the $k = 0, ..., n_r$ summation is to allow for survival into age group r from more than one preceding age group (Wilson 1971a, 1971b). The accounting equation for age groups into which persons born over the study period can survive is

$$W_r^{iXE}(t+T) = \sum_{k=0}^{n_r} S_{r-kr}^{iiXE}(t,t+T) + \sum_{k=0}^{m_r} B_{r-kr}^{i'iXE}(t,t+T)$$

$$+ \sum_{\substack{j=1 \\ j \neq i}}^{n} \sum_{k=0}^{n_r} M_{r-kr}^{jiXE}(t,t+T) + \sum_{\substack{j=1 \\ j \neq i}}^{n} \sum_{k=0}^{m_r} B_{r-kr}^{j'iXE}(t,t+T). \tag{64}$$

Table 7. A closed demographic matrix for a single period for an ethnic population disaggregated by age and sex.

Location at time t	State at time t	Location at time $t+T$				Totals
		Zone i	Zone i'	Zone R	Zone R'	
		State at time $t+T$				
		Survival (e)[a]	Death (ne)[b]	Survival (e)	Death (ne)	
Zone i	Survival (e)	S^{iiXE}	$D^{ii'XE}$	M^{iRXE}	$D^{iR'XE}$	$w^{iXE}(t)$
Zone i'	Birth (ne)	$B^{i'iXE}$	$B^{i'i'XE}$	$B^{i'RXE}$	$B^{i'R'XE}$	$B^{i' \cdot XE}(t,t+T)$
Zone R	Survival (e)	M^{RiXE}	$D^{Ri'XE}$	S^{RRXE}	$D^{RR'XE}$	$w^{RXE}(t)$
Zone R'	Birth (ne)	$B^{R'iXE}$	$B^{R'i'XE}$	$B^{R'RXE}$	$B^{R'R'XE}$	$B^{R' \cdot XE}(t,t+T)$
Totals		$w^{iXE}(t+T)$	$D^{\cdot i'XE}(t,t+T)$	$w^{RXE}(t+T)$	$D^{\cdot R'XE}(t,t+T)$	$F^{\cdot \cdot XE}(t,t+T)$

[a] (e) is existence.   [b] (ne) is non-existence.

The symbols have the same substantive meaning as those in table 1 except that each refers to a matrix of flows between age groups over the time period $(t, t+T)$. The marginal totals are row or column vectors disaggregated by age group at the beginning of the period or at its end.

The m_r in the births summation acts like the n_r in the survivors and migrants summation (Wilson, 1971a, 1971b), and enables account to be taken of short time interval information on the number of births. The exact methods for defining m_r and the B_{r-kr} terms are given in the appendix.

Survivors in equation (64) are defined as follows:

$$S_{r-kr}^{ii\mathrm{XE}}(t,t+T) = W_{r-k}^{i\mathrm{XE}}(t) - D_{r-k(r)}^{ii'\mathrm{XE}}(t,t+T) - \sum_{j=1}^{n} M_{r-kr}^{ij\mathrm{XE}}(t,t+T)$$

$$- \sum_{\substack{j'=1' \\ j' \neq i'}}^{n'} D_{r-k(r)}^{ij'\mathrm{XE}}(t,t+T) - S_{r-k\bar{r}}^{ii\mathrm{XE}}(t,t+T)$$

$$- \sum_{j=1}^{n} M_{r-k\bar{r}}^{ij\mathrm{XE}}(t,t+T) - D_{r-k(\bar{r})}^{ii'\mathrm{XF}}(t,t\mid T)$$

$$- \sum_{\substack{j'=1' \\ j' \neq i'}}^{n'} D_{r-k(\bar{r})}^{ij'\mathrm{XE}}(t,t+T) . \tag{65}$$

The bracketed age subscripts in the deaths terms refer to the age group which those persons would have been in had they not died. The notation $\bar{r}$ is used to denote age groups other than r. The concept is explained in more detail in the appendix. The last four terms in equation (65) are necessary in the age disaggregated model in its general form. Their full implications for the generalized demographic model have yet to be worked out. Similar residual equations are necessary for the births terms in equation (64), though not for the migration term which can usually be directly estimated.

Equations (63) and (64) can be converted into a rate form to be used in projection:

for $r > m$

$$W_r^{i\mathrm{XE}}(t+T) = \sum_{k=0}^{n_r} s_{r-kr}^{ii\mathrm{XE}}(t,t+T) W_{r-k}^{i\mathrm{XE}}(t)$$

$$+ \sum_{\substack{j=1 \\ j \neq i}}^{n} \sum_{k=0}^{n_r} m_{r-kr}^{ji\mathrm{XE}}(t,t+T) W_{r-k}^{j\mathrm{XE}}(t) , \tag{66}$$

and for $r < m$

$$W_r^{iXE}(t+T) = \sum_{k=0}^{n_r} s_{r-kr}^{iiXE}(t,t+T) W_{r-k}^{iXE}(t)$$

$$+ \sum_{k=0}^{m_r} b_{r-kr}^{i'iXE}(t,t+T) B_{r-k*}^{i'*XE}(t,t+T)$$

$$+ \sum_{\substack{j=1\\j\neq i}}^{n} \sum_{k=0}^{n_r} m_{r-k}^{jiXE}(t,t+T) W_{r-k}^{jXE}(t)$$

$$+ \sum_{\substack{j=1\\j\neq i}}^{n} \sum_{k=0}^{m_r} b_{r-kr}^{j'iXE}(t,t+T) B_{r-k*}^{j'*XE}(t,t+T), \tag{67}$$

where

$$s_{r-kr}^{iiXE}(t,t+T) = \frac{S_{r-kr}^{iiXE}(t,t+T)}{W_{r-k}^{iXE}(t)}, \tag{68}$$

$$m_{r-kr}^{jiXE}(t,t+T) = \frac{M_{r-kr}^{jiXE}(t,t+T)}{W_{r-k}^{jXE}(t)}, \tag{69}$$

$$b_{r-kr}^{i'iXE}(t,t+T) = \frac{B^{i'iXE}\{t+[-(r-k)]\tau, t+[-(r-k)+1]\tau\}}{B^{i'*XE}\{t+[-(r-k)]\tau, t+[-(r-k)+1]\tau\}}, \tag{70}$$

unless $r-k = m_r$ when

$$b_{m,r}^{i'iXE}(t,t+T) = \frac{B^{i'iXE}[t+(-m_r)\tau, t+T]}{B^{i*XE}[t+(-m_r)\tau, t+T]}, \tag{71}$$

and

$$b_{r-kr}^{j'iXE}(t,t+T) = \frac{B^{j'iXE}\{t+[-(r-k)]\tau, t+[-(r-k)+1]\tau\}}{B^{j'*XE}\{t+[-(r-k)]\tau, t+[-(r-k)+1]\tau\}}, \tag{72}$$

unless $r-k = m_r$ when

$$b_{m,r}^{j'iXE}(t,t+T) = \frac{B^{j'iXE}[t+(-m_r)\tau, t+T]}{B^{j'*XE}[t+(-m_r)\tau, t+T]}. \tag{73}$$

The problem of estimating the survival, migration, and birth rates in the model equation has been discussed in connection with the aggregate model and by Wilson (1971a, 1971b). Here we need only comment on the characteristics of the model equations peculiar to the ethnic groups case. Total births are used, in preference to aggregate population or the number of women in the reproductive age groups, as the birth rate divisor because allowance for ethnic group interaction can then be made in a separate equation.

The number of births in a zone of babies of ethnic group E, where E may be a pure or mixed ethnic group (say E = A, B, C, ..., BC in the case of England and Wales), is a function of the number of inter-racial couples in the zone and of their age, marital status, and present family size. In other words, we can model total births in the following way:

$$B^{i'*XE}(t, t+\tau) = \sum_k \sum_m \sum_f b^{N'*XE}_{kmf}(t, t+\tau) Z^{iE_1 E_2}_{kmf}(t) + \Delta^{iXE} , \qquad (74)$$

where

$B^{i'*XE}(t, t+\tau)$ is the estimated or projected number of births in zone i, of persons of sex X and ethnic group E, in short time period $t, t+\tau$;

$Z^{iE_1 E_2}_{kmf}(t)$ is the number of couples with the man in ethnic group E_1, the woman in ethnic group E_2 in zone i with age characteristic k, marital status m, and number of children f;

$b^{N'*XE}_{kmf}$ is the national birth rate of persons of sex X and ethnic group E, born to couples with age characteristic k, marital status m, and number of children f,

$$= \frac{B^{N'*XE}(t, t+T)}{Z^{NE}_{kmf}(t)} ;$$

Δ^{iXE} is the residual or error term specific to zone i, sex X, and ethnic group E.

Now information on the ethnic composition of families is rarely given, so that we must estimate the number of couples in each ethnic group from information about the separate ethnic distribution of men and women. The way to determine the ethnic mix of couples in a zone is to use national probabilities of inter-marriage of groups, such as those implied in section (f) of table 6. A number of alternative probability models exist to estimate the number of couples in each of the ethnic groups, and the empirical fit of these would need to be explored.

The error term in the equation would also need to be investigated, though the data needed for its estimation and for the detailed validation of equation (72) might be difficult to assemble. In principle, birth registration forms carry all the information necessary.

The migration rates needed in equations (66) and (67) have also to be modelled. The linking of population and housing sectors of the city via migration models are discussed in a later section, but here it may be noted that such a model for ethnic groups would have to take into account not only the housing opportunities offered in an urban zone but also the influence of its ethnic composition. Minority group members may meet resistance and discrimination when attempting to move into majority group areas; ethnic group families may be attracted to areas where community facilities have already been set up by members of their group. Morrill (1965) has built a successful simulation model for the expansion of the Seattle ghetto incorporating these features, and the Monte Carlo methods he uses may have to be applied in the sex, age, and ethnic group model in British cities, given the relatively small numbers involved in any one ethnic group in most urban zones.

Summary of the components needed for a successful social group model
Some six building blocks are needed for a successful model of the
distribution of social groups within cities over time. These are as
enumerated below.

1. We need a *set of population accounting tables and equations* together
   with a parallel set of *demographic model equations.* The *rates* in the
   model equations can be established from the accounts for an historical
   test period or periods. However, to project those rates into the future
   and, often, even to estimate them for the past, we need some four sets
   of models.
2. A *migration model* that describes and predicts the movement of members
   of the social groups distinguished within the city, and between the city
   and the rest of the world.
3. A *transition model* that describes and predicts the movement of persons
   from one social group to another. This may be a very simple model in
   some cases.
4. A *natality model* that describes and projects the number of births in
   each social group.
5. A *mortality model* that describes mortality trends for the social groups
   and projects these into the future.
6. Finally, *a set of estimation techniques* is needed that links together the
   information available from published sources and the data needed in
   each of the models listed.

The first of these building blocks has been specified in some detail, in the
cases of social classes and ethnic groups, and some preliminary suggestions
have been made concerning the other five components. Now we shall
turn to the housing sector of the city and examine the applicability to
housing types of the demographic concepts developed for social groups.

A housing model [6]
We adopt a very simple classification of housing by age to begin with and
then disaggregate by dwelling unit type.

The closed demographic matrix for housing (table 8) turns out to be
much simpler than the social group equivalents because we can regard the
migration of dwelling units as being of no practical importance [7]. The
number of housing units in a zone at the end of a study or projection
period is therefore

$$H^i(t+T) = {}^H S^{ii}(t, t+T) + {}^H B^{i'i}(t, t+T) \tag{75}$$

---

[6] This exposition of a housing model is based in part on work by Dear (1971).

[7] There are, of course, dwelling units that do move location, namely caravans or
mobile homes. In Britain these are numerically insignificant; in parts of the US they
are more numerous, but migrate only between specially prepared mobile home sites.

or, breaking this down by age groups,

$$H_r^i(t+T) = \sum_{k=0}^{n_r} {}^H S_{r-kr}^{ii} \, t, t+T) \,, \tag{76}$$

for age groups where $r > m$ and, for age groups where $r \leqslant m$,

$$H_r^i(t+T) = \sum_{k=0}^{n_r} {}^H S_{r-kr}^{ii}(t, t+T) + \sum_{k=0}^{m_r} {}^H B_{r-kr}^{i'i}(t, t+T) \,. \tag{77}$$

The ${}^H S$ terms represent housing units that survive from the opening stock into the closing stock, aging in the process; the ${}^H B$ terms represent houses newly constructed in the period, which also age during the period, and n_r and m_r are the parameters associated with the sex and age group model described earlier. The numbers of surviving housing units can be estimated by subtracting losses of houses from the opening housing stock: for ages $r > m$

$$^H S_{r-kr}^{ii}(t, t+T) = H_{r-k}^i(t) - {}^H D_{r-k(r)}^{ii'}(t, t+T) - {}^H S_{r-k\bar{r}}^{ii}(t, t+T) \,, \tag{78}$$

and for ages $r \leqslant m$

$$^H B_{r-kr}^{i'i}(t, t+T) = {}^H B_{r-kr}^{i'i}(t, t \mid T) \quad {}^H B_{r-k(r)}^{i'i'}(t, t+T) - {}^{II} B_{r-k\bar{r}}^{i'i}(t, t+T) \,, \tag{79}$$

where the notation (r) refers to the age group the housing lost in the period would have survived into had it not been demolished, and $\bar{r}$ refers to all the age groups, other than r, into which housing stock aged $r-k$ at time t could have aged by $t+T$. Where age group intervals and period length are all equal, equation (78) simplifies to

$$^H S_{r-1r}^{ii}(t, t+T) = H_{r-1}^i(t) - {}^H D_{r-1*}^{ii'}(t, t+T) \,, \tag{80}$$

and equation (79) simplifies to

$$^H B_{01}^{i'i}(t, t+T) = {}^H B_{0*}^{i'i}(t, t+T) - {}^H B_{0*}^{i'i'}(t, t+T) \,; \tag{81}$$

Table 8. A closed demographic matrix for a single period for housing stock disaggregated by age.

Location at time t	State at time t	Location at time $t+T$				Totals
		Zone i	Zone i'	Zone R	Zone R'	
		State at time $t+T$				
		Survival (e)[a]	Death (ne)[b]	Survival (e)	Death (ne)	
Zone i	Survival (e)	${}^H S^{ii}$	${}^H D^{ii'}$	–	–	$H^i(t)$
Zone i'	Birth (ne)	${}^H B^{i'i}$	${}^H B^{i'i'}$	–	–	${}^H B^{i'}{}_*$
Zone R	Survival (e)	–	–	${}^H S^{RR}$	${}^H D^{RR'}$	$H^R(t)$
Zone R'	Birth (ne)	–	–	${}^H B^{R'R}$	${}^H B^{R'R'}$	${}^H B^{R'}{}_*$
Totals		$H^i(t+T)$	${}^H D^{*i'}$	$H^R(t+T)$	${}^H D^{*R'}$	${}^H F^{**}$

[a] (e) is existence. [b] (ne) is non-existence.

The symbols are defined in same way as those in table 1 except that an H symbol has been added to represent housing. Each term is understood to be between time t and time $t+T$, except where otherwise noted.

though in all probability there will be no losses of housing built within the period if the period is short, as long as the builders or planners have not made any serious mistakes.

The housing losses represented in the ^HD terms can be broken down into demolitions and changes from residential to non-residential uses. However, it is probably more useful to disaggregate all the model components by housing types, one of which will be a non-residential 'bin'. This allows for conversions between different dwelling types (tenure changes, for example) as well as for conversions into and out of residential use.

Dwelling types are defined only in a general sense here. In operationalising a model of housing stock changes one would have to define the same sort of compromise typology of houses as had to be done for ethnic groups. This typology should use as differentiating characteristics at least information on housing unit tenure (owner-occupied, publicly rented, privately rented, etc.), condition (full amenities, outside wc, no hot water, etc.), and structure type (flat, terrace house, semi-detached, detached, etc.), and also, if available, information on price and size.

So, if the possibility of conversion between dwelling types is recognised, the closed demographic matrix for a single period for housing takes on the form of table 9, in which we use the 'all other types' device employed in previous tables. The housing stock accounting equation becomes,

Table 9. A closed demographic matrix for a single period for housing stock disaggregated by age and type.

Category		4	Zone i		Zone i'		Totals
		5	Survival (e)[a]		Death (ne)[b]		
		6	g	H	g	H	
1	2	3					
Zone i	Survival (e)	g	$^HS^{iigg}$	$^HS^{iigH}$	$^HD^{ii'gg}$	$^HD^{ii'gH}$	$H^{ig}(t)$
		H	$^HS^{iiHg}$	$^HS^{iiHH}$	$^HD^{ii'Hg}$	$^HD^{ii'HH}$	$H^{iH}(t)$
Zone i'	Birth (ne)	g	$^HB^{i'igg}$	$^HB^{i'igH}$	$^HB^{i'i'gg}$	$^HB^{i'i'gH}$	$^HB^{i'\bullet g\bullet}$
		H	$^HB^{i'iHg}$	$^HB^{i'iHH}$	$^HB^{i'i'Hg}$	$^HB^{i'i'HH}$	$^HB^{i'\bullet H\bullet}$
Totals			$H^{ig}(t+T)$	$H^{iH}(t+T)$	$^HD^{ii'\bullet g}$	$^HD^{ii'\bullet H}$	$^HF^{\bullet\bullet\bullet}$

[a] (e) is existence. [b] (ne) is non-existence.

The categories 1–6 are as defined in table 3:
1 Location at time t, or at first existence
2 State at time t
3 Housing type category at time t, or at time of birth
4 Location at time $t+T$, or at last existence
5 State at time $t+T$
6 Housing type at time $t+T$, or at time of death
g Housing type
H All housing types except g
The symbols within the body of the table are as defined in table 8.

for age groups $r > m$

$$H_r^{ig}(t+T) = \sum_{k=0}^{n_r} {}^H S_{r-k\,r}^{iigg}(t,t+T) + \sum_{k=0}^{n_r} \sum_{\substack{h=1 \\ h \neq g}}^{p} {}^H S_{r-k\,r}^{iihg}(t,t+T), \qquad (82)$$

and for age groups $r \leqslant m$

$$H_r^{ig}(t+T) = \sum_{k=0}^{n_r} {}^H S_{r-k\,r}^{iigg}(t,t+T) + \sum_{k=0}^{n_r} \sum_{\substack{h=1 \\ h \neq g}}^{p} {}^H S_{r-k\,r}^{iihg}(t,t+T)$$

$$+ \sum_{k=0}^{m_r} {}^H B_{r-k\,r}^{i'igg}(t,t+T) + \sum_{k=0}^{m_r} \sum_{\substack{h=1 \\ h \neq g}}^{p} {}^H B_{r-k\,r}^{i'ihg}(t,t+T). \qquad (83)$$

The terms in these accounting equations must be established from opening stock, conversion, demolition, and construction records. Thus,

$${}^H S_{r-k\,r}^{iigg}(t,t+T) = H_{r-k}^{ig}(t) - \sum_{\substack{h=1 \\ h \neq g}}^{p} {}^H S_{r-k\,r}^{iigh}(t,t+T) - {}^H D_{r-k\,r}^{ii'gg}(t,t+T)$$

$$- \sum_{\substack{h=1 \\ h \neq g}}^{p} {}^H D_{r-k\,r}^{ii'gh}(t,t+T) - {}^H S_{r-k\,\bar{r}}^{iigg}(t,t+T)$$

$$- {}^H D_{r-k\,\bar{r}}^{ii'gg}(t,t+T) - \sum_{\substack{h=1 \\ h \neq g}}^{p} {}^H D_{r-k\,\bar{r}}^{ii'gh}(t,t+T), \qquad (84)$$

that is, the housing that survives from age group $r-k$ to age group r in zone i in type g is equal to the opening stock of housing in zone i in type g, less conversions of age group $r-k$ houses surviving to age r from type g to all other types h, less demolitions to houses in age group $r-k$ at time t which would have survived into age group r had they not been demolished, less demolitions of the same kind in which the house had been converted before demolition, less three terms equivalent to the third, fourth, and fifth in which the housing in age group $r-k$ would have survived age groups other than r over the period. The other terms of equations (82) and (83) can be similarly specified as residuals working from the rows of table 9.

It might be possible to simplify this set of equations if the age group intervals for housing were equal in length and of the same span in time as the study or projection period (for example Rees, 1971b). However, this is unlikely to be the case, especially at the older end of the housing stock, and the generalised model developed by Wilson (1971a, 1971b) makes the use of such uneven data feasible.

The accounting equations can be converted into model equations in the usual way. For age groups $r > m$, the model equation is

$$H_r^{ig}(t+T) = \sum_{k=0}^{n_r} {}^H S_{r-kr}^{iigg}(t,t+T) H_{r-k}^{ig}(t)$$

$$+ \sum_{k=0}^{n_r} \sum_{\substack{h=1 \\ h \neq g}}^{p} {}^H S_{r-kr}^{iihg}(t,t+T) H_{r-k}^{ih}(t), \tag{85}$$

where

$${}^H S_{r-kr}^{iigg}(t,t+T) = \frac{{}^H S_{r-kr}^{iigg}(t,t+T)}{H_{r-k}^{ig}(t)}, \tag{86}$$

and

$${}^H S_{r-kr}^{iihg}(t,t+T) = \frac{{}^H S_{r-kr}^{iihg}(t,t+T)}{H_{r-k}^{ih}(t)}. \tag{87}$$

The model equation for age groups $r \leqslant m$ is

$$H_r^{ig}(t+T) = \sum_{k=0}^{n_r} {}^H S_{r-k}^{iigg}(t,t+T) H_{r-k}^{ig}(t) + \sum_{k=0}^{n_r} \sum_{\substack{h=1 \\ h \neq g}}^{p} {}^H S_{r-kr}^{iihg}(t,t+T) H_{r-k}^{ih}(t)$$

$$+ \sum_{k=0}^{m_r} {}^H b_{r-kr}^{i'igg}(t,t+T) {}^H B_{r-k*}^{i'ig*}(t,t+T)$$

$$+ \sum_{k=0}^{m_r} \sum_{\substack{h=1 \\ h \neq g}}^{p} {}^H b_{r-kr}^{i'ihg}(t,t+T) {}^H B_{r-k*}^{i'*h*}(t,t+T), \tag{88}$$

where

$${}^H b_{r-kr}^{i'igg}(t,t+T) = \frac{{}^H B_{r-kr}^{i'igg}(t,t+T)}{{}^H B_{r-k*}^{i'*g*}(t,t+T)}, \tag{89}$$

and

$${}^H b_{r-kr}^{i'ihg}(t,t+T) = \frac{{}^H B_{r-kr}^{i'ihg}(t,t+T)}{{}^H B_{r-k}^{i'*h*}(t,t+T)}, \tag{90}$$

remembering that the $r-k$ term refers to a pseudo-age group in this case. The advantage of making the row totals from the accounting table, rather than the opening stock population, the denominator in the rate equation is clear in this instance. Houses do not give birth to other houses, and the size of the existing housing stock in a zone would be a very poor predictor of housing growth because housing growth takes place in 'empty' or cleared land.

The housing construction process has often been described as wavelike. The housing commencements in a zone within the city are small when its development cycle begins. They soon build up rapidly to a peak, after which construction activity moderates because the land available within a zone is being filled up (figure 3). Such situations have often been modelled as logistic curves. The cumulative total of housing units constructed in a zone up to time (t), $H^i_{cum}(t)$,

$$H^i_{cum}(t) = \frac{U^i}{1 + \exp(a - bt)} \tag{91}$$

its simplest form. U^i on the right hand side represents the maximum number of units that could be built in the zone, a number set by the land available for residential development in a zone and the maximum density at which planning regulations allow it to be developed. The a parameter establishes the base level from which growth begins, and the b parameter measures the rate at which new housing is added. New dwellings constructe in a study or projection period would then be modelled as

$$^H B^{i'i}(t, t+T) = \int_{v=t}^{v=i+T} \frac{U^i \, dv}{1 + \exp(a - bv)} . \tag{92}$$

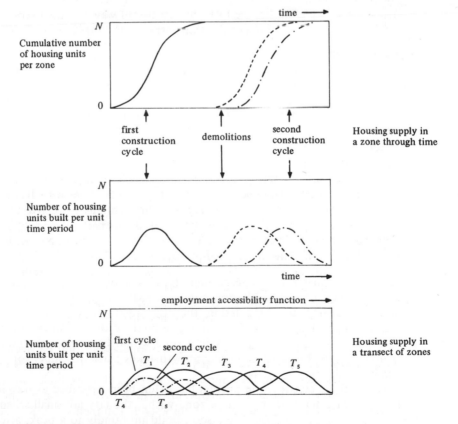

Figure 3. Housing construction cycles.

The point in calendar time at which the model time clock starts running would have to be established. The clock would be started when demand for housing in the city builds up to an extent that makes development of the particular zone under consideration, with its particular accessibility-to-workplace characteristics, profitable. Given that housing tends to be developed in fairly large chunks related to the way land comes on the market, and the way housing authorities and large private developers schedule development, it might not be possible to describe the housing construction process in such a fashion. But at least some explanation is indicated.

The other rates in equations (85) and (88) which need to be modelled are the survival and conversion or transition rates. Simple extrapolation into the future might suffice. Stone (1971, pp.117–118), however, suggests that logistic curve models might give better approximations. The age dependence of housing survival and transition rates is clear: the older the housing the more likely it is to move from a 'fit' to an 'unfit' condition, and the more likely it is to be demolished. This age dependence might well prove to be a very useful way of filling serious information gaps concerning transition rates.

Links between the social group and housing models

The primary link between the social group and housing sectors of the urban system would be via migration between urban zones, and between the urban system and the rest of the world—a variety of such models has been outlined by Wilson (1971a, 1971b). A necessary key feature of the intraurban migration model would be variables used as attractiveness factors in the destination zones. Housing classified by age and type is the primary attracting feature of any zone to intraurban migrants, and at least a secondary attracting feature to job seeking interurban migrants. Housing of a particular type is attractive to households of a particular type, or rather housing of various types is differentially attractive to the various social groups. Forrester (1969) solved this particular problem by simple assignment of the underemployed to underemployed housing, labour to worker-housing, and managerial-professional workers to premium housing. Similarly Stouffer (1940), in his paper on the intervening opportunity model, used as attractiveness factors in destination zones the number of housing units in the rental class which families occupied in the origin zone. Families were classified by housing class rather than social group in Stouffer's model.

However, in practice there is not a one-to-one association between social group and housing type at any point in time, and households move between social groups in the course of migrating. For example, one of the main forces behind intraurban migration is the progressive increase in family size in the early part of the family cycle (Simmons, 1968). This increase causes families to reappraise the utility of their present dwelling and to look for a better solution to their housing problem. If the move that results is an inter-zonal migration, then our accounting system should record not only a geographical but also a social move. This kind of process would probably have to be modelled as a chain-like process in which the probability of a household moving into a new social group within the system is multiplied by the probability of a household in the (new) social group moving between zones in the urban area. Of course, many characteristics of destination zone rather than those of housing stock would have to be taken into account in an intraurban migration model.

It has been implicitly recognised in the discussion above and in Wilson (1971a, 1971b) that the best behaviour unit to use in an intraurban migration model is the household. This in turn implies that we need to develop an accounting system and associated demographic models for households—a much more difficult task from both the conceptual and from the information point of view. Most of the information available for building the accounts is based on the individual as a unit, and methods of converting information on individuals in urban zones into information on households will have to be found.

Given successful specification of household accounts, and a rough and ready operationalization of them, it should then be possible to link the population and housing accounts into a more general framework. At the city-wide level these accounts should provide very interesting cross-tabulations of household and housing unit characteristics. At the zonal level such cross-classifications should make possible the identification of serious mismatches between households and the housing they occupy.

Conclusion
This paper has been concerned principally with the elaboration of a fairly simple accounting system and its associated dynamic models for a variety of sub-populations whose different distributions go to make up the social variety of the city. Intervening between the theoretical specifications of these accounts and models and an operational model of sub-population distribution in the city, there yawns a vast gap that will probably be filled partly by directly available information, partly by estimation based on other information, and partly by calculated guesswork. In many cases the operational model may take on the character of a probabilistic simulation model rather than that of a set of accounting identities. Also the model will be less than general, since connections to the business and employment sector will not have been specified. Notwithstanding all these difficulties we can say with R. A. Fisher (1930, quoted in Keyfitz, 1968, page v):

"The inexactitude of our methods of measurement has no more reason in statistics than it has in physics to dim our conception of that which we measure".

References

Babcock, D. L., 1970, *Analysis and Improvement of a Dynamic Urban Model,* Ph. D. dissertation, University of California.

Blau, P. M., Duncan, O. D., 1967, *The American Occupational Structure* (John Wiley, New York).

Bogue, D. J., 1969, *The Principles of Demography* (John Wiley, New York).

Brown, L. A., Horton, F. E., 1970, "Social area change: an empirical analysis", *Urban Studies,* 7 (3), 271-288.

Dear, M. J., 1971, "A model for predicting the growth of London's housing stock", in *Housing Models,* report of a Planning and Transport Research and Computation Seminar (Planning and Transportation Research and Computation Co. Ltd., London).

Forrester, J. W., 1969, *Urban Dynamics* (MIT Press, Cambridge, Mass.).

Herbert, D. T., 1970, "Principal components analysis and urban social structure: a study of Cardiff and Swansea", in *Urban Essays: Studies in the Geography of Wales,* Eds. H. Carter, W. K. D. Davies (University of Wales Press, Cardiff).

Hester, J., Jr., 1969, *Systems Models of Urban Development* (Urban Systems Laboratory, MIT, Cambridge, Mass.).

HMSO, 1971, *The Registrar General's Statistical Review of England and Wales, 1969,* Part II, Tables, Population (HMSO, London).

Keyfitz, N., 1968, *Introduction to the Mathematics of Population* (Addison-Wesley, Reading, Mass.).

Keyfitz, N., Flieger, W., 1971, *Population: An Introduction to the Facts and Methods of Demography* (Freeman, San Francisco).

Leicester, C., 1970, "Manpower planning in the national economy", University of Cambridge, Department of Applied Eonomics, Reprint Series No. 304, reprinted from *Manpower Research,* Ed. N. A. B. Wilson (English Universities Press, 1969).

Lipset, S. M., Bendix, R., 1962, *Social Mobility in Industrial Society* (University of California Press, Los Angeles).

Morrill, R. L., 1965, "The negro ghetto: problems and alternatives", *Geographical Review,* 55, 339-361.

Murdie, R. A., 1969, "Factorial ecology of metropolitan Toronto, 1951-1961: an essay on the social geography of the city", research paper No. 116, Department of Geography, University of Chicago.

Rees, P. H., 1970, "Concepts of social space: toward an urban social geography", in *Geographic Perspectives on Urban Systems,* Eds. B. J. L. Berry, F. E. Horton (Prentice-Hall, Englewood Cliffs, New Jersey), Chapter 10, pp.306-394.

Rees, P. H., 1971a, "Constructing a set of population accounts for a region", working note, Department of Geography, University of Leeds.

Rees, P. H., 1971b, "How to make the Rogers' version of the demographic model operational for an English or Welsh county in about one hundred easy steps", working paper No. 8, Department of Geography, University of Leeds.

Rees, P. H., 1972, *Residential Patterns in American Cities,* Ph. D. dissertation, Department of Geography, University of Chicago (in preparation).

Robson, B. T., 1969, *Urban Analysis* (Cambridge University Press, Cambridge).

Rogers, A., 1966, "Matrix methods of population analysis", *Journal of the American Institute of Planners,* 32, 40-44.

Rogers, A., 1967, "Matrix analysis of interregional migration", *Papers, Regional Science Association,* 18, 177-196.

Rogers, A., 1968, *Matrix Analysis of Interregional Population Growth and Distribution* (University of California Press, Los Angeles).

Shevky, E., Williams, Marianne, 1949, *The Social Areas of Los Angeles: Analysis and Typology* (University of California Press, Los Angeles).

Simmons, J. W., 1968, "Changing residence in the city: a review of intraurban mobility", *Geographical Review,* **58**, 622-651.

Stone, R., 1971, *Demographic accounting and model-building* (O.E.C.D. Technical Reports in Education and Development, Paris).

Stouffer, S. A., 1940, "Intervening opportunities: a theory relating mobility and distance", *American Sociological Review,* **5**, 845-867.

Wilson, A. G. (Ed.), 1971a, "Multi-regional models of population structure and some implications for a dynamic-residential location model", in *London Papers, Volume 3, Patterns and Processes in Urban and Regional Systems* (Pion, London).

Wilson, A. G., 1971b, "Demographic models", in *Mathematical Models in Geography and Planning* (John Wiley, London), forthcoming.

APPENDIX
Some additional age group concepts
The m_r and $r-k$ devices in the births terms

In the generalised demographic model developed by Wilson (1971a, 1971b), persons are allowed to survive from some prior age groups $r-k$ into age group r over a period T. The youngest age from which they can survive into r is $r-n_r$. The index number n_r is a function of the length of the period T and the lengths of the various age groups up to and including r, the Δ_r. The index number n_r is defined as the largest integer that will satisfy

$$\Delta_{r-n_r+1} + \Delta_{r-n_r+2} + ... + \Delta_{r-1} < T , \tag{93}$$

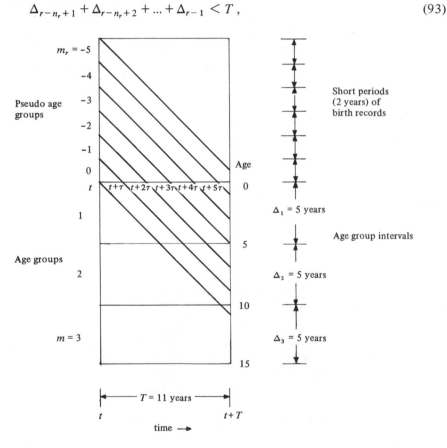

Key

m The oldest age group into which persons can be born
Δ The age group interval or length
t The starting point of a study or projection period
T The length of the period
τ The length of a short period in which births are recorded

Figure 4. A Lexis diagram showing how use is made of short period birth information.

subject to the constraint that

$$r - n_r + 1 > 1 . \tag{94}$$

That is, the earliest age from which people are allowed to survive into an age group r is the first.

However, persons can be born *and* survive into the earlier age groups $r \leqslant m$. An index number m_r, similar to n_r above, can be defined to allow births and survival to take place into age groups $r \leqslant m$:

$$\Delta_{r-m_r+1} + \Delta_{r-m_r+2} + \dots + \Delta_{r-1} < T . \tag{95}$$

No constraint is placed on the value of $r - k$, which can become negative. The meaning of these age groups with non-positive integer labels is made clear in figure 4. This is a Lexis diagram (Lexis, 1875, cited in Keyfitz, 1968) in which age is plotted against time. Diagonal lines from top left to bottom right represent lifelines. The pseudo-age groups with integer labels less than 1 correspond to births in given small time intervals within the larger period T. The correspondence can be listed thus:

pseudo-age group $r - k$	equivalent births time interval in period $(t, t+T)$
0	$t, t+\tau$
-1	$t+\tau, t+2\tau$
-2	$t+2\tau, t+3\tau$
.	.
.	.
.	.
m_r	$t+(-m_r)\tau, t+[(-m_r)+1]\tau$.

Births in pseudo-age group $r - k$ take place in time interval $\{t + [-(r-k)]\tau, t + [-(r-k)+1]\tau\}$ where $r - k \leqslant 0$. This assumes that births are counted in equal length short periods, which is generally the case.

The (r) and $\bar{r}$ notation
This notation has to be adopted to take into account the possibility that some of the persons in an $r - k$ age group may survive into age group r and some may not. An example of such a situation is portrayed in figure 5. The period length is one and a half times the age group interval. Persons surviving in age group r at time $t + T$ could have originated in age groups $r - 2$ or $r - 1$. But the younger half of age group $r - 2$ and the older half of age group $r - 1$ cannot survive into age group r; they survive into age groups $r - 1$ and $r - 2$ respectively. These are the persons designated $S_{r-k\bar{r}}$ in equation (65).

Similarly persons aged $r - 1$ and $r - 2$ who die but who could have survived into age group r must be distinguished from those who could not have survived into age group r.

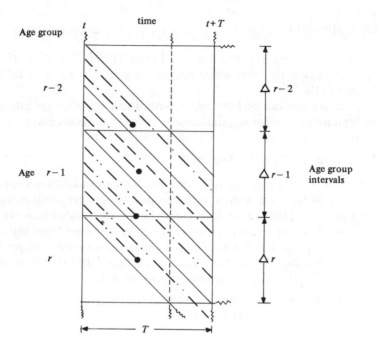

Age group

Key

Lifeline of person who

——— · ——— · ———   survives from age group $r-2$ into $r-1$

——— · ——— · —●   dies but who could have survived from $r-2$ into $r-1$

— — — · — — —   survives from $r-2$ into r

— — — · — — —●   dies but who could have survived from $r-2$ into $r-1$

— ·· — — ·· —   survives from $r-1$ into r

—·· — — ·· —●   dies but who could have survived from $r-1$ into r

— — · · — — —   survives from $r-1$ into $r+1$

— — · · — —●   dies but who could have survived from $r-1$ into r

For definitions of the other symbols see figure 4 and text

Figure 5. A Lexis diagram illustrating the age concepts (r) and $\bar{r}$.

Multi-regional models of population structure and some implications for a dynamic residential location model

A.G.WILSON
University of Leeds

1 Introduction: the Rogers' framework

The basic principles of building demographic models are well known. Matrix methods have been formally developed by Rogers in a series of articles (Rogers, 1966, 1967, for example) where he cites earlier references on which this kind of analysis is based. In this introductory section, we outline the basic Rogers' model. It turns out that the Rogers' model, in its present form, can only be used if data for calibration and testing are made available in a particular, rather restrictive form. Thus, in section 2 of the paper, a generalised demographic model is presented. In section 3, a model is given in which time is treated as a continuous variable and this gives an alternative way of resolving the difficulties described. In section 4, we briefly discuss the task of building migration models so that, together with the generalised demographic model, we can form a complete migration–demographic model. This general model can be applied at a variety of spatial scales, most of which are familiar, but in section 5, we consider the possibility of applying it at a rather fine spatial scale and note some implications for the task of building a dynamic residential location model.

We consider the Rogers model in three forms—the single region model; the multi-region model; and the multi-region male–female model. For a single region, let $w(t)$ be a vector giving the age distribution of a single region population at time t. That is, $w_r(t)$ is the number of people in the rth age group at time t. Then we can define a *survivorship matrix*

$$S = \begin{bmatrix} 0 & 0 & \dots & b_1 & b_2 & \dots & 0 \\ s_{21} & 0 & & & & & \\ 0 & s_{32} & 0 & & & & \\ 0 & 0 & s_{43} & & & & \\ 0 & & & & & s_{nn-1} & 0 \end{bmatrix} \tag{1}$$

where the b_r's are birth rates, and s_{rs} is the probability of survival from the sth age group to the rth age group in a unit time interval.

We can also define a migration matrix

$$M = \begin{bmatrix} 0 & \dots \\ m_{21} & 0 & \dots \\ 0 & m_{32} & 0 \\ \cdot & \cdot & \cdot \\ \cdot & \cdot & \cdot \end{bmatrix}, \tag{2}$$

where $m_{r+1\,r}$ is 'the rate of net migration' *into* the region from age group r into age group $r+1$. We can then define a *growth* matrix G, such that

$$G = S + M,$$ (3)

and

$$Gw(t) = w(t+1).$$ (4)

Now suppose there are N regions: $1, 2, 3, ..., N-1$ in the system of interest, and N (the 'rest of the world') to close the system. Now let $w^i(t)$ be the population of region i at time t, and let S^i be the survivorship matrix of the ith region. The *migration matrix* now takes the form M^{ij}, and has elements of the form $m^{ij}_{r\,r-1}$ which are the rates at which, in the projection period, members of the $(r-1)$th age group in j will migrate *into* i into the rth age group[1]. Strictly speaking, this must be the rate of migrating *and* of surviving.

We can then form a growth matrix for the multi-region system of the form

$$G = \begin{bmatrix} S^1 & M^{12} & M^{13} & \cdots \\ M^{21} & S^2 & M^{23} & \cdots \\ M^{31} & M^{31} & S^3 & \cdots \\ \cdot & \cdot & & \\ \cdot & \cdot & & \\ \cdot & \cdot & & S^N \end{bmatrix},$$ (5)

and if

$$w(t) = \begin{bmatrix} w^1(t) \\ w^2(t) \\ \cdot \\ \cdot \\ \cdot \end{bmatrix},$$ (6)

then

$$Gw(t) = w(t+1).$$ (7)

The model as explained so far applies to populations subdivided by age groups only. There is a strong case for applying it to the male and female populations separately, and Rogers and McDougall (1968) have done this for a 2 region system in Yugoslavia.

Firstly, however, a preliminary comment: there may be other sub-groupings of the population in which we are interested—income groups, ethnic groups, and so on—but generally demographic analyses of such groups can be carried out by applying the above model to each group separately (possibly with some 'correction mechanism' to allow for

[1] Note that this migration matrix includes *in-migration* only. Out-migration probabilities must be incorporated into the *survivorship* terms.

transition between groups). In the case of males and females, however, this is not possible because *both* males and females are born to females only! Rogers and McDougall show how to handle this as follows.

The notation employed is the same as before, but additional superscripts are used to denote male and female—M, F. Thus $w^{iM}(t)$ is the male and $w^{iF}(t)$ is the female population in region i at time t. $S^{iM}, S^{iF}, M^{ijM}, M^{ijF}$ are the survivorship and migration matrices which apply to males and females separately. The survivorship matrices have a special feature, however: the births in S^{iF} are female only, and *no* births are incorporated in S^{iM}. We define an additional matrix B^{iM} which records probability of male births, and is applied to the female population. It takes the form

$$B = \begin{bmatrix} 0 & 0 & \dots & b_1 & b_2 & \dots & 0 & 0 \\ 0 & 0 & & 0 & 0 & & 0 & 0 \\ . & . & & . & . & & . & . \\ . & . & & . & . & & . & . \\ . & . & & . & . & & . & . \end{bmatrix} . \tag{8}$$

The multi-region growth matrix now takes the form

$$G = \begin{bmatrix} S^{1F} & 0 & M^{12F} & 0 & \dots \\ B^{1M} & S^{1M} & 0 & M^{12M} & \dots \\ M^{21F} & 0 & S^{2F} & 0 & \dots \\ 0 & M^{21M} & B^{2M} & S^{2M} & \dots \\ . & . & . & . \\ . & . & . & . \\ . & . & . & . \\ . & . & . & . \end{bmatrix} , \tag{9}$$

$$w(t) = \begin{bmatrix} w^{1F} \\ w^{1M} \\ w^{2F} \\ w^{2M} \\ . \\ . \end{bmatrix} , \tag{10}$$

and we can write

$$Gw(t) = w(t+1) \tag{11}$$

in the usual way.

This completes what might be called the basic Rogers' framework.

2 A generalised demographic model[2]
Curiously, although the Rogers' matrix framework has been in existence for five years or so, British planning studies have apparently never utilised

[2] Susan Costello has written a computer program to represent the model described in this section and I am grateful to her for several discussions which showed up weaknesses in an earlier form of the model.

it for their population projections. However, there is an implicit
assumption in the Rogers' model that the age group differentials are all
equal to one another and to the projection period. Data for calibration
and testing are not usually available in this form and this, in part,
probably explains why the model has not been used very much. Of
course, it is possible to take Census information and interpolate to derive
the appropriate 'data', but it is better in general to construct a model
which will use any available data and which will work, in principle at any
rate, for any projection period. It is the task of this section to construct
such a model.

So far, we have used t as a calendar time label and a unit projection
period. We will now take T to be the projection period and consider
populations at t and $t+T$.

Let $\Delta_1, \Delta_2, ..., \Delta_R$ be the age group intervals covering age ranges $(0, \Delta_1 - 1)$,
$(\Delta_1, \Delta_1 + \Delta_2 - 1)$, $(\Delta_1 + \Delta_2, \Delta_1 + \Delta_2 + \Delta_3 - 1)$, ..., and so on. Note that the
projection period T can bear an arbitrary relationship to the Δ_i's. In the
Rogers' case, during a projection period T, people always aged from one
age group to the next, or were born into the first age group. In the
general case, there are many additional possibilities, as illustrated in
figure 1. The Rogers' case is shown as figure 1(a). Figures 1(b) and 1(c)
show a variety of other cases. In figure 1(b), the arrow A shows that
someone whose age group puts him at the 'beginning' of age group $r-1$
will remain in $r-1$ at the end of time T when Δ_{r-1} and T bear the
relationship shown in figure 1. Arrow B shows someone surviving from
age group $r-1$ to age group r, but because Δ_r is short compared to T, it is
also possible (arrow C) for someone to survive into age group $r+1$ from
$r-1$ in time T. Arrows A and B in figure 1(c) show that if T is large

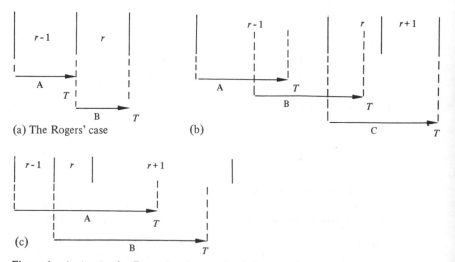

(a) The Rogers' case   (b)

(c)

Figure 1. Ageing in the Rogers' and generalised demographic models.

compared to Δ_{r-1} *and* Δ_r, then survivors from age group $r-1$ may jump age group r and survive directly into age group $r+1$. Many other cases are possible.

Figure 2 shows that if T is large compared to $\Delta_1, \Delta_2, ..., \Delta_m$, then children may be first recorded as being 'born' into any of the age groups $1, 2, ..., m$ during the projection period T.

We can set up a number of variables so that we can handle this variety of cases as follows (in most cases, time period t to $t+T$ should be understood). Let b_{rk}^{iF}, b_{rk}^{iM} be female and male birth rates, to females in age group k, which are first recorded in age group r; let s_{rr-k}^{iF} and s_{rr-k}^{iM} be female and male survival rates from age group $r-1$ ($k = 0, 1, 2, ..., n_r$) into age group r; let m_{rr-k}^{ijF} and m_{rr-k}^{ijM} be female and male migration rates of people from age group $r-k$ ($k = 0, 1, 2, ..., n_r$) in j into age group r in i. $r-n_r$ is the most distant age group from age group r from which people can survive into age group r in the projection period. It is illustrated in figure 3.

n_r is the largest integer to satisfy

$$\Delta_{r-n_r+1} + ... + \Delta_{r-1} < T \tag{12}$$

provided

$$r-n_r > 1 . \tag{13}$$

If the value of n_r obtained from the inequality (12) infringes the inequality (13), then it should be set to

$$n_r = r-1 . \tag{14}$$

This simply ensures that no one 'survives' from an age group earlier than the first. (Note that if $r = 1$ in this case, then n_r is formally set to zero. We shall use this symbol later to ensure that no one 'survives' from the zeroth group!)

Figure 2. Births in the generalised model.

Figure 3.

There is one other special case: if

$$\Delta_{r-1} > T,\tag{15}$$

then we also set

$$n_r = r-1 .\tag{16}$$

Note that some of the s_{rr-k}'s and m_{rr-k}'s for $k = 0, 1, 2, ..., n_r$ may be zero because of the 'jumping' situation illustrated by arrows A and B of figure 1(c).

We also calculate m (see figure 2) as the smallest integer such that

$$\Delta_1 + \Delta_2 + ... + \Delta_m > T,\tag{17}$$

and this gives the age groups into which people can be born.

The birth rates, survival rates, and migration rates for the generalised model will typically be calculated from data on total births, survivors, and migrants in some period T. We now show how to calculate the model rates from this kind of information. The method turns on the notion of finding the proportion of survivors (or migrants) who pass from one given age group at the beginning of the period into one of several age groups by the end of the period. Consider figure 4.

This shows that survivors of age group r end up in an age group in the range $r_1(r)$ to $r_2(r)$. $r_1(r)$ is the largest integer such that

$$\Delta_r + \Delta_{r+1} + ... + \Delta_{r_1(r)-1} < T,\tag{18}$$

with the special case

$$r_1(r) = r\tag{19}$$

if

$$\Delta_r > T.\tag{20}$$

$r_2(r)$ is the largest integer such that

$$\Delta_{r+1} + ... + \Delta_{r_2(r)-1} < T,\tag{21}$$

with special cases that

$$r_2(r) = r+1\tag{22}$$

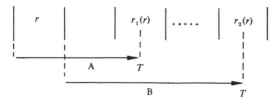

Figure 4.

if

$$\Delta_{r+1} > T , \tag{23}$$

and

$$r_2(r) = R \tag{24}$$

if

$$r = R . \tag{25}$$

The non-zero values of the rates of the form s_{rr-k} and m_{rr-k} can now be expressed as $s_{r'r}$ and $m_{r'r}$ for $r' = r_1(r) ... r_2(r)$. We can then calculate quantities p_{rr-k} $(k = 0, ..., n_r)$ which give the proportion of survivors (or migrants) who are in age group r at time $t + T$. These proportions can be expressed as follows. p_{rr-k} is zero [the 'jumping' case of figure 1(c)], except for terms of the form $p_{r'r}$ $[r' = r_1(r), ..., r_2(r)]$, and these are given in the general case (see figure 4) by

$$p_{r_1(r)r} = \frac{\Delta_r + \Delta_{r+1} + ... + \Delta_{r_1(r)-1} - T}{\Delta_r} , \tag{26}$$

$$p_{r'r} = \frac{\Delta_{r'}}{\Delta_r} , \qquad r_1(r) < r' < r_2(r) , \tag{27}$$

$$p_{r_2(r)r} = \frac{T - (\Delta_{r+1} + ... + \Delta_{r_2(r)-1})}{\Delta_r} . \tag{28}$$

In the special case where

$$r_1(r) = r , \tag{29}$$

equation (26) is to be interpreted as

$$p_{r_1(r)r} = \frac{\Delta_r - T}{\Delta_r} ; \tag{30}$$

and in the special case

$$r_2(r) = r + 1 , \tag{31}$$

equation (28) is to be interpreted as

$$p_{r_2(r)r} = \frac{T}{\Delta_r} . \tag{32}$$

Finally, in the special case where

$$r_1(r) = r_2(r) , \tag{33}$$

then

$$p_{r_1(r)r} = p_{r_2(r)r} = 1 . \tag{34}$$

Births are easier to allocate to age groups. Defining quantities π_r, $(r = 1, ..., m)$ we now have (see figure 2)

$$\pi_r = \frac{\Delta_r}{T}, \qquad r < m, \tag{35}$$

$$\pi_m = \frac{T - (\Delta_1 + \Delta_2 + ... + \Delta_{m-1})}{T} \tag{36}$$

as the proportions being 'born' into different age groups.

Suppose now that we are given our data in the form $B_k^{iF}(t, t+T)$ and $B_k^{iM}(t, t+T)$, being the total number of female and male births to mothers in age group k at time t, and $M_r^{ijF}(t, t+T)$ and $M_r^{ijM}(t, t+T)$ being the number of migrants from region i to region j, who were in age group r at time t, in t to $t+T$. Then, using the quantities p_{rr-k} $(k = 0, ..., n_r)$ and π_r $(r = 1, ..., m)$ we can calculate the model rates as follows:

$$b_{rk}^{iF} = \frac{\pi_r B_k^{iF}(t, t+T)}{w_k^{iF}(t)}, \tag{37}$$

$$b_{rk}^{iM} = \frac{\pi_r B_k^{iM}(t, t+T)}{w_k^{iF}(t)}, \tag{38}$$

$$s_{rr-k}^{iF} = \frac{p_{rr-k} S_{r-k}^{iF}(t, t+T)}{w_{r-k}^{iF}(t)}, \tag{39}$$

$$s_{rr-k}^{iM} = \frac{p_{rr-k} S_{r-k}^{iM}(t, t+T)}{w_{r-k}^{iM}(t)}, \tag{40}$$

$$m_{rr-k}^{ijF} = \frac{p_{rr-k} M_{r-k}^{jiF}(t, t+T)}{w_{r-k}^{jF}(t)}, \tag{41}$$

$$m_{rr-k}^{ijM} = \frac{p_{rr-k} M_{r-k}^{jiM}(t, t+T)}{w_{r-k}^{jM}(t)}. \tag{42}$$

We are now almost in a position to write down the equations of the generalised model. At this point, the matrix notation no longer seems helpful and it is discarded (indeed, it is not strictly necessary in the Rogers' model itself).

If equation (11) was written without matrix notation, it would take the form of the following equation system:

$$w_1^{iF}(t+1) = \sum_{k=\alpha}^{\beta} b_k^{iF} w_k^{iF}(t), \tag{43}$$

$$w_1^{iM}(t+1) = \sum_{k=\alpha}^{\beta} b_k^{iM} w_k^{iM}(t), \tag{44}$$

$$w_r^{iF}(t+1) = s_{rr-1}^{iF} w_{r-1}^{iF}(t) + \sum_{j \neq i} m_{rr-1}^{ijF} w_{r-1}^{jF}(t), \qquad r > 1, \tag{45}$$

$$w_r^{iM}(t+1) = s_{rr-1}^{iM} w_{r-1}^{iM}(t) + \sum_{j \neq i} m_{rr-1}^{ijM} w_{r-1}^{jM}(t), \qquad r > 1, \tag{46}$$

where α and β are the limits of the child bearing age groups.

In the generalised model, the equations take the same form, except that (1) 'births' can now occur in age groups $r = 1, 2, ..., m$; (2) survival and migration is possible in the 'birth' age groups for some values of T; and (3) in general, survival and migration into an age group is possible from groups other than the immediately preceding one. The reader can easily check that, using the various rates just defined, the generalised model can be written

$$w_r^{iF}(t+T) = \sum_{k=\alpha}^{\beta} b_{rk}^{iF} w_k^{iF}(t) + (1-\delta_{n_r o}) \sum_{k=0}^{n_r} s_{rr-k}^{iF} w_{r-k}^{iF}(t)$$

$$+ (1-\delta_{n_r o}) \sum_{j \neq i} \sum_{k=0}^{n_r} m_{rr-k}^{ijF} w_{r-k}^{jF}(t), \qquad r < m, \qquad (47)$$

$$w_r^{iM}(t+T) = \sum_{k=\alpha}^{\beta} b_{rk}^{iM} w_k^{iF}(t) + (1-\delta_{n_r o}) \sum_{k=0}^{n_r} s_{rr-k}^{iM} w_{r-k}^{iM}(t)$$

$$+ (1-\delta_{n_r o}) \sum_{j \neq i} \sum_{k=0}^{n_r} m_{rr-k}^{ijM} w_{r-k}^{jM}(t), \qquad r < m, \qquad (48)$$

$$w_r^{iF}(t+T) = \sum_{k=0}^{n_r} s_{rr-k}^{iF} w_{r-k}^{iF}(t) + \sum_{j \neq i} \sum_{k=0}^{n_r} m_{rr-k}^{ijF} w_{r-k}^{jF}(t), \qquad r > m, \qquad (49)$$

$$w_r^{iM}(t+T) = \sum_{k=0}^{n_r} s_{rr-k}^{iF} w_{r-k}^{iM}(t) + \sum_{j \neq i} \sum_{k=0}^{n_r} m_{rr-k}^{ijM} w_{r-k}^{jM}(t), \qquad r > m. \qquad (50)$$

In equations (48) and (49), δ is a Kronecker delta which is 1 when $n_r = 0$ and 0 otherwise. It formally removes survival and migration from the 'zeroth' age group when $r = 1$ and $n_r = 0$.

To use this model it needs to be calibrated, by estimating the various rates from historical data, and testing the model. These rates themselves need then to be projected forward before the model can be used for forecasting. The migration rates themselves can be estimated from a model such as one of those described for this purpose in section 4. The birth rates and survival rates can be estimated only by trend projections of historical data combined with detailed demographic study.

3 A continuous variable model [3]
In the models built in previous sections of this paper, we have had considerable difficulty in handling age groups, and especially in the generalised case where people may survive into more than one age group in a projection period. One way of overcoming this difficulty is to treat

[3] The idea of working on a continuous variable version of the generalised model was suggested in chapter 2 by Watt (1968) which contains a very simple—one region, one age group—continuous variable model. His equation does, however, build in the notion of a limited population capacity, which may be appropriate for the model presented here.

time as a continuous variable—both in the sense of age, and as calendar time. In a continuous variable model, birth is to be interpreted as being born in the next infinitesimal interval of time, while survival and migration are to be interpreted as 'surviving into' and 'surviving into and migrating during' the next period of time.

Since we are going to treat age as a continuous variable, as well as calendar time, we no longer write it as a subscript, and we write our populations as $w^{iF}(r, t)$ and $w^{iM}(r, t)$, the female and male populations in region i age r at time t. [Strictly, these are population density functions, and we should speak of $w^{iF}(r, t)\delta r$ as the female population of region i aged between r and $r + \delta r$.] If we now define $b^{iF}(r, t)$ and $b^{iM}(r, t)$ to be the female and male birth rates to females age r at time t, then the birth equations are simply

$$w^{iF}(0, t) = \int_\alpha^\beta b^{iF}(r, t) w^{iF}(r, t) \, dr , \tag{51}$$

$$w^{iM}(0, t) = \int_\alpha^\beta b^{iM}(r, t) w^{iF}(r, t) \, dr , \tag{52}$$

where α and β are again the limits of the child bearing age ranges. Then, approximately, $w^{iF}(0, t)\delta t$ and $w^{iM}(0, t)\delta t$ are the number of births between t and $t + \delta t$.

In order to obtain the survival and migration equations, let us manipulate equation (49) from the generalised discrete model. It is repeated here for convenience:

$$w_r^{iF}(t + T) = \sum_{k=0}^{n_r} s_{rr-k}^{iF} w_{r-k}^{iF}(t) + \sum_{j \neq i} \sum_{k=0}^{n_r} m_{rr-k}^{ijF} w_{r-k}^{jF}(t) . \tag{49}$$

We transform this to the continuous notation for an increment t to $t + \delta t$ in which the population ages from r to $r + \delta r$. Of course,

$$\delta r = \delta t \tag{53}$$

in this case. Recall that the survival and birth rates were functions of t and $t + T$ as well as r, and so we define them to be $s^{iF}(r, \delta t, t)$ and $m^{ijF}(r, \delta t, t)$—the rate of survival of r age people to $r + \delta r$ in projection period $\delta t (= \delta r)$, and the corresponding migration rate. We can expand these rates about $\delta t = 0$:

$$s^{iF}(r, \delta t, t) = s^{iF}(r, 0, t) + \delta t \frac{\partial s^{iF}}{\partial \delta t} + 0(\delta t^2) , \tag{54}$$

$$m^{ijF}(r, \delta t, t) = m^{ijF}(r, 0, t) + \delta t \frac{\partial m^{ijF}}{\partial \delta t} + 0(\delta t^2) ; \tag{55}$$

however, by definition

$$s^{iF}(r, 0, t) = 1 , \tag{56}$$

since everyone survives in a zero time interval, and

$$m^{ijF}(r, 0, t) = 0 , \tag{57}$$

since no one migrates in a zero time interval. Equation (49) can be written, using the continuous variables as

$$w^{iF}(r+\delta r, t+\delta t) = s^{iF}(r, \delta t, t)w^{iF}(r, t) + \sum_{j \neq i} m^{ijF}(r, \delta t, t)w^{jF}(r, t) . \tag{58}$$

We can now substitute from equations (56) and (57) into (54) and (55) and then from the latter pair into (58). This gives

$$w^{iF}(r+\delta r, t+\delta t) = w^{iF}(r, t) + \delta t \frac{\partial s^{iF}}{\partial \delta t}w^{iF}(r, t) + \sum_{j \neq i} \delta t \frac{\partial m^{ijF}}{\partial \delta t}w^{jF}(r, t) . \tag{59}$$

Define

$$\sigma^{iF}(r, t) = \frac{\partial s^{iF}}{\partial \delta t}(r, \delta t, t)|_{\delta t = 0} , \tag{60}$$

$$\mu^{ijF}(r, t) = \frac{\partial m^{ijF}}{\partial \delta t}(r, \delta t, t)|_{\delta t = 0} , \tag{61}$$

and substitute in equation (59):

$$w^{iF}(r+\delta r, t+\delta t) = w^{iF}(r, t) + \delta t \sigma^{iF}(r, t)w^{iF}(r, t)$$
$$+ \sum_{j \neq i} \delta t \mu^{ijF}(r, t)w^{jF}(r, t) + 0(\delta t^2) . \tag{62}$$

This can be rearranged as

$$\frac{w^{iF}(r+\delta r, t+\delta t) - w^{iF}(r, t)}{\delta t} = \sigma^{iF}(r, t)w^{iF}(r, t)$$
$$+ \sum_{j \neq i} \mu^{ijF}(r, t)w^{jF}(r, t) + 0(\delta t) . \tag{63}$$

Now let $\delta t \to 0$, when equation (63) becomes

$$\frac{\partial w^{iF}}{\partial t}(r, t) = \sigma^{iF}(r, t)w^{iF}(r, t) + \sum_{j \neq i} \mu^{ijF}(r, t)w^{jF}(r, t) , \tag{64}$$

so that we now have a set of simultaneous linear differential equations in $w^{iF}(r, t)$. An exactly similar equation could be written down for $w^{iM}(r, t)$.

This is an awkward equation system to handle, for it contains two time variables, r and t, but $\delta r = \delta t$. The next step is to write the equation in terms of a single time variable. Put

$$r = r_0 + \hat{t} \tag{65}$$

and

$$t = t_0 + \hat{t} \tag{66}$$

so that $\hat{t}$ represents elapsed time from some base t_0. We can later consider the equation system for a range of values of r_0. Equation (64) can now be written in full (dropping the $\hat{\ }$ on $\hat{t}$ and the 0 on r_0) as

$$\frac{\partial w^{iF}}{\partial t}(r+t, t_0+t) = \sigma^{iF}(r+t, t_0+t)w^{iF}(r+t, t_0+t)$$

$$+ \sum_{j \neq i} \mu^{ijF}(r+t, t_0+t)w^{jF}(r+t, t_0+t) . \qquad (67)$$

The equivalent equation for males is

$$\frac{\partial w^{iM}}{\partial t}(r+t, t_0+t) = \sigma^{iM}(r+t, t_0+t)w^{iM}(r+t, t_0+t)$$

$$+ \sum_{j \neq i} \mu^{ijM}(r+t, t_0+t)w^{jM}(r+t, t_0+t) . \qquad (68)$$

These equations can be solved as linear simultaneous differential equations in a function of t for a (continuous) set of values of r. At $t = 0$, the solution has to satisfy the boundary condition $w^{iF}(r, t_0)$ and $w^{iM}(r, t_0)$ which are assumed to be given. The values of $w^{iF}(0, t_0+t)$ and $w^{iM}(0, t_0+t)$ are given for all t by equations (51) and (52) with t replaced by t_0+t.

The next step is to explore the nature of the coefficients $\sigma^{iF}(r, t)$ and $\mu^{ijF}(r, t)$. We shall see that they are not rates in the usual manner, but derivatives of rates. Consider $s^{iF}(r, \delta t, t)$ as a function of δt and r for given t. The δt and r dimensions are shown in figure 5; s^{iF} can be considered to be plotted as a surface in a third dimension at right angles to these. As shown on the figure, s^{iF} decreases as r increases and as δt increases. If we fix r and cut sections through the figure 5 surface, say at $r = r_1, r_2$, and r_3, then we can show a plot of $s^{iF}(r, \delta t, t)$ against δt for given values of r. This is shown in figure 6.

We now see that $\sigma^{iF}(r, t)$ is the gradient of one of these curves at $\delta t = 0$.

Similarly, we can plot $m^{ijF}(r, \delta t, t)$ against δt as shown in figure 7. μ^{ijF} is the gradient of these curves (for given r) at $\delta t = 0$. Note that in

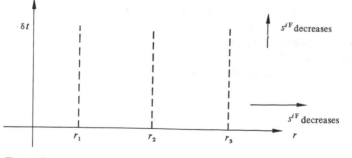

Figure 5.

the case shown in figure 7, r_1 represents an age group with a higher migration propensity than r_2, and r_2 a higher propensity than r_3. They are not necessarily in any particular numerical order of course.

Now assuming that $\sigma^{iF}(r, t)$, $\sigma^{iM}(r, t)$, $\mu^{ijF}(r, t)$, and $\mu^{ijM}(r, t)$ can be estimated from empirical studies, and then projected forward on the basis of trends or a range of assumptions, how do we solve the differential equation system given by equations (67) and (68)? They are a very unusual set of differential equations since, although t is the main independent variable, r and t_0 can vary also. The first task is to *organise* the solution of the equations. We do this by noting that r and t_0 between them determine the cohort structure of the population. If we assume we are given the initial distributions of population $w^{iF}(r, t_0)$ and $w^{iM}(r, t_0)$, and that we are given births at all future times from equations (51) and (52)— that is $w^{iF}(0, t_0+t)$ and $w^{iM}(0, t_0+t)$ for all t—then we see that our task is to solve the differential equation system for each cohort in turn for $t > 0$: that is, to project $w^{iF}(r, t_0)$, $w^{iM}(r, t_0)$, $w^{iF}(0, t_0+t)$, and $w^{iM}(0, t_0+t)$ forward. In the case of future births, we start from $t = t_1 > 0$, not $t = 0$, for a full range of t_1. Although r and t_1 and t vary continuously, it will perhaps help fix understanding if we consider them to vary in one year intervals, and then we can exhibit the cohorts which are being modelled as in table 1 (shown for the female population). A similar table could be drawn up for males.

It can easily be seen that table 1 exhibits a number of discrete (r, t) points from a continuous array, which shows that estimates will be made for all the population for all combinations of r and $t > 0$, and without repetition. The equation (67) is solved for r and t_0 values (or t_0 and t_1) given for each row of table 1 in turn. The first population shown in each row of the table is given and provides a boundary condition.

For a given (r, t_0, t_1) combination, and a given sex, the differential equation system takes the form

$$\frac{\partial y_i(t)}{\partial t} = \sum_j a_{ij}(t) y_j(t) \tag{69}$$

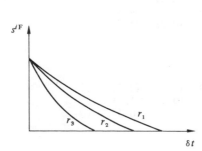

Figure 6.

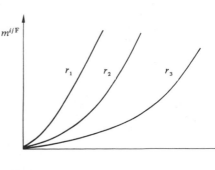

Figure 7.

and such equation systems are well known, for example, in the literature of theoretical biology and control engineering. Much of the discussion in this literature relates to equation systems of the form of (69), but in which the coefficients a_{ij} are time-independent. This could be useful for us if we are projecting forward for relatively short periods, in which case we may obtain a set of a_{ij}'s for each (r, t_0, t_1) combination which could be assumed independent of t. How short the projection period would have to be before the approximation was sound is a matter of empirical investigation. In general, though, we will be interested in the time-dependent case. However, we indicate for time-independent and time-dependent cases in turn how equation systems of the form of equation (69) can be solved. The time-independent case is

$$\frac{\partial y_i}{\partial t} = \sum_j a_{ij} y_j . \tag{70}$$

A general solution can be obtained in this case. Our first task is to transform the matrix a_{ij} to a particular canonical form using the contragredient transformation (and in this case we are following Rosen, 1970, and Birkhoff and MacLane, 1953). Equation (70) can be written in an obvious matrix notation, dropping the subscripts:

$$\frac{\partial y}{\partial t} = ay . \tag{71}$$

We wish to find a non-singular transformation T, so that we have new variables y^* given by

$$y^* = Ty , \tag{72}$$

and a matrix of coefficients a^* given by

$$a^* = TaT^{-1} . \tag{73}$$

Table 1. Distribution of female population $w^{iF}(r, t)$ for progressive values of r, t.

t_1	Initial value of $w^{iF}(r, t)$ represented by (r, t) shown	Predicted value of $w^{iF}(r, t)$ represented by (r, t) shown			
0	(0,0)	(1,1)	(2,2)	(3,3)	...
	(1,0)	(2,1)	(3,2)	(4,3)	...
	(2,0)	(3,1)	(4,2)	(5,3)	...
	.				
	.				
	.				
1	(0,1)	(0,1)	(1,2)	(2,3)	...
2	(0,2)		(0,2)	(1,3)	...
3	(0,3)			(0,3)	...
	.				
	.				
	.				

Then, equation (71) can be written

$$\frac{\partial}{\partial t} T^{-1} y^* = a T^{-1} y^* ,$$
(74)

and so premultiplying by T, and using equation (73), we have

$$\frac{\partial y^*}{\partial t} = a^* y^* .$$
(75)

Our task is to choose T so that a^* takes an appropriately simple form. This task is dealt with in an appendix. It is shown there that we can find a vector α, a cyclic vector of a, such that $\alpha, a\alpha, a^2\alpha, ..., a^{n-1}\alpha$ can be taken as a new basis leading to a coordinate transformation T, the contragredient transformation, which gives

$$a^* = T^{-1} a T = \begin{bmatrix} 0 & 0 & \cdots & -\beta_n \\ 1 & 0 & \cdots & \beta_{n-1} \\ 0 & 1 & \cdots & -\beta_{n-2} \\ \cdot & \cdot & & \\ \cdot & \cdot & & \\ \cdot & \cdot & & \\ 0 & 0 & \cdots & 1-\beta_1 \end{bmatrix}.$$
(76)

The β_n's are given by

$$\beta^n = A_{N-n+1} ,$$
(77)

where the A_n's are the coefficients of the characteristic polynomial of a. Then, on substituting from equation (76) into equation (75), the transformed equation system can be written out in full as

$$\frac{\partial y_1^*}{\partial t} = y_2^*$$

$$\frac{\partial y_2^*}{\partial t} = y_3^*$$

.

.   (78)

.

$$\frac{\partial y_N^*}{\partial t} = \sum_{i=1}^{N} A_i y_i^*$$

We can then substitute for y_2^* from the first of equations (78) into the second, and so on, and these N first order differential equations are then seen to be equivalent to a single Nth order differential equation:

$$\frac{d^n y_1^*}{dt^n} + A_1 \frac{d^{n-1} y_2^*}{dt^{n-1}} + ... + A_N y_1^* = 0 .$$
(79)

The general solution of this equation can be obtained in the usual way. Writing D for the operator d/dy, and writing equation (79) in the following form, we get

$$f(D)y_1^* = 0 . \tag{80}$$

Then we note

$$f(D)\exp at = f(a)\exp at , \tag{81}$$

and so

$$y_1^* = \exp at \tag{82}$$

is a solution if

$$f(a) = \sum_{i=1}^{N} A_i a^i = 0 \tag{83}$$

and this is the characteristic polynomial of a. If $\lambda_1, \lambda_2, \lambda_3, ..., \lambda_N$ are the possible solutions for a, then

$$y_1^* = \sum_{i=1}^{N} c_i \exp \lambda_i t \tag{84}$$

is the general solution. $y_2^*, y_3^*, ..., y_N^*$ can be obtained from the family of equations (78), and y^* from equation (72), given T from the appendix. If some of the λ_i's are equal, special steps must be taken (Rosen, 1970, p.101). In general, some of the values of λ_i may be complex, and then the imaginary parts of $\exp \lambda_i t$ cause damped oscillations.

We can now deal with the time-dependent case. Since the functions $a_{ij}(t)$ are to be determined empirically, and we have no reason to think that they can be well fitted by simple analytical functions, at this stage we look for general formal solutions to the equation.

As with most differential equation systems of this kind, the general solution is usually expressed as a function of a number of particular solutions. Rosen (1970), for example, notes that if $y^{(n)}(t)$ form N linearly independent particular solutions, and we form the matrix $\Xi(t)$ whose columns are the vector $y^{(n)}$, then the general solution is

$$y(t) = \Xi(t)\Xi^{-1}(t_0)y(t_0) , \tag{85}$$

where $y(t_0)$ is the boundary condition. It is also sometimes convenient to apply the contragredient transformation. Rosenbrook and Storey (1970)—from another field—give a similar general solution in a different notation. They go on to discuss the *stability* of solutions, which has obvious implications in the study of populations.

An alternative approach is to convert the differential equation system into integral equations, following Bellman (1970). Equation (71) integrates to

$$y = y(t_0) + \int_{t_0}^{t} a(t^1)y(t^1)dt^1 , \tag{86}$$

and this can be solved by successive approximations. Given $y(t_0)$, then the $(n+1)$th approximation is

$$y^{(n+1)} = y(t_0) + \int_{t_0}^{t} a(t^1) y^{(n)}(t^1) \mathrm{d}t^1 \ . \tag{87}$$

This procedure obviously lends itself to numerical analysis more easily than does the search for particular solutions to the differential equation.

4 A note on migration models

A considerable amount of development work has been carried out on models of migration flows (for example, see Lowry, 1966, and Masser, 1969). In this section however, a formalised and general spatial interaction model of migration is presented which can be transformed into almost any specific model of migration.

Models have been developed of net, gross, and directional flows. Obviously, the most general case will be achieved by attempting to build a model of directional flows, and so we begin by defining $M_{ij}(t, t+T)$ to be the migration flow from region i to region j in the time period t to $t+T$ [4]. This will be written M_{ij} for short, though the time period should always be understood to be referred to implicitly. This also applies to most other variables to be defined below. Clearly, migration flows will depend on age, on characteristics such as occupation, and so on. Thus we shall subdivide M_{ij} from time to time: for example, we might employ M_{ij}^r as the flow of migrants in age group r at time t. For the time being, however, we will use M_{ij} and disaggregate later.

We will begin by building a production constrained model. This is based on the assumption that propensity to leave—to out-migrate—is predictable as a function of the region and its population. We might proceed as follows: let μ_i be the propensity to migrate per thousand population from region i; let P_i be the population of i; let O_i be the number of migrants leaving i; let λ be the system-wide propensity to migrate; let X_i^k be the number of variables which characterise region i (unemployment, etc.); and let Y_j^k be a number of factors which characterise region j. Then we might hypothesise that

$$\mu_i = \lambda + \sum_k a^k X_i^k \ , \tag{88}$$

$$O_i = \mu_i P_i \ , \tag{89}$$

and that for each region an 'attractiveness to migrants' term exists of the form

$$W_j = \sum_k b^k Y_j^k \ . \tag{90}$$

[4] Note that the flow is i to j; in the previous sections of this paper, the flows implied by the rates m^{ij} were from j to i to facilitate building the matrix form of the model.

Then, for some given projection, $\mu_i - \lambda$ can be measured, and the coefficients a^k in equation (88) estimated by regression analysis; we can assume

$$W_j = KM_{*j} \qquad (91)$$

for the same period, and estimate the coefficients b^k by regression analysis. Then we can build a spatial interaction model of the form

$$M_{ij} = A_i O_i W_j \exp(-\beta c_{ij}) , \qquad (92)$$

where

$$A_i = \frac{1}{\sum_j W_j \exp(-\beta c_{ij})} , \qquad (93)$$

and estimate β in the usual way.

If we were particularly interested in migration flows by age group, we could carry out such an analysis for the model:

$$M_{ij}^r = A_i^r O_i^r W_j^r \exp(-\beta^r c_{ij}) \qquad (94)$$

where

$$A_i^r = \frac{1}{\sum_j W_j^r \exp(-\beta^r c_{ij})} , \qquad (95)$$

using obvious extensions of the definitions of the variables.

Clearly, there is a wide variety of choice of the variables X_i^k and Y_j^k, and in this way many models can be developed and tested. Further, the relationship between these variables need not necessarily be additive as in equations (88) and (90), though log–linear regression or other methods of estimation would then have to be used.

If migration flows can be estimated in this way, they can then be used to estimate rates which form inputs to the demographic model. We would then have relationships of the form[5]

$$m_{rr-k}^{jiF}(t, t+T) = \frac{p_{rr-k} M_{ij}^{(r-k)F}(t, t+T)}{w_{r-k}^{jF}(t)} , \qquad (96)$$

and

$$m_{rr-k}^{jiM}(t, t+T) = \frac{p_{rr-k} M_{ij}^{(r-k)M}(t, t+T)}{w_{r-k}^{jM}(t)} \qquad (97)$$

(assuming that we could estimate migration models disaggregated by age and sex). Thus, if equations (96) and (97) are added to equations (47) to

[5] Note that in equations (96) and (97) the age groups index in the migration terms on the right hand side refer to the *beginning* of the period t to $t+T$. In practice adjustments usually have to be made because in the Census the corresponding age group refers to the end of the period.

(51) together with the associated migration model equations, we then have a reasonably complete migration-demographic model.

5 Some implications for a dynamic residential location model

Migration–demographic models are usually applied to systems of regions in which the 'regions' are either countries or large areas within a country (such as the Economic Planning Regions of the UK). There is no reason in principle, however, why the regions should not be small area units such as the analysis zones of some urban study area. Then, the migration–demographic model becomes the basis of a residential location model—and one which is basically dynamic, as the migration–demographic model is explicitly concerned with change over time.

The migration–demographic model needs as inputs for each region, the initial population by age and sex, survival rates, birth rates, and migration rates. Population data by age and sex are easily available for small urban analysis zones such as Census Enumeration Districts; survival, birth, and migration data are typically available only for larger area units, but, at least survival and birth rates can be estimated which may be applicable to small areas. Special sources of migration data would probably be needed. The heart of the modelling problem, however, would be the task of building an intra-urban migration model.

Following Rees (1970), we might argue that intra-urban migration is a function of household characteristics (income, job, age, stage in life cycle, preference structure), housing characteristics (type, price), and zone characteristics (job accessibility, access to services, environmental quality, community characteristics). We might also distinguish a variety of reasons for moving, associated with home quality, home size, community structure, access to services, and job. It might be appropriate to distinguish a number of special migrant types, such as servicemen, students, and people who are retiring.

There is no difficulty in principle in building such an array of factors into a migration model. The difficulties would be associated with the quality of small area migration data available and associated household, home, and zone information, with which a model could be calibrated. The migration model presented in section 4 could be used. It would be preferable if it was disaggregated further according to household or person type, and then the X_i^k's and Y_j^k's could be used to represent zone and housing characteristics. (It is probably better in principle not to mix personal and zone characteristics in an additive formulation, though it may be feasible in a multiplicative one if model disaggregation is not possible.)

Other possibilities come to mind. In the model just referred to, all the different types of migration are in effect lumped together, though various zone variables, which modify the average propensities, will reflect different reasons for moving. It would be possible to run the model separately for each of the different types of move, but there would almost certainly be an identification problem on calibration.

A different type of model would be one which used some kind of utility construct. Let h represent person or household type, and let π_i^h be the probability of a person being of this type in zone i. Then $\pi_i^h w_r^{iF}(t)$ may be taken as the number of females in zone i of this type. Let a^h be the migration propensity for this type per unit time. Let u_r^{ih} be the perceived utility of residence in i—and this could be a function of all the characteristics mentioned earlier. Then we might have for $M_{ij}^{rF}(t, t+T)$ used in equation (96)

$$M_{ij}^{rF}(t, t+T) = \sum_h M_{ij}^{rFh}(t, t+T) , \tag{98}$$

where

$$M_{ij}^{rFh} = (a^h T)[\pi_i^h w_r^{iF}(t)] \frac{\exp[\beta_r^h (u_r^{jh} - u_r^{ih})]}{\sum\limits_{j \neq i} \exp[\beta_r^h (u_r^{jh} - u_r^{ih})]} , \tag{99}$$

where β_r^h is a set of parameters.

It should be clear by now that a rich intra-urban migration model could be built in principle—rich in the sense that a great variety of different type of move for different people in different circumstances could be represented, and the rates of move would be sensitive to the propensity-coefficients and parameters of the model. The migration–demographic model which incorporates such a migration model, therefore, has a good chance of success as a dynamic residential location model. It would be rooted in the set of small area demographic data which is available but underutilised at the present time, though there would also be data difficulties associated with the task of building the model. It seems to have as much chance of success, and perhaps more, than a dynamic model based on the more traditional elementary residential location model [6] (for example, as described in Wilson, 1970, chapter 4).

References
Bellman, R., 1970, *Methods of Nonlinear Analysis,* Volume 1 (Academic Press, New York).
Birkhoff, G., MacLane, S., 1953, *A Survey of Modern Algebra* (Macmillan, London).
Lowry, I. S., 1966, *Migration and Metropolitan Growth* (Chandler, San Francisco).
Masser, I., 1969, "A test of some models for predicting intermetropolitan movement of population in England and Wales", CES-WP-9, Centre for Environmental Studies, London.

[6] We should note, however, that the two models could be incorporated together in an iterative scheme: a dynamic elementary residential location model based on the home-workplace interaction could be used to predict change, and the resulting migration rates incorporated and tested in a migration–demographic model. The outputs of the latter model could then be used to constrain a new run of the former!

Rees, P. H., 1970, "Concepts of social space: toward an urban social geography", Eds. B. J. L. Berry, F. E. Horton in *Geographic Perspectives on Urban Systems*, chapter 10, pp.306-394 (Prentice Hall, Englewood Cliffs, New Jersey).

Rogers, A., 1966, "Matrix methods of population analysis", *Journal of the American Institute of Planners*, **32**, 40-44.

Rogers, A., 1967, "Matrix analysis of inter-regional migration", *Papers, Regional Science Association*, **18**, 177-196.

Rogers, A., McDougall, S., 1968, "An analysis of population growth and change in Slovenia and the rest of Yugoslavia", Working Paper 81, Center for Planning and Development Research, University of California, Berkeley.

Rosen, R., 1970, *Dynamical System Theory in Biology*, Volume 1 (Wiley-Interscience, New York).

Rosenbrook, H. H., Storey, C., 1970, *Mathematics of Dynamical Systems* (Nelson, London).

Watt, K. E. F., 1968, *Ecology and Resource Management* (McGraw-Hill, New York).

Wilson, A. G., 1970, *Entropy in Urban and Regional Modelling* (Pion, London).

Appendix

The algebra of the companion matrix transformation

All the references checked so far on companion matrices seem inadequate in their explanation in the sense that they take a lot of results in linear algebra as given. This appendix is an attempt to state the results in more detail.

Let $e_1, e_2, ..., e_n$ be the *basis* of some n dimensional vector space. Then a vector x has *coordinates* $(x_1, x_2, ..., x_n)$ in this space, and

$$x = x_1 e_1 + x_2 e_2 + ... + x_n e_n . \tag{A1}$$

We can think of this basis as

$$e_1 = \begin{pmatrix} 1 \\ 0 \\ 0 \\ . \\ . \\ . \\ 0 \end{pmatrix} \qquad e_2 = \begin{pmatrix} 0 \\ 1 \\ 0 \\ . \\ . \\ . \\ 0 \end{pmatrix} \qquad e_3 = \begin{pmatrix} 0 \\ 0 \\ 1 \\ 0 \\ . \\ . \\ 0 \end{pmatrix} \qquad e_n = \begin{pmatrix} 0 \\ 0 \\ 0 \\ . \\ . \\ . \end{pmatrix}. \tag{A2}$$

Suppose we now transform to a new basis $e_1^*, e_2^*, ..., e_n^*$. The coordinates of this basis with respect to the first basis system are

$$e_i^* = \sum_j \hat{T}_{ij} e_j , \tag{A3}$$

and it can be shown that the new coordinates of x, written as x^*, are

$$x^* = Tx , \tag{A4}$$

or

$$x_i^* = \sum_j T_{ij} x_j . \tag{A5}$$

In equation (A3), $\hat{T}_{ij}$ is the (ji)th element of the *inverse* of T in (A5). The new basis, and the coordinates, are said to transform *contragrediently*.

Suppose a linear transformation with respect to the first basis is given by the matrix A, so that a relationship between vectors y and x may be expressed as

$$y = Ax . \tag{A6}$$

In the system with respect to the new basis, this relationship is

$$y^* = A^* x^* . \tag{A7}$$

But

$$y^* = Ty , \tag{A8}$$

and

$$x^* = Tx . \tag{A9}$$

So substituting from equations (A8) and (A9) into (A6) we have

$$T^{-1}y^* = AT^{-1}x^* \; ;$$

on pre-multiplying by T

$$y^* = TAT^{-1}x^* \; , \tag{A10}$$

and comparison of (A7) and (A10),

$$A^* = TAT^{-1} \; , \tag{A11}$$

shows how A transfers into A^* under the shift to a new basis given by T.

Suppose now that a_{ij} is the (ij)th element of a matrix a in equation (69). We wish to find a transformation T such that with a new basis, TaT^{-1} is a more convenient form. The most familiar of such canonical transformations is the diagonalisation of a matrix. This can be achieved by taking each column of T as the eigenvectors of a. In this case, however, it is most useful to obtain the *companion matrix* of a—what Birkhoff and MacLane call the "first natural form" of a matrix. This is done as follows.

We seek a vector α (given in the *old* coordinates) so that we can take

$$f_1^* = \alpha, f_2 = a\alpha, f_3 = a^2\alpha, f_4 \ldots, f_n = a^{n-1}\alpha \tag{A12}$$

(in the old coordinates) as the *new basis*. (For the *new coordinates*, we shall have

$$f_1^* = \begin{pmatrix} 1 \\ 0 \\ 0 \\ \cdot \\ \cdot \\ \cdot \\ 0 \end{pmatrix} \qquad f_2^* = \begin{pmatrix} 0 \\ 1 \\ 0 \\ \cdot \\ \cdot \\ \cdot \end{pmatrix} \qquad f_n^* = \begin{pmatrix} 0 \\ 0 \\ 0 \\ \cdot \\ \cdot \\ \cdot \\ 1 \end{pmatrix} \tag{A13}$$

in the usual way.)

Let T be the matrix of the transformation from the old basis to the new, so that

$$a^* = TaT^{-1} \; . \tag{A14}$$

The coordinate transformations are given by

$$x^* = Tx \tag{A15}$$

in the usual way. Let $\hat{T}$ be the transpose of T^{-1}. Then

$$f_i = \sum_j \hat{T}_{ij} e_j \tag{A16}$$

so that the columns of $\hat{T}$ are the elements of f_i in the old coordinates as given in equation (A12). This enables T to be obtained.

From equation (A12), we see that

$$f_2 = af_1 , \quad f_3 = af_2 , \quad \dots , \tag{A17}$$

and so in the new coordinates

$$f_2^* = a^*f_1^* , \quad f_3^* = a^*f_2^* , \quad \dots . \tag{A18}$$

We can use equations (A18) directly to obtain a^*: from the first of these

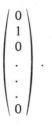

This means that the first column of a^* must take the form

Similarly, the second equation tells us that the second column of a^* must be

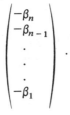

and so on up to and including the $(n-1)$th row. The final column can be specified arbitrarily and for convenience we take it in the form

$$\begin{pmatrix} -\beta_n \\ -\beta_{n-1} \\ \cdot \\ \cdot \\ \cdot \\ -\beta_1 \end{pmatrix} .$$

Hence

$$
a^* = \begin{pmatrix}
0 & 0 & 0 & & -\beta_n \\
1 & 0 & 0 & & -\beta_{n-1} \\
0 & 1 & 0 & & . \\
& & & . \\
& & & . \\
& & & . \\
& & & -\beta_1
\end{pmatrix} .
\tag{A19}
$$

Since the elements of the new basis must be linearly independent, any other vector can be expressed in terms of it. In particular, we can express $a^n \alpha$ in this form. We can write

$$
a^n \alpha = -\beta_1 \alpha - \beta_2 a\alpha - \ldots - \beta_n a^{n-1} \alpha
\tag{A20}
$$

in the old coordinates. In the *new* coordinates, the same equation would be

$$
a^{*n} T\alpha = -\beta_1 T\alpha - \ldots - \beta_n T^{n-1} \alpha = -\beta_1 f_1^* - \beta_1 f_2^* - \ldots - \beta_n f_n^* .
\tag{A21}
$$

However, we know that the left hand side can be written

$$
a^* f_n^*
$$

and this shows that $\beta_1, \beta_2, \ldots, \beta_n$ in equation (A21) can be identified with $\beta_1, \beta_2, \ldots, \beta_n$ in equation (A19). [Note that Rosen (1970) has the signs wrong in his polynomial (4.2.10) on page 94 for all the β's.] Equation (A20) can be written

$$
(a^n + \beta_n a^{n-1} + \beta_{n-1} a^{n-1} + \ldots + \beta_1)\alpha = 0 .
\tag{A22}
$$

The β's turn out to be related to the characteristic roots (eigenvalues) of a. We can see this as follows: let $g(a)$ be the polynomial

$$
g(a) = a^n + \beta_n a^{n-1} + \ldots + \beta_1 ;
\tag{A23}
$$

then $(-1)^n g(\lambda)$ is the characteristic polynomial of a^*. [Since *similar* matrices have the same eigenvalues, a also has the same characteristic polynomial (Birkhoff and MacLane, p.318).] The characteristic polynomial is

$$
g(\lambda) = \det |a^* - \lambda I|
\tag{A24}
$$

and an expansion of the determinant shows that the above stated result is correct. Thus, the β's are $(-1)^n$ times the coefficients of the characteristic polynomial, and can be found from a directly.

We now, at last, have a scheme of calculation.

(1) Given a, find the characteristic polynomial, and hence the β_i's using equations (A24) and (A23).

(2) (A22) is then a set of n linear equations in α which can be solved for the elements of α.

(3) The column vectors α, $a\alpha$, $a^2\alpha$, ..., $a^{n-1}\alpha$ form the columns of the matrix $\hat{T}$ which gives the transformation from the old basis to the new.

(4) We can next get the coordinate transformation T, since

$$T = \hat{T}'^{-1} ,$$
(A25)

where $'$ indicates transposition.

We now have all the equipment to put the equation system in canonical form using the companion matrix.

Inter-sectoral Contact Flows and Office Location in Central London

L.L.H.BAKER†, J.B.GODDARD
London School of Economics and Political Science

Introduction

An important theme in the development of location policy for economic activities has been the search for criteria of locational efficiency, that is measures of the appropriateness of particular types of activities for certain areas (for example, Greater London Council, 1970). One approach to this problem has suggested labour productivity differentials as an index but this has proved to be generally unsatisfactory, especially for non-manufacturing activities (Manners, 1970, Goddard, 1970a). In this paper the focus is on office-based activities and the concept of linkage, expressed in terms of information flows via personal contacts as a possible criterion for assessing which types of office activity most need to remain in central locations within cities.

It is a well-established fact that one of the principal advantages of a central location is the ease with which personal contacts can be maintained between customers and suppliers. In addition, the office is often involved in contacts not directly related to sales or purchases of goods or services: it is often through these information links that many offices derive important external economies for their firms by locating in a city centre (Thorngren, 1967). Through its contacts with the economic environment a firm is able to adjust to changing economic circumstances and so ensure its long-run profitability.

The central areas of large cities consist of complex communications networks made up of information flows between different activities. Within such networks flows are unlikely to be random; there must exist meaningful sets of patterned relationships. One would expect that certain groups of functions are closely linked to one another but have far weaker connections with functions that fall into other groups. In other words, the network of linkages between functions defines a system within which there are a number of interrelated sub-systems. Such sub-systems might be defined as office complexes analogous in many respects to industrial complexes. The object of this paper is to attempt to identify such complexes within the contact network of a sample of London offices, and then to specify the strength of the linkages to this network of different groups of offices.

In previous studies linkages have been inferred from analyses of patterns of locational association within the centre, or from analyses of movement patterns (Goddard, 1968; Goddard, 1970b). This form of inference is

† Now at Greater London Council, Department of Planning and Transportation.

plausible because the high cost of inter-office communication, especially where face-to-face meetings are involved, leads to linked functions having a propensity to locate in similar parts of the city centre. A correspondingly structured pattern of movement follows from this ordering of activity locations. In this paper a direct analysis of linkages based on an examination of the volume of face-to-face and telephone contacts between different office sectors is presented. With its aim of defining groups of strongly interconnected functions, the problem is in some respects methodologically similar to that of defining functional regions (Berry, 1966; Brown and Horton, 1970). However, since there is no direct locational component in the data matrix, the problem is probably more analogous to that of identifying clique structures from sociometric matrices, a problem that has been of continuing concern in the sociological literature (cf.Coleman, 1964).

It might be argued, following from the identification of functionally linked groups, that the loss of employment through decentralisation of an activity belonging to a particular complex might seriously undermine the viability of that complex as a whole, since each activity offers important external economies to other members of the group. In contrast, the loss of employment in weakly connected sectors is likely to have less far-reaching repercussions on the rest of the system. However, before developing a locational policy based on linkage, account also has to be taken of the strength of these linkages in terms of how far they demand close spatial proximity. One of the chief criticisms of a linkage approach is that existing patterns of contact might in no way reflect an optimal location with respect to currently available communications technology. An attempt is therefore made in the final section of this paper to examine some of the characteristics of the communications links to ascertain whether in fact they exhibit features of sub-optimality. That is, how far can existing links be stretched over space by the use of telecommunications facilities without serious diseconomies to the activities concerned? By adding features of the contact like length, number of people involved, and subject matter discussed, to the analysis of inter-office communications, an attempt is made to devise some weighting of these linkages in terms of the need for contacts to take the form of face-to-face meetings. Such considerations are likely to be of increasing importance with the introduction of advanced telecommunication facilities like videophones, document transmission, and conference vision (Reid, 1970; Goddard, 1971a).

The data
For a period of three days, a sample of 705 business executives, from a selection of commercial offices in Central London, recorded details of their telephone and meeting contacts with other firms in a specially designed contact diary. Examples of the contact record sheets are given in figures

1 and 2. The offices were sampled from a full list of all establishments in Central London, with the probability of selection proportional to the size of establishment and with the sample stratified according to office sector. Within each firm the sample of respondents to complete diaries was selected so that each identifiable organisational unit was represented.

MEETING RECORD

1 How long did the meeting last?

1 ☐ 2-10 minutes
2 ☐ 10-30 minutes
3 ☐ 30-60 minutes
4 ☐ 1-2 hours
5 ☐ more than 2 hours

2 Was the meeting arranged in advance?

1 ☐ Not pre-arranged at all
2 ☐ Arranged on the same day
3 ☐ Arranged the day before
4 ☐ Arranged 2-7 days in advance
5 ☐ Arranged more than 1 week in advance

3 Who initiated the meeting?

1 ☐ Myself/another person in my firm
2 ☐ Any person outside the firm or any other organization

4 How many people, apart from you, were at the meeting?

1 ☐ One other person
2 ☐ 2-4 people
3 ☐ 5-10 people
4 ☐ over 10 people

IF there was only one other person at the meeting:-

5 What is the work address of that person?

....

....

6 What is the nature of business of his firm?

....

....

IF there was more than one other person at the meeting, please complete the details overleaf

7 How often on average do you have a meeting with this person or particular set of people?

1 ☐ Daily
2 ☐ About once a week
3 ☐ About once a month
4 ☐ Occasionally
5 ☐ First contact

8 What was the main purpose of the meeting?

1 ☐ To give an order or instruction
2 ☐ To receive an order or instruction
3 ☐ To give advice
4 ☐ To receive advice
5 ☐ For bargaining
6 ☐ To give information
7 ☐ To receive information
8 ☐ To exchange information
9 ☐ For general discussion
10 ☐ Other (please specify)................
....

9 What was the range of subject matter discussed?

1 ☐ One specific subject
2 ☐ Several specific subjects
3 ☐ A wide range of general subjects

10 Was the meeting concerned with the purchase or sale of goods or services?

1 ☐ Directly concerned with purchases or sales
2 ☐ Indirectly concerned with purchases or sales
3 ☐ Not at all concerned with purchases or sales

IF the meeting took place outside your place of work:-

11 What is the address of the meeting place?

....

....

12 What was your principal method of transport from your office or previous meeting place?

1 ☐ Walk
2 ☐ Bus
3 ☐ Private car
4 ☐ Taxi
5 ☐ Underground
6 ☐ Train
7 ☐ Plane

13 How long did this journey take?

1 ☐ Less than 10 minutes
2 ☐ 10-30 minutes
3 ☐ 30-60 minutes
4 ☐ 1-2 hours
5 ☐ More than 2 hours

Figure 1. Meeting record sheet.

For as many of the people at the meeting as you have details, please state their work address and the nature of business of their firms (there is no need to name the people)

Firm's Business	Address
1	....
2	....
.	
)	....

Figure 1 (contd.)

Table 1. Size and sector distribution of firms cooperating in the survey of office communications.

Sector	Size of groups				% sample	No. of diaries	% of diaries	% office employment
	1–25	26–100	100+	total				
Primary industry	–	1	–	1	1·4	1	0·1	0·4
Food, drink, and tobacco	–	–	1	1	1·4	9	1·3	0·8
Chemicals and allied industries	–	3	4	7	9·7	135	19·1	5·2
Metals and other metal goods	1	–	–	1	1·4	1	0·1	0·8
Engineering	1	–	4	5	6·9	54	7·7	3·6
Other manufacturing	–	–	2	2	2·8	31	4·4	1·0
Printing, paper, and publishing	1	–	1	2	2·8	24	3·4	5·2
Construction	–	2	1	3	4·2	26	3·7	2·7
Gas, electricity, and water	–	–	2	2	2·8	19	2·7	1·4
Transport and communications	–	2	–	2	2·8	3	0·4	8·6
Wholesale distribution	–	1	1	2	2·0	5	0·7	4·8
Retail distribution	2	1	1	4	5·5	14	2·0	2·9
Commodity dealing	3	–	1	4	5·5	11	1·6	4·8
Insurance	–	3	3	6	8·3	44	6·2	10·7
Banking	–	2	4	6	8·3	113	16·0	10·3
Other finance	1	2	2	5	6·9	67	9·5	6·1
Professional and scientific services	1	1	2	4	5·5	44	6·2	11·6
Business services	1	1	4	6	8·3	49	7·0	7·3
Societies and associations	1	1	1	3	4·2	8	1·1	4·5
Entertainment	2	–	3	5	6·9	44	6·2	5·3
Miscellaneous offices	1	–	–	1	1·4	3	0·4	0·8
Total number of firms	15	20	37	72				
% of sample in each size group	21	29	50					
% of employment in each size group	23	27	50					

TELEPHONE CONTACT RECORD

1 How long did the contact last?

    1 ☐   2-10 minutes
    2 ☐ 10-30 minutes
    3 ☐ 30-60 minutes
    4 ☐ 1-2 hours
    5 ☐ More than 2 hours

2 Was the contact arranged in advance?

    1 ☐ Not pre-arranged at all
    2 ☐ Arranged on the same day
    3 ☐ Arranged the day before
    4 ☐ Arranged 2-7 days in advance
    5 ☐ Arranged more than one week in advance

3 Who initiated the contact?

    1 ☐ Myself/any other person in my firm
    2 ☐ Any person outside the firm or any other organization

4 What is the work address of the person with whom you talked?

....

....

5 What is the nature of business of his firm?

....

....

6 How often on average do you have contact with this person or firm, whichever is the most frequent?

    1 ☐ Daily
    2 ☐ About once a week
    3 ☐ About once a month
    4 ☐ Occasionally
    5 ☐ First contact

7 What was the main purpose of this contact?

    1 ☐ To give an order or instruction
    2 ☐ To receive an order or instruction
    3 ☐ To give advice
    4 ☐ To receive advice
    5 ☐ For bargaining
    6 ☐ To give information
    7 ☐ To receive information
    8 ☐ To exchange information
    9 ☐ For general discussion
    10 ☐ Others - please specify...

8 What was the range of subject matter discussed?

    1 ☐ One specific subject
    2 ☐ Several specific subjects
    3 ☐ A wide range of general subjects

9 Was the contact concerned with purchase or sale of goods or services?

    1 ☐ Directly concerned with sales or purchases
    2 ☐ Indirectly concerned with sales or purchases
    3 ☐ Not at all concerned with sales or purchases

Figure 2. Telephone contact record sheet

Because of variations of response, the degree of coverage varied considerably between office sectors. Some sectors, like chemicals, including fuel and oil, were over-represented by respondents, and others, such as transport, under-represented (table 1). Altogether, these businessmen recorded details of 5266 telephone contacts and 1549 meetings. From the diaries, the question on initiation can be used to give a directional component to the communication; with this question as a filter, intersectoral contact flow matrices can be constructed with each column representing a destination or chosen sector, each row an origin or choosing sector, and diagonal elements intra-sectoral flows. Separate contact matrices have been constructed for telephone calls and meetings in which the entries represent the number of contacts recorded between pairs of sectors. Each participant in meetings involving more than two people had to be counted as a separate contact, since large meetings could involve people from several different business sectors. Matrices have also been constructed with each contact weighted by its frequency according to the categories on the diary record sheets (times 1 for a first contact, and times 5 for a daily contact).

For the purposes of this analysis 42 office sectors have been identified, representing a considerable aggregation of a more detailed initial classification of nature of business (table 2). Sectors not sampled in the survey, like central and local government, can appear in the inter-sectoral contact flow matrices, since individuals in the sampled firms could initiate a contact with, or receive a contact from, another individual in one of these sectors. The sector groupings were defined in order to obtain a minimum of 25 meetings and 25 telephone contacts originating and terminating in each sector. Clearly the pattern of transactions will depend on the way in which sector groupings are defined: too broad a classification will mask critical functional differences between office activities, while too fine a classification creates data difficulties and a transaction matrix with an excess of zero entries. The classification that has been adopted is essentially pragmatic; sectors that are poorly represented in Central London and in the sample are broadly classified— like many of the industrial sectors—while sectors that are strongly represented by employment in the centre, like professional services, are more finely sub-divided.

Nevertheless, even given that the most appropriate classification of the data is given by this list of 42 sectors, it can still be argued on theoretical grounds that the business sector of a firm is not the most relevant unit of aggregation for the analysis of contact flows (Törnqvist, 1970). In the first instance an individual's patterns of contacts are most likely to depend on his job type; a computer manager's function and related contacts are likely to be similar whether he works in a bank or in an advertising agency However, the business sector will have some bearing: the computer manager is most likely to contact other computing personnel in his own sector. Also the requirements of policy making suggest the need for familiar classifications that can be related to other more readily available data.

Table 2. Office sectors.

1	Primary industry (including mining and quarrying)
2	Food, drink, and tobacco
3	Fuel and oil
4	Chemicals (including pharmaceuticals and rubber)
5	Metals and metal goods
6	Mechanical engineering and machinery (including industrial plant and steelworks)
7	Precision engineering (including office equipment)
8	Electrical engineering
9	Transport equipment (including shipbuilding and vehicles)
10	Textiles, leather, and clothing
11	Bricks, pottery, glass, and cement
12	Other manufacturing (and office fitting)
13	Paper, printing, and publishing
14	General construction (including civil engineering)
15	Specialist contracting (including concrete and plant hire)
16	Gas, electricity, and water
17	Transport and communications (including postal services and telecommunications)
18	Transport services (including shipping and forwarding agents)
19	Food wholesaling
20	Other specialist wholesaling (including clothing and footwear; paper, stationery, and books; machinery and equipment; chemicals)
21	General wholesale merchants
22	Retailing
23	Export and import merchants
24	Commodity brokers (including grain; metal; tea and coffee; wool and fur)
25	Insurance companies (including life assurance and accident insurance)
26	Other insurance (including insurance brokers and underwriters)
27	Banking (including merchant banks and foreign exchange)
28	Stockbroking and jobbing
29	Other finance (including building societies and investment trusts)
30	Property (including estate agents, surveyors, and valuers)
31	Accounting
32	Legal services
33	Consulting engineers
34	Architects
35	Other specialist consultancy (including management, production and marketing consultants)
36	Non-profit services (including research and educational institutes)
37	Advertising and public relations
38	Office services (including E.D.P. services; employment agencies; security services; translating)
39	Miscellaneous business services (including drawing and photographic services; news agencies and press services; equipment rental)
40	Societies and associations (including employers and trade associations; professional membership associations; trades unions; political organizations; charities)
41	Entertainment (including radio and television)
42	Central and Local Government

Approaches to the identification of functional sub-systems
Our first objective is to seek out functional sub-systems within the
meeting and telephone contact networks defined by the transaction
matrices; and, given the supposition that such sub-systems do exist, to
assign each sector to a group such that within-group linkages are maximized.
A variety of numerical procedures suggest themselves. Although most
succeed in reducing the complexity of interaction matrices through the
highlighting of incipient group structures, all suffer from the disadvantage
that the final decision as to which individual to allocate to each group
depends on the specification of usually arbitrary thresholds for group
membership. Some element of subjectivity is therefore inevitably involved
(Johnston, 1968).

Berry's original work on commodity flows has suggested factor analysis
as a technique for identifying functional regions (Berry, 1966). This
technique can be applied to the contact matrices by the correlation of
columns and the extraction of factors that indicate chosen sectors with
similar patterns of linkages to sets of choosing sectors. High factor
loadings identify the common chosen sectors, and high factor scores the
choosing sectors. Specifying some arbitrary cut off for the definition of
high factor loadings and high factor scores, and then linking the two
sectors together defines the interacting groups. The analysis can be
inverted (Q-mode analysis) to provide groupings of choosing sectors in
terms of common patterns of choice. Differences in the grouping
according to R-mode and Q-mode analysis are indicative of assymetric
relationships, or contacts, that are not reciprocated.

Russett has criticised the application of conventional factor analysis to
the correlation matrix derived from the transaction data, on the grounds
that it does not define interacting groups but only individuals with similar
patterns of connections (Russett, 1967). Following MacRae and Horst, he
suggests direct factor analysis of the original square transaction matrix,
with R-mode analysis defining the chosen individuals, and Q-mode analysis
the choosing individuals (MacRae, 1960; Horst, 1965). In this study,
questions concerning the reliability of the data in an absolute sense
unfortunately do not justify the use of direct factor analysis.

While suggesting groupings of sectors, factor analysis has no theoretical
underpinning. However, the indifference model of transaction flow
analysis, although basically only a simple data transformation, does seem
particularly suitable for the prediction of flows that are relatively
unconstrained by distance—such as intra-city contacts (Savage and Deutsch,
1960). The transaction flow model requires a comparison of the actual
flows (A_{ij}) between two sectors with that which would be expected given
the chosen sector's share of all received contacts. Thus expected
interaction (E_{ij}) between a choosing sector i and a chosen sector j is

defined as:

$$E_{ij} = O_i\left(\frac{D_j}{\sum_i D_j}\right),$$

where:

$$O_i = \sum_j A_{ij}, \quad \text{and} \quad D_j = \sum_i A_{ij}.$$

With assymetric relationships between sectors, the expected interaction between a chosen sector j and a choosing sector i would be:

$$E_{ji} = D_j\left(\frac{O_i}{\sum_j O_i}\right).$$

Absolute and relative differences (D_{ij} and R_{ij} respectively) between observed and expected interaction may then be defined:

$$D_{ij} = A_{ij} - E_{ij}, \qquad\qquad R_{ij} = \frac{A_{ij} - E_{ij}}{E_{ij}}.$$

Absolute values of relative differences between observed and expected contacts, that exceed specified thresholds, can be defined as salient flows. These indicate sectors having strong interconnection relative to the whole system.

Neither factor analysis nor transaction flow analysis will define a complete assignment of sectors to groups. In the case of factor analysis this can be achieved by applying some grouping algorithm to a similarity matrix derived from the factor scores. This approach has been adopted by Goddard in a study of functional regions within a city centre (Goddard, 1970b). However, this will only define groups according to the pattern of choice, not according to interconnected choosing and chosen sectors. Similarly a binary matrix indicating salient connections, derived from the transaction flow analysis, can be subjected to some grouping procedure like dissimilarity analysis (McNaughton-Smith et al., 1964). As this connection matrix is likely to be assymetrical, the problem of whether to group on the basis of choosing or chosen sectors still arises. In view of these difficulties we have used conventional factor analysis to suggest incipient groups, and transaction flow analysis as a guide to the assignment of residual sectors to these groups.

The telephone contact network

Six factors provide the best description of the telephone contact network. Together the six factors account for 62% of the total variance. A normal varimax rotation was performed upon an initial principal components solution to give the factor structures described in table 3. Factor 1 can be described as a civil engineering group, including architects, consulting engineers, and brick and cement manufacturers. The group focuses on general construction companies as the principal choosing sector. It is well

Table 3. Factor analyses of inter-sectoral telephone contacts matrix.

Factor	Chosen sector	Factor loading[a]	Choosing sector	Factor score[b]
1 Civil engineering	Architects	0·868	General construction	5·103
	General construction	0·844	Consulting engineers	1·463
	Consulting engineers	0·833	Bricks, pottery, glass,	
	Specialist construction	0·763	and cement	1·309
	Metals and metal goods	0·689		
	Primary industry	0·673		
	Bricks, pottery, glass, and cement	0·662		
	Explained variance:	12·54%		
2 Fuel and oil	Fuel and oil	−0·904	Fuel and oil	−5·858
	Non-profit services	−0·904		
	Transport and communications	−0·876		
	Mechanical engineering and machinery	−0·797		
	Central and local government	−0·648		
	Office services	−0·516		
	Explained variance:	12·25%		
3 Banking and finance	Stockbroking	−0·885	Banking	−3·876
	Property	−0·870	Property	−4·300
	Banking	−0·862		
	Legal services	−0·848		
	Other finance	−0·658		
	Accounting	−0·524		
	Explained variance:	10·95%		
4 Publishing and business services	Chemicals and pharmaceuticals	0·881	Chemicals and pharmaceuticals	4·518
	Retailing	0·859	Advertising and public relations	2·696
	Food, drink, and tobacco	0·805	Paper, printing, and publishing	2·100
	Other special services	0·747		
	Paper, printing, and publishing	0·716		
	Advertising and public relations	0·691		
	Explained variance:	10·56%		
5 Official agencies	Electrical engineering	−0·906	Entertainment	−5·454
	Entertainment	−0·901	Paper, printing, and publishing	−1·663
	Societies and associations	−0·711	Miscellaneous business services	−1·191
	Miscellaneous business services	−0·675		
	Explained variance:	9·05%		
6 Commodity trading	Food wholesaling	−0·790	Export and import merchants	−4·980
	Textiles, leather, and clothing	−0·772	Property	−1·438
	Export and import merchants	−0·609	Commodity brokers	−1·426
	Transport services	−0·600	Food wholesaling	−1·181
			Retailing	−1·064
	Explained variance:	6·70%		
	Total explained variance:	62·05%		

[a] Only factor loadings greater than ±0·5 are shown.
[b] Only factor scores greater than ±1·00 are shown.

known that many aspects of a civil engineering project are contracted out to different types of firms; inevitably this procedure will lead to a substantial volume of contact between the various contractors.

Factor 2 centres on fuel and oil companies, and is partly a reflection of over-representation of this sector in the initial sample. The major links maintained by fuel and oil companies include those with the transport industry, engineering firms, and central government. Factor 3 covers the closely related activities of banking and finance; surprisingly insurance loads only moderately (0·42) on this factor. Factor 4 includes industries very directly concerned with publicity—for example, advertising agencies, public relations consultants, management consultants, pharmaceutical manufacturers, retailers, and food manufacturers. Factor 5 isolates the activities of public and semi-public agencies, including broadcasting (here classified under entertainment), Government offices, and professional associations. Finally factor 6 suggests a small group of activities concerned with commodity trading.

On the leading factors, factor scores are generally confined to a few sectors. These sectors are the principal sources for contacts within each group. The high scores also indicate the skewed nature of the underlying distributions; normalizing transformations of the data would partly suppress this basic fact. To some extent this highly nodal structure reflects the sampling procedure, the choosing sectors tending to be those with a large number of respondents. This bias is reinforced by the greater likelihood of respondents recording telephone contacts they have initiated, rather than incoming calls. Thus, whereas the choosing sectors are predominantly those sampled, the chosen sectors are often those not included in the sample, or with small sample fractions. For example, Government offices are major choices for contacts in certain groups but, because these offices were not included in the sample, they are not recorded as a major chooser. In fact very few respondents recorded contacts that had been initiated by the Government sector.

Another data difficulty concerns inter-sectoral contact flows; these are contained in the diagonal elements of the contact matrices and represent contacts received from, or addressed to, other firms within the same business sector. The volume of inter-sectoral contacts, expressed as a proportion of total telephone contacts, varies considerably from sector to sector; it is a figure partly influenced by the sampling procedure, since sectors with no respondents will have no inter-sectoral contact flows. In an attempt to eliminate this problem the diagonal elements in the contact matrices were set to zero and the R-mode factor analysis repeated, again extracting 6 factors. The same basic structure emerges, with the exception of a separate public agencies group and the division of the financial factor into two groups, one with banking as its principal source, and the other focusing on accounting (table 4). A separate trading factor focussed on export and import merchants is more clearly identifiable.

Table 4. Factor analyses of inter-sectoral telephone excluding inter-sectoral contacts.

Factor	Chosen sector	Factor loading[a]	Choosing sector	Factor score[b]
1 Fuel and oil	Transport and communications	−0·866	Fuel and oil	−5·221
	Non-profit services	−0·862	Entertainment	−2·129
	Gas, electricity, and water	−0·841	Paper, printing, and publishing	−1·317
	Societies and associations	−0·814		
	Central and local government	−0·723		
	Mechanical engineering	−0·699		
	Office services	−0·656		
	Miscellaneous business services	−0·503		
	Electrical engineering	−0·500		
	Explained variance:	15·0%		
2 Civil engineering	Architects	0·805	General construction	5·217
	Consulting engineers	0·781	Fuel and oil	1·681
	Specialist construction	0·754	Chemicals	1·1203
	Metals and metal goods	0·692	Consulting engineers	1·134
	Bricks, pottery, glass, and cement	0·683		
	Transport services	0·657		
	Primary industry	0·692		
	Mechanical engineering	0·598		
	Explained variance:	11·50%		
3 Publishing and business services	Retailing	0·778	Chemicals	4·049
	Food, drink, and tobacco	0·706	Paper, printing, and publishing	3·217
	Advertising and public relations	0·652	Advertising and public relations	2·354
	Other specialist consultancy	0·634		
	Miscellaneous business services	0·598		
	Fuel and oil	0·572		
	Explained variance:	9·04%		
4 Accountancy	Stockbroking	−0·873	Accountancy	−5·670
	Legal services	−0·851		
	Banking	−0·785		
	Export and import overheads	−0·560		
	Explained variance:	7·76%		
5 Banking	Property	−0·816	Banking	−5·365
	Accountancy	−0·800	Insurance	−1·362
	Legal services	−0·609		
	Other manufacturing	−0·556		
	Explained variance:	7·48%		
6 Commodity trading	Textiles, leather, and clothing	0·841	Export and import merchants	4·707
	Food wholesaling	0·771	Retailing	1·832
	Transport services	0·581	Commodity brokers	1·121
	Other specialist wholesaling	0·510		
	Explained variance:	7·24%		
	Total explained variance:	58·00%		

[a] Only factor loadings greater than ±0·50 are shown.
[b] Only factor scores greater than ±1·00 are shown.

Table 5. Factor analyses of inter-sectoral meeting contacts.

Factor	Chosen sector	Factor loading[a]	Choosing sector	Factor score[b]
1 Banking and finance	Stockbroking	0·908	Banking	5·595
	Banking	0·870		
	Office services	0·806		
	Legal services	0·754		
	Other finance	0·658		
	Explained variance:	11·21%		
2 Entertainment	Entertainment	0·756	Entertainment	5·781
	Electrical engineering	0·825		
	Non-profit services	0·820		
	Other specialist wholesaling	0·805		
	Food wholesaling	0·633		
	Societies and associations	0·563		
	Food, drink, and tobacco	0·533		
	Transport and communications	0·513		
	Explained variance:	10·36%		
3 Fuel and oil	Fuel and oil	−0·882	Fuel and oil	−5·609
	Mechanical engineering	−0·745		
	Other specialist consultancy	−0·692		
	Societies and associations	−0·617		
	Accountancy	−0·530		
	Explained variance:	9·74%		
4 Publishing and business services	Advertising and public relations	−0·847	Paper, printing, and publishing	−3·00
	Paper, printing, and publishing	−0·795	Advertising and public relations	−3·310
	Retailing	−0·735	Chemicals	−3·173
	Chemicals	−0·651	Precision engineering	−1·005
	Miscellaneous business services	−0·527		
	Explained variance:	8·91%		
5 Civil engineering	Consulting engineer	0·807	General construction	3·076
	General construction	0·783	Property	2·651
	Architects	0·612	Architects	2·640
	Specialist contracting	0·783	Consulting engineers	2·290
	Explained variance:	7·40%	Office services	1·212
6 Trading	Transport equipment	−0·732	Export and import merchants	−4·218
	Textiles, leather, and clothing	−0·652	Transport equipment	−1·792
	Accountancy	−0·639	Other insurance	−1·569
	Explained variance:	5·56%	Precision engineering	−1·263
	Total explained variance:	53·18%		

The meeting network

Six factors also provide the best description of the inter-sectoral meeting contacts, accounting for 52% of the total variance (table 5). The lower level of explanation achieved by the same number of factors suggests that the meeting network is less structured than that maintained by telephone contacts. Three of these factors, namely those associated with civil engineering, publishing and business services, and banking and finance, can be equated with the similar groupings derived from the analysis of telephone contacts. These three groups, therefore, appear to be the most readily identifiable contact sub-systems. As the leading factor, the banking and finance group is the most inter-connected according to meeting contacts, whereas it ranks third according to telephone contacts. From this it might be inferred that, relative to all other groups, this group makes greater use of the meeting for communication. This and other differences between telephone contacts and meetings suggest that each communication channel is used for somewhat different contact networks.

However, in view of the nature of the data, inferences about the nature of meeting contacts need to be considered cautiously. Meetings take place with a much lower frequency than telephone contacts. For the full sample, 41% of the telephone contacts took place more than once a week, compared with only 24% of the meetings; if the financial sectors, with a high frequency of meetings are excluded, the latter figure is substantially reduced. The three days of the diary survey therefore represent a much smaller sample of meetings than of telephone contacts. In addition the problem of dealing with meetings involving two respondents, and our convention of treating each participant as a separate contact, may bias the meeting network towards sectors with a high proportion of large meetings. For these reasons the analysis of telephone contacts can be taken as more representative of the basic pattern of functional groupings.

The pattern of spatial linkages

It has frequently been suggested that groups of functionally related office activities would tend to locate in similar parts of the city centre (Goddard, 1968). These spatial linkages can be determined from patterns of locational association. A factor analysis of a spatial data matrix, consisting of 64 office employment categories measured over 70 traffic zones within Central London, was carried out to test this hypothesis. (The 42 sectors used in constructing the contact matrices were aggregated from the 64 employment categories of this spatial analysis.) The 5 orthogonally rotated factors shown in table 6 indicate groups of employment categories with similar patterns of locational association within Central London. Although ordered differently in terms of explained variance, all groups (with the exception of fuel and public agency) derived from the functional analysis of telephone contacts appear to have approximate spatial equivalents—a fact which lends support to a long standing theory of urban structure.

Table 6. Factor analysis of three digit employment categories (by traffic zone).

Factor 1: Trading

Other insurance	−0·938
Commodity brokers, merchants, and dealers	−0·937
Transport services	−0·932
Postal services and telecommunications	−0·920
Agriculture, forestry, and fishing	−0·831
General wholesale merchants	−0·829
Food wholesaling	−0·744
Food	−0·689
Transport	−0·667
Export and import merchants	−0·666

Explained variance = 18·54%

Factor 2: Clothing and business services

Management, production, marketing, and costing consultants	−0·788
Drugs, chemicals, and other non-food wholesaling	−0·746
Clothing and footwear wholesaling	−0·737
Textiles	−0·689
Clothing and footwear	−0·664
Advertising and public relations	−0·594
Leather, leather goods, and fur	−0·578
Vehicles	−0·573
Drawing and photographic services	−0·571
Miscellaneous manufacturing industries	−0·533
Property	−0·529

Explained variance = 12·72%

Factor 3: Civil engineering

Employers' and trade associations	−0·824
Consulting engineers	−0·781
Bricks, pottery, glass, cement	−0·757
Charitable organisations	−0·739
Other specialist consultants	−0·649
General construction and contracting	−0·600
Professional membership organisations	−0·593
Specialist contracting	−0·537
Architects	−0·525

Explained variance = 7·45%

Factor 4: Banking and finance

Accounting, auditing, and bookkeeping	0·943
Stockbroking and jobbing	0·888
Other banking	0·867
Central banking	0·855
Insurance companies	0·806
Other finance	0·755
Office services	0·633
Head offices of offices operating abroad	0·601
Legal services	0·599

Explained variance = 6·84%

Factor 5: Publishing

Printing and publishing	−0·725
Paper, stationery, and books wholesaling	−0·618
Drawing and photographic services	−0·508

Explained variance = 5·27%

Total variance accounted for by five factors = 50·78%

The pattern of 'within and between' group linkages

From the result of the factor analyses of contact patterns, it cannot be assumed that all chosen sectors loading high on a particular factor are both significantly connected with each other or with each of the principal choosing sectors indicated by the high factor scores. In previous studies of functional regions this assumption has been made, and all high loadings and high scoring places have been linked together in mapping the regionalisation. This exact pattern of linkage is best examined through transaction flow analysis.

In developing the final grouping that is displayed in figure 3 the sectors highly connected according to telephone contacts have been formed into clusters as suggested by the factor analysis, with the final assignment of residual sectors being made according to the pattern of salient transactions. In this procedure greater weight has been given to two way linkages. Heavy lines in the diagram indicate linkages where either or both R_{ij} and R_{ji}

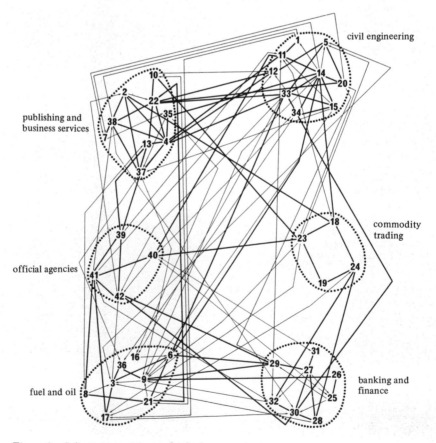

Figure 3. Salient transactions of telephone contacts.

exceed $0 \cdot 50$, and D_{ij} and D_{ji} exceed $2 \cdot 0$. Lighter lines indicate linkages where there is a one way connection exceeding the same threshold for both R_{ij} and D_{ij}. These particular thresholds indicate pairs of sectors that have 50% more interaction than expected (relative saliency), and where this involves more than 2 actual contacts (absolute saliency).

The diagram highlights a substantial number of between group linkages and so illustrates a basic conceptual limitation of factor analysis when applied to transaction data. This is that the factor analysis model seeks to

Table 7. Within and between group telephone contacts.
(a) Absolute number of calls.

From	To						Total	%
	A	B	C	D	E	F		
A	317	121	23	127	50	97	735	14·5
%	43·1	16·4	3·1	17·3	6·8	13·1		
B	83	1000	45	116	53	107	1404	27·7
%	5·9	71·2	3·2	8·3	3·8	7·6		
C	34	50	111	35	11	26	267	5·3
%	12·7	18·7	41·6	13·1	4·1	9·7		
D	115	177	38	646	109	137	1222	24·1
%	9·4	14·5	3·1	52·8	8·9	11·2		
E	61	65	11	85	207	94	523	10·3
%	11·6	12·4	2·1	16·2	39·5	18·0		
F	97	109	28	126	85	462	907	17·9
%	10·7	12·0	3·1	13·2	9·4	50·9		
Total	707	1522	256	1135	515	923	5058	
%	13·9	30·0	5·1	22·4	10·1	18·2		

(b) Number of calls weighted by frequency.

	A	B	C	D	E	F	Total	%
A	899	364	87	358	127	266	2101	
%	42·7	17·3	4·1	17·0	6·0	12·6		13·5
B	248	3427	171	319	136	374	4675	
%	5·3	73·3	3·6	6·8	2·9	8·0		30·1
C	103	164	412	109	34	82	904	
%	11·4	18·1	45·6	12·0	3·8	9·1		5·8
D	299	488	113	2083	281	392	3656	
%	8·2	13·3	3·1	56·9	7·6	10·7		23·5
E	181	207	31	214	606	257	1496	
%	12·0	13·8	2·0	14·3	40·3	17·2		9·6
F	259	332	84	387	232	1404	698	
%	9·5	12·3	3·1	14·3	8·6	52·0		17·3
Total	1989	4974	898	3470	1416	2775	15 530	
%	12·8	32·0	5·7	22·2	9·2	17·8		

Key: Group A – Civil engineering   Group D – Publishing and business services
      Group B – Banking–finance   Group E – Public agencies
      Group C – Commodity trading   Group F – Fuel and oil

reduce the data into the minimum number of statistically independent groups, whereas complex interaction systems are composed of interdependent or overlapping systems (Johnston, 1970). Oblique factor rotation solutions can only improve marginally on this basic orthogonality, which is imposed by the initial factoring procedure. In this instance promax rotation of the varimax factor loadings only suggested a slight degree of correlation between factors, in spite of the strong evidence to the contrary (Hendrickson and White, 1964).

The pattern of within and between group linkages by telephone is summarised in table 7 and figure 4. According to both the absolute volume of contact and the number of two-way salient transactions, within group linkages exceed the number of linkages to any other single group. Overall, 54·2% of telephone contacts are within the groups. The most strongly internalised group is that composed of the financial sectors, with 71·2% of contacts originating in the group being destined for other sectors in the same group. In contrast another major group, civil engineering, has only 43·1% of its telephone contacts internal to the group, with substantial volumes of communication to the financial group and to the publishing and business services group. Examination of figure 3 suggests that the former connections can be attributed to links between property companies and architects, and the latter to links between consulting

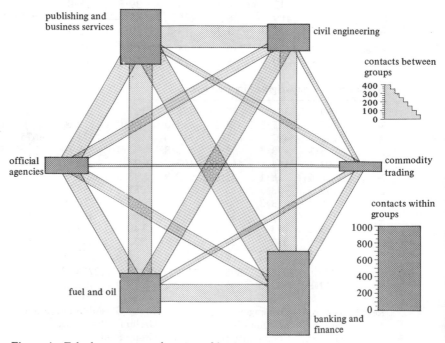

Figure 4. Telephone contacts by type of business.

engineers and chemical manufacturers. The trading group also has a large
number of external links, particularly to trading and finance, while the
public agencies group has strong links with publishing and business services.

Weighting of the contacts according to frequency (times 5 for a daily
contact and times 1 for a first contact) surprisingly makes little difference
to the pattern of within and between group linkages (table 7b). It might
have been expected that within group contact would occur more
frequently but this does not appear to be the case. A separate factor
analysis of the weighted contacts also produced similar groupings.
However, if regular and occasional contacts had been considered separately,
a somewhat different contact network might have been identifiable.

Within and between group meeting contacts are summarised in figures 5
and 6 and table 8. In figure 5 the sectors are clustered into groups
defined from the analysis of telephone contacts. The pattern of salient
transactions at once confirms the different nature of the meeting network

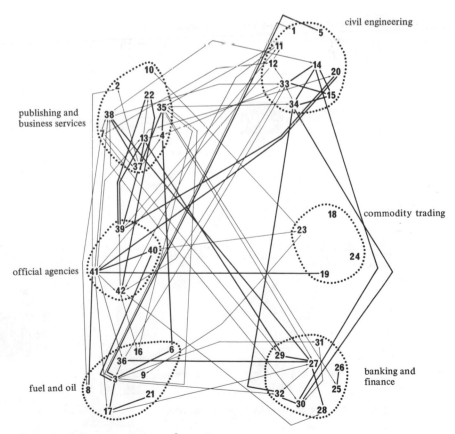

Figure 5. Salient transactions of meeting contacts.

and the overall lower degree of connectivity at the same saliency level. Some sectors are completely unconnected, with the number of between group links often exceeding the number of within group links. However, when the absolute volume of contacts within and between groups is considered, the proportion of meetings that are confined to the group (60%) exceeds the equivalent figure for telephone contacts (54%) (see table 8a). Again the pattern of flows for weighted contacts does not alter this picture (see table 8b). We can therefore conclude that the meeting network is the less interconnected, simply because contacts are more tightly confined to a few sectors. This fact can be confirmed by examining how far the proportion of contacts received by a chosen sector j from every other sector i deviates from each of the choosing sector's share of all contacts.

An index of concentration C, closely related to the familiar coefficient of localisation, can be defined for each chosen sector j as:

$$C_j = \sum (X_i - Y_j) \qquad \sum \text{ for all } X_i > Y_j \, ,$$

where

$$X_i = \frac{A_{ij}}{\sum_i D_j} \, , \qquad\qquad Y_j = \frac{O_i}{\sum_j O_i} \, ,$$

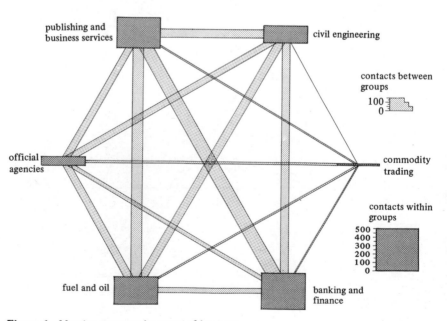

Figure 6. Meeting contacts by type of business.

and

$$O_i = \sum_j A_{ij}, \qquad\qquad D_j = \sum_i A_{ij},$$

and A_{ij} = actual interaction between choosing sector i and chosen sector j.

The mean value of C for meetings for all sectors j is $0\cdot693$ compared with a mean of $0\cdot553$ for telephone contacts. About this mean there is a considerable variation between sectors in the degree of concentration of their contact flows.

Table 8. Within and between group meetings.
(a) Absolute number of meetings.

From	To						Total	%
	A	B	C	D	E	F		
A	209	35	0	41	44	47	376	15·2
%	55·5	9·3	0 0	10·9	11·7	12·5		
B	50	472	9	60	15	21	627	25·3
%	8·0	75·2	1·4	9·6	1·6	3·3		
C	3	8	27	8	15	15	76	3·1
%	3·9	10·5	35 5	10·5	17·7	19·7		
D	52	90	8	348	48	54	600	24·3
%	8·6	15·0	1·3	58·0	8·0	9·0		
E	26	34	13	35	95	48	251	10·1
%	10·3	13·5	5·2	13·9	37·3	19·1		
F	50	44	6	68	44	329	541	21·9
%	9·2	8·1	1·1	12·6	8 1	60·8		
Total	390	683	63	560	261	541	2471	
%	13·7	27·6	2·5	22·6	10·5	21·9		

(b) Number of meetings weighted by frequency.

	A	B	C	D	E	F	Total	%
A	572	98	0	98	118	125	1011	15·3
%	56·6	9·6	0·0	9·6	11·6	12·3		
B	140	1387	17	172	35	60	1811	27·5
%	7·7	76·6	1·0	9·5	1·9	3·3		
C	4	15	88	16	3	34	160	2·4
%	2·5	9·3	55·0	9·3	2·2	21·2		
D	119	216	13	981	126	127	1582	24·0
%	7·5	13·6	0·8	62·0	7·9	7·9		
E	76	95	36	79	219	124	629	9·5
%	12·1	15·1	3·7	12·5	34·8	19·7		
F	104	111	15	185	104	873	1392	21·1
%	7·8	8·3	1·1	13·9	7·4	65·7		
Total	1015	1922	169	1531	605	1343	6585	
%	15·4	29·1	2·6	23·2	9·1	20·4		

Key:	Group A – Civil engineering	Group D – Publishing and business services
	Group B – Banking–finance	Group E – Public agencies
	Group C – Commodity trading	Group F – Fuel and oil

Indirect linkages

Both factor analysis and transaction flow analysis can be criticised on the grounds that they consider only direct linkages in the system. Where flows are unconstrained, as is the case of inter-sectoral contacts, linkages are most likely to be direct. However, in certain instances, indirect linkages from intermediate sectors may be significant. For example, a firm wishing to place an advertisement usually approaches the medium, such as a newspaper publisher, through an advertising agency. There is therefore only an indirect link between the firm and the newspaper publisher.

Indirect linkages can be considered through the closely related procedures of Markov chain analysis and graph theory. Each sector may be considered as a state of a system, and flows between sectors as movements between states. The transaction matrix can therefore be considered as a transition probability matrix, and this matrix solved for the mean first passage time between states. Low values in the mean first passage time matrix will indicate sectors with a high level of direct and indirect connection. These indices can be treated as measures of 'functional distance' (Brown and Horton, 1970). Again this transformation will not directly yield a grouping of sectors; this can be achieved by factor analysis or a grouping algorithm (Johnston and Kissling, 1971; Brown and Holmes, 1971; Brown et al., 1970). Unfortunately with a contact matrix containing a large number of zero entries, the mean first passage times between states can be very unstable and exhibit very large variances. For this reason the technique has not been applied here.

In a similar way a directed graph, derived from the transaction flow analysis or some other transformation, can be analysed for indirect connections by powering the matrix of direct linkages. Penalties on indirect links can be built into the analysis by dividing each direct link by a constant and so converting the values into decimal numbers (Nystuen and Dacey, 1961). Alternatively, each successive powering of the matrix can be preceded by multiplication by an arbitrary attenuation constant. Powering can continue until the diameter of the graph is reached. The elements in the sum of the powered connection matrices indicate the total number of indirect and direct linkages between pairs of sectors. However, this matrix does contain redundant linkages that involve doubling back. No known way exists for extracting these redundancies beyond the third level, while at the same time yielding all of the n step links between pairs of individuals (Coleman, 1964). The powered connection matrix has to be subjected to some grouping procedure like factor analysis in order to define the various sub-systems, or thresholds of connectivity have to be specified for group membership (Gauthier, 1968; Hubbel, 1969).

No attempt has been made to provide an alternative partitioning of the contact matrices on the basis of indirect connections. However, the graph theoretic analysis can be used to derive a measure of ultimate connectivity of each sector to the contact system. It is to this question of connectivity of individual sectors that we now turn.

The connectivity of business sectors to the contact network

A number of distinctive functional groupings of office sectors have been identified and the volume of within and between group contacts specified. In terms of locational policy some summary measures, that suggest the degree of involvement of each sector in the functional groups, are required. One such index is provided by the final communality of each variable derived from the factor analyses of the contact data. The sectors with high communalities will be those with high factor loadings and hence a heavy involvement in one or more groups.

Some sectors may not be involved in any particular functional group and therefore have a low communality, yet still be well connected to the contact network, especially through indirect links. To take account of this situation, an index of connectivity can be derived from the powering of the connection matrix that has been defined from the transaction flow analysis. The two-way salient transaction, displayed in figure 3, defines a symmetrical graph (C^1) with a diameter of 6. From the sum of the power series, $C^1 + C^2 + C^3 \dots C^6$, a new matrix of total connectivity can be determined. Summing the columns of the matrix gives a measure of connectivity for each sector, which considers both direct and indirect links. This analysis cannot be carried out for the meeting network, since at the same saliency level a completely connected graph cannot be defined.

The converse of a high degree of connectivity is that a particular sector has a large proportion of its contacts with a limited number of other sectors. Because the connectivity measure is based on a crude binary generalisation of this contact network, a supplementary measure is provided by the index of concentration outlined earlier. The sectors with a low concentration index will be those connected directly to a large number of other businesses.

All three indices are relevant measures of the attachment of each business sector to the Central London contact system. These measures are summarised in table 9. Each index has been ranked and divided into quartiles, and the sectors divided into three groups on the basis of their combined ranking. At the extreme of the ranking the various measures are broadly similar. Sectors like primary industry, textiles, commodity broking, and insurance fall into the bottom halves of the distributions according to all five indices: that is, these sectors have highly concentrated contact flows, few indirect linkages, and have little involvement in any of the groups. Sectors such as general construction, retailing, banking, and central government fall into the top halves of all of the distributions, with dispersed contacts, numerous indirect connections, and high group involvement. In the intermediate group some sectors, for example specialist

Table 9. Connectivity of business sectors to the contact network.

Sector	Telephone contacts			Meetings	
	Concentration index	Communality	Connectivity index (C^6)	Concentration index	Communality
Highly connected					
Fuel and oil	0·45 (1)	0·85 (1)	306 (2)	0·56 (1)	0·78 (1)
Metals and metal goods	0·55 (2)	0·73 (2)	344 (1)	0·64 (2)	0·53 (3)
Mechanical engineering and machinery	0·52 (2)	0·90 (1)	365 (1)	0·67 (2)	0·64 (2)
Paper, printing, and publishing	0·43 (1)	0·72 (3)	298 (2)	0·44 (1)	0·79 (1)
General construction	0·40 (1)	0·85 (1)	622 (1)	0·63 (2)	0·64 (2)
Retailing	0·46 (1)	0·76 (2)	319 (1)	0·76 (3)	0·61 (2)
Banking	0·46 (1)	0·75 (2)	160 (3)	0·52 (1)	0·78 (1)
Legal services	0·44 (1)	0·85 (1)	140 (3)	0·60 (2)	0·83 (1)
Consulting engineers	0·51 (2)	0·73 (2)	546 (2)	0·59 (1)	0·75 (2)
Other specialist consultancy	0·48 (2)	0·67 (3)	288 (2)	0·49 (1)	0·81 (1)
Advertising and public relations	0·57 (3)	0·57 (3)	271 (2)	0·50 (1)	0·83 (1)
Office services	0·34 (1)	0·74 (2)	119 (3)	0·55 (1)	0·81 (1)
Societies and associations	0·40 (1)	0·74 (2)	195 (2)	0·63 (2)	0·80 (1)
Central and local government	0·39 (1)	0·86 (1)	160 (3)	0·52 (1)	0·60 (3)
Moderately connected					
Food, drink, and tobacco	0·65 (4)	0·69 (3)	206 (2)	0·61 (2)	0·62 (2)
Chemicals	0·57 (3)	0·81 (2)	507 (1)	0·64 (2)	0·59 (3)
Precision engineering	0·47 (2)	0·12 (4)	139 (3)	0·70 (2)	0·17 (4)
Electrical engineering	0·60 (3)	0·84 (1)	51 (4)	0·69 (3)	0·78 (1)
Bricks, pottery, glass, and cement	0·57 (3)	0·54 (3)	405 (1)	0·75 (3)	0·16 (4)
Other manufacturing	0·55 (3)	0·31 (4)	417 (1)	0·57 (1)	0·29 (4)
Specialist contracting	0·57 (3)	0·71 (3)	410 (1)	0·79 (4)	0·40 (3)
Transport and communications	0·61 (3)	0·90 (1)	119 (4)	0·79 (4)	0·52 (3)
Transport services	0·60 (3)	0·72 (2)	203 (2)	0·81 (4)	0·09 (4)
Other specialist wholesaling	0·43 (1)	0·57 (3)	306 (2)	0·79 (4)	0·71 (2)
Stockbroking and jobbing	0·64 (4)	0·85 (1)	47 (4)	0·75 (4)	0·84 (4)
Other finance	0·54 (1)	0·48 (1)	222 (4)	0·56 (4)	0·75 (2)
Architects	0·54 (2)	0·82 (2)	345 (1)	0·81 (4)	0·39 (4)
Non-profit services	0·49 (2)	0·91 (1)	59 (4)	0·82 (4)	0·78 (2)
Miscellaneous business services	0·55 (2)	0·62 (3)	165 (3)	0·77 (3)	0·35 (4)
Entertainment	0·57 (3)	0·83 (2)	129 (3)	0·61 (2)	0·76 (2)
Weakly connected					
Primary industry	0·75 (4)	0·51 (4)	73 (4)	0·78 (3)	0·40 (3)
Transport equipment	0·63 (4)	0·22 (4)	226 (2)	0·74 (3)	0·59 (3)
Textiles, leather, and clothing	0·70 (4)	0·61 (3)	92 (4)	0·98 (4)	0·45 (3)
Gas, electricity, and water	0·67 (4)	0·21 (4)	125 (3)	0·70 (3)	0·05 (4)
Food wholesaling	0·74 (4)	0·66 (3)	50 (4)	0·80 (4)	0·51 (3)
General wholesale merchants	0·76 (4)	0·04 (4)	135 (3)	0·86 (4)	0·09 (4)
Export and import merchants	0·63 (4)	0·48 (4)	162 (3)	0·76 (3)	0·09 (4)
Commodity brokers	0·49 (4)	0·16 (4)	82 (4)	0·84 (4)	0·36 (4)
Insurance companies	0·55 (3)	0·19 (4)	8 (4)	0·78 (4)	0·10 (4)
Other insurance	0·62 (4)	0·09 (4)	43 (4)	0·82 (4)	0·05 (4)
Accounting	0·53 (2)	0·54 (4)	56 (4)	0·79 (4)	0·72 (2)

(Numbers in brackets refer to quartile of each sector according to ranking of each index)

construction, have numerous indirect connections, yet with a relatively weak involvement in any group and a concentrated pattern of contact flows. Some sectors, notably banking, other finance, and advertising, rank higher according to meetings than to telephone contacts.

These indices are only suggestive of the sort of measures that might provide guide lines in forming a location policy for office sectors. With such a relatively small sample of contacts and the variations of response, too much significance cannot be attached to the specific results. The data were not collected with the sole purpose of measuring the volume of inter-sectoral contact flows. Rather, the primary objective was to establish how far particular information linkages demanded the close spatial proximity of the activities concerned. By examining the characteristics of the communications, it may be possible to identify information links that might be carried out by present or future forms of telecommunications over a considerable distance. By breaking down the crude volumes of contacts within and between sectors and sector groups, some weighting of these linkages might be possible.

The characteristics of inter-personal communication

The features of personal contact that influence the choice of communication medium (that is telephone or face-to-face meeting) have been reviewed elsewhere (Goddard, 1971a). The questions on the contact record sheets (figures 1 and 2) attempt to measure some of these characteristics. They were selected so as to be generally applicable to all types of organisation. In the main, the questions try to avoid purely subjective ratings of contacts, using semantic scales to identify nebulous concepts like 'importance' and 'urgency'. Rather, the questions concentrate on the more directly quantifiable characteristics of the contacts.

Duration can be shown to be an important dimension, since long contacts are difficult to maintain with telecommunications. Arrangement could be used *in conjunction with* other characteristics as a proxy for concepts like 'urgency' and 'importance'. Urgent matters tend to crop up quickly and lead to unarranged contacts; in this situation the telephone has an advantage, especially over long distances. On the other hand many routine contacts are unarranged because of the trivial nature of the transactions involved. At the other end of the scale, important subject matters are often discussed at meetings that have to be arranged a long time in advance *because* a number of busy people are likely to be involved. In the case of meetings, the number of people that need to be involved in a contact is also a vital factor when considering the possibility of using telecommunications, although developments like confra-vision and conference phone calls are likely to change this situation. The frequency with which contacts take place between particular individuals or groups of individuals can be related to their 'familiarity'. People familiar with each other generally find it easier to assess the other person's reaction on the telephone. Giving or receiving of orders, information, and advice are uni-directional communications, while exchanging information, bargaining, and general discussion implies some interplay between the participants. Again face-to-face contacts have been shown to be more effective for communications involving a substantial amount of feed-back. The range of subject matter discussed is also an important variable, since wide-ranging discussions are generally more difficult to maintain on the telephone. Finally, the question of sales and purchases on the contact record sheet was introduced on the assumption that, while ultimately all contacts are concerned with the sales of a firm's goods or services, some are more directly related to the day-to-day process of selling, while others are more concerned with the longer term search for new markets and products. This question therefore relates to the position of the contact on the time continuum with respect to selling.

Differences in the characteristics of business communications, that lead to the selection of either a face-to-face meeting or a telephone contact, stem from the decision making processes in which individuals are involved. In this respect, Simon has drawn an important distinction between 'programmed' and 'non-programmed' decision processes (Simon, 1960). Programmed decisions are routine, repetitive, and standardised. We can postulate that these are likely to give rise to regular contacts between familiar individuals about fairly specific subjects. The purpose of these contacts is likely to be to give or receive orders and, in the case of contacts external to the firm, these are therefore likely to be concerned with sales or purchases. At the other extreme, non-programmed decisions are novel, unstructured, and complex. They are likely to give rise to contacts between unfamiliar participants, often in large meetings; these meetings are likely to take the form of wide-ranging discussions about a number of subjects not specifically related to sales or purchases. And whereas programmed contacts are most suited to telecommunications, unprogrammed contacts generally require a large amount of feedback, and therefore are likely to be associated with face-to-face meetings.

Thorngren (1970) has labelled contacts related to non-programmed decision processes as orientation contacts. It is through its orientation contacts that a firm adjusts to changing economic circumstances, scanning its environment for new alternatives (e.g. new products, markets, supplies, etc.). While orientation processes often suggest new alternatives, existing resources are usually managed through programmed processes. These levels of decision process give rise to different levels of contact between the firm and its environment; whereas orientation processes often involve wide-ranging diversified patterns of contacts, programmed processes are more narrow and restricted in scope.

Can such distinctive types of contacts, corresponding to orientation and programmed processes, be identified from the Central London sample? If so, are there significant differences between sectors or sector groups in the proportion of contacts that are of each type? If this is the case, it can be argued that groups linked predominantly by orientation contacts most require the linked functions to remain in close proximity in the city centre, whereas groups linked predominantly by programmed contacts can be more readily dispersed. Also, if the programmed contacts include a large number of meetings, this would be indicative of sub-optimisation in the meetings system. Unlike the telephone, the meeting is an extremely flexible medium and can be used for a range of purposes, from simple information exchanges to complex problem-solving discussions. Meetings of the programmed variety could easily be carried out by telecommunications from a decentralised location.

Contact patterns: a multivariate classification
Two approaches to the analysis of inter-sectoral variations of contact patterns are possible. First, the data could be divided into sector groups and within group variations established; or, the characteristics of the contacts themselves could be allowed to define a multivariate classification. Sector and sector groups can then be compared according to the proportion of contacts assigned to each class. We have chosen this second approach.

In the light of the earlier discussion, a multivariate classification is required that considers higher order interrelationships—for instance, the possibility of contacts being short, unarranged, *and* between familiar participants. For binary data this requirement is met by Latent Structure Analysis (LSA) (Lazerfeld, 1954; Isard, 1960). This would involve treating the categorised responses to each question as a separate variable taking on either 'zero' or 'one' values. Alternatively, since each of the categories into which the diary questions have been divided represents an explicit or implicit numerical ordering, these questions can be treated as quantitative variables and the data analysed using Latent Profile Analyses (LPA). LPA is a generalisation of LSA to quantitative data (Gibson, 1959; Lazerfeld and Henry, 1968). LPA is akin to factor analysis but, instead of yielding factors, it yields typologies, each type being represented by a specific average score on each of the variables. However, unlike factor analyses, LPA considers the higher order intercorrelations between the variables. Further details of latent profile analyses are given in the appendix.

For the purposes of this classification, both telephone contacts and meetings have been entered together into the analysis. Eight characteristics are common to both. These are length, prearrangement, frequency, purpose, range of subject matter discussed, concern with sales or purchases, number of participants, and the media involved. Telephone contacts were entered through the creation of an additional variable 'media', which takes on the value 'one' for a telephone contact and 'two' for a meeting. The number of people involved in a telephone contact is coded as 'two'. For the purposes of this analysis, the scale for frequency of contact was reversed from that on the contact record sheet, so that the value 'one' equals a first contact, and value 'five' equals a daily contact. The question on purpose, as categorised on the contact record sheets, could not be entered into the analysis as a quantitative variable. It was therefore recoded to indicate whether the contact involved one-way or two-way interaction—in other words whether some feedback was necessary. Orders, advice, and information given and received—that is, one-way interaction— were coded 'one', and bargaining, exchanging information, and general discussion were coded 'two'—that is, two-way interaction. This variable is henceforth referred to as 'feedback'.

Three latent profiles give the best fit to this data, composed altogether of 6680 contacts. The latent profiles and the associated observed profiles are given in table 10. 971 contacts (14·5% of the total) can be assigned to class 1, the bulk (81·2%) to class 2, and a small proportion (2·4%) to class 3. The three observed profiles are summarized in figure 7, where each axis, scaled in standardised units, represents one of the original eight variables. Thus contacts in class 1 are characterised by having a mean length of 1·90 standard deviations above the mean length of all contacts in the sample (1·21), while those in class 2 are −0·37 standard deviations below the grand mean. Contacts in class 1 are therefore meetings of above

Table 10. Latent profile analysis: telephone contacts and face to face meetings.

Variable	Latent profiles			Observed profiles			Observed	
	I	II	III	I	II	III	grand mean	discrim- inability
Media	2·00	−0·38	−0·13	1·90	−0·37	0·59	1·21	0·718
Length	2·08	−0·36	−0·52	2·01	−0·34	−0·29	1·49	0·776
Arrangement	1·86	−0·35	−0·09	1·62	−0·34	0·94	1·77	0·627
Frequency	−0·65	−0·09	2·83	−0·58	0·03	1·41	2·93	0·542
Feedback	1·10	−0·27	0·73	0·76	−0·18	0·87	1·36	0·269
Range	1·02	−0·30	1·33	0·79	−0·18	0·84	1·25	0·331
Trading	0·10	0·18	−2·61	0·10	0·04	−1·14	2·04	0·429
Participants	1·80	−0·30	−0·63	1·58	−0·27	−0·27	1·13	0·586
F	1016·6	5269·2	394·2	971	5429	280		
P	0·152	0·789	0·059	14·5	81·2	4·2		

Observed and latent profile tests

Profile	Distance[a]	Difference[b]
1	0·542	1·12
2	0·231	0·25
3	2·490	2·06
Mean distance	1·088	

[a] Distance between observed and theoretical profiles.
[b] Absolute difference between sum of latent profile elements and sum of observed profile elements.

average length, arrangement, and number of people involved; also, these contacts are concerned with above average range of subject and above average degree of feedback. These contacts take place with below average frequency and hence generally involve unfamiliar participants. In complete contrast, contacts in class 2 are generally made by telephone, and are below average in length, arrangement, and the number of people involved; these contacts also have below average feedback, and are concerned with a below average range of subject matter. On the other hand, contacts in class 2 take place with above average frequency. In terms of the previous discussion, class 1 can be labelled as containing orientation contacts, and class 2, programmed contacts. Class 3 represents a small but distinctive group. It is characterised by contacts that are generally short, very infrequent, involve only two participants, but are arranged a long time in advance. These contacts require a fair amount of feedback, and are directly concerned with sales or purchases.

The differences between observed and latent profiles are indicative of the goodness of fit of the model. Of the three profiles, profile 2 provides the best fit to the data, and profile 3 the poorest fit. Of the eight variables, media, length, and prearrangement are the most effective in

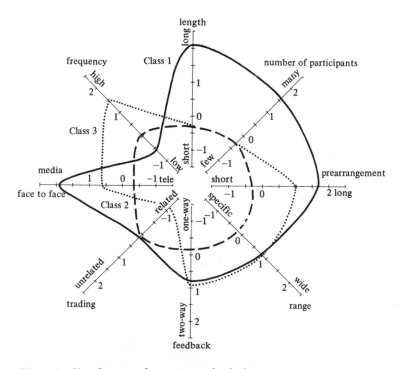

Figure 7. Classification of meetings and telephone contacts using Latent Profile Analysis (3 profiles).

Table 11. Characteristics of contacts in each class in relation to original variable categories.

	Class I		Class II		Class III	
	No.	%	No.	%	No.	%
Media						
Telephone	6	0·2	5093	93·8	152	54·2
Face to face	965	99·8	336	6·2	128	45·7
Length						
2–10 min	17	1·7	4624	85·2	222	79·3
10–30 min	213	21·9	773	14·2	58	20·7
30–60 min	225	26·3	30	0·5	0	0·0
1–2 h	268	27·6	1	0·1	0	0·0
Over 2 h	218	22·5	1	0·1	0	0·0
Arrangement						
Unarranged	40	4·1	4455	82·1	112	40·0
Same day	98	10·1	500	9·2	22	7·8
Day before	118	12·2	241	4·4	21	7·5
2–7 days	392	40·1	167	3·0	4	0·1
Over 1 week	323	33·2	66	1·2	121	43·2
Initiation						
Myself	526	53·7	2759	50·8	118	20·8
Other	439	45·1	2654	48·8	168	79·2
Frequency						
Daily	30	3·1	884	16·2	231	82·6
Weekly	99	10·1	1217	22·4	46	16·4
Monthly	139	14·3	787	14·4	1	0·0
Occasional	421	43·3	1915	35·2	1	0·0
First	282	29·0	625	11·5	1	0·0
Purpose						
Give order	49	5·0	730	13·4	25	8·9
Receive order	9	0·9	224	4·1	3	1·0
Give advice	48	4·9	328	6·0	6	2·0
Receive advice	33	3·3	480	8·8	1	0·3
Bargaining	72	7·4	210	3·8	119	42·5
Give information	45	4·6	851	15·6	7	2·5
Receive information	84	8·6	1335	24·9	16	6·4
Exchange information	281	28·9	812	14·9	66	23·5
General discussion	242	24·7	302	5·6	32	11·4
Other	107	11·0	153	2·8	1	0·3
Range						
One subject	461	47·5	4622	85·1	123	43·9
Several subjects	394	40·5	766	14·1	137	48·9
Wide range	116	11·9	41	0·8	17	6·1
Sales or purchases						
Directly related	284	29·2	1876	34·5	271	96·7
Indirectly	276	28·4	1284	23·7	8	2·8
Unrelated	410	42·2	2268	41·8	7	0·3

discriminating between the three types of contact. Surprisingly the degree
of feedback is a poor discriminator between the groups.

It is possible to be more specific about the nature of the contacts in
each class by examining their characteristics in terms of the original
variable categories. Instead of a single figure representing the mean of all
of the contacts in each class, the number of contacts falling into each of
the categories of the original variables can be calculated. These frequencies

Table 12. Inter-sectoral variations in contact characteristics.

	Contacts assigned to latent profile I (orientation contacts) (%)	Total number of contacts	Group according to connectivity measures (see table 9)
Group One			
Electrical engineering	30·8	13	II
Mechanical engineering	29·4	17	I
Gas, electricity, and water	26·9	93	III
Food, drink, and tobacco	26·6	73	II
Food wholesaling	21·4	28	III
Precision engineering	19·2	182	II
Transport equipment	18·8	69	III
Fuel and oil	18·1	1092	I
Banking	17·0	985	I
Consulting engineers	17·0	224	I
Group Two			
Paper, printing, and publishing	15·3	203	I
Chemicals	14·6	178	I
Bricks, pottery, glass, cement	14·4	194	II
Transport services	14·3	28	II
Entertainment	14·1	347	II
General wholesale merchants	14·0	57	III
Advertising and public relations	13·7	278	III
Insurance companies	13·1	367	I
Retailing	11·9	267	I
Miscellaneous business services	11·8	169	II
General construction	11·6	266	I
Societies and associations	11·5	61	I
Other manufacturing	11·3	177	II
Group Three			
Architects	11·1	81	II
Metals and metal goods	10·0	30	I
Export and import merchants	9·7	93	III
Property	9·3	593	II
Other finance	9·0	156	II
Other insurance	8·8	68	III
Commodity brokers	7·0	128	III
Office services	6·8	48	I
Primary industry	5·9	34	III

are given for the contacts in each class in table 11. In this table the original responses to the question on purpose are given, rather than the combined values for the generated variables referred to as 'feedback' in the latent profile analysis. Amongst other things, this table shows that contacts in class 1 are predominantly face-to-face meetings and those in class 2 are predominantly telephone contacts, although there are in the latter class a number of meetings with characteristics broadly similar to the telephone contacts that dominate the class as a whole. It is these contacts that can be described as suboptimal, even with current communications technology. Class 3 contains telephone contacts and meetings in fairly even proportions. Many of the other characteristics follow from this basic differentiation according to media. For instance, in terms of the original categories of purpose, most of the contacts in class 1 involve information exchanges or general discussion (53% of the total)—that is, contacts involving two-way interactions. Contacts in class 2 are most frequently concerned with giving or receiving information (35·5%), and also giving orders (13·4%). The biggest group of contacts in class 3 are those involving bargaining (42·5%).

Inter-sectoral variations in contact characteristics

The critical question now is, are there significant variations between sectors in the proportion of contacts that are of each type? Clearly the orientation contacts of profile 1 are the most important, since these exhibit characteristics that most require face-to-face meetings.

In table 13, sectors are ranked according to proportion of contacts assigned to this profile. As the latent profile analysis is based on all contacts, as recorded by the respondents, and not on the derived inter-sectoral matrices, sectors not represented in the initial sample are not included in this table. Those sectors with the highest proportion of their contacts of the orientation variety are largely represented by the offices of industrial concerns: the highest ranking pure office sector is banking. Table 9 also shows the group of each sector according to its rank on the various measures of connectivity. This reveals that there is little relationship between the connectivity of the sector to the contact network, and the strength of the linkages. It therefore does not follow that, if a business sector is strongly linked to the contact network, these linkages are necessarily of a variety demanding close spatial proximity. Finally, table 13 confirms that there is little variation between the sector groups identified in the earlier part of this paper and the proportion of contacts that are of each type. The only exception is banking and finance, where a significant proportion of the contacts can be assigned to profile 3: that is, frequent contacts between familiar participants that are concerned with bargaining. These contacts clearly represent regular dealings at fixed times in the various financial markets.

Because contacts in latent profile 1 are predominantly face-to-face meetings, we are in effect examining, in these last two tables, variations between sectors in the proportion of meetings to total contact. Of greater significance are the meetings assigned to profile 2—that is meetings that are of the programmed variety. However, as there are only 300 such meetings for the whole sample, detailed examination of inter-sectoral variation would not be justified.

Table 13. Inter-group variations in contact characteristics.

Group	% of contacts latent profile I	% of contacts latent profile II	% of contacts latent profile III	Total number of contacts
Civil engineering	13·1	85·3	1·6	1032
Banking and finance	13·5	77·5	8·9	2093
Commodity trading	10·1	88·5	1·4	278
Publishing and business services	14·8	81·5	3·7	1314
Public agencies	12·4	86·3	1·3	622
Fuel and oil	18·9	79·9	1·2	1341
Total	14·5	81·2	4 2	6630

Conclusion

It has been possible to identify a number of functionally related groups of business sectors in Central London, and to suggest a number of measures of connectivity of these sectors to the contact network, that could be of relevance in assessing locational priorities. However, connection in the sense of the absolute volume of contact is not the only important criteria. Of equal significance is whether these links can be carried out by some form of telecommunication and so are relatively unconstrained by distance cost considerations. In this respect it appears that the business sector is not a significant indicator of communications characteristics. Although distinctive types of contacts can be distinguished, these are more closely related to the status of the individual and to his job function (Goddard, 1971b). Those types of contacts that require face-to-face meetings (that is, orientation contacts) are usually confined to higher status levels and decision-making functions. Contacts most suited to telecommunications (that is, programmed contacts) are confined to lower status levels. This suggests that a location policy can only operate at the firm level, taking account of not only the business sector but the job levels, functions, and organisational units which make up that firm. Studies of individual firms have shown that the same typology of contacts can be identified at this micro level, and that blocks of work can be identified whose contact links, although of the programmed variety, are maintained through face-to-face meetings (Goddard, 1971b). It is these functions that are the most likely candidates for relocation outside the city centre.

References

Anderson, T. W., 1954, "On estimation of parameters in Latent Structure analysis", *Psychometrika*, **19**, 151–166.

Berry, B. J. L., 1966, "Commodity flows and the spatial structure of the Indian economy", Department of Geography, Research Paper 111, University of Chicago.

Brams, S. J., 1966, "Transaction flows in the international system", *The American Political Science Review*, **60**, 880–898.

Brown, L. A., Holmes, J., 1971, "The delimitation of functional regions, nodal regions and hierarchies by functional distance approaches: an unconnected network example and overview", *Journal of Regional Science*, **11**, 57–72.

Brown, L. A., Horton, F. B., 1970, "Functional distance: an operational approach", *Geographical Analysis*, **2**, 76–83.

Brown, L. A., Odland, J., Golledge, R. G., 1970, "Migration, functional distance and the urban hierarchy", *Economic Geography*, **46**, 472–485.

Coleman, J. S., 1964, *Introduction to Mathematical Sociology* (Free Press, New York).

Gauthier, H., 1968, "Transport networks and the spatial structure of the Sao Paulo economy", *Journal of Regional Science*, **8**, 77–94.

Gibson, W. A., 1959, "Three multivariate models: factor analysis, latent structure analysis and latent profile analysis", *Psychometrika*, **24**, 54–76.

Goddard, J. B., 1968, "Multivariate analysis of office location patterns in a city centre: a London example", *Regional Studies*, **2**, 69–85.

Goddard, J. B., 1970a, "Greater London development plan: Central London, a key to strategic planning", *Area*, **3**, 52–54.

Goddard, J. B., 1970b, "Functional regions within the city centre: a study by factor analysis of taxi flows in Central London", *The Institute of British Geographers, Transactions*, **49**, 161–182.

Goddard, J. B., 1971a, "Office communications and office location: a review of current research", *Regional Studies*, **5**, 263–280.

Goddard, J. B., 1971b, *Office Linkages in Central London*, South-east Economic Planning Council, London.

Greater London Council, 1970, *Greater London Development Plan: Statement* (Greater London Council, London).

Green, B. F., 1951, "A general solution for the latent class model of latent structure analysis", *Psychometrika*, **16**, 151–166.

Hendrickson, A. E., White, P. O., 1964, "Promax: a quick method for rotation to oblique simple structure", *British Journal Statistical Psychology*, **17**, 65–70.

Horst, P., 1965, *Factor Analysis of Data Matrices* (Holt, Rinehart and Winston, New York).

Hubbel, C. H., 1969, "An input–output approach to clique identification", *Sociometry*, **32**, 377–399.

Isard, W., 1960, *Methods of Regional Analysis* (MIT Press, Cambridge, Mass.).

Johnston, R. J., 1968, "Choice in classification: the subjectivity of objective methods", *Annals Association of American Geographers*, **58**, 575–589.

Johnston, R. J., 1970, "Components analysis in geographical research", *Area*, **4**, 68–71.

Johnston, R. J., Kissling, C. C., 1971, "Establishment use patterns within central places", *Australian Geographical Studies*, **9**, 116–132.

Lazarfeld, P. F., 1954, "A conceptual introduction to latent structure analysis" in *Mathematical Thinking in the Social Sciences*, Ed. P. F. Lazarfeld (Free Press, Glencoe, Illinois).

Lazarfeld, P. F., Henry, N. W., 1968, "The application of latent structure analysis to quantitative ecological data", in *Mathematical Exploration in the Behavioural Sciences*, Eds. F. Massarik, P. Ratoosh (Dorcey Press, Homewood, Illinois).

Mardberg, B., 1967, "Description of latent profile analysis programme", Swedish Council for Personal Administration.

Manners, G. F. G., 1970, "Greater London development plan: locational policy for manufacturing industry", *Area,* **3**, 54-56.

McNaughton-Smith, T., Williams, W. T., Dale, M. B., Mockett, L. G., 1964, "Dissimilarity analyses: a new technique of hierarchical sub-division", *Nature,* **202**, 1034-1035.

MacRae, D., 1960, "Direct factor analysis of sociometric data", *Sociometry,* **23**, 360-371.

Nystuen, J., Dacey, N. F., 1961, "A graph theory interpretaion of nodal regions", *Papers and Proceedings, Regional Science Association,* **7**, 29-42.

Reid, A., 1970, "Proposals for a study of the effectiveness and impact of future systems of persons/person telecommunications", Joint Unit for Planning Research, University College, London, mimeo.

Russett, B. M., 1967, *International Regions and the International System* (Rand McNally, New York).

Savage, R., Deutsch, K. W., 1960, "A statistical model of the gross analysis of transaction flows", *Econometrica,* **28**, 551-572.

Simon, H. A., 1960, *The Shape of Automation for Men and Management* (Harper and Row, New York).

Thorngren, B., 1967, "External economies and the urban core", in *Urban Core and Inner City* (E. J. Brill, Leiden).

Thorngren, B., 1970, "How do contact systems affect regional development?", *Environment and Planning,* **2**, 409-427.

Tornquist, G., 1970, *Contact Systems and Regional Development* (Gleerup, Lund).

APPENDIX

Latent Profile Analysis

In the discrete class model of latent structure analysis (LSA), the population is assumed to be clustered into homogeneous latent classes: the division is not directly observable. The manifest or observable data are the proportions of the population who possess particular characteristics and combinations of characteristics. Thus p_i is the proportion of the population with characteristic i, p_{ij} is the proportion with characteristic i and j, and p_{ijk} the proportion with i, j, and k. The latent parameters are the relative size classes: v^1, v^2, ..., v^q (where v is the proportion of the population in each of the q latent classes), and the probability of an individual i, given in a class x, possessing a particular characteristic is p_i^x.

An assumption of local independence is made. In other words, within a particular class, the possession of any characteristic is independent of the possession of any other characteristic. The equations relating manifest and latent parameters are:

$$1 = \sum_x v^x \;,$$

$$p_i = \sum_x v^x p_i^x \qquad \text{for all } i \;,$$

$$p_{ij} = \sum_x v^x p_i^x p_j^x \qquad \text{for all } i, j \;,$$

$$p_{ijk} = \sum_x v^x p_i^x p_j^x p_k^x \qquad \text{for all } i, j, k \;,$$

(A.1)

$\sum$ is taken over all q latent classes.

The first equation sums to unity, since the terms are the proportionate sizes of each class and all individuals are discretely assigned to a class. The second, defines the proportion of individuals in each of the classes possessing characteristic i; the third, the proportion in each class possessing i and j, and so on.

A variety of solutions for the latent parameters, v^x, p_i^x, have been suggested (Anderson, 1954; Green, 1951). On the basis of the actual pattern of characteristics, an individual can be assigned to the class to which it most probably belongs. Thus, with four characteristics and two classes, an individual with the pattern $(0, 1, 0, 1)$ might have a $0 \cdot 8$ probability of belonging to Class I, and a $0 \cdot 2$ probability of belonging to Class II.

Gibson has shown that the latent class model can be generalised to consider quantitative variables (Gibson, 1959). With q quantitative characteristics of N individuals, individual i's score on variable j would be $Y_{j,\,i}$. The mean score on variable j is $\overline{Y_j}$, and the variance is

$$(s_j)^2 = \frac{1}{N} \sum_i (Y_{j,\,i} - \overline{Y_j})^2 \;.$$

The raw scores must be standardized to have zero mean and unit variance

$$Z_{j,i} = \frac{Y_{j,i} - \overline{Y_j}}{s_j} .$$

The following equations then define the manifest parameters of the latent profile model

$$\frac{1}{N}\sum_i Z_{j,i} = m_j = 0 ,$$

$$\frac{1}{N}\sum_i Z_{j,i}Z_{k,i} = r_{jk} , \qquad (A.2)$$

$$\frac{1}{N}\sum_i Z_{j,i}Z_{k,i}Z_{m,i} = r_{jkm} ,$$

$\sum$ is taken over all N individuals.

r_{jk} is simply the product moment correlation between variables j and k, and r_{jkm} is the average triple product or third order correlation. The model therefore uses the same manifest parameters as factor analysis, with the addition of higher order correlations like r_{123}.

As with the latent structure model, the population of individuals is assumed to be divided into several homogeneous groups. In this case the latent parameters are v^x, which is the relative size of class x, and m_j^x, which is the average standard score on variable j for member of class x. The equations are therefore

$$1 = \sum_x v^x ,$$

$$m_j = 0 = \sum_x v^x m_j^x ,$$

$$r_{jk} = \sum_x v^x m_j^x m_k^x , \qquad (A.3)$$

$$r_{ijk} = \sum_x v^x m_j^x m_k^x m_i^x .$$

Again the proportions in each class sum to unity; the sum of the within class means defines the grand mean of each variable, which for standard scores is zero; the products of within class means, summed over all classes, define the observed inter-correlations between the variables.

The equations of LSA were derived on the assumption of within class independence. The same assumption must be made to derive the LPA equations, with each class being homogeneous in the sense that the inter-correlations between the variables observed over the group members are all zero. Since the equations (A.3) are identical with those of LSA (A.1), the same solutions for the parameters can be applied. We have used Green's solution and a program supplied by Mardberg (Mardberg, 1967).

The assignment of individuals to classes is different in LPA from LSA, since the parameters are means and not probabilities. One solution is to assign the individuals to classes to which these are nearest in euclidean space. In an m characteristic space, each individual would be located according to its observed Z score on all the m variables. Each latent class can be located according to its standardized means on the m variables and every individual assigned to the nearest class. This assignment will be only approximately accurate. The observed standardized means and standard deviations of the individuals in each class can be used to define the *observed profile*. The observed within class inter-correlations should be zero, but this may not be the case due to the possibility of mis-allocation.

Measures of goodness of fit of the classification are given by the differences between latent and observed profiles. These include a low euclidean distance between the observed and latent profile means. Another goodness of fit criterion is low within class standard deviations. An index D, measuring how effectively each variable discriminates between the individuals in each group, can be defined for both observed and latent profile as

$$D_i = \sum_{s=1}^{k} v_s x_i^2$$

where x_i is the latent/observed profile element for variable i, v_s is the proportion of individuals belonging to profile s, and k is the number of profiles.

All these criteria can be used to define the number of latent classes that best describe the data. This can be automatically defined when no individuals can be assigned to a particular latent class because all are nearer to one of the other classes.

The Structure of Activity Patterns †

I.CULLEN, VIDA GODSON, SANDRA MAJOR
Joint Unit for Planning Research, University College, London

For some time now it has been widely accepted that our early theories of spatial form based on profit maximization and 'economic man' assumptions were inadequate. As a result we have seen a major shift towards 'behavioural' studies. On the one hand attempts have been made to construct models with less rigid versions of the classical economic assumptions of rationality. The goal of optimality itself has been questioned (Wolpert, 1964), likewise the assumptions of perfect knowledge and synthesizing ability (Pred, 1967), and recognition has been given to the uncertain environment in which individual decisions must be made (Isard and Dacey, 1962). Coupled with this has been a tendency towards the use of stochastic models as a method of overcoming our inadequate knowledge of spatial behaviour (Olsson and Gale, 1967; Curry, 1964). On the other hand, there has also been a shift from studying spatial form —location models—to studying the actual spatial processes themselves (Harvey, 1969). Notable examples of this are the great wave of diffusion and migration models (Hägerstrand, 1953; Brown, 1968), the rise of environmental perception studies (Gould, 1967; Downs, 1970; Harrison and Sarre, 1972), and the development of learning models of spatial behaviour (for example, Golledge, 1967; Horton and Reynolds, 1971).

In many ways these various channels of thought are quite different from each other but in one rather important respect they are alike, for whether they are focused on spatial form or social process they are mostly directed towards the analysis of either the location of a single activity or the decision process governing a single unit of behaviour. For example, the migration models focus on the decision process relating to a single move; many of the perception and learning models are concerned with the single decision of where to shop; other models commonly isolate the residential location decision. Even the more general discussions of the spatial decision process are cast in terms of a single decision—the amount of information available about a particular situation, the certainty of outcomes, and so on (Isard *et al.*, 1969). In all the cases we have mentioned so far the discussions have ignored the fact that any event in an individual's day is part of a sequence of interdependent events and that the decisions governing these events must therefore also be interdependent owing to the necessity of continuity of action in both time and space.

The inadequacy of this fragmented view of people's decisions has not, of course, passed entirely unnoticed, and discussions suggesting ways of improving these models have come from various quite different quarters.

---

† This research was sponsored by the Centre for Environmental Studies, London.

Some of the earliest and least clearly formulated discussions of the interdependence of decisions came from the direction of locational agglomeration studies. These were expressed in terms which stressed the importance of the 'interweaving' of city processes, the 'web' or 'fabric' of urban activities and the 'networks of linkages' which bind together the different aspects of urban life. Meier (1962) presented his communications theory of urban growth and Webber (1964) developed his ideas of 'place' and 'non-place' communities. Gradually these ideas crystallized into studies of flows of materials, finance, traffic, and, particularly, information between companies, institutions, and other activity centres. In particular many studies of office location patterns have done a great deal of detailed work on the communication patterns associated with such institutions. However, although these generally start from a holistic view of people's behaviour patterns and often use diary techniques of data collection which suggest a concern with the interdependence of parts of the individual's day (Goddard, 1969; Thorngren, 1970), they ultimately retain a radial view of contacts between activities which perpetuates the partial approach to urban structure.

The generally acknowledged shortcomings of the Lowry and other allocation models are another indication of the need for a broader view of behaviour patterns, for almost all of these (Lowry, 1964; Alonso, 1966; Wingto, 1961) generate residential distributions on the basis of a simple two-way relationship between residence and employment. The Lowry model also distributes services in relation to the residential pattern in a similar manner. In no case is account taken of the fact that houses are usually occupied by families, the members of which may work in as many as three or four different places and go to school in yet another place. Shopping may have to be done near the wife's work place or the primary school. In short, the action space of the household, in the framework of which the residential location decision is made, is not merely a work place–home dumbbell but a complex joint action space structured by the commitments of all the members of the family.

Chapin and the Chapel Hill school have tried to overcome the weaknesses of the allocation and other simple accessibility based models of urban structure by a comprehensive approach to urban behaviour based on the identification of patterns of basic daily activity (see, for example, Chapin, 1965; Chapin and Logan, 1967; Chapin and Brail, 1969). Although Chapin does not view space use as a direct outcome of daily activities but rather as the outcome of location behaviour, he feels that the latter is itself prompted by the basic daily activity pattern and that the identification of these patterns is, therefore, of prime importance. Unfortunately, the task of developing these ideas operationally has presented rather more problems than had been envisaged at the start. The studies have made considerable progress in quantifying the amounts of time which different groups spend on various sorts of activity and many interesting ideas have been generated—notably the trading stamp concept of activity choice. But again, despite the group's use of time budget diary techniques to collect information, there has been very little development of either ideas or data relating explicitly to the question of the interdependence between activity choice decisions over time. The task of pattern recognition has not yet taken the form of identifying sequences of activities which can be viewed as activity modules or of trying to understand the processes which govern the integration of the individual's time-space behaviour.

Before going any further, we would like to stress that the limitations which we have pointed out in the contact pattern view of office location factors, allocation models, and Chapin's work are certainly not meant as criticisms of these approaches. In a field as underworked as this it is inevitable, and indeed healthy and potentially productive, that researchers should make many and varied attempts at the problem. All of these will be partial and must have limitations. We have no quarrel with the usefulness of, say, the Lowry model, and would take no part in an argument over the question of whether we should pursue aggregate or micro-behavioural models. Each has its role in a mixed strategy of long and short term, pure and applied research, and each will benefit from the further development of the other. Our only objective in highlighting the limitations of each of these studies is to draw similarities between them and thus use them as a springboard for ideas about possible new lines of research.

But returning from that digression to the development of the theme, how do an individual's decisions about his time-space behaviour interrelate? In his address to the European meetings of this association in 1969, Hägerstrand (1970) suggested an extremely interesting model of daily behaviour. Envisaging the individual's day to be undertaken in a two-dimensional time and space framework, he noted that a person's path through the day was structured by the fact that at certain times he had to be at particular places and that in order to meet these commitments his area of potential movement in the intervening periods was limited to varying extents depending on the type of transport available to him. His choice of activities in the periods between those activities which were time and space fixed was limited to those which could be undertaken within the time-space 'prism' defining the feasible region of activity.

The main features implicit in this model of daily behaviour are, therefore, the idea that certain activities are fixed in both space and time, the division of the day into two sorts of period, fixed and unfixed, and the demarcation of feasible prisms within which the entire day is confined, but more particularly within which unfixed activities may be undertaken. Thus an explicit demonstration of the vital interdependence of time-space decisions is at the very core of the model. The decision of where to shop at three o'clock in the afternoon is no longer taken in the context of a purely theoretical action space surrounding the individual's residence but is taken in terms of a highly specific time–space prism anchored between the individual's location at that time and his next forecast commitment.

Some of the work which has been going on at the Joint Unit for Planning Research over the past three years has been moulded along very similar lines to Hägerstrand's model. It has, however, had at least a semi-independent inception and thus differs in some respects. It has hinged on an empirical study of activity patterns and our objectives have been limited simply to finding out more about the way in which the individual's time–space decisions are structured.

The framework for the empirical study was a tentative model of the individual's activity–time–space decision process based on a set of propositions which are set out below. Before presenting these propositions however it should be made clear that they are not so much viewed as factual components of a theory of the decision process but as a useful way of looking at the problem for research purposes. By breaking the factors down into a number of separate items one immediately suggests a process which is far more objective than it actually is, for the propositions inevitably suppose that people always consider these items separately and objectively when in fact they rarely, if ever, do.

1 Organized behaviour

We propose that the purposeful element in individual behaviour varies in strength both between individuals and amongst the different activities undertaken by a single individual so that some behaviour appears to be virtually instinctive whereas other is obviously highly calculated. We do not comment on the rationality of this behaviour for we would contend that all behaviour is to some degree purposeful and that the assessment of rationality by an observer is a dubious process which must be subject to a variety of cultural, ideological, and personal biases. Whether or not we construe a pattern of behaviour to be rational depends on how well we understand the values, goals, or purposes towards which that behaviour is directed. We have, therefore, preferred to avoid the concept of rationality and have tried instead to isolate merely that behaviour which demonstrates recurrent patterns. We of course accept, along with other authors, that the individual inevitably operates with imperfect knowledge in conditions of uncertainty and has bounded cognitive ability. Thus, although we do not see behaviour as consistently rational and well informed in the classical economist's sense, we see it as containing highly organized episodes which give structure and pattern to the whole stream of behaviour.

2 The action space

The individual operates within a framework which is fundamentally structured by physical patterns and needs. These are now to a large extent institutionalized both by the availability of services and by the norms, expectations, and habits acquired by the individual himself.

3 Priorities

Within the framework outlined above, the individual selects amongst possible alternative activities by an order of priorities which he assigns to them in accordance with their attributes. Some activities may take a different priority according to the planning horizon within which a decision is being made. A meeting, for example, may feature as a priority when a person tries to arrange activities a week in advance and would hold this priority in all shorter term planning periods which include that time slot, but answering the telephone would only take priority in a decision situation governing the choice of activity in the next few seconds.

Some of the factors which contribute to an individual's assessment of an order of priorities might be the following.

(a) The 'importance' of the activity as measured in financial, strategic, physical, or other terms.

(b) The presence of participants and their characteristics—relationship to the decision maker, frequency of contact, distance travelled, etc.

(c) The order in which activities were planned. When participants are involved, order of commitment places a semi-institutionalized order of priorities on activities but even when there are no participants the sheer 'inertia' of a plan worked out in an individual's mind often results in activities which were thought out first acquiring a certain priority. Similarly, routine activities may attain more stability than is strictly necessary.

(d) Finally, actual likes and dislikes for some activities will enter into a person's ranking of alternatives to complement and perhaps even override the previous considerations.

4 Constraints

As with priorities, constraints on choice operate differently in different planning horizons, but whereas priorities are self-generated, constraints are imposed externally. We have said that at the broadest level the individual's action space is limited by economic, physical, institutional, conventional, and accessibility constraints. But within this framework all these factors operate within much finer limits—the money in one's pocket, the opening hours of one particular shop, the location of a certain theatre—and constrain the individual's choice of location and timing of specific activities to a small subset of points within the action space. In extreme cases where there are rigid constraints, as in a prison, the individual activity choice is effectively overruled.

5 Flexibility of activities

As a result of the constraints and priorities felt by the individual, any specific activity has a subjective fixity rating according to the degree of commitment associated with it and the extent to which it is constrained in time and space. These two dimensions of flexibility, commitment, and time or space fixity are, of course, highly correlated with one another, but they are theoretically independent aspects of the problem which can be approached separately. The degree of commitment primarily governs the flexibility of choice of type of activity, but this is naturally intimately related to its timing. Four main categories of commitment can be readily distinguished.

(a) Arranged activities where joint action with other people has been planned and the time and place of the activity are therefore usually fixed.

(b) Routine activities which often seem to acquire almost Pavlovian mental and physical associations and which frequently attain the status of virtually immovable points in a person's day.

(c) Planned activities which the individual decides to undertake some time in the future. The degree of flexibility associated with these planned activities may vary widely from a vaguely formulated idea to get one's hair cut this week to an avowed intention to buy the wife's birthday present at lunchtime today. Thus the degree of flexibility attached to planned activities may be greater or less than that of routine or even arranged activities, but would generally be greater.

(d) Unexpected activities which either 'just happen' as the individual drifts into some pursuit such as reading a magazine, or which are sprung on a person by chance meetings, accidents, and so on and which have no fixity in a long term planning horizon, but may override all previously arranged or planned activities instantaneously.

Once the degree of commitment to an activity is established, its time and space fixity are determined by a combination of this and the personal, physical, and institutional constraints peculiar to that event. The activity may be either fixed in time or fixed in space, or both.

6 Scheduling

A variable proportion of the individual's day is scheduled in order to facilitate synchronization of activities and movements and to conserve time. The scheduling is carried out in accordance with the fixity ratings discussed above and with estimates of activity durations and travel times. Although much of the required scheduling process is doubtless entirely automatic, the ordering of more complicated, unfamiliar, or crowded combinations of activities is objectively calculated. Activities to which the individual is strongly committed and which are both space and time fixed, or just time fixed, tend to act as pegs around which the ordering of other activities is arranged and shuffled according to their flexibility ratings. Any periods of the day which are left free after this process are either scheduled in a later, shorter planning period, or are ultimately occupied by 'spur of the moment' activities or 'doing nothing'.

   It can be seen that these propositions represent a fairly considerable elaboration of Hägerstrand's basic model and in fact include some differences in opinion, or at least emphasis. Most significantly we see in place of Hägerstrand's simple fixed-unfixed dichotomy a much more elaborate range of flexibility defined by the degree of commitment to the activity and the time and space fixity of it.

In the empirical study we have attempted to collect information to substantiate or illuminate our propositions. In particular, we have been concerned to examine the relationship between prearrangement, time and space fixity, and the sequencing of activities. The data were collected by means of augmented time budget diaries administered by interviewers and backed up by self-administered questionnaires recording the socioeconomic attributes of the respondents. At this point it should be said that the work we are describing here formed only part of a wider study and the survey had, therefore, to serve more than one purpose. This meant that we were severely restricted in the number and type of questions which we could ask on the fixity topic and in the type of population which we chose to sample. For reasons relating to the wider context of the study our sample (of 336 respondents) was drawn from the academic staff and students of a college of London University. In many ways this might, of course, be expected to be a highly unique sample, for university personnel are generally thought to have a degree of freedom governing their working hours far in excess of the majority of the working population. The variation between individuals in the ways in which they structure their days would be expected to be much larger than within other homogeneous groups of working people. In many ways, however, this extreme population is particularly interesting, for the emergence of clearly defined patterns of behaviour amongst this group, despite its apparently loosely structured action space, might be at least suggestive about people's habit of structuring their days in a standardized form regardless of the lack of direct constraints. It must also be remembered that only about half the population is employed in any sort of regular job and that there are many housewives, old people, and children who have even fewer hard and fast commitments imposed upon them from outside than these supposedly unfettered students and dons. In some respects university people, although atypical, are perhaps quite middle-of-the-road in terms of the degree of freedom which they have to structure their own time.

The core of the time budget diary contained the usual questions concerning start and end times, nature, and location of each activity, and also included the number and type of participants present. To these normal questions two extra ones were added with the objective of establishing the degree of commitment and spatial and temporal fixity of each episode. The first question was fairly straightforward and respondents seemed to find no difficulty in answering it. To the question: "To what extent was this activity planned?", four possible responses were offered in line with our proposition of four main categories of commitment— arranged with other people, planned independently, routine, and unexpected. The definitions of these were spelled out to respondents in some detail but only a couple of points need mention here. First of these is the fact that both the length of the planning horizon and the degree of precision of the plan were left open. So long as a respondent claimed to have planned to do a particular activity at some time during the day it was counted as planned. Second, the degree of regularity of routine activities was left flexible. Any activity which almost always occurred in a particular set of circumstances and thus involved little conscious choice, even though the set of circumstances as a whole might only recur at intervals of a week or more, was considered to be routine.

The other supplementary question, applicable to all episodes except travel, was in four parts, each with simple yes or no answers, and was asked after the initial recording of the complete day on a rerun through the diary. The four parts of the question were asked as follows: "Could you have (1) Done anything else at that time?
                                (2) Done this at some other time?
                                (3) Done this elsewhere?
                                (4) Been elsewhere at that time?".
The phrasing of this question was rather difficult, for any direct question on the subject of fixity of activities must immediately allow the introduction of the issue of free will. After a certain amount of experimentation it was decided that, since interviewers would be present to remind respondents of interpretation, it was best to ask the question in the simplest, most direct manner, guarding against pedantic interpretations by a preliminary explanation to respondents that they should answer in terms of the degree of responsibility which they would normally have felt about the activity in such circumstances. In the actual interviews it was explained at some length that we anticipated that the degree of compulsion which people felt about certain activities would differ quite a bit but that we wished to have their subjective opinions so that we could examine the way in which they viewed the structure of their day.

We are, of course, fully aware that this was an extremely difficult question to ask and one which could easily be misinterpreted, but since it is impossible to get away from the subjectivity of people's structuring of their own activities, we felt it was worth experimenting with the question in this form for a trial run. Doubtless it will be possible with a less overcrowded questionnaire to develop subtler and more reliable ways of measuring these factors but for the moment we hope that this first crude attempt will be of some interest. Actually, having done much of the interviewing ourselves, we feel rather more confident in the reliability and consistency of the interpretation than we might otherwise have done, for respondents appeared to have little difficulty in answering the questions and the answers generally appeared to be entirely reasonable. The only major doubt is whether the interviewers may have been a little over zealous in their desire to help respondents in their interpretation of the questions and thus indirectly suggested the sorts of answers we were expecting.

The first part of the question—"Could you have done anything else at that time?"—was aimed at finding out whether the individual had any choice of activity open to him. It was phrased in this way rather than the apparently more direct form: "Did you have to do that activity at this time?", because the latter leaves it ambiguous as to whether the question refers to the timing of the activity or the choice of a particular type of activity. The timing of a chosen activity is the subject of the next part of the question which is also phrased in the inverse format of: "Could you have done this at some other time?" so that the respondent was forced to isolate the timing from the choice of activity.

The third and fourth parts of the question are related in a similar manner for both are concerned with the spatial fixity of the episode. The third part is the direct spatial equivalent of the second—"Could you have done this elsewhere?", being similarly dependent on the activity choice. The fourth mirrors the first in the sense that whereas the first focused on a unit of time and the choice of activity available to the individual at that time, the fourth focuses on the same unit of time but on the individual's potential choice of location in it—"Could you have been elsewhere at that time?". The importance of this may not be immediately obvious but an example will help to show the significance of it. The clearest case is probably that of a mother tied to the house in the evenings by a sleeping child. She can do almost anything she likes within that location but cannot move from it. At a less extreme level a sequence of events may effectively tie a person to a particular place for short periods simply because there is not time to go elsewhere in the period between, for example, two classes in the same place.

In many cases the four parts of this question become interdependent and some combinations of response are very rare, but they are theoretically independent and it is useful to be able to treat them as such for certain purposes. One can use the last question either as four separate binary variables or as one variable with sixteen possible responses (combinations of responses).

In addition to these two questions we had one other shot at establishing the fixity of episodes because we wanted a simple measure to act as a yardstick against which to assess the detailed fixity question and to fall back on if that blew up. Before answering the four part fixity question on the rerun through the diary respondents were asked to look back on the day which they had just recorded and to pick out those episodes which stood out in their opinions as important in the sense of having to be done at a fixed time or location and having thus been points about which they felt their day had been organized. At this stage interviewers made no attempt to remind respondents of any activities which they might have thought were important in this sense so the responses to this question represent highly impressionistic snap decisions.

The data set generated from this questionnaire presented a variety of problems when analysis was attempted. The propositions outlined earlier provided us with an immensely comprehensive framework within which to perform analysis. They suggested a whole battery of questions each of which might illuminate one or more of the various facets of behaviour which we were interested in. The problems derived both from the complicated nature of the questions which were asked and from the structure of the data from which the answers had to be sought, for before each piece of analysis it was necessary to make a decision as to the appropriate unit of study. In most survey research this is not a problem. A sample of individuals is asked a series of questions whose answers are converted into a vector of information in cardinal, ordinal, or nominal form. The vector is of fixed length and the unit of analysis is the sampled individual throughout the study. When the information is drawn from a diary based questionnaire this is not the case. There is one fixed length vector, as in the case of an ordinary study, which describes the socioeconomic status of the respondent and some contextual information relevant to the interpretation of the diary, such as the day of the week, available transport, and certain important addresses. But there is also the diary information itself which may best be thought of as a matrix, one dimension of which is of fixed length, and the other is variable. The length of the first is determined by the number of indices chosen to describe each activity episode while that of the second varies with the number of episodes performed. Again each element of the matrix may be of cardinal, ordinal, or nominal form depending on the aspect of the episode being described. Thus one is inevitably faced with a choice in the performance of any analysis of behaviour patterns as to which is the most meaningful unit of analysis. In many cases the question one asks implies the unit of study but this is not always the case. Suppose one's interest were in time allocations to various categories of behaviour. For some activities which are performed by only a few people it may be most appropriate to look at data describing the duration of activity episodes, for a figure of 4·2 minutes per day spent by the average student sailing is not very meaningful. However, for other activities which tend to be performed by most, if not all, of the sample, especially activities spread throughout the day, the most appropriate unit of study may be the individual. Thus one would concentrate not on data describing the duration of episodes, but rather on those describing the amount of time that the *individual* allocates per day to activities of that sort (say eating meals, personal hygiene, etc.). In many cases the decision as to the most meaningful unit of study may be less obvious. Even when the selection is theoretically easy, this ideal choice is in practice often precluded by the form of the data. For instance, when the question involves comparing one attribute of an activity episode (say its location) with another (perhaps the number of participants involved), then the prime focus of interest is the episode which has these characteristics. But, in order to convert such ordinal or nominal data into a common cardinal measure for comparative purposes, one is forced to convert it into amounts of time spent in certain locations or with certain size groups by each member of the sample. That is, one has to transform the problem into one with the individual as the unit of study.

These related problems had their most marked impact on the general question of devising a methodological strategy. All readily available library software capable of performing the sorts of analysis required is designed to accept only the simplest forms of input—namely a sequence of fixed length vectors of information. Each phase of the analysis presented us, therefore, with a choice of either regenerating the data in a fixed length format or writing the software from scratch in a form that would accept the variable length input. In fact the former alternative was only adopted in situations where it would have been infeasible to write software specifically for the time diary information. Writing our own programmes enabled us to keep our options open upon the question of selecting the unit of study and to minimize the necessary loss of information, for all the ways of recreating the data inevitably meant accepting a considerable loss of information about the sequence in which activities were performed.

A suite of computer programmes was written to perform all the required simple analysis upon the original data set. Each programme was designed to accept the data structured in the manner described earlier, and any restructuring that was necessary for a particular piece of analysis was performed automatically as an integral part of the analysis process. Although designed specifically to suit time budget data, each programme was also written in a manner which allowed for maximum flexibility of analysis. Thus wherever appropriate as much as possible in the way of option control over the details of the analysis was left open to the user faced with a particular problem. Many programmes allowed selection of different units of analysis for different sub-problems, user control over analysis options, boolean selection of cases, and the stacking of variables one on top of the other. In this short paper it is impossible to present any of our results in detail, but it will be useful to outline the sorts of analysis we have performed.

(1) *Frequency counts*

During the current phase of the project this procedure has been used largely with the activity episode as the unit of study in order to examine interesting cross-classifications of episodes. Our interest has been focused upon patterns of behaviour which are relatively unaffected by socioeconomic background. To this end we have been concentrating on the dimensions of pre-arrangement and subjective fixity and cross-tabulating responses to these questions against other attributes of each episode such as type of activity, number of participants, duration, time of day, etc.

(2) *Time allocation analysis*

This programme, designed to provide a statistical description of the distributions of cardinal variables through the first four moments about their respective means, has provided the chief method for looking at the question of time allocation. It has enabled us to answer certain questions. Do people spend most time in the morning, afternoon, or evening on activities which they describe as routine? Is the mean time spent on activities regarded as totally fixed in both time and space greater or less than that regarded as totally free? (The results in fact show them to be almost exactly the same.) Are the deviations about the means small, suggesting among other things perhaps that there is a consensus in the sample's interpretation of the terms commonly used to describe behaviour? Do people spend more time doing things where the location is the critical factor or where the timing is the more important? (Here the results are rather intriguing. 40% more time is devoted to space fixed activities than to time fixed ones.) These and many other time allocation questions have been tackled using this programme.

(3) *Simple time series generation and analysis*

Besides time allocations, we have also looked at the absolute times at which different sorts of activities occur throughout the day. In the first place, it is interesting for its own sake to look at where the peaks and troughs of performance of various activities occur over a daily and weekly cycle. But in addition, it is often very revealing to attempt to compare two differently defined time series since this can lead to insights into the manner in which people structure their days. Thus a programme was written to generate fixed length time series in which the observations are equally spaced records of the number of people doing any particular sort of activity (for example, social, small group, or prearranged activities) at time t. The programme plots these as histograms and then computes auto-covariance and cross-covariance functions appropriately lagged. The histograms are plotted as a series of up to five parallel vertical bands. Each band refers to a particular type of activity and the width of the band at any point in the vertical dimension reflects the number of people who are performing that activity (say socializing or working) at a given time of day. As one moves down the page the time interval is incremented by a given and constant amount. Thus by reading vertically and horizontally it is possible to see, for instance, how people change from personal activities and eating meals between about nine and ten o'clock to predominantly formalized work until about one o'clock, when they break off for lunch and social activities. In the afternoon socializing falls off at first and the balance between formal and informal work becomes more even. From about three o'clock, however, socializing increases regularly until it reaches a peak between ten and eleven p.m. Other attributes of activities, such as the number of participants present and the degree of pre-planning, have also been compared in this way.

(4) *Transition probability analysis*

Another way of looking at the manner in which a person's day is integrated or scheduled is to look specifically at the probability of occurrence of given sequences of activities. To this end a programme was written to compute the frequencies of occurrence of changes between one activity and another, to convert these into transition probabilities, and to compute second and third powers of the probability matrices so as to provide an indication of second- and higher order linkages. It is also possible to pass each matrix through a filter so that flows are only included under given conditions—say that the preceding activity is of a certain sort. Thus it is feasible to test the disorientation which results from, for example, the occurrence of an unexpected event by comparing the differences in transition probabilities with and without the appropriate filter. With two or more of these filters on the preceding and earlier activities it is possible to build up counts of the frequency of occurrence of three and four way sequences.

Apart from these fairly standard forms of analysis, some multivariate statistical tests were performed using the method described earlier of generating from the basic information an intermediate data set which was appropriately structured for the problem in hand. Amongst the analyses performed to date in this way are the following:

(1) *Stepwise multiple regression*

One major interest at this point in the project was to test for interrelationships amongst the variables which were used to describe an individual's time utilization. In particular we wished to test the hypothesis that differences in the way people described episodes as free or constrained might be closely related to less subjective attributes of these items of behaviour such as the presence or absence of other participants, the location or the prearrangement of the events and so on. However, we were not able to take the individual episodes as our observations (an instance of the problem mentioned previously) since at this level the attributes are in nominal or ordinal form and therefore unsuitable for use with parametric models. Thus the data had to be regenerated using the respondents as the unit of study and percentages of time relative to each method of classifying behaviour as the variables. Regression tests were made with the four successive dependent variables being the amounts of time spent on 'fixed' activities of the sorts referred to in the four parts of the last question (the amount of time during which the individual could have been elsewhere, could have been doing something else, etc.). Independent variables were the amounts of time spent at home and at college, the amounts alone or with others, and the amounts devoted to planned, arranged, routine, or unexpected activities. To ensure

the best possible selection of explanatory variables an optimal regression
model (programmed by Boyce *et al.,* 1969), which tests various possible
combinations of independent variables, was used, yet even after the
inclusion of the five most significant variables on the right hand side the
proportion of the variance of the independent variable explained never
rose above $0 \cdot 2$. The lack of explanatory power is, no doubt, in part due
to the fact that episodes could not be used as the unit of study but the
results also suggest that responses to the fix questions do not merely
represent redefinitions or combinations of other ways of looking at
behaviour patterns.

(2) *Factor analysis*
Further evidence in favour of this conclusion was amassed when all the above
variables (including all four independent ones) were incorporated in a factor
analysis. The original 12 variables were reduced to a rotated factor matrix
in which the first four factors accounted for 70% of the variance of the
original data set (see table 1). The factors are surprisingly easy to interpret.
The interesting thing to note about the first is the interdependence of the fix
questions, suggesting that the majority who perform a high number of
constrained activities feel them to be fixed in both space and time.
Moreover, no other variable has a high positive relation with any of the fix
questions, and the only negatively related variable is the amount of time
spent on unexpected activities. This factor then accounts for the subjective
fixity in the data describing time use. The second accounts primarily for the
locational aspects, since it obviously isolates those individuals who spend
more time at home and alone. The third factor reflects the extent to which
an individual defines his day in advance (whether others are involved or not)
contrasting those days which are highly planned with those which are
mostly routine. And finally, the fourth relates to the extent to which
people arrange in advance to do things with others or on the other hand
act alone or just let things happen. Thus, so far, it would appear that the
four key factors describing an academic sample's time allocation are the
feeling of constraint associated with its behaviour, the locational
orientation, the premeditation of activities, and the level of prearranged
participation. Of course it is currently impossible to generalize upon
these findings, and even with respect to our current data base much more
in the way of testing is still required. We have, however, gathered a
considerable body of evidence establishing the independence of responses
to the last four fix questions from other simple ways of classifying
behaviour, such as by the presence of participants, type of activity and so
forth. On the other hand, we are beginning to find that the complex
process whereby people schedule their activities is heavily conditioned by
the manner in which they conceive activities as variously important as
constraints upon their days.

It is, in fact, for this reason that we have not attempted a simulation. It is not that we believe a simulation to be a valueless exercise. It is rather that we feel that if it is to have any real descriptive or explanatory value it would have to incorporate this important notion of constraint or subject fixity. However, this is a very difficult principle to build into an operational simulation since at the very least it implies complete rejection of Markovian assumptions. It would, in fact, mean that the simulation would have to be based upon complex feedbacks taking the form of oscillations about pre-fixed high priority activities. Our analyses have not yet reached a level which would warrant attempting such a problematic simulation.

Table 1. Rotated factor matrix.

Variables[a, b]	Factors[c]			
	Subjective fixity	Locational orientation	Solo premeditation	Prearranged participation
1 Fixed location given this time	0·858[d]	0·108	0·036	0·041
2 Fixed activity given this time	0·862[d]	0·177	0·046	0·039
3 Fixed location given this activity	0·737[d]	0·206	0·046	0·082
4 Fixed timing given this activity	0·889[d]	0·050	0·025	0·007
5 Activity arranged with others	0·094	0·078	−0·068	0·957[d]
6 Activity occurred unexpectedly	−0·179[d]	−0·034	−0·056	−0·104
7 Activity planned alone	−0·045	−0·098	−0·809[d]	−0·347
8 Routine activity	0·096	0·074	0·884[d]	−0·311
9 Activity located at home	−0·092	−0·793[d]	−0·048	−0·281
10 Activity located at college	0·129	0·853[d]	0·060	0·026
11 Activity performed alone	−0·069	−0·367	−0·228	−0·465[d]
12 Activity performed with others	0·233	0·684[d]	0·035	−0·063

[a] All variables are in the form of: "% of time spent doing (at) ...".
[b] Sample size is 336, all being academic members of Bedford College (staff or students).
[c] The cumulative proportions of variance accounted for by the first four factors, prior to orthogonal rotation using the Varimax criterion, were:

1 0·3056   2 0·4754
3 0·5944   4 0·6931

[d] The factor loadings with superscripts are the maximum absolute row values.

References

Alonso, W., 1966, *Location and Land Use* (Harvard University Press, Cambridge, Mass.).

Boyce, D. E., Farhi, A., Weirschedel, R., 1969, "A computer program for optimal regression analysis", Discussion Paper number 28, Regional Science Research Institute, Philadelphia.

Brown, L. A., 1968, *Diffusion Processes and Location: A Conceptual Framework and Bibliography* (Regional Science Research Institute, Philadelphia).

Chapin, F. S., 1965, *Urban Land Use Planning* (University of Illinois Press, Urbana).

Chapin, F. S., Logan, T. H., 1969, "Patterns of time and space use", in *The Quality of the Urban Environment*, Ed. H. S. Perloff (Johns Hopkins Press, Baltimore).

Chapin, F. S., Brail, R. K., 1969, "Human activity systems in the metropolitan United States", *Environment and Behaviour*, **1**, 107-130.

Curry, L., 1964, "The random spatial economy: an exploration in settlement theory", *Annals of the Association of American Geographers*, **54**, 138-146.

Downs, R. M., 1970, "The cognitive structure of an urban shopping centre", *Environment and Behaviour*, **2**, 13-39.

Goddard, J., 1969, "Contacts between people in the City", Mimeo, London School of Economics, London.

Gould, P. R., 1967, "Structuring information on spatio-temporal preferences", *Journal of Regional Science*, **7**, 259-274.

Golledge, R. G., 1967, "Conceptualizing the market decision process", *Journal of Regional Science*, **7**, 239-258.

Hägerstrand, T., 1953, *Innovation Diffusion as a Spatial Process*, translated from the Swedish, 1967 (University of Chicago Press, Chicago).

Hägerstrand, T., 1970, "What about people in regional science?", *Papers, Regional Science Association*, **24**, 7-24.

Harrison, J., Sarre, P. V., 1971, "Measurement of environmental perception: a problem in psychometrics", *Environment and Behaviour*, **3**, 351-374.

Harvey, D., 1969, "Social processes and spatial form: an analysis of the conceptual problems of urban planning", *Papers, Regional Science Association*, **25**, 47-70.

Horton, F. E., Reynolds, D. R., 1971, "Effects of urban spatial structure on individual behaviour", *Economic Geography*, **47**, 36-48.

Isard, W., Dacey, M., 1962, "On the projection of individual behaviour", *Journal of Regional Science*, **4**, 1-34, 51-83.

Isard, W., 1969, *General Theory: Social, Political, Economic and Regional* (MIT Press, Cambridge, Mass.).

Lowry, I., 1964, *Model of Metropolis*, RM-4125-RC, Rand Corporation, Santa Monica.

Meier, R. L., 1962, *A Communications Theory of Urban Growth* (MIT Press, Cambridge Mass.).

Olsson, G., Gale, S., 1967, "Spatial theory and human behaviour", *Papers, Regional Science Association*, **21**, 229-242.

Pred, A., 1967, *Behaviour and Location—Part I*, Lund Studies in Geography, Series B, number 27, Lund.

Thorngren, B., 1970, "How do contact systems affect regional development?", *Environment and Planning*, **2**, 409-427.

Webber, M., 1964, "The urban place and the non-place urban realm", in *Explorations into Urban Structure*, Ed. M. Webber (University of Pennsylvania Press, Philadelphia).

Wingo, L., 1961, *Transportation and Urban Land* (Resources for the Future Inc., Washington, D.C.).

Wolpert, J., 1964, "The decision process in spatial context", *Annals of the Association of American Geographers*, **54**, 537-558.

The Objectives and Methodology of Transport Assessment

J.M.CLARK
Cranfield Institute of Technology, Cranfield, Bedford

1 Introduction

The broad concept of technological assessment is by no means a new one. The development and implementation of modern technological innovations frequently involve extremely large investments of national resources. Furthermore the economic and social implications of these programmes are generally complex and far reaching. Under such circumstances it has long been recognised that decision making cannot safely be based on experience and intuition alone: it is highly desirable to develop some procedure for formal analysis. It is probably in the defence field that organised assessment studies are most firmly established. Particularly in the design and procurement of modern weapons systems, assessment teams play a central role in the development and application of the latest technological ideas.

In many respects the defence field is a simple one from the assessment point of view, involving clearly defined objectives and little concern with social implications. The application of assessment techniques in other areas of public sector decision making is much less coherently organised. Certainly a number of investment appraisal studies have been undertaken in a wide variety of fields—water supply, transport, land usage, health, and education to name but a few. However these studies have generally been 'one-off' exercises related to specific projects, and although they provide a useful store of background experience for the assessment analyst there appear to have been few attempts to establish assessment as a coherent and on-going study area in its own right.

This paper attempts to outline the role and process of assessment in one particular field of public investment, namely transport. This field has emerged over the last few decades as one of the major national problem areas, both in this country and in many other parts of the world. Two aspects of the field render it particularly suitable for initiating the search for a general assessment methodology. Firstly it represents an increasingly hectic area of activity for engineers and designers, who are busily engaged in the development of many and diverse solutions to modern transport problems—short and vertical take-off and landing aircraft, various forms of high speed tracked vehicles, automatically guided and routed urban taxi systems, high speed moving pavements, and so on. With such large numbers of novel systems needing to be assessed it is inevitable that the various assessment exercises will contain a great many common elements. Secondly it is in this field perhaps more than any other that the public at large is becoming most strongly aware of the powerful social and

environmental implications which such technological developments leave in
their wake. The fierce debates surrounding the location of the third
London airport and the building of motorways in and around our major
conurbations are excellent examples of this growing environmental
awareness. Probably in no other area is the possibility of trading off
economic and material resources against the preservation or enhancement
of our national environmental heritage (a very scarce resource in so small
a country) so clearly perceived by so many people. These two aspects
alone make transport a natural starting point for general assessment studies.

No further reference will be made here to the application of assessment
in investment areas other than transport. However it seems very likely
that the objectives of, and framework developed for, transport assessment
will have close analogues in these other fields, and it is hoped that the
way in which transport methodologies are being developed will be of
direct value in developing assessment studies in the wider context.

2 Objectives of transport assessment

Before proceeding to discuss the objectives of transport assessment, it
should be mentioned that we intend to give the phrase 'technological
innovation' a rather broad interpretation. The improvement of existing
transport facilities may be attempted in a variety of different ways. The
simplest is the construction of additional facilities using existing
technology, for example, new road programmes or the extension of an
underground rail network. Alternatively existing systems may be improved
by modifying their design or operation, as with the Advanced Passenger
Train and demand responsive bus systems. Again, the innovation may be
radical and amount to a completely novel mode of transport as with
automatic taxis (Cabtrack) and high speed moving pavements. It is
probably for only the last case that the term 'technological innovation' is
truly apt, but in all cases a new transport situation is produced whose
social and economic implications need to be assessed. We shall accordingly
describe all of these situations as innovations and regard them as amenable
to assessment.

It is now straightforward to define one of the objectives of transport
assessment—to provide the decision maker with information which will
help him determine which technological innovations (in the sense used
above) are capable of generating the greatest benefits to the community as
a whole.

Such an objective clearly implies a detailed study of the technological
properties of the innovation. These properties include the costs of its
development and construction (and particular attention must be paid to
the comparative costs of achieving various technical design specifications),
the characteristics of its performance, and the amount of land which its
structure and associated facilities will require. Equally, however, the
objective implies an investigation of the operating environment in which

the innovation will ultimately be used. Central to this aspect of the study is the determination of the relationship of the innovation to general planning objectives. How will the system fit into existing policies on housing, land-use, health, education, and so on? Will it be compatible with the existing transport systems which it is intended to complement? What are the specific management problems of operating the innovation as part of a real transport undertaking? In this connexion, of course, transport is being considered in its general sense as providing the means of communication between the various forms of activity which constitute modern life.

Viewed from this standpoint, assessment can be seen as capable of providing a link between technological development on the one hand and the planning and operation of transport systems on the other. This suggests that assessment studies in addition to providing a service for decision makers may also have a valuable role to play in enhancing the development of both technological and planning studies. This represents a different but by no means incompatible type of objective from the one stated in the paragraph before last. The requirements of the decision maker are in a sense 'static', in that he seeks specific information at discrete points in time to assist him in finding answers to (hopefully) clearly defined questions. The additional role we are proposing is a 'dynamic' one of providing a continuous exchange of information between the two disparate activities of technology and planning. It is the size of the gulf which exists at present between technologists and planners which establishes an urgent need for the development of assessment studies of this 'dynamic' kind. We shall return to this point after we have described the methodology for assessment and argue that this 'dynamic' function is a much more fundamental and useful one than the 'static' approach related to individual decisions.

3 Methodology of transport assessment
In describing the methodology of transport assessment, we shall, for convenience, consider first the 'static' case of assessing a particular technological innovation which has already been specified. At the end of this section we shall consider how the 'static' framework is applicable to the 'dynamic' objective we have just outlined, and in the next section go on to discuss the general problem of the origins of technological innovations.

In general a transport system will have impacts upon three distinct, but closely related, classes of people—the operator of the system, the user of the system, and what we shall call the non-user whose environment may be affected by the existence of the system. In the case of private transport systems the operator and user classes overlap, but in all forms of public transport these classes are distinct and perceive the system in quite different ways. It is of course true that many individuals may find themselves moving from one class to another several times during any given day. The concept of these classes is none the less valuable, since it enables us to list the attributes of the system as they are perceived by those people whom they affect. We list some of the most important attributes in the next three paragraphs.

Operator attributes consist of:

(1) total operating costs of the system. These are frequently subdivided into direct operating costs (which include amortisation and interest on capital, labour costs, insurance, power costs, and vehicle maintenance) and indirect operating costs (which include such items as terminal costs, track costs, building rents, advertising, and staff training);

(2) revenue which the system can attract. Whatever the policy of the operator (developing profit for shareholders or breaking even with or without the aid of subsidies) he is concerned with the relationship between the costs of operation and the revenue which the system can attract from the market. A particular aspect of this attribute is the adaptability of the system to the land-use environment and to long- and short-term changes in that environment.

User attributes consist of:

(1) out of pocket costs, such as fares, car running costs;

(2) travel time, including in-vehicle time, various categories of excess times (walking, waiting etc.), freedom of selection of departure time, reliability;

(3) safety of himself and his property;

(4) comfort, including privacy, security, exposure to weather, scenic aspects;

(5) convenience, for example flexibility in changing trip plans after starting, provision for parcels, fare payment methods.

Non-user attributes consist of:

(1) aesthetic features of the vehicles and rights of way;

(2) noise and air pollution;

(3) safety of persons and property;

(4) effect on Government taxation;

(5) changes in land-use activity which a large and comprehensively utilised system may bring about if implemented.

It will be realised that many of these attributes are closely related. For example any innovation aimed at making a system more safe from the point of view of passers-by (non-user attribute) may affect the costs of operating that system (operator attribute), which in turn may affect the out-of-pocket costs which must be charged to the user. It is further clear from this simple example that the objectives of the three classes of people are conflicting, and accordingly that any innovation will in general provide benefits to some of the classes and disbenefits to others.

This brings us to the central feature of the process, which is to evaluate these attributes and enumerate the people in each class who will be affected by the proposed system. If the quality of each attribute and the quantity of people affected can be determined, it becomes in principle possible to draw up a balance sheet for the system indicating whether or not it will provide an overall benefit for the community as a whole.

At this point it is tempting to digress at length on the relative merits of various cost-benefit techniques, and indeed on the applicability of cost-benefit analysis to this type of situation. We do not propose to do this for two reasons: firstly because this is a complex and well documented field, and the reader is referred to the literature for an extensive discussion of it, and secondly because only in the 'static' assessment situation is it necessary to carry out the balance sheet analysis with full rigour. We shall return to this latter point when we come to considering this methodology in the context of 'dynamic' assessment. Suffice it to say at this stage that the process must contain some means (which may well be crude) of comparing the various impacts with a view to forming judgments.

Returning to the discussion of methodology, it is clear that, before any form of balance sheet can be drawn up, the system under study must be placed into an operating environment so that the response of the transport market may be studied. We shall refer to this environment as a scenario, and would stress that although it may well be a real one (a particular town, a conurbation, a specific rural area) it is frequently desirable to specify only the main characteristics of a particular scenario type and analyse what is in effect a hypothetical scenario. This latter approach is especially valuable when assessing systems which are as yet only imperfectly specified (as for example the magnetically suspended high speed train). On the one hand the technical information is not sufficiently detailed to support or justify extensive data analysis of a real situation, and there is further the danger that specific and untypical aspects of a particular scenario may have an unjustified effect on the assessment of the system.

In the context of assessment, the relevant properties of a scenario are, firstly, the disposition and nature of its land-use activities, and secondly, the socioeconomic characteristics of its population. Once these are known it is possible to employ the well known models of travel demand forecasting (trip generation, trip distribution, modal split, and assignment) which have been developed for use in transportation studies. These models provide much needed information both on the values of the system attributes (the use of modal split models in determining values of time is well known) and of the numbers of users and non-users who will be affected. It is worth noting that the development of generalised forecasting models related to concepts such as utility maximization[1]

[1] See, for example, McLynn and Watkins (1965), Quandt and Baumol (1966), and Beckmann and Golob (1971).

appears both more relevant and more practical in the assessment context than does the orthodox approach of treating the modelling process in four discrete stages.

We have attempted in figure 1 to illustrate diagrammatically the relationships which exist between the various elements of the transport assessment process which have been described in the preceding paragraphs. Although there is a tendency in 'static' assessments to progress from top to bottom of the diagram, it is less intended as a flow diagram than as a description of the relationships between the various elements of assessment, and the arrows indicate which elements provide inputs for which other elements. Furthermore in some assessments certain aspects of the process may be unnecessary and can be ignored.

It will be noticed that the diagram is presented in closed form with the final analysis of costs and benefits suggested as inputs to the specification of the innovation. This represents our view that a single pass of the process as described so far is only of limited value in itself, since it provides information in the light of which alterations may be made both to the technological specification and to the general planning objectives (land-use or otherwise), and consideration may well be felt necessary of alternative scenario types. Even in the 'static' assessment case it is frequently necessary to make several passes of the process before a final balance sheet can be drawn up and a decision suggested. In the sense in which we defined 'dynamic' assessment, it is clear that continuous passes of the assessment process in the context of several different lines of technological research and development and several different planning strategies and situations can provide valuable information to both of these activities and greatly enrich their progress.

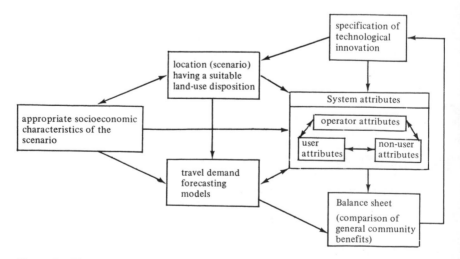

Figure 1. The transport assessment process.

We therefore see the primary objective of an assessment team as working simultaneously in close contact with planning and technological research teams, and regard the provision of information on a 'one-off' basis to decision makers as a subsidiary activity.

4 Origins of technological innovations

In the previous section we presented the methodology for transport assessment as if it started from a 'God-given' technological innovation. It is useful now to consider two closely related questions:
(1) who is 'God'?
(2) does the innovation really initiate the process?

In answer to the first question we would suggest that innovations or specifications for innovations can arise from four main sources:
(1) planning authorities or research workers, whose overall planning objectives necessarily imply some requirement for transport as a means of physical communication;
(2) operators of existing transport systems, who are constantly subjected to economic pressures to maintain or increase market shares, and who are frequently faced with obsolescence of their existing equipment;
(3) manufacturers of existing systems who are continually committed by pressure from their competitors and requests from transport operators to the search for new developments;
(4) technological research organisations (frequently academic or government sponsored) who are in many cases developing technological ideas for their own sake.

In the light of this answer it is now clear that the second question exposes a 'chicken and egg' situation. Each of the sources listed above can obtain useful information from the assessment process itself. For example the ideal travel demand forecasting models provide detailed information on user responses to existing transport systems, and are thus of value to planners, operators, and manufacturers in their search for new systems which will be acceptable. Furthermore there is emerging within the technological research organisations a demand for guidance as to what will be the best areas into which to concentrate their limited resources so as to produce innovations which will be of direct application. This situation reinforces our view that the primary objective of assessment is to provide a continual flow of relevant information to the advantage of planners, operators, and technologists.

However the second question posed at the beginning of this section can be seen to have some meaning when we consider that of the four sources listed above only the planner has direct concern with and responsibility to all three classes of people who are affected by developments in transport technology, that is operator, user, and non-user. This suggests that there should be some sort of hierarchy in the ideal formulation of technological specifications, with the planner providing the initial impetus for a specification to emerge, and the operator, manufacturer, and research organisation (not necessarily in that order) providing inputs to the specification as it develops and becomes more precise. This is not to say that the last three sources should not be capable of, nor encouraged to, produce innovation on their own initiative, but one might expect that the majority of successful innovations would be first specified as a result of a definite planning requirement. It is salutory to consider how difficult it is to think of a technological innovation whose specification was really developed in this way.

5 Conclusion

In addition to presenting a methodology for transport assessment this paper has also discussed the role which assessment should play in the transport context. It may be useful in conclusion to restate the objectives which have emerged from the discussion.

Only a finite quantity of any nation's resources can be made available for the provision of transport facilities. The basic objective of assessment is to help to see that these resources are allocated in the optimum manner. We have stressed that much of this assessment work will be concerned with the allocation of resources into competing forms of transport based on existing technologies. This is not to preclude the assessment of genuinely novel developments, but it is important to recognise that assessment does not only apply itself to the latest brainchild of the inventor.

In interpreting this basic objective we have distinguished between what have been referred to as 'static' and 'dynamic' applications of assessment, the former being concerned with helping in the taking of 'one-off' decisions, the latter aiming to provide a continuous link between technological and planning activities. We have suggested that the 'dynamic' application, wherein planners can be helped to make better use of the current state of technology by being actively aware both of its limitations and of its potentialities and wherein technologists are guided to concentrate their efforts into those areas which will be of the most direct application, is by far the more important one.

The distinction between these applications is in no way clear-cut, and it has only been emphasised to counteract the popular interpretation of assessment, namely the 'static' one. We believe that assessment has a much wider role to play than this and is emerging as an important and on-going interdisciplinary study area, whose impact on both planning and technology will become increasingly marked over the next few years.

Acknowledgements. The author wishes to thank his colleagues Mr. R. A. F. Seaton and Mr. J. W. Perdue for their help in the development of the assessment methodology, and for their critical and constructive comments on this paper. None the less, the shortcomings of the paper are entirely the responsibility of the author.

References
Beckmann, M. J., Golob, T. F., 1971, "On the metaphysical foundation of traffic theory—entropy revisited", mimeo, presented to the Fifth International Symposium on Traffic Flow Theory and Transportation, University of California, Berkeley, USA.
McLynn, T. M., Watkins, R. H., 1965, "Multi-mode assignment model", mimeo (Davison, Talbird and McLynn, Inc., New York).
Quandt, R. E., Baumol, W. J., 1966, "The demand for abstract transport modes—theory and measurement", *Journal of Regional Science,* **6**, 13-26.

Land Use Planning in Urban Growth Areas— Evaluation: a Compromise

A.METCALF, B.PILGRIM
Local Government Operational Research Unit, Reading

Introduction

Recent months have seen several press reports of the growing rift between the decision makers in local authority planning departments and model builders in the authorities themselves, universities, and consultancies. For example, in a report on the conference of the Royal Town Planning Institute held recently in Edinburgh, the Guardian quoted the solution offered by Mr. John Boynton, Clerk to Cheshire County Council, who urged planners "to concentrate on things which they could influence" and suggested that "they should go back to land use planning and development control". Mr. Boynton went on to question whether planners had been unsuccessful in raising the quality of the environment because too much effort, and the most able people, had been "solving interesting intellectual problems instead of contributing to the quality of the life of the people".

The government's action on structure planning may have heightened this conflict by forcing individuals to take 'views'—but in principle the problem lies in a lack of understanding between the two groups.

This paper looks at some of the reasons for this lack of understanding, and describes an approach that is designed to make computers and models more attractive to planners. The approach is deliberately simple, but it is designed to fit the current requirements of planning departments while providing a framework on which the model builder may hang his models.

Elements of the problem

A good understanding of the nature of the conflict between planners and model builders can be gained by looking at how it manifests itself in the design and preparation of structure plans. It shows up in three main areas: in the philosophy underlying the approach used by each side; in the aspects of planning they concentrate on; and in the degree of control over the implementation stages.

Philosophy

One of the main tasks of a planning department is the creation of structure plans. Usually, alternative proposals are considered and a choice is made by examining the important planning factors. For example, the cost of supplying new development in one plan may be low at the expense of building on valuable agricultural land, whereas another may preserve the agriculture but require considerable capital to provide the necessary sewage disposal.

To tackle this problem the planner requires measures of all the crucial factors. Some of these measures can only be approximate, since they must be based on values for certain benefits which convert them into cost terms to allow comparisons to be made. In practice, these values are not usually given explicitly but are implied once one of the alternative plans is chosen. The process is thus one of surveying all the factors together and does not require refined measures of the more easily quantifiable elements.

This approach is in marked contrast to that used in many of the present planning models. These concentrate on a subset of planning factors (sometimes only one of them) and try to achieve either a very accurate mathematical representation of the observed facts, or an optimum solution for the sub-problem. For example, in land use and transport studies a great deal of effort may be taken to optimise the transport network on the generalised cost of travel, to serve a land-use plan which has in fact been devised with little or no evaluation.

Of course, advances in any field are made by developments in technology preceeding their application, often by a large period of time. What is really required is a means of making the rapidly advancing models more relevant to the planning process as it is now. To fail to do this denotes a failure on the part of both the model builder and the decision maker.

Direction of effort
Different planning factors are important at different scales of planning. Except for the large conurbations and in *ad hoc* regional studies, the local authority planner is directly concerned with three scales of structure plan, which are linked by well defined quantities:
1 The largest scale is that of the sub-regional plan. In this, planners aim to produce major communication networks and predictions of urban growth areas in terms of population and employment expansion.
2 The middle scale is that of the urban plan. The urban structure plan tries to define in which direction the urban area should grow to accommodate the extra people and jobs.
3 Finally, the lowest scale is that of local area plans. Here concern is with individual developments of housing and industry, and the requirement is that of consistency with policies laid out in the higher level plans.

Generally, the models that have been developed have been directed to local authority structure planning at only the highest of these scales. A good example is the work described in "An Operational Urban Development Model of Cheshire" (Barras *et al.*, 1971), which shows clearly the use of molecular theory in developing planning models. As a result the local authority planner, who is concerned with planning at the lower levels, is given little help. And, although the planner is able through his training and the planning committee system to cope with the third level (local planning), he faces real difficulties at the second level (urban planning). Attempts to improve the planning process at these lower levels have in some cases shown real benefits (Friend and Jessop, 1969), but the local authority planner is aware that further improvements are required. How much this action will cost, how it will affect growth, and what else might be done are often unanswered questions.

Use of control
At each scale the planner is concerned with two things: forecasting those elements that he cannot control, and producing the best policies for operating those that he can. At the *local scale,* policies of control predominate, since control by the local authority is directly exercised by the acceptance or refusal of individual planning applications. At the other end of the spectrum, at the *sub-regional scale,* it is debatable whether there is significant control.

Since the model builder is concerned with providing practical planning tools, the extent of a planner's control must be considered. In local scale planning models, the planner's individual response to a problem is unique and as a result the models developed have to be evaluative. On the other hand, at the sub-regional level individual decisions have less influence and the forecasting models used may place less emphasis on planning control and more on 'mass behaviour'.

In between these extremes, at the *urban* level, the balancing of forecasting and control elements presents a particularly difficult problem. As a result it is at this level above all others that the model builder and the decision maker must communicate. It is for this reason that we put forward the Local Government Operational Research Unit's (LGORU) work at this level as an example of the sort of model that could help to close the present rift.

An example at the urban scale
A joint study by the LGORU and Cheshire County Council Planning Department examined how computer techniques could assist in urban structure plan making. This study produced a computer program designed to answer three questions about a given land use plan (Local Government Operational Research Unit, 1970a):
What are the effects of the plan?
How much does it cost?
How could the plan be improved?

What are the effects of the plan?
A planning department uses much of its resources on calculating population, employment, and trip distribution statistics which are associated with the plans it designs. Much of this work involves simple conversion of data from one unit to another—for example, acreage of housing to people. The use of a computer greatly speeds up this process and thus allows more alternative plans to be considered. In addition, such simple work helps to persuade the local authority planner that the computer is no more than a giant adding machine—and no better than the man operating it.

How much does the plan cost?

The plans are costed by the program for those planning factors which are vital at the urban scale. Those included at present are as follows:

construction costs of housing and industry;

demolition costs of housing and industry;

benefits of housing associated with the sites on which it is built;

'locational benefit'—the additional benefit derived from people being able to exercise freedom of choice about where they live;

transport costs—the capital cost of roads and the user cost of travel;

environmental factors—the socially undesirable consequences of having conflicting land uses next to each other;

sewerage costs—the capital cost of laying trunk sewers;

agricultural benefits—the benefit, in terms of agricultural production, derived from the land.

A brief description of how these factors were represented mathematically in the program is given in the appendix at the end of the paper.

The evaluations were not combined to produce an overall measure of the plan for two reasons. First, some of the costs are capital items and can only be combined with the benefits—which extend continuously over time—if assumptions are made about interest rates and write-off periods. To include these as input parameters initially could easily obscure the meanings of the results obtained. Second, the costing of benefits will not be the same for all planners. To show the sensitivity of the results to variations in any of the values used and the level of human control, the costs and benefits are kept separate.

How could the plan be improved?

The most useful feature of the program is its ability to suggest improvements that can be made in the plan. The relatively simple form of the formulae used can be differentiated with respect to the acreage of land use of each type in each zone of the urban area. This enables the program to show the increase or decrease in each cost and benefit that is produced by a small amount of additional development on each site. Using this facility it is possible to devise land use plans by a step-by-step approach. For a potential growth area the *existing* development is evaluated to show which zones can be developed at lowest cost with the highest benefit. This development is then included and the new plan re-evaluated. More zones are then identified in the same way and additional development introduced. The process continues until all the anticipated growth has been catered for. To help planners interpret the results of this process, Cheshire County Council have been able to link the program with the computer mapping program SYMAP to give visual displays of the costs associated with additional development.

Next steps

As we have shown, our approach is to produce a tool which aids the planner in the daily task of urban structure plan design. We now intend to develop the program further, but would stress that in doing so we hope to avoid making the model so complex that it becomes less useful to the planning departments. Individual applications will involve specific planning factors which have not yet been included, but we believe these can be added to the program in such a way as to present no greater difficulties to the model users, in terms either of the data required or the manageability of the program.

Obviously from the model builders' viewpoint the present program leaves a lot to be desired. The ultimate goal is a model for urban structure plans that includes all the relevant factors with accurate mathematical representations, and that optimises the overall cost (including benefits) to produce the best plan in one step. Attempts were made originally in this study to produce an optimising model (Local Government Operational Research Unit, 1970b), but these failed for two reasons. First, the model became too big for the available computers (the largest being an IBM 360/50) and second, the mathematical form—particularly for transport—could not be made simple enough for solution by the mathematical programming techniques presently available.

The developments we are currently considering concentrate on refining the various sub-models used in the program. We hope by this approach to make sure of maintaining the simplicity of the program while at the same time providing a generally more satisfactory model. Five modifications in particular are planned:

1 It is intended to provide a better representation of the effects on the land use of various levels of transport investment, in particular investment in public transport. The use of Compact (Mackinder et al., 1971) is being considered for this purpose. Because of the sensitivity of this model at the distribution stage to modal split effects, it is thought that this will provide a much more realistic interface between the effects of transportation on land use than has previously been achieved. The flexibility obtained will allow the testing of several transportation systems on many land use patterns. Naturally, one would eventually like to iterate back from the land use into the transport system, and this will be attempted, computer space permitting.

2 It is intended to integrate a shopping model (Eilon et al., 1969) into the main model's structure, since at present the treatment of shopping provision is inadequate. This again should help to satisfy basic location theory (Alonso, 1964, Wingo, 1961) in that yet another factor of significance to residential location is being considered.

3 In a new formulation of the model a more general consideration of the environment will be included, since although environmental factors are

included to some extent in the main model's 'neighbourhood' costs their treatment is extremely inadequate. In particular, noise evaluation will be taken into account and the question of marginal land values examined. The evaluation of the environment is of course subjective, and a considerable range of valuations is possible. In formulating the sub-model, therefore, greater weight will be placed on ease of use than on the relatively small gains from more complex formulations.

4 It is hoped that eventually models relating to other important factors of residential (and to a lesser extent, industrial) location, such as recreation facilities, may be introduced to the general model. Investigations of these factors are already being carried out by the LGORU (Brookes and Metcalf, 1970). However, at present this is regarded as rather a long-term development; the developments suggested above will represent the bulk of the new work on the model.

5 Finally, the research program will concern itself with questions of scale. Although in its present form the model is designed for the urban scale, we believe that planners have the right to determine their own levels of scale for the various factors when using the model, and to this end we hope to compile a guide to the effects of varying the scale that is used. Such a guide, we believe, will help not only to speed the 'learning process', but will also help prevent misunderstandings over which factors were relevant at particular levels of planning.

Conclusion

In developing the program described in this paper one of our main aims was to breach the rift that has recently opened up between local authority planners and professional model builders. Clearly we have so far taken only a very small step in this direction. However, in the course of the work we have learned a great deal about practical planning, and believe that we have also helped planners to gain a better understanding of the objectives and problems of the model builder. There is, of course, a lot of distance still to be covered. However, we are certain that, if both sides make the effort to cooperate, very substantial achievements are possible, which can only be good for the planning profession as a whole.

References

Alonso, W., 1964, *Location and land use* (Harvard University Press, Cambridge, Mass.).
Barras, R., Broadbent, T.A., Cordey Hayes, M., Massey, Doreen B., Robinson, Krystina, Willis, J., 1971, "An operational urban development model of Cheshire", *Environment and Planning*, 3, 115–234.
Brookes, T.E., Metcalf, A.E., 1970, "Recreation pricing policy study", Discussion paper prepared for the Sociological Survey Study Group of the Ministry of Housing and Local Government, Internal paper, Local Government Operational Research Unit, Reading.

Cheshire County Planning Department and Local Government Operational Research Unit, 1969, "Systems design project: design procedure;" progress report, Chester and Reading.

Eilon, S., Tilley, R., Fowkes, T., 1969, "Analysis of a gravity demand model", *Regional Studies*, **3**, 115-122.

Escritt, L.B., 1965, *Sewerage and sewage disposal* (Contractors Record Ltd., London).

Friend, J.K., Jessop, W.N., 1969, *Local government and strategic choice* (Tavistock Publications, London).

Houghton, A.G., 1971, "The simulation and evaluation of housing location", *Environment and Planning*, **3**, 383-394.

Local Government Operational Research Unit, 1970a, "Systems design project: a computer program to evaluate urban land use plans: general description", Report C. 70, Reading.

Local Government Operational Research Unit, 1970b, "Systems design project: land use plans by linear program: towards a solution", Report T.23, Reading.

Mackinder, I.H., Rafferty, J., Singer, E.H., Wagon, D.J., 1971, "Compact II: a simplified program for transportation planning studies", Internal M.A.U. Note No. 201. Ministry of Transport, London.

Appendix

In this section we look at each of the planning factors that have been included in the program and describe the mathematical representation and the data required to run the program.

Construction costs of housing and industry

These were considered to be linearly dependent on the area developed, since no economies of scale are significant with the areas involved at this level of planning. The costs per unit area must be defined for each housing and industrial type in each zone, and must depend on physical attributes of the sites—such as slope and soil. The zonal pattern for the urban area must be defined to avoid too much variation of these construction costs within each zone.

Demolition costs of housing and industry

These involve any existing development which is planned for demolition, and can be estimated relatively easily.

Benefits of housing associated with the site

Housing benefits include three factors. Two of these are combined together and include those benefits which are independent of the location of other land uses. The first of these is the intrinsic benefit of having a house which can house a family; this depends on the type of house, and, in particular, the density of development. The second expresses the benefit of developing a house on a particular site—in a nice area, for example. These two benefits are not easy to cost and work is required to estimate them. It may be possible to link them in some way with house prices.

Locational benefits

The third benefit of housing is derived from people being able to exercise freedom of choice about where they live. The evaluation program uses a mathematical form derived by Houghton (1971). We give here a very brief outline of the ideas.

We hypothesise that all people choose where they live to maximise their net benefit (including the benefit of the house, less the cost of travelling to work). Complex travel patterns arise because different people place different benefits on a house in a particular zone. Of those people who work in zone j, the number of people P_i who place a benefit of more than k on living in a house in zone i is given by a negative exponential form:

$$P_i = O_{ij}\exp(-\beta k) \ . \tag{1}$$

With this form of demand curve Houghton has shown that the total costs and benefits associated with the people who live in zone i is given by:

$$B_{ij} = T_{ij}\left[b_i - C_{ij} + \frac{1}{\beta}\ln\left(\frac{E_j}{T_{ij}}\right)\right], \tag{2}$$

where:

B_{ij} is the total benefit derived by people living in i and working in j;

T_{ij} is the number of people living in i and working in j (trips);

b_i are the benefits associated with zone i, independent of development in other zones;

C_{ij} is the cost of travel to work from i to j;

E_j are the employment opportunities in j;

β is a constant.

This equation is a simple form for one house type and one job type, and in practice extensions are necessary.

The first term in equation (2) represents the housing benefits described above which are not related to the location of other land uses, and the second term represents the cost of travel to work. The third term is the additional benefit obtained by people choosing the site most favourable to *them* and is the locational benefit. It can be calculated without requiring the costing of any benefits—once the trip distribution is known.

If equation (2) is maximised with population and employment fixed in each zone, the doubly constrained gravity model is obtained. The constant β is then the exponent of the gravity model and can be obtained by calibration in the usual way. With the demand curve in equation (1) and the hypothesis of individuals maximising their net benefit, we have a theoretical basis for the gravity model of trip distributions.

Transport costs

The costs of transport are of two types; the cost of providing the necessary services and the cost of use by the travellers. Provision of the service includes both a capital element and a running cost. User costs are the costs of travelling time, petrol, wear and tear of vehicles, and so on.

The present program only includes journey to work by road since at the present time this gives the major cost of transport provision. Other types of trip (such as work-to-shop, home-to-shop, and so on) are not crucial to the planning of the location of housing and industrial development. Even with these restrictions, transport is one of the most complex parts of the program. To provide estimates of travelling costs between each pair of zones a separate procedure takes a planned network of roads and finds costs for the shortest distances, assuming no congestion. User costs can then be found once the trips have been calculated.

Trips are found with the simplest form of doubly constrained gravity model. This was considered to be sufficiently accurate for zone sizes greater than, say, one quarter of a square mile, particularly if the program is used for comparing alternative land use configuration rather than for a detailed evaluation of the transport network.

Environmental factors

The program considers the costs of having housing and industry next to each other. It was shown (Cheshire County Planning Department and

Local Government Operational Research Unit, 1969) that, except for heavy industry, the costs are not important at this scale if the areas of each development of land use are sufficiently large (more than about 10 acres). For existing development this may not be easy to define and further research work is required.

Notable omissions from the program at present are the costs of noise and pollution from roads, and the benefits of recreational facilities. Here, too, further work is required.

Sewerage costs
The study examined the importance of all public utilities, defined as those services that are to and from a house by way of pipes or wires. For each service (gas, water, sewerage, etc.), two types of distribution can be defined: a primary distribution from the major source to an area of land use and a secondary distribution within the development. This secondary distribution can be treated as part of the construction costs of the development.

In the case of the primary network it was felt that cost differences between alternative land use patterns were only likely to be significant in the case of sewerage. This results from the basic inflexibility of sewerage systems. The program evaluates the costs of the trunk sewerage network necessary to cater for the land uses in the plan, for a combined system where both foul sewerage and storm water flow through the pipes. To do this a network covering the whole urban area is defined with the costs of construction (for new pipes) and speeds of flow. Construction costs are approximated to an initial set-up cost plus a linear relationship with flow. Flows are calculated by considering the effects of sewerage combining at each junction and are based on the Lloyd-Davis method (Escritt, 1965).

Agricultural benefits
Benefits of agriculture are calculated in a straightforward manner from a given figure for the benefit per acre.

Some Remarks on People's Evaluation of Environments

P.STRINGER
University College, London

In the case of the author, whose work in the past has been principally confined within the territory staked out by psychology, the most interesting aspect of recent research in regional studies, and more generally in geography and planning, has been the growing interest in environmental perception and evaluation (Craik, 1970; Downs, 1970; Goodey, 1971; Hoinville, 1971). One may detect a variety of motives for studies in which lay people are invited to evaluate parts of their physical environment. For example, a justification might be sought for action taken by planners of the environment; or a test made of whether their goals have been achieved. Or the purpose may be proleptic, to discover what people value now, on the assumption that repeating it and emphasising it will produce maximum future satisfaction. Or one may be attempting to find out quite generally what kind of value systems operate in relation to the environment, and in what ways they correspond to other and higher-order value systems.

In the justificatory approach the environment is sometimes evaluated by observing people's behaviour and the extent to which it matches the planner's intentions. However this must be distinguished from any methods that one would employ for the lay evaluation of the environment. It might be argued that people's behaviour in the environment represents their evaluation of it. For example, that when people spend a Bank Holiday in traffic jams and on over-crowded beaches they are demonstrating that they place a positive value upon these things as such. And yet it is not simply that this is implausible; rather that there is nothing that requires that any behaviour of this type be consonant with a value system. Although we may often validly infer values from behaviour, strictly speaking they are different realms. By 'evaluation', therefore, is meant at this point a direct and explicit ascription of positive or negative value to a part of the environment.

The first of these approaches, that is the justificatory approach, may well be nonsense as I have stated it. For if the environmental planners share the appropriate set of values with lay people, there is no need to have recourse to their evaluations. The rules are known. One can do the sum oneself, and arrive at the same answer. If they do not share the same values, and if their actions have been governed by their own perhaps rather specialised values, it may be very unlikely that lay people will be able to make an appropriate evaluation. If the purpose of the exercise is to see whether lay people understand the values of the specialists, one is of course adopting the third approach—exploring the nature of environmental value systems with respect to their match or mismatch between two groups of people.

The proleptic approach depends rather crucially on several assumptions. One must assume that people's values once ascertained should be actualised to the highest degree possible; or alternatively one must have a set of rules that enable one to decide when to ignore lay values, or how to aggregate values and other considerations when the former cannot or are not allowed to be wholly superordinate. In other words one has either to bypass or to make assumptions about higher-order values. In general, however, an individual or group's statement of values, their attachment of values to elements, or their ordering of elements by relative preference, is not the same thing as voting. It does not confer any authority on another party to use or interpret their statement as a legitimation of action which might affect them in any way.

The third approach, the attempt to arrive at a general understanding of people's values, may appear to be rather academic and divorced from empirical problems. But in fact it offers an acceptable way of obtaining the information required to clarify empirical problems, while avoiding any unnecessary assumptions. It says nothing about the identity or otherwise of the values of different groups, nor about what one might do when understanding has been attained. Very likely one will use the understanding in some way, and it is preferable to be clear about this as early as possible in one's search; but this is a purely external matter which does not carry with it any implications that are germane to the search.

One can criticise the justificatory and proleptic approaches, not only on the assumptions they make, but also on the methods they adopt—which, of course, reflect those assumptions. The justificatory approach commonly uses a technique in which subjects are asked to rate a number of elements, that is parts of the physical environment, on a number of descriptive-cum-evaluative scales. The elements will include one or more in which the investigator is particularly interested, which he hopes will receive more favourable ratings than the remainder. I have called the scales 'descriptive-cum-evaluative' because there is no way that one can guarantee in advance that they will be used evaluatively as intended. The difficulty in this approach is that not only can one not know how people will interpret the scales, it is also a matter of conjecture that one is offering them scales that are at all personally meaningful. This might be overcome to some extent by using a semantic differential—that is in the form in which Osgood and his colleagues (1957) actually developed it, rather than the unrecognisable mutants which are found in most of the studies claiming to use it. But in this case, it would still be necessary to show that the structure of meaning in relation to the physical environment was similar for lay people and experts; and the experts would have to accept the semantic differential as an adequate expression of their environmental semantic structure. This is rarely done, and is probably difficult to carry through in a meaningful way.

The proleptic approach of asking people to compare a number of environments or aspects of the environment, with a view to providing them with what they say they most prefer, generally proceeds by way of preference rankings. It is very difficult to see, however, in what situations a preference ranking of any sizeable set of elements is an operation that anyone would perform. Much more likely is that one would, on occasions, express preferences for one or two elements over the rest of the set. In certain cases, over a long enough period of time, one might come to express simple preference orders within all possible, or the majority of, subsets of two or three elements. This is transformable into a rank order. But it does not justify the straightforward production of a rank order as a meaningful psychological operation. Another difficulty is that, even if one were to accept it as a meaningful operation, unless it entails some commitment or carries some implications for action, it becomes game-like, in a trivial sense. In the context of environmental studies very few situations are readily apparent in which an extended ranking of preferences would not be trivially game-like.

The third approach distinguished above avoids the problems of the other two because it does not contain the same sort of prior assumptions. Within the context of reaching for an understanding of environmental value systems, there is no suggestion that one should confine oneself to evaluatory responses in the sense in which I have defined them. Studies of evaluation can be integrated into more general perceptual studies, for example. It has been very consistently found in investigations of person or object perception, or the construing of more abstract entities, that one of the major components, usually *the* major component, is evaluation. This obtains even in cases where great care has been taken not to suggest to subjects in any way that their perceptions should or should not be evaluatory. It is quite unnecessary therefore to assume that one has to resort to such highly specific response modes as preference rankings. Decisions in fact have to be made first about the extent to which one is interested in people's responses *qua* responses; or whether one is more interested in the relationships between the elements that are implied by people's responses; or whether again one is more interested in the types of people that are revealed by their differing responses to a set of elements.

Firstly, one may be interested in individuals, so as not to assume the validity of aggregating responses across subjects, nor even across groups of subjects based on such *a priori* classifications as age, sex, or social class. If different people respond to the environment in different ways (whether the nature of their response or its 'value' is different) one may wish to be able to identify them first and only then look for other differentiating characteristics.

One may be interested in elements as such, that is in more than one element, and in specific elements. There are strong grounds for assuming that perception is basically a comparative operation; that a construct can only be meaningfully ascribed to an element in the world when it is perceived in relation to a least one other element. Indeed the construct can only be formed upon experience with positive and negative instances of its ascription to elements. In the same way, then, I am unlikely to understand your response to something if that is the only thing to which I see you respond.

It is important also to ask subjects to respond to a particular set of elements rather than any set. This is especially so in the case of environmental perception, where I suspect we are usually interested in people's perception and evaluation of particulars. One might be interested in their perception of universals or classes, but that is again a higher-order consideration. Asking people to evaluate the concepts 'shady country lane' or 'metropolitan sprawl' is asking them to construe constructs rather than elements. The use of particular elements is also an important consideration if one wishes it to be clear both to oneself and one's subjects what it is they are responding to. For example, a heterogeneous collection of photographs of dwellings or a list of the counties of the UK are very likely to be ambivalent stimuli. I doubt in the first place that they are valid elements to represent the physical environment as such; and secondly people's experiences of many of them will be scant or non-existent. It would be nonsense as it happens to ask me to evaluate Ross and Cromarty in the same context as Cornwall, or an 18th Century terrace house in Islington, in the same breath as a semi-detached house in Barnet. I could however, manage Cornwall and Sussex; or 18th Century houses in Islington, Bristol, or Edinburgh. One might object that this is what one is trying to find out. But that being so, there are much simpler, more direct and honest ways to find it out.

Thirdly, the same considerations apply to responses, as to elements to be construed. I should find it difficult to understand what you mean by, let us say, 'good' and 'bad' in relation to a set of environmental elements if that was the only response you made. I could certainly infer your meaning. But it would be far preferable if you were to define its meaning operationally in relation to other constructs, so that I could see whether or not 'bad' was, say, correlated with 'crowded', 'noisy', 'tall', 'dry', and so on. Again, as in the case of elements, I would want you to understand the response constructs you were using; so that you only evaluated a transportation plan, for example, in terms of 'flexibility', 'affording mobility', or 'ease of implementation' if those constructs were part of your personal system for perceiving such things.

These assumptions and requirements are expressed in the following way in a research study I am currently doing. First of all a basic three-dimensional data matrix is preserved, with coordinates corresponding to subjects, elements, and responses. The elements chosen are six alternative proposals for the redevelopment of a medium-size shopping centre in South London. The proposals are presented in map-form to a random sample of 200 housewives living within the centre's catchment area. The proposals are initially equally unfamiliar to the majority of subjects. But since they are real possibilities as to the nature of the physical environment in which the housewives will have in future to do much of their shopping, and since by definition they cannot represent environments with which the housewives are familiar, they are not impermissible objects of evaluation. There is a great difference between this and being asked to evaluate an actual environment of which one has no direct experience. There is no plausible psychological reason why one's construct system should include within its scope or range of convenience an astronomically large set of elements. On the other hand once a set of elements has been convincingly presented as urgently needing to come within the scope of this system their evaluation presents no insuperable problem to the average person.

In order to obtain responses from the housewives which are as meaningful as possible, constructs are elicited separately from each individual. The terms in which they perceive potential environments are determined by asking them to compare the proposals two at a time; more specifically to compare first of all each of the proposals with the *status quo*, also in map form, and then pairs of proposals. They are asked to describe what they perceive as the major point of dissimilarity in each comparison; and are encouraged as the comparisons proceed to make fresh perceptions, that is not to repeat constructs. This particular sample has on average produced 15 to 16 constructs per individual. When the subject's constructs appear to be exhausted, a different kind of judgement begins. The set of proposals is ranked on each of the constructs in turn. It is important to emphasise, however, that subjects do not simply rank the elements. For any construct, they nominate the element which most clearly exemplifies that construct. That map is then removed from sight and the procedure repeated successively for the remaining subset, until a ranking has been produced. The mode of response is presented not so much as an ordering, but as a succession of salience judgements. It has in most cases been performed by the sample, which represents a broad cross-section of the adult female general public, without any difficulty. The procedure is repeated for all the individual's constructs and finally for a supplied construct—'the proposal I would like to see put into effect'.

It must be admitted that in educing the rank orders I am making an assumption about underlying psychological processes that I could not defend. It seems much more likely that subjects cluster elements on a construct, perhaps in simple binary categories as possessing or not possessing the attribute, or in three or more categories which could be considered as scalar points. The problem, however, is that binary categorisation produces a rather small amount of information in each individual's grid, and makes a principal components analysis, which I wanted to do, a dubious possibility. Multiple or scalar categories introduce snags because individuals can show considerable differences in the way in which they use them, and this can have an unduly large influence on the way the data look when they have been subjected to multivariate analysis. In this situation one ought obviously to allow subjects to use their own strategy, and to do the necessary variety of analyses depending on what kind of data they produce.

The basic method of analysis in the event is a principal components analysis of each subject's grid, in which the grid and its transpose are decomposed into principal components within the same space. Graphically speaking, this enables one to map the position of either the elements or the constructs on a number of orthogonal dimensions in such a way that the two sets of dimensions can be directly related to one another. In other words any observed relationship between elements, say, whether of similarity, opposition, or orthogonality, can be described in terms of construct dimensions; contrariwise any observed relationship between constructs can be interpreted in terms of corresponding element dimensions. There are many advantages to having both sets of dimensions describe collinear spaces. Among them is the emphasis it puts upon the grid as a closed system, at least in so far as the investigator's viewpoint is concerned. It underlines the fact that element relationships are defined solely within the framework of the constructs used, and that construct relationships cannot be validly generalised beyond a particular set of elements without further evidence of a different kind.

The goals of the justificatory approach, outlined above, are strictly unrelated to this particular project. However, one might imagine that instead of asking housewives to construe proposals for the redevelopment of a particular shopping centre, one asked them to construe a number of existing centres including a newly developed one. Provided that one could decide upon a criterion of sufficient familiarity with, or use of, the centres this should be a reasonable task. The relative disposition of the centres within an individual's construct space would be compared with their disposition in the planner's space, particularly perhaps on the dimension that appears most clearly to be evaluative or preferential. The argument would have to be that any close match between the lay and expert perception of the centres, although the two parties may be looking at the environment in different terms as far as one could judge from the verbal expression of their constructs, nevertheless represents agreement as to the relative merits of the centres considered as closed systems, and as, let us say, 'places to go shopping'.

An elaboration of the justificatory approach would be to have both lay and expert subjects construe the shopping centres on their personal constructs, and the lay subjects also on the constructs of the experts— provided of course that they could use them. The elements would be disposed, in the case of the latter group, in three construct spaces—lay, expert, and a combination of both. Several interesting comparisons could then be performed between these dispositions and those of the experts. This procedure could, incidentally, be of considerable educational potential for individual subjects and ultimately for any larger groups of which they are found to be representative. Given that one wished to teach lay people the meaning of the experts' constructs in perceiving and evaluating the physical environment this could be done by showing them how their own constructs related to those of the experts in particular contexts. Perhaps in some forms of participatory democracy the reverse might even occur.

The proleptic requirements of environmental evaluation are extremely well served by the method I am describing. The housewives, when looking at the maps and construing the proposals, quite clearly imagined what they would like if they had actually been constructed. They were giving anticipatory responses. An indication of which proposal they would like to see put into effect can be taken from the disposition of elements on whichever dimension is interpreted as the evaluation dimension and usually this will be the first dimension or component. In this research the supplied construct 'the proposal I would most like to see put into effect' might be taken as a marker to indicate the evaluation component. That is, the component on which this construct has its highest loading is taken as the evaluation component. The elements with the highest loading in the direction of positive evaluation can be taken as the most preferred; and contrariwise for the least preferred. In addition the constructs with high loadings on what is taken as the evaluation component can be taken to indicate the meaning of positive and negative evaluation. One does not have to make do with the mysteries of a simple and isolated statement of preference. One can, of course, also point to aspects of the subjects' environmental perception which are independent of evaluation—purely descriptive one might say—by reference to construct components other than the evaluative. One of the most interesting aspects of tackling the proleptic approach through components is that the order of elements on the component on which the supplied 'implementation preference' construct has its highest loading is sometimes not identical with the preference ordering. The ordering on the component—if it is the largest— is the ordering on the greatest part of the shared variance between the preference construct and other constructs. One might interpret this ordering as the most valid ordering of the elements in terms of the subject's construct system, at least as it has been elicited and as it can be interpreted by the investigator. Since one can only be concerned with the elicited constructs, and since much of the burden of the method is on eliciting those constructs, the component ordering is the one which best meets methodological assumptions.

Since this study has been concerned more with an exploration of the way in which people perceive and evaluate possible future environments than with trying to answer specific questions or solve particular planning problems, it is only assumed that the results might be useful as giving some general understanding of people's responses. They are not intended to answer specific empirical questions nor solve the planners' problems. The evaluations that can be inferred from the housewives' construing of the alternatives will not be taken as a referendum on the planning of their shopping centre. It is very important that planners should not attempt to give the status of 'hard information' to information that is essentially and crucially 'soft'.

The 'softness' of people's environmental value systems is brought out most clearly by preserving the basic three-dimensional data matrix, which I referred to earlier. By not aggregating individuals one appreciates the diversity of individual responses. I suspect that the social sciences give too much attention to aggregate-type propositions, and too often treat them as though they had the force of general-type propositions. Responses vary to such an extent that one of the alternatives may be approved of for quite different and even incompatible reasons; or two individuals may place opposite evaluations on an alternative, while using nominally identical constructs. Eliciting responses to a set, and a limited set, of alternatives, rather than attempting to infer people's values simply from their remarks on their present environment, suggests the drawbacks of not using a representative set of elements for people to judge. In the context of my research this was brought out by the responses to sub-sets of alternatives produced by independent planning authorities. These were very different and often polarised people's evaluations. In most everyday planning situations only one body produces proposals, and these usually have a rather homogeneous look. But any set of proposals that falls far short of being representative of the total population of possible solutions is unlikely to generate valid or reliable information about environmental value systems.

It should be trivial to point out that information about values is 'soft information'. But that it is information at all seems to be ignored very often. And many of the assumptions built implicitly in to much of the work on environmental evaluation, let alone the more ludicrous excesses of cost benefit analysis, seem determined to petrify it quite out of its essential character. How one can use 'soft information' is a question which would need considerable time to discuss but since the use of soft information is commonplace in human affairs I see no reason to be unduly pessimistic about one's chances.

Acknowledgement. While this paper was prepared the author was supported in part by a research grant from the Centre for Environmental Studies.

References
Craik, K.H., 1970, "Environmental psychology", in *New Directions in Psychology*, Vol.4, (Holt, Rinehart and Winston, Inc., New York), pp. 1-121.

Downs, R.M., 1970, "Geographic space perception: past approaches and future prospects", in *Progress in Geography,* Eds. C. Board, R.J. Chorley, P. Haggett, D.R. Stoddart, Vol.3, (Edward Arnold, London), pp. 67–108.

Goodey, B., 1971, "Perception of the environment", Centre for Urban and Regional Studies, University of Birmingham.

Hoinville, G., 1971, "Evaluating community preferences", *Environment and Planning,* **3**, 33–50.

Osgood, C.E., Suci, G.J. Tannenbaum, P.H., 1957, *The Measurement of Meaning,* (University of Illinois Press, Urbana).